Christian Social Ethics

Christian Social Ethics

Elmar Nass

ROWMAN & LITTLEFIELD
Lanham • Boulder • New York • London

Published by Rowman & Littlefield
An imprint of The Rowman & Littlefield Publishing Group, Inc.
4501 Forbes Boulevard, Suite 200, Lanham, Maryland 20706
www.rowman.com

86-90 Paul Street, London EC2A 4NE

Copyright © 2023 by Elmar Nass

All rights reserved. No part of this book may be reproduced in any form or by any electronic or mechanical means, including information storage and retrieval systems, without written permission from the publisher, except by a reviewer who may quote passages in a review.

British Library Cataloguing in Publication Information Available

Library of Congress Cataloging-in-Publication Data

Names: Nass, Elmar, 1966- author.
Title: Christian social ethics / Elmar Nass.
Description: Lanham : Rowman & Littlefield Publishers, [2023] | Includes bibliographical references and index.
Identifiers: LCCN 2022027730 (print) | LCCN 2022027731 (ebook) | ISBN 9781538165263 (cloth) | ISBN 9781538165270 (ebook)
Subjects: LCSH: Christian sociology. | Christian ethics. | Ethics. | Postmodernism—Religious aspects—Christianity.
Classification: LCC BT738 .N335 2023 (print) | LCC BT738 (ebook) | DDC 261.8—dc23/eng/20220906
LC record available at https://lccn.loc.gov/2022027730
LC ebook record available at https://lccn.loc.gov/2022027731

∞™ The paper used in this publication meets the minimum requirements of American National Standard for Information Sciences—Permanence of Paper for Printed Library Materials, ANSI/NISO Z39.48-1992.

Contents

List of Abbreviations … vii
List of Tables … ix
List of Figures … xi
Preface … xiii
Introduction: Christian Social Ethics in the World Today … xvii

PART I: THE MISSION … 1
1 The Search for Good … 3
2 Sanctification of the World … 11
3 Ecumenical Perspective … 33
4 Mission in Crisis … 51

PART II: IN DIALOGUE … 59
5 Theological Humanism beyond Christianity … 61
6 Normative Humanism beyond Theology … 79
7 Ethics beyond Normative Humanism … 95
8 World Authority for Unconditional Human Dignity … 117

PART III: APPLICATION … 123
9 Creation, Justice, and Peace … 125

10	Life, Work, and Death	155
11	Economy and Economic Order	215
12	Leadership and Organizational Culture	281
13	Future Issues	307
Conclusion: Relevance of the Christian Perspective		319
Bibliography		321
Index		343
About the Author		351

Abbreviations

AAL	Ambient Assisted Living
AI	Artificial Intelligence
AK	Academy Edition (*Akademie-Ausgabe* / Immanuel Kant)
AL	Post-Synodal Apostolic Exhortation *Amoris Laetitia*
BGB	*Bürgerliches Gesetzbuch* (German Civil Code)
BVerfGE	*Entscheidungen des Bundesverfassungsgerichts* (German Federal Constitutional Court decisions)
CA	Encyclical *Centesimus Annus*
Can	Canon (in CIC)
CCC	Catechism of the Catholic Church
CDA	*Christlich Demokratische Arbeitnehmerschaft* (Christian Democratic Employees' Organization)
CIC	*Codex Iuris Canonici* (Code of Canon Law)
CiV	Encyclical *Caritas in Veritate*
CSR	Corporate Social Responsibility
DBK	*Deutsche Bischofskonferenz* (German Bishops' Conference)
DCE	Encyclical *Deus Caritas Est*
DFG	*Deutsche Forschungsgemeinschaft* (German Research Foundation)
EC	European Community
EG	Apostolic Exhortation *Evangelii Gaudium*
EKD	*Evangelische Kirche in Deutschland* (Protestant Church in Germany)
EMI	European Monetary Institute
ESCB	European System of Central Banks
ESF	European Social Fund
EV	Encyclical *Evangelium Vitae*

FC	Encyclical *Familiaris Consortio*
Fed	Federal Reserve System (central bank of the United States of America)
GDP	Gross Domestic Product
GG	*Grundgesetz* (Basic Law for the Federal Republic of Germany)
GS	Constitution *Gaudium et Spes*
HICP	Harmonized Index of Consumer Prices
HO	*Homo oeconomicus* (Homo economicus)
IGFM	International Society for Human Rights
IS	"Islamic State"
KAB	*Katholische Arbeitnehmer-Bewegung* (Catholic Workers' Movement)
LE	Encyclical *Laborem Exercens*
LS	Encyclical *Laudato Sí*
LThK	*Lexikon für Theologie und Kirche* (Encyclopedia for Theology and Church)
MEESTAR	Model for the Ethical Evaluation of Socio-Technical Arrangements
MM	Encyclical *Mater et Magistra*
NA	Constitution *Nostra Aetate*
PGD	Preimplantation Genetic Diagnosis
PiT	Encyclical *Pacem in Terris*
PP	Encyclical *Populorum Progressio*
q.	Quaestio
QA	Encyclical *Quadragesimo Anno*
QALY	Quality Adjusted Life Year
RN	Encyclical *Rerum Novarum*
SED	*Sozialistische Einheitspartei Deutschlands* (Socialist Unity Party of Germany)
SGB	*Sozialgesetzbuch* (German Social Security Code)
sine anno, loco, sine nomine	no indication of year/place/author (for sources)
SRS	Encyclical *Sollicitudo Rei Socialis*
STEM	Science, Technology, Engineering and Mathematics
StGB	*Strafgesetzbuch* (German Criminal Code)
STh	*Summa Theologica*
SVD	*Societas Verbi Divini*
TARGET	Trans-European Automated Real-Time Gross Settlement Express Transfer System
TFEU	Treaty on the Functioning of the European Union
WeimVerf.	*Weimarer Verfassung* (Weimar Constitution)

Tables

Table 2.1: Biblical reasons for the humane ethos   21
Table 9.1: Four order-ethical contexts of social justice   138
Table 9.2: Concepts of social justice beyond normative humanism   140

To Joe

Figures

Figure 6.1: Phenomenological Transcendental Revelation   89
Figure 10.1: Just Price for a Kidney in Economic Imperialism   190
Figure 11.1: Economic Ethics System   220
Figure 12.1: Leadership Ethics System   285

Preface

The understanding of values in Western countries is in a state of upheaval. Christian orientation is losing importance. Secular ethics is gaining ground. Christian ethics is seeking to make its own contribution. The Catholic tradition, in particular, is now increasingly on the defensive when it comes to answering society's most fundamental ethical questions. We are currently witnessing a general trend toward quantitative analyses in the social sciences. Material relevance for social life is lost from view in the process, as is a fundamental understanding of society. The question of the (ethical) principles and values of the social order has thus lost much of its significance. Wrongly so. For only such a qualitative ethics of order reveals the reasons for concrete political and moral decisions and rules. Empirical pragmatism should give way to ethical programmatics if we are to give freedom and democracy a future. This volume is committed to this task. Consequently, the form of social ethics developed here offers a powerful blueprint for shaping a liberal order based on a view of humanity and society, in honest dialogue with alternative worldviews and with orientations for tangible social issues. The result is a welcoming compass of social values. This guide can enrich the liberal-democratic soil of Western culture and fortify it against totalitarian ambitions (such as those of Russia, China, and others).

This book was first published in German by the Kohlhammer Verlag publishing company in 2020. Some specific examples in the application part of the book refer to discussions in German-speaking countries. Depending on the region of the world, other major social issues that might certainly have had more urgency for the application part of this book may be missing here. Each of these issues would undoubtedly have deserved its own chapter. This lack of completeness owes to the German origin of the work. At the same time, however, it should be understood as an invitation to identify and answer precisely such regionally charged questions following the logic of this socio-ethical outline (including critical race theory, DEI, the Black Lives Matter movement, colonialism, neo-imperialism, corruption, hunger, LGBTQAI+, society's fight against sexualized violence, autonomous weapons systems, the international peace order, migration and refugees, energy politics of the future, pandemic ethics, and others). Therefore, from a Christian perspective, this book offers a universal socio-ethical basis for argumentation. Application to real-world social questions is thus only in the early stages of development. It should be carried forward with the respective regional competence. It is my hope that this will help make this work a starting point for globally effective Christian social ethics that justifies liberal democracy and continues to advance it to address concrete social questions. This claim automatically counters a widespread self-secularization of Christian social ethics.

ACKNOWLEDGMENTS

I would like to express my sincere appreciation to the Rowman & Littlefield publishing company for their confidence in me and for including this book in their program. I am delighted and truly honored by this. I would also like to extend a special thanks to the publisher for the outstanding support provided in conjunction with this project. In particular, I wish to thank Ms. Natalie Mandziuk, Ms. Sylvia Landis, and Ms. Rebecca Anastasi. I am also grateful for the seamless cooperation with the Kohlhammer Verlag publishing company. I am indebted to Ms. Julie Cornillie for her swift and highly professional work in preparing the English version of this book along with countless important references. My thanks also go to my research assistant, Mr. Igor Tadic, for the many hours he invested in transcribing the bibliography, to Ms. Roberta Schlüter for compiling the keyword index, to my office manager, Ms. Maria Gross, for her invaluable assistance, and to the "Zabel Foundation," which covered part of the translation costs.

A NOTE ABOUT QUOTATIONS

Quoting historical texts in English translation poses a particular challenge due to conventions that once used masculine pronouns for God and tended to refer to people, in general, as men. The original quotations have largely been retained here, even in instances where today terms such as "humanity" or "humankind" would be more appropriate than "man" or "mankind."

All quotations from Scripture are from the New Revised Standard Version (NRSV) unless otherwise indicated. Quotations from the Koran are based on the Arberry translation. Immanuel Kant's writings are cited from the Berlin Academy Edition ("AK"). English translations of German-language texts are the author's own unless otherwise noted.

Introduction
Christian Social Ethics in the World Today

Ethics seeks to impart values on people to guide them toward responsible decisions and help them find answers when faced with dilemmas. Social ethics focuses primarily on rules and human relationships. It promulgates its own normative foundations as a set of values (view of humanity and society, concept of human dignity, freedom, justice, etc.), inferring answers for such decisions from them. This makes ethics vulnerable to attack because, in a pluralistic society, there are different views regarding these values on the one hand and regarding the specific answers in dilemmas to the other. Not all people share these views. Nevertheless, this heightened awareness is the very essence of an ethics that offers a moral compass to humankind. It is presented here with a form of Christian social ethics that seeks to persuade people with sound reasoning, arguments, and position statements to facilitate decisions in social dilemmas. As such, this volume is not a textbook that comparatively juxtaposes different models of social ethics. There is also no shortage of works focused on the general principles of socio-ethical reflection or postmodern variants with specific references to applications.[1] These texts will not be elaborated upon here. Rather, the time has come to formulate valid Christian answers to the unresolved social questions of our time, above and beyond the (post-)modern guidelines of the present. (Post-)modern contexts and a widespread defense of explicitly Christian-ethical reasoning point in a direction that differs greatly from the systematic nature of an argumentative orientation such as this, which defines its own values with confidence and subjects them to controversial debate. The relevance of such an approach to the present is the topic of this brief introduction.

(POST-)MODERN CONTEXTS

In contemporary society, value is placed on normative consensus models that smooth the rough edges of ethics. Thus, it follows that contentious ethics would no longer be in keeping with the times in a pluralistic society. Here are two examples:

- On the occasion of its tenth anniversary in July 2018, the German Ethics Council met in Berlin to discuss whether, in the field of ethics, it still makes sense to fill the concept of human dignity with semantics. If this effort is abandoned and an agreement is reached merely on a consensual concept, then this concept loses its power of orientation in critical decision-making situations (for example, with regard to concrete questions concerning the beginning and end of life, the distribution of scarce resources, etc.).
- With respect to the ethics of the currently popular subject of behavioral economics as it relates to private law,[2] lawyer Philipp Hacker proposes the following normative axiom:

> In general, recourse to substantive theories has become problematic in the age of postmodernism. There is no longer an overarching, acceptable normative theory. Therefore, it seems advisable to rely on procedural theories instead. Such theories have the advantage of being able to cope constructively with the factum of value pluralism in modern Western societies. . . . Procedural theories in particular are not committed to any specific substantive moral or ethical goal.[3]

Hacker proposes the principle of communicability as a foundation for ethics, which he derives primarily from the postmodern discourse ethics of Jürgen Habermas and combines with elements of John Rawls' theory of justice. In doing so, Hacker follows the paradigm of theory that sees itself as contemporary ethics. The abandonment of substantive ethics is characteristic of postmodernist thinking.[4] It is assumed to be a determining cognitive horizon of our time and, thus, an important social sounding board, which the model of Christian social ethics presented here aims to influence and for which it wishes to regain followers. Postmodernism is understood in the sense of Wolfgang Welsch as "a radicalized modernity."[5] Accordingly, it is the unquestioned successor to so-called Modernism and continues its program unabated—without, however, one epoch having completely replaced the other. Modern as well as postmodern perspectives remain present today and build on the thus understood achievements of secular enlightenment: "Freedom, emancipation, autonomy of the subject, establishment of societies based on the principle of autonomy."[6] Religiosity is initially seen here as a heavy burden: "Secularism means that society should reject and exclude religion and religious considerations in making laws and political decisions."[7]

Secularity is a unifying concern of modernity and postmodernity. When Habermas, as a representative of postmodern discourse ethics, nevertheless speaks of the present as a post-secular age and in the meantime even grants religion its own potential for articulation in discourse,[8] this should in no way be interpreted as a means of relativizing essential religious skepticism. Rather, it is an admission of deficiencies in its own project of secular postmodernism, which actually seeks to overcome religion along with ethical references to transcendence. Religion tolerated in the postmodern era, however, at least brings roots of secular reason to mind.[9] Their deconstruction nevertheless remains (in contrast to the view of the equally secular, but not [post-]modern Canadian social philosopher Charles Taylor)[10] the goal of a postmodern secularism that would distance itself from religion.

In contrast to modernity, what is new in postmodernity, which was first outlined as such for the social-philosophical dialogue by Jean-François Lyotard, is in this tradition the renunciation of universal concepts with their metanarratives of truth, justice, dignity, freedom, and so on.[11] All these *inter alia* elusive concepts would now always require the plural form. The essential commonalities of modern and postmodern perspectives compared to such differences are the reason this book generally makes overarching references to (post-)modern ethics to separate it from Christian social ethics. An even more differentiated sociological view of the peculiarities of modernity and postmodernity is only undertaken where the distinguishing features are of central importance for the respective line of reasoning.

SUBSTANTIVE POSITIONING IN DIALOGUE

This book does not follow a postmodern communicative system[12] that renounces substantive ethics. While secular orientations of the present (such as those of Yuval N. Harari et al.) assume matter-of-factly that there is no God, the alternative represented here expressly starts with the antithesis: "Imagine there is a God." This foundation of values for the guiding compass is neither excluded nor included to make it compatible with discussions that go beyond theology. Such contemporary theological thinking attaches itself to given secular patterns and leaves behind the metaphysical moment that constitutes them.[13] The claim of universalizability is also abandoned and, out of consideration for ethical plurality, translated by what is known as transparticularization. Theological ethics can thus still claim to say the right things even outside the realm of the Church, but it can then no longer claim to provide orientations for all people. That would move it away from the understanding of sanctification of the world advocated here: "If it wants to have a say, if it wants to appear orientational and competent, it must not emphasize its theologicity, but instead must show itself capable of secular and interdisciplinary connection."[14]

To prevent exactly this, Pope Francis admonishes: "May the religions be wombs of life, bearing the merciful love of God to a wounded and needy humanity: may they be doors of hope helping to penetrate the walls erected by pride and fear."[15]

Religious ethics can and should derive answers to the social questions of our time from its respective views of humanity and society. In the social-scientific dialogue of the present, this openly communicated commitment to a specific *Weltanschauung*, or philosophical-ideological worldview, prompts reservations among those who wish to keep worldviews out of social science in accordance with the doctrine on *Werturteilsfreiheit*, or freedom from moral value judgments. However, the explicit philosophical-ideological transparency is also a strength because the origins and claims of one's own reasoning are clearly laid out. Even non-religious social ethics, such as Kantian, utilitarian, contractualist, communicative, or collectivist approaches, begin with unproven postulates or secular commitments to reason, the collective, individualism, or the like. Seen in this light, a Christian position can easily compete in dialogue with these forms of ethics and others with a nod toward the very values that form the foundations of the social order. Thus, the Christian social ethics represented in this volume, with its core values, first and foremost follows Jesus' command to be leaven (Matthew 13:33), light and salt of the earth (Matthew 5:13 et seq.). As such, the Christian view of humanity and the concept of dignity, which is closely linked to it, are substantive (i.e., semantically rich) starting points of ethical reasoning. Social values, principles, and further guidance on ethical applications are inferred from this to produce thought-provoking answers to some of the most pressing questions of our time. These answers can and should demonstrate the topicality and relevance of Christian orientation.[16] The use of such a system emphasizes internal coherency over broad social acceptance and is thus bound to encounter resistance. This is accepted in the spirit of a healthy democratic culture of debate, in which competing ethical profiles and answers to social questions, in particular, should respectfully strive for well-reasoned, positive solutions.

Substantive Christian social ethics joins other equally distinguished alternatives, whether religious or secular, with this same confidence. It is communicative in the sense that it allows itself to be the subject of democratic dialogue and must be expressible as a result. Dialogue, in this case, should not be understood in the postmodern sense as discourse governed by the rules of secular discourse ethics and, thus, as normative consensus.[17] Rather, this dialogue is concerned with successful communication and a culture of debate centered around well-founded values and positions. It must reflect on and accept secular facticity as a sounding board for its line of reasoning; yet it must also never fail to question the conditions on which it is built. Dialogue thus also means—in keeping with society's evolving value systems—constructively calling into question the very sounding board that has enjoyed immense power until now.[18] This form of communication has both a systematic and a political side. This line of reasoning, which provides socio-ethical guidance in dilemmas, must be systematically developed and articulated as a decision compass based on a transparent set of values, guided by proper knowledge of the respective areas of application, and with a fair view of alternative solution proposals, and yet it should be as clearly defined as possible. Since some of social ethics' specific areas of application also always involve politically controversial topics (such as social justice, family, currency crises, organ donation, etc.), the orientation suggested here is also at times political in nature. This should never be understood in terms of party politics. The failure to exclude it is the price for taking a socio-ethically relevant position but not retaining an open stance of accepting "one as well as the other," fully cognizant of the fact that the subsequently proposed answers are vulnerable to attack precisely because of their political volatility. The orientation understood in this way, whose aim is to regain followers with sound Christian reasoning, thus has many steps and stages upon which the structure of this volume is based:

- In its constructive opposition to (post-)modernity, the form of substantive Christian social ethics represented here is simultaneously firmly rooted in today's world. It must be aware of its normative goals and, considering the prevailing conditions of communication, create a system of values that is coherent in and of itself and open to discussion and debate. Here, the focus is on Jesus' command, which is first examined from a Catholic perspective, but is immediately elaborated upon to reveal an ecumenical dimension. The Catholic perspective was chosen based on my background as the author; it is the common thread that winds through this outline of Christian social ethics. The emphasis on an ecumenical perspective is intended to overcome a narrow and purely Catholic understanding and to highlight corresponding commonalities in the view of humanity and in the resulting value systems. Part I focuses on the ascertainment made in the beginning with a Christian take on humanity and society.
- In a searching dialogue with competing religious or secular ethics, it then considers how they can be linked to Christian goals and, at the same

time, seeks new insights that help us better understand our own views of humanity and society along with the ideas of dignity, justice, freedom, responsibility, creation, and others derived from them. Our own values and justifications are not abandoned in dialogue or relativized under pressure of consensus. Rather, the idea is to better understand or enhance them as part of a dialogue with other positions under the conditions of the Great Commission of Jesus to His disciples to spread the Gospel. This open dialogue with other perspectives and ethics is a key topic in part II. Non-Christian positions are also free to engage in a constructive dialogue with Christian ethics in order to sharpen or clarify their own values and positions.

- However, beyond this is also the hope that contemporary individuals who are searching will be able to (re)identify in substantive Christian social ethics a preferable program that serves as a moral compass to help them navigate social dilemmas. As such, dialogue understood in the spirit of a positive democratic culture of debate undoubtedly also has the aim of convincing people with sound reasoning and persuading them to examine more closely the Christian stance outlined here. This is expressly meant to be an invitation.[19] The areas of application covered in part III in particular pursue this objective. Related topics include creation, social justice, peace, family, the culture of dying, property, financial and currency crises, organ donation, digital technologies, and more.

The concluding outlook ventures a visionary prognosis regarding the future response to Christian social ethics[20] in the world at large and seeks possible allies with whom essential, socially relevant positions of Christian social ethics might also be enforced politically.

NOTES

1. Cf. from the Catholic perspective, e.g., J. Höffner (1962/1997).
2. Cf. the section on rethinking economic ethics in the chapter "Economy and Economic Order" in Part III.
3. P. Hacker (2017): 391.
4. Cf. the chapter "Ethics beyond Normative Humanism" in Part II.
5. W. Welsch (1988): 35.
6. U. Kropač (2019): 28.
7. The term secularism is first found within this meaning in G. J. Holyoake (1896), cited in D. W. Mitchell (2018): 70.
8. Cf. J. Habermas (2001), ibid. / J. Ratzinger (2005).
9. Cf. U. Kropač (2019): 31.

10. C. Taylor (2009) urges Christians to embrace transcendence and mystery in secular society because recourse to this is precisely what provides a good rationale for truth, forgiveness, love, and justice that secular philosophy is unable to produce on its own. Thus, from this secular perspective, Christianity and possibly other religions contribute to the stabilization of social peace.

11. Cf. e.g., J.-F. Lyotard (1988). Taylor's metanarrative thus fits neither secularism (which seeks to overcome religion) nor postmodernism because the latter wished to relegate grand narratives to the past. Cf. the section on phenomenological humanism in the chapter "Normative Humanism beyond Theology" in Part II.

12. Cf. the above quote from P. Hacker (2017): 391.

13. The ability of theological thinking to connect with secular ethnology, social, and literary studies, etc. could, for example, offer the appropriate hermeneutic framework for theology to gain a new understanding of itself by allowing itself to be enriched by its other, its counterpart, in order to later absorb this difference in a process of convergence. Cf. e.g., M. Heimbach-Steins (2015): 13.

14. R. A. Klein (2018): 308.

15. Pope Francis, Address to Representatives of Various Religions, quoted by D. M. Mitchell (2018): 73.

16. Values are social goals (such as dignity, justice, freedom, etc.), whereas social principles are laws of order used as a means of achieving these goals (solidarity, subsidiarity, etc.).

17. Cf. the section on postmodern discourse ethics in the chapter "Ethics beyond Normative Humanism" in Part II.

18. Cf. J. Coleman (1986).

19. Thus, the identity of a welcoming form of Christianity represented here is explicitly in the tradition of the letter *"Proposer la foi dans la société actuelle"* written by the French bishops to the French Catholics.

20. Whenever Christian social ethics is referred to here in this sense, the addition of the term "substantive" is generally omitted to improve readability. Differing positions in the realm of Christian social ethics are identified accordingly.

Part I

THE MISSION

> I am convinced that our concern for people is an offer that, if properly conveyed, has inestimable value and can deliver ultimate, unassailable meaning.
>
> —Karl Cardinal Lehmann[1]

Christians are in the world but not of the world. They are to bring inspiration to the world as leaven in the spirit of the Gospel. This is their missionary calling. This mission of Christianity, which is documented countless times in the Bible (cf. Matthew 28:19, for example), seems suspect to many people today, evoking memories of forced conversions in the past on the one hand and raising concerns about a form of Christianity that questions the secular state on the other. However, secular contemporaries are not alone: many Christians and theologians also struggle with these concepts. The classical *Societas Verbi Divini* (SVD) still uses the term mission, now interpreting it mainly in a socio-humanitarian sense, which is also undoubtedly aligned with the commands of Christ. However, any understanding of mission or what it means to be a missionary in the world that goes beyond this faces difficulties in terms of public perception and in (post-)modern theology.

In part I, it is presented as the sense of being a Christian and the sense of being a Church with which Christians confidently stand in support of their faith and whose message Christians spread to welcome others into the fold. Many pastoral and missiological or missional concepts from recent years are on the table. These are not the focus of this book. Rather, the main purpose of this work is to bring about an awareness of the ethical guiding compass and apply it to contemporary issues throughout the book. Following a general exploration of basic ethical questions, part I first presents a Catholic perspective on the sanctification of the world. What is meant here is a fundamental concretization of Jesus' command to be leaven, light, and salt of the earth.[2] This includes becoming aware of the Christian idea of humanity, human dignity, and responsibility to invite contemporaries to share in these ideas and use them as the foundation on which society and coexistence may be built.

This is followed by an ecumenical discussion that primarily points out the bridges between Protestant and Catholic social ethics, which—confessional autonomy notwithstanding—underpin the common Christian set of values and the common mission in and for the world derived from it. Part I concludes with a summary of some of the crisis phenomena of this mission and an attempt to provide initial basic responses.

NOTES

1. K. Lehmann (2005): 14.
2. Sanctification aims to bring that which is holy into the world, the first step being a correspondingly authentic (holy) life. E. Schockenhoff (2013): 258 sees in the sacred, according to the Word, that which "belongs to God and is intrinsically valuable." Cf. ibid: 259: "In its original sense, 'holiness' means belonging to God, from which the mandate to lead a life aligned with this dignity is inferred."

Chapter One

The Search for Good

On the one hand, ethics offers a moral compass for individual decisions in dilemmatic situations where neither pure expertise nor gut feeling suffice. On the other hand, this yardstick of human utility can be used to evaluate rules, even beyond efficiency, mere acceptance, or technical feasibility. Ethics, whether Christian or not, is fundamentally about the search for good. In contrast to morality as the living compass of values in life, ethics is about a reflection of morality and its orientations. The objective of all forms of ethics is to consistently translate coherent—i.e., well-founded—normative theory into practice. In the search for good, it is the systematic reflection of what humans ought to be. Since there are as many competing perceptions of good as there are conceived approaches to it, there are also many different types of ethics and thus variants between which a moral compass such as this must distinguish. Three central questions always arise in relation to the respective compass profile:

1. What is good?
2. How can it be identified?
3. How can it be made the standard of good living, as a compass to direct individual decisions or frame the rules of a society?

All ethical concepts must go through this three-step process. Social ethics focuses on the rules that govern people and the ways in which they live together, while virtue and individual ethics focus on decisions of conscience on the part of those involved. The first principle of both is "good is to be pursued and evil avoided"—a statement that can be traced back to Doctor of the Church Thomas Aquinas as early as the Middle Ages. Every form of ethics is tasked with infusing this principle with practical meaning.

This book focuses on social ethics, which is inherently interdisciplinary. It is in constant dialogue with economic, legal political, environmental, cultural, biological, and other sciences. The prerequisites for the success of such interdisciplinary communications are, for social ethics, immersion in the respective language games of the partner disciplines on the one hand and a clear confrontation between these disciplines and relevant values and normative principles on the other. Where such an encounter succeeds, the way is paved for the so-called hyphenated ethics, such as bio-ethics, cyber-ethics, or neuro-ethics; business, corporate, and leadership ethics; legal, family, and gender ethics; environmental, medical, and health ethics; cultural and peace ethics; and so on. The question of good, of meaning, of what is just and legitimate—ultimately, the question of human dignity in human coexistence—is the pivotal point of all social ethics. The answer to the human question has an impact on the normative assessments of how order and social rules are shaped in law, politics, economics, and so on. Social ethics inquires after an order rooted in human dignity seen from an order-ethical perspective and justifies designs of social justice and freedom on this basis. In doing so, ethics itself must be rooted in views of humanity shaped by *Weltanschauung*, whether these are of religious or secular origin. After all: "Tell me your view of humanity and I will tell you what view of human society belongs to it."[1]

In this context, social ethics encompasses questions of normative reasoning and its application. Normative ethics questions the justification of good, while virtue ethics concerns itself with concrete expression in individual behavior and in the shaping of relationships, which are defined by individuals but nevertheless form their own social entities.

First, some basic points concerning normative ethics: It seeks values as desirable goals for informed decision-making. Social values include, for example, human dignity, (social) justice, and freedom. In the social sphere, social principles should be used as tools to offer guidance on practicing values, such as personhood, solidarity, and subsidiarity. In terms of distribution, they call for concepts that "help people help themselves" as a measure of justice, yet they leave ample room for interpreting and prioritizing the social claims and obligations that can be inferred from them in a legal sense. Although there is a great deal of agreement in the Western world on the importance of acknowledging the values and social principles mentioned here, this consensus quickly fades when it comes to concretizing their content. From its very inception, this form of ethics must ask: What are humans in the first place? Discussing human dignity is futile as long as this question remains unanswered. The supposedly self-evident value of human dignity quickly falters depending on whom I count as human or not and why. In the process, personal dignity may be defined in a semantically counterintuitive way. For instance: The Spanish conquistadors did not initially see the Indigenous people of South America as truly human. Defined in this way—following a line of thought that would be inconceivable today—they would not be shielded by the concept of human dignity. Islamic jihadists see infidels as fair game and justify ruthless killing with a supposedly divine mandate. Based on this ideology, only the presumedly orthodox would be granted full dignity. Radical right- and left-wing ideologies argue similarly in favor of violent race or class warfare. Depending on how I define when dignified human life begins and ends, whether I accept cerebral or cardiac death or neither, I will arrive at completely different conclusions when evaluating prenatal diagnostics, abortions, organ donations, euthanasia, social transfers, etc. These few examples alone show how controversial the topic of human dignity is. As such, from a normatively accurate and categorical standpoint, it would be better to say that: Human dignity is vulnerable and must therefore be protected at all costs.

Weltanschauung, as a fact of normative plurality, need not inevitably lead to a form of relativism that views the various ethics with equal validity. Presumably, all adherents who support specific approaches to ethics are convinced that their perspective is the right one, and the one that will ultimately help them honor Aquinas' imperative to do good. To evaluate the respective, possibly mutually exclusive, perceptions of good, dignity, (social) justice, freedom, and so on along with all their consequences in turn requires a metaperspective, detached from the internal views of the respective representatives of such ethics. Adam Smith recognized this when, for humankind's inclination toward good, he relied not solely on the verdict of the judge within (i.e., the voice of the conscience) but rather on an imaginary external, impartial spectator as an additional instance for the probing of one's conscience. Immanuel Kant also understood the conditionality of conscience as *norma normata*[2] and the dangers of a purely internal perspective of ethics, which can quickly blind the observer to objective moral law prescribed to humanity (as a deontologically founded representative of objective good).[3] Religious ethics in particular assumes this type of metaperspective, whether God, the divine, or the like. Notions of transcendence can be seen as the standard of all that is good. If it is assumed either with a transcendent good such as this or with Smith and Kant that there is indeed an objective metaperspective, then the subjective conceptions of good that are immanent to the world can be evaluated based on how closely their content is aligned with what is objectively good. Then the fascist, jihadist, and cannibal could be countered with: "You may have your own idea of what is good. And you may even think it is the right and ethically good view. But it is nevertheless not only ethically bad but also wrong because it contradicts what is objectively good."

It is plausible to assume an ethical metaperspective of what is good to substantiate such distinctions. The challenge here remains to continually subject them to conscientious review. The vicious circle of endless relativization of ethics is then countered by the bold attempt to find rational plausibility for a semantically rich good, which exists and can be identified and practiced. For a Christian moral compass, it follows that the triune God is this objective good, which has been made recognizable to humankind through Holy Scripture, Jesus Christ, revelation, and reason. This cannot be proved empirically, just as, for example, the existence of the Kantian moral law or the categorical denial of an objective good cannot be proved. Therefore, all individuals who are capable of reflection, including professing Christians, must remain willing to question their own internal viewpoint critically and constantly from an external perspective. For the dialogue with other forms of ethics, the reference to a philosophical-ideological confession is undoubtedly also a weakness in the justification of a meta-idea of what is good. If it remains self-critical when roles are reversed with the external perspective of an impartial observer, it nevertheless does not fall prey to dogmatic ideology.

Now, let us turn to another important area of ethics that occasionally receives short shrift in the context of social issues: Virtue ethics probes the practical consequences of good in practiced morality and in ethos, whether interpreted individually or socially. The question here is: Which specific attitudes toward values determine people's behavior? In 1848, Bishop Wilhelm von Ketteler of Mainz described a fundamental problem of virtue ethics something like this:

> The two great evils of the soul that afflict our social relations are partly insatiable greed and avarice and partly selfishness, which has destroyed charity and compassion. This disease has consumed both the rich and the poor. What effect can tax distributions and savings banks have as long as this mindset persists? The world with all its teachings is utterly powerless in the face of this inner relationship, while Christianity directs the full force of its teachings precisely to the conviction, the inner soul of humankind.[4]

Von Ketteler targeted all social strata equally with this criticism of the prevailing attitudes of his time. Virtue ethics is about the concrete implementation of what is recognized as good or what is considered good in practical life. The classic personal virtues are temperance, prudence, fortitude, and justice; the latter is not to be confused with the value of righteousness. Justice as a value describes the (actionable) right corresponding to human dignity in normative ethics, while justice as a virtue describes just persons who, in their behavior toward others, are always concerned with what is appropriate for the other person. Christian virtues include faith, hope, and love as the basic guiding principles. Moral coherence thus means that ideally conscience, as an individual compass for decision-making, should be able to put into practice what has theoretically been recognized as good with the help of the virtues by which it lives. In individual ethical decisions, a distinction is generally made between the perspective of ethics of conviction (*Gesinnungsethik*) and ethics of responsibility (*Verantwortungsethik*). Ethics of conviction demands unconditional adherence to the values recognized in normative ethics. In addition, a responsible ethical attitude attaches considerable importance to the possible consequences of the specific decision.

The socio-ethical side of virtue ethics comes into play when we examine the way in which humans live together, which is shaped by individual behavior, or when we inquire after the agents and their values, which determine the rules in society or in a business, for example. Evaluating existing or proposed rules is then the task of institutional ethics.

Christian social ethics expressly "sees and evaluates the entire realm of human coexistence in the light of Christian revelation."[5] It is not only a reflection of the normative but also takes a normative position itself and seeks answers to the definitive questions of our time. This applies consistently to application in all its sub-areas. There are different names for this discipline, and there can also be very different designs in terms of content. The initial starting point in this book is Catholic social teaching. It is "an integral part of the Christian doctrine of humanity"[6] and sees itself as

> the totality of socio-philosophically (from the essentially socially predisposed human nature) and socio-theologically (from the Christian order of salvation) obtained knowledge concerning the nature and order of human society and the norms and tasks of order that result from this and are to be applied to the respective historical conditions.[7]

Based on this, all that is (i.e., everything that exists) is created by God and has its reason and justification in Him. It is thus in the nature (essence) of the created being to be deeply grounded in the uncreated being of God. The precursor of such ethics, in the so-called Western world, at least, includes the Aristotelian conception of an ordered world as a whole, which has its origin in an unmoved mover of the universe.[8] Thus, a supreme absolute principle is assumed, which is interpreted by Aquinas from a Christian perspective as a personal, triune God. God is understood in such a way that He exists as an absolute being from Himself and in Himself and does not need the created world in order to exist. God can exist without the created being, but the created being cannot exist without God. Thus, God becomes the ground from which the created being springs, in which the created being may only share. God Himself requires no further justification. He is the absolute reason in everything, just as He is the absolute being in all created beings.[9] Justificatory recourse for legitimate norms is dispensed with in this absolute, thus obviating the problem of infinite regress. Against this backdrop, it becomes understandable that all beings are part of a divine plan and are given a context of meaning that draws on natural law (*lex aeterna*). This is the core of the theonomic Christian approach. What people ought to do (their moral mandate to do good) is not deduced from being. It is already immanent in being. People thus carry within themselves a normatively effective goal or ideal purpose. "*Bonum enim et ens convertuntur*,"[10] says Aquinas. This normativity is taken into account whenever a Christian view of human nature is discussed in this book.

Therefore, it can be stated: Social ethics, as it relates to humankind, concerns itself with what is good and with offering good justification for it. This is the normative orientation for rules and coexistence. The value basis of social ethics is the concept of humanity and human dignity from the perspective of *Weltanschauung* with the interpretations of justice, freedom, and responsibility derived therefrom. Human-centric, humane social ethics asks normative questions about how orders, rules, and relationships serve humanity. It must provide an answer as to whom, to what extent, and why humanity and/or society is responsible for what and with what consequences. This is the litmus test for the respective understanding of legitimacy. Depending on the semantics of the concept of human dignity and responsibility, competing ethical approaches each have their own contents, justifications, and practical consequences, as well as different weightings of the relationship between virtue ethics and institutional ethics. This book proposes Christian social ethics from a Catholic perspective as a means of resolving contemporary issues and offers at least a partial further ecumenical discussion. It addresses the three questions of the existence, knowability, and practicability of good in the sense of the Christian confession and not from normative sources derived in any other way. A compass identified in this way is based on demonstrably good Christian reasons and can thus offer answers that provide guidance on important social questions that may differ from the answers offered by alternative forms of ethics.

Thus, there is no denial of the ethical plurality of the present. Nor is there any effort to seek ethical consensus based on the lowest common denominator. Rather, the moral compass profiled here places the stringency of Christian reasoning above general acceptability. This profile can not only be used to identify answers to specific dilemmas; it can also point out the limits of alternative models of ethics, which are ultimately rooted in different conceptions of humanity, human dignity, and society. This form of Christian social ethics is aware of its role as one among many and its need to defend itself in the struggle and dispute surrounding social orientation. The outlines of the Christian profile identified here offer a kind of clarity that can only be of benefit to any earnest democratic culture of debate.

NOTES

1. O. von Nell-Breuning (1987): 49.
2. Translated, *norma normata* means "standardized norm." Conscience is thus considered a norm that is itself normed, that is, conditioned and influenced by contexts. On anthropology in Adam Smith and Immanuel Kant, cf. the corresponding sections in the chapter "Normative Humanism beyond Theology" in part II.
3. Here, the term "objective" expresses that there is a truth of good that is predetermined and hence unattainable to humankind. This can be interpreted subjectively (i.e., according to the respective view of the observer), which may lead to different interpretations. However, this diversity is no argument for relativism. Rather, what is objectively good retains its normative validity, even independent of subjective and possibly diverse interpretations.
4. W. von Ketteler (1848): 109.
5. F. J. Stegmann and P. Langhorst (2005): 605.
6. MM 222.
7. J. Höffner (1962/1997): 22 et seq.
8. Cf. Aristotle, *Metaphysics* XII, chapters 6–7. The concept of an objective good and its knowability as the starting point of ethics is found in Plato and Aristotle. As representatives of what is objectively good, Plato's idea of good and Aristotle's notion of an unmoved mover establish a transcendent objectivity. The task of humankind—as in Christian ethics—is to recognize this normative objectivity and derive from it a reliable compass for leading a good life, whether this is conceived of in terms of individual or social ethics. Aristotle compares the virtuous person to an archer, who must recognize and aim his reason like an arrow at the target of a transcendently defined good. In Plato, the transcendent good is immanently given as the eidos in human reason. With this incarnation of good, humans are now able to recognize objective good and align themselves with it. The Islamic humanism of Ibn Rush (Averroes) and the Christian scholasticism of Thomas Aquinas continued this thinking in religious contexts and identified the henceforth abstractly conceived good with the personally conceived one God. The Christian notion is an integral part of the substantive ethical profile presented here. On Islamic humanism, cf. the corresponding section in the chapter "Theological Humanism beyond Christianity" in part II. Immanuel Kant can also justify such absoluteness independently of transcendence and knowledge of God. On Kantian universalist ethics, cf. the corresponding section in the chapter "Normative Humanism beyond Theology" in part II.
9. Cf. Thomas Aquinas: II Sententiae, 16.
10. Thomas Aquinas, STh I–II, q. 18, a.1.

Chapter Two

Sanctification of the World

A Christian moral compass for good cannot be reduced to a purely internal perspective with no contact with the non-Christian world. On the contrary: Christian social ethics cannot be understood without considering Jesus' command to share this message of good with as many people as possible. This involves conveying well-founded Christian values on the one hand and applying these values to solve specific questions related to society on the other. With this transparency and relevance, Christian social ethics offers orientation for winning over new converts. It always has a missionary side because its objective is to be instrumental in the sanctification of the world. Sanctification, in this sense, means more than proclaiming a philosophical idea of good. It should be understood as Jesus' command to Christians because, from a Christian standpoint, good assumes material form in the discipleship of Jesus. This type of mission is reflected in good reasons and good people, who, in their commitment to the triune God, appeal to the reason and soul of humankind for the Christian idea of humanity and society. Both are considered here. Thus, to understand the mission, one's gaze is directed not first to a theory but to the person in whose service and responsibility sanctification stands.

THE MISSION

The origin of the command to sanctify the world is the mission of Christians through Jesus Christ and the mission of the Holy Spirit. The aim is to realize Christians' responsibility to the world before God in today's increasingly secular environment. Christianity and the world are inseparably interrelated through anthropology and creation. The task of Christians is to show the way to a meaningful life in the eyes of God and to contribute to the preservation of creation.[1] Christians are not merely of the world. Their origin and purpose are given by God. Their identity is therefore eschatological. At the same time, Christians are in the world. They themselves should be leaven,[2] light, and salt of the earth. They should recall the reality of creation and demand the ethical consequences resulting from it.[3] This requires a dialogue with the earthly realities (politics, economy, natural and social sciences, etc.).[4] Christians are not conformed to this world (Romans 12:2). If they were, Christian theology, for instance, would merely be an adjunct to other sciences. Nor is the Christian community—like the Church—a ghetto that has turned its back on the world. After all, it proclaims the message of Jesus for the people and the preservation of creation in the here and now. Christians thus recognize an autonomy of the world,

> if by the autonomy of earthly affairs we mean that created things and societies themselves enjoy their own laws and values which must be gradually deciphered, put to use, and regulated by men. . . . But if the expression, the 'independence of temporal affairs', is taken to mean that created things do not depend on God, and that man can use them without any reference to their Creator, anyone who acknowledges God will see how false such a meaning is. For without the Creator the creature would disappear.[5]

The goal of Christian social ethics is always to create paths that lead to a meaningful life before God in this world and to enable people to follow these paths.[6] Origin and goal, systematics and practice are inseparable. Christian social ethics also seeks ways to reconcile human behavior and social rules with the virtues of love of God, self, and neighbor. From the Christian view of humanity follows not only the measure of a legitimate order but also a viable path to a good life before God, marked by the use of one's conscience and the spirit of love.[7]

God alone is the source of all holiness. People should—as taught by Francis de Sales, for example—fully embrace the will of God in this life. This is a moral command. However, Christians are not only called upon to do this through baptism. The gift of the Holy Spirit also makes the command to fulfill this mission an essential characteristic of Christian existence in terms of being. It is true that humans, who, according to the story of creation, were created in God's image, lost their original nearness to God through the Fall. But Christ has restored this dignity so that the essence of the *human condition* and the universal call to holiness, which always remains eschatological, do not fundamentally contradict each other. The christened individual is thus also an eschatological existence in which perfect love through God's grace is equally grounded as a commandment and a form of empowerment. Here, then—especially in infant baptism—God's grace precedes human action, a view that largely also coincides with Protestantism.[8] The ontic share in holiness through baptism is imparted on people through sacrament. This is because holiness comes from God alone and not from humankind and the normative constructs developed by humans, whether constructivistically or otherwise. It is not first the result of virtuous deeds performed individually but an expression of fully potentialized sacramental human existence. The baptized share in the sacred by being called to holiness and empowered by the Holy Spirit to respond to God's call.[9] A perfect life from God based on this is holy in its ethical, ontic, eschatological, and, from the Catholic perspective, also social-ecclesiological dimension.[10] The command to holiness is obeyed through the radical discipleship of Jesus. This command is directed equally to all Christians. Nevertheless, there is no simple template for concretizing holiness. The worship of Jesus is the expected response to the call of God by those who are called upon. People's callings or vocations are not always the same, just as not all people or their talents are the same. The diversity of charisms or spiritual gifts—among canonized saints, for instance—is only one simple piece of evidence of the myriad ways of understanding holiness in practice.[11]

But what human being can achieve this holiness in full? Does it not remain the exclusive vocation of a select few after all? No, because all who are baptized are destined for holiness.[12] Now, this does not mean that whoever is unable to live a perfect life from God is lost. Here Christians hope for a gracious God who knows that beyond such perfection, people are also sinful. Nevertheless, this vocation remains as a goal and thus as a reliable compass that points the way to a successful life in the eyes of God and in the world. The Christian tradition recognizes the saints in their sheer perfection as models for all those called to holiness. For they have radically succeeded in following Christ. Christians can and should use them as orientation. Saints are good examples of this, making them a compass for what it means to live a good life today, if people succeed in emulating the holiness of the saints and using their own talents and charisms to follow in their footsteps.

Even if only a few baptized persons are saints themselves, all Christians have the non-delegable mission to sanctify the world by imbuing it with the Holy Spirit. The idea of the world being imbued with the Spirit of the Trinity makes the baptized, through their share in holiness, the leaven, light, and salt of the earth. The diverse nature of the vocations involved is a visible expression of God's versatility in His holiness. As the baptized engage with the world through the development of their different talents and charisms, each bestowed upon them by God, ever new facets of the greater holiness are revealed. Sanctification is thus the sacramental imbuement of the world with the Holy Spirit, which is ontically present in those who have been baptized and is morally and personally effective and thus always also a revelatory event.

THE AGENTS

The representatives of the official church, theology, associations, church agencies, and congregations could be mentioned classically first as agents called upon to sanctify the world. All of this is true. More comprehensive than a purely functional attribution is the view of the inner attitude of the agents who are called upon to be protagonists of sanctification even beyond any office or function. In this regard, we must first distinguish between the saints and those called to holiness.

The call to holiness reaches its perfect culmination in the *imitatio Christi*. Saints achieve this supreme goal of Christian life, which is also important for the Reformation tradition of Martin Luther and Philipp Melanchthon, for example.[13] In spite of the Fall, it presupposes the ability of humankind to encounter God, to observe Him (for example, in prayer, mysticism, etc.) and to live a perfect life in the worship of Jesus. *Imitatio*, in this sense, refers to more than a directional ethic. Those who succeed are credible role models. The first prerequisite is the vision of God or beatific vision *(visio Dei)*. The starting point for this is again God's grace: a gift to which people can and should respond. God can be seen because God sees humankind. The most important examples of this in Catholicism are the holy mystics. This immediate approach can also be considered in the Reformation, even if it remains controversial in the reformative tradition. According to Melanchthon, humankind 1.) with the natural light *(lumen naturale)* carries an inherent natural ability to see God in spite of the Fall. This is illuminated 2.) by the decalogue and reaches its perfect culmination 3.) in the Gospel of Christ. God then offers humanity these three perspectives from which to observe God. However, people are personally responsible for how they use them. This is the answer that people must give themselves—and, again, this must not arise exclusively from a previously bestowed grace but from a freely rendered decision. Melanchthon develops

> the doctrine of 'natural light' *(lumen naturale)*, which enables all men to think and to recognize natural law. The later Old Lutheran teachers held on to this idea. This doctrine of the *lumen naturale* proves to be the bridge that leads Melanchthon to the Erasmine views in certain fundamental dogmatic questions, including the doctrine of 'free will.'[14]

Thus, in an ecumenically significant way, Melanchthon opens the door for people's active participation in the fulfillment of their mission.[15] One must say "yes" to God of one's own volition. Humans are capable of developing these characteristics. For Jesus Christ has made a new covenant with humankind and sent the Holy Spirit into the world for this purpose. With the order of creation and this new covenant, God steps forward to enable humans, as free and moral beings, to respond to their call to holiness. Based on Christian understanding, people walk this path in responsibility both before God and always with God. The second step of *imitatio* (besides *visio Dei*) is now to become completely one with Christ and thus live a perfect life—something that is reserved for a chosen few. This perfection, which humans can attain through grace and the acceptance of grace as becoming one with Christ, still requires redemption because humans cannot be equal to God. It shows versatility in different vocations. But some essential characteristics can be determined in the concrete realization of Christian virtues of faith, love, and hope:

- *Imitatio* means that people accept the Gospel of Christ as an inner habitus and live entirely from it. Christ is the reliable path to inner freedom and, at the same time, a compass of conscience for good. That is: Jesus' spirit wants to be, should be, and can be the habitus of the Christian.
- Freedom in the sense of *imitatio* follows precisely from the *visio Dei* and the divine revelation in Jesus Christ. Liberation happens through the internalization of His message and thus through the acceptance of the transcendence effective in the world.
- Piety in the sense of *imitatio* is not limited to asceticism and the mere recital of prayers. Added to this is a life that is convincingly credible because it loves Jesus Christ more than itself.
- According to Melanchthon, reason in the sense of *imitatio* juxtaposes the logic of Jesus (*ratio Christi*) in the Word of God as its own rationality with the worldly one. Human use of reason must ultimately be aligned with this *ratio*, openly profess it, and expressly develop it as an independent metaphysical epistemology and introduce it into the discussion with alternative epistemologies.
- Martin Luther, experiencing his own fear, contemplated the human relationship to self, neighbor, and God. Here we find the idea of the human being who is damaged as a whole by the Fall but who is not lost. Everything that makes humans lovable comes from God alone. This mercifully opens the door to *imitatio*. From this follows the call to an attitude of humility.

Reformed theologian Walter Nigg even cites very specific guidelines for holiness,[16] according to which all saints (for example, Augustine, Paul, etc.)

experience turning points. They are not born saints. These turning points allow them to experience an immediate calling that they wrestle with until they come to accept it and recognize their own affinity for obedience. This enables them to experience and recognize the meaning of their lives and use their own existence to point the way to eternity. For Christ lives in them (Galatians 2:20). The veneration of saints leads those who are called upon to Scripture and to Christ. This also makes them credible role models for the young. Countless people have found and continue to find guidance in the saints, discovering the presence of God in their lives for the world. Moreover, the veneration of saints can also challenge *de facto* human coexistence in a socio-ethically effective way. Pope Francis challenges the tendency toward materialism, Thomas More challenges opportunism and nepotism, Mother Theresa challenges indifference toward the poor, and so on. Taking these ideas to their logical ecumenical conclusion also brings role models such as Dietrich Bonhoeffer, Brother Roger, Martin Luther King Jr., and many others to mind. Depending on how saintly perfection is conveyed, it can also be a barb against practiced social or religious circumstances. Its root is never primarily political but transcendent. As long as veneration is alive in people's faith, the saints will also be the mouthpiece of *ratio Christi* in express opposition to earthly imperfection. Take, for example, these telling words regarding St. Nicholas of Myra in a legend of the saint that was widely circulated in Germany around 1935:

> From afar he rescues the innocent who are unjustly condemned to the executioner's sword. . . . Always and everywhere he is the friendly helper, who never fails the oppressed. . . . In recognition of what is truly great, our people have never inquired after kind or origin—they followed faith and faith never betrayed them.[17]

It can thus be said: An encounter with God in *visio* and becoming one with Christ constitute saintly perfection. In this, they are an example to all who are called upon. Nevertheless, the path that leads there is not arbitrary. To follow the call to holiness means walking the path with God and toward Him. God's providential love and its acceptance on the part of those who are called upon come together here. The personal God expects each person to respond to His loving call.

The call to holiness is aligned with God's command to open up the paths for all persons to worship Jesus in as many areas of life as possible (in individual ethics in the orientation of their personal lives, e.g., through values and principles, in their thinking, in the ethos by which they live, in how they interact with God and themselves, in social ethics in the respective manner of shaping rules, and in concrete encounters with others and creation).

Non-baptized individuals should also be included, even if, from a Catholic perspective, they cannot share in holiness because they do not take part in the sacraments. For God is free to call them to holiness as well.

Even secular politicians (or business leaders, etc.) may act in accordance with this call if they allow such freedoms in society or business.[18] In this sense, leaders should trust in their reason, provided it follows their conscience, which—with an open and sympathetic ear toward the Word of God—will prevent them from going astray. Leaders live, make decisions, and seek guidance differently with this ear for "creative reason" that precedes humankind than without it. Christianity understands this as *ratio Christi*. When he referenced this during his address to the German Bundestag on September 22, 2011, Pope Benedict encouraged non-Christians not to rely solely on their own reason or that of their advisers but to at least consider the possibility that there could be an objective instance of good (whether it may be conceived of as God, reason, an idea, or something similar). The pope did not mince words, underscoring the direct responsibility of all regulators (in the body politic, the economy, etc.) and comparing them to the biblical King Solomon. Parliamentarians and other policymakers should be open to transcendence in the hereafter, seek (sacred) role models, and conscientiously align their own reasoning with a source of good that predates humankind. Thus, even those who help shape secular society can adopt responsible regulations and pass laws that ultimately allow sanctity to unfold. This means that they can contribute to the sanctification of the world. Well-founded Christian social values, for example, provide a reliable compass to guide these responsibilities. While values such as freedom, equality, humanity, human dignity, and so on receive overwhelming approval even in the secular world, those who are in charge have failed to sufficiently substantiate them and infuse them with meaning. The former pope extended an invitation to approach ethically good and socially effective policymaking marked by an openness to the idea of transcendence to achieve the necessary, practically effective materialization. This invitation is directed toward basic human sentiment, so it does not offer a template for easily establishing and reproducing monosemy. Each individual decision-maker would be obliged to personally examine their own conscience—an examination which could also be preserved beyond political decision-making as an ethos of responsibility toward an objectively conceived human truth. The Solomonic quote cited by the pope, in which the king refers to himself as a "servant," emphasizes the fact that this examination should be accompanied by an attitude of humility or at least modesty in the face of both the human and political temptations of a primary orientation toward goals such as "power-wealth-longevity-destruction of enemies." By listening to conscientious reason and using humility as their guide, decision-makers should contemplate coexistence and state legislation in light of the Law of Transcendence, whereby Benedict's focus is on the personal Holy Creator Spirit who established the *lex aeterna* and expressed Itself in creation.

THE OBJECTIVE GOOD AND ITS REALIZATION

The Christian view of humanity and society gives the responsible agents a socially effective value compass as a tool for shaping the world around them. According to this, as written in the biblical book of Genesis, humans possess an unconditional dignity that they owe to their Creator because they were created by God and in His image. This is affirmed by the incarnation of God in the form of Jesus Christ.[19] This dignity, founded in God, cannot be relativized. It is thus objective, timeless, and universally valid.[20] In Catholic social doctrine, such justification is understood to be

> a service to the truth which sets us free. Open to the truth, from whichever branch of knowledge it comes, the Church's social doctrine receives it, assembles into a unity the fragments in which it is often found, and mediates it within the constantly changing life-patterns of the society of peoples and nations. (CiV 9)

Unconditional dignity as objective good thus becomes concrete in the sanctification of the world. As a result, contemporary society "presents us with choices that cannot be postponed concerning nothing less than the destiny of man, who, moreover, cannot prescind from his nature" (CiV 21). The compass for shaping the world for the purpose of sanctification is thus related to the destiny of humankind, to human nature. As moral people, humans receive a social mandate from God to shape society in a manner that ensures this unconditional dignity is respected and brought to bear. This compass is used to assess responsibilities, rights, and duties.

Human knowledge of the content of this mandate lies in discovering God-given destiny as absolute human dignity but not in creatively constructing it.[21] From a Catholic frame of reference, agents need not depend on the Bible alone for this realization of the compass—in this case, the Christian image of people and society. After all, reason and conscience are considered truthful: "Man has become like one of us, knowing good and evil" (Gen 3:22).

Reason can also help us identify timelessly valid rights and duties: "The Church's social teaching argues on the basis of reason and natural law, namely, on the basis of what is in accord with the nature of every human being" (DCE 28).

The active mind (the νοῦς as *intellectus agens*) can recognize God-given destiny through its participation in the divine spirit with the help of abstraction (as *Wesensschau*, or the intuition of essences and essential structures). It uses the inherent guide of the "right reason" (as ὀρθός λόγος, or *ratio recta*) for this purpose.[22] What is meant by this is the right reason that, following conscience, recognizes what is in alignment with natural law and thus absolute human dignity.[23] In this *Wesensschau*, it is possible for right reason to touch upon natural human destiny through understanding, but it cannot grasp it in its entirety. However, right reason is only part of divine reason; it is not identical. Thus, the knowledge of human dignity and personhood (and other social values) that are regarded as true are not identical to divine truth, yet not completely different from it either. This is why they are called analogous. However, questions remain about this knowledge of reason:

- How can reason be directed toward God at all?
- Even right reason remains human. Therefore, how can it recognize something absolute, even if only analogously?

The answer is: The Holy Spirit present in the world enables humans, as *caritas in veritate*, to direct loving reason toward God and His eternal order (*lex aeterna*), to recognize it analogously,[24] and thus to make timelessly valid statements about the nature of humanity, human dignity, and the essential rights and duties of humankind. Knowledge of good, however, cannot rely on reason alone: "There is no true humanism but that which is open to the Absolute" (PP 42, CiV 16). The basic attitude of love enables such an opening: "Charity is at the heart of the Church's social doctrine" (CiV 2). "'*Caritas in veritate*' is the principle around which the Church's social doctrine turns" (CiV 6). Love is a vehicle for the knowledge of good, directing reason toward God: "It is about . . . making [reason] capable of knowing and directing these powerful new forces, animating them within the perspective of that 'civilization of love' whose seed God has planted in every people, in every culture" (CiV 33).

Knowledge of good succeeds with a basic attitude of reason in love. A habitus of love liberates reason toward the love first given to humankind by God. It frees humans from greed and makes them ready to share (poverty before God). It frees humankind from hubris and opens people's minds to the truth that transcends the material (obedience to God). It liberates people from the addiction of uncontrollably giving in to urges and gives them creativity and self-worth (passion before and for God).[25] People should understand themselves as being given by God's love and therefore as being called to love. With its openness to transcendence made possible by reason in love,

Christianity can thus open itself to the truth of God: "The greatest service to development, then, is a Christian humanism that enkindles charity and takes its lead from truth" (CiV 78).

In his address to the Bundestag, Benedict XVI reminded the audience that—from a Catholic perspective—in addition to right reason, living tradition also conveys truth.[26] Following Benedict's line of thought, knowledge of good has a dynamic and a stable side.

- Recognized good (for example, as content for dignity, justice, family, economy, education, etc.) is not a monolithic block in an ivory tower because its understanding is in a spirited dialogue with the world. In the search for truth and justice, humanity's gaze should "again be directed to the vastness of the world, heavens, and the earth." Finding objective truth remains a dynamic process. Augustine would give a different testimony of justice than the resistance fighters in the Third Reich. Both testimonies and many others open windows with equally valuable perspectives on truth, which is a reliable standard of good. This perspective is understood as a dynamic dialogue with the world based on the premise that God exists (*etsi deus daretur*).
- Objective normative ethics for the determination of good as a Christian compass for good has little tolerance for normative relativisms, but at the same time, must remain modest in its only analogous and thus deficient understanding of semantics. Likewise, it must always reaffirm whether its objectively recognized content actually corresponds to the law of God.

This search for good is never-ending because it requires an enduring exegesis in accordance with reason, with constant critical examination of this supposedly discerning reason. And this protects it from dogmatism.

ESSENTIAL CONTENT OF THE GOOD

Humanity and Responsibility

Besides the question of God, Christian ethics always begins with the following question: What is humanity from the Christian point of view? Humankind is first loved by God and called to love—free, social, dialogical, sinful, and seducible with inclinations such as egoism and a desire for power, driven by urges, and yet reconciled with God.[27] Humans carry an essential purpose within themselves—a purpose that gives rise to a moral existence that can arrive at good decisions with the help of an honestly examined conscience. In the Christian view, humans are living beings and the image of God. The resulting unconditional dignity establishes with personal *individualitas* and *socialitas* the unconditional rights of every human being to allow creativity and communality to unfold. According to biblical testimony, God acts as a model and expects the appropriate responses from humankind, as can be seen in some normative formulations in Scripture.

Table 2.1. Biblical reasons for the humane ethos

God's instructions in the covenant with humanity	Appropriate human responses	Biblical sources
Freedom, friendship, and judgment	Moral responsibility for one's own life/ overcoming coercion	I do not call you servants any longer. . . . But I have called you friends (John 15:15). So then, each of us will be accountable to God (Romans 14:12).
Love for people	Love of self, neighbor, and God	You shall love the Lord your God with all your heart. . . . And: You shall love your neighbor as yourself (Luke 10:27).
Human talents	Creative development of the talents bestowed	Like good stewards of the manifold grace of God, serve one another with whatever gift each of you has received (1 Peter 4:10).
The earth's scarce resources	Sustainable use and appreciation of creation	The Lord God took the man and put him in the garden of Eden to till it and keep it (Gen 2:15).

God gives dignity and freedom to every human being. He establishes fellowship with people in His covenant. He entrusts creation to humankind. He gives people grace and forgiveness on the cross and, through the resurrection, the certainty of new life. The vocation to holiness—unlike in esoteric thinking, for example—does not correspond to an ennobling process of self-redemption that prepares people for an earthly rebirth.[28] Rather, the unfolding of the personal qualities of being is considered a human response to God's gift of personhood. Humankind's salvation is not first the result of its own achievements[29]; ultimately, it is granted to humans by God. Thus, even the human existence broken in its weakness (the fragmentary) retains the same full dignity. Consequently, both the saint and the sinner, the devout Christian and the atheist, have unconditional human dignity and so on. From a Christian standpoint, humans have a non-delegable duty to God and to themselves to realize the full potential of their individual and social personhood and to value every human life, especially the lives of the weak and the vulnerable. So, responsibility toward one's fellow human beings is a mandate of love of neighbor, which is also realized, for example, in an affective spirit of social cohesion. As a moral existence, humankind bears a threefold responsibility according to the triune commandment of love in the Bible:

- Thy God: This love is manifested in the understanding of our life in the light of God, our Creator, and our being thankful for what He gives to us and, as moral beings, realizing freedom in this light;
- Thyself: This love is manifested in accepting ourselves in the image of God as persons with unconditional dignity and in recognizing the undivided dignity precisely in the experience of our own weakness; and
- Thy neighbor: This love is manifested in tangible acts of compassion on the one hand and in our commitment to living together in an affective spirit of social love on the other.

Such responsibility bestows true freedom and is meant to permeate the world: "Each person finds his good by adherence to God's plan for him, in order to realize it fully: in this plan, he finds his truth, and through adherence to this truth he becomes free."[30]

In this responsibility, Christian ethics calls for the development of individual virtue in all areas of life, as well as for social participation in creating such rules and frameworks and living such relationships, so that the development of the vocation is achievable, or at least unhindered, for as many people as possible. Humankind follows God's moral command by developing its own dispositions of freedom and sociality in response to the work performed by God in an independent and socially responsible manner.

Social responsibility is the moral duty to love one's neighbor. This can now be interpreted as a powerful duty in the sense of Franz Böckle.[31] According to "Good Samaritan" laws (Luke 10, 30–7), the burden of proof would then always lie with the person who fails to help another in an emergency (illness, financial need, refuge, or similar). The Christian spirit of social love[32] required to coexist is thus expressed in the normality of helping others. The alternative Christian interpretation of charity establishes a weak duty in the sense of Eberhard Schockenhoff. No one should be obliged to do something they cannot do for good reasons. Following this principle of *ultra posse nemo posse tenetur*, it is up to the personal self-determination of humans in their responsibility before God to concretize the commandment of loving their neighbors in the sense of the Golden Rule (Matthew 7:12). There may also be good ethical and Christian reasons for not helping another in a specific emergency because doing so would exceed one's own strength.[33] For the culture of coexistence, this does not give us carte blanche to be self-centered; instead, it reinforces a culture of personal responsibility. In the awareness of being a human family of individuals created by God, it is then incumbent on moral decision-making to shape life in a self-determined way, in accordance with God's command.[34] I share Schockenhoff's reasoning in the following, understanding fully that there are good Christian reasons for the corresponding counterposition.

The idea of God's plan of salvation is not to be understood as predestination but instead as God's desire, founded in love for humankind, for humans to be saved at the Last Judgment (that is, when they enter eternal life). To this end, people are commanded and empowered to follow Jesus and thus to make the good a reality.[35] By fulfilling this mission, humans bring salvation to the world and may also hope for salvation in eternal life. God's plan of salvation thus has an earthly as well as an eschatological dimension, since the material world is never the Kingdom of Heaven until the Day of Judgment and thus salvation in the world always remains imperfect. Salvation does not simply mean a healing from illness, from evil, and so on but stands on its own as a positive and, at the same time, perpetually lacking term for God's plan with humankind and creation. This inadequacy is a consequence of human limitations.[36] What is recognizable, however, from a Christian point of view is the following: God is love (1 John 4:8), God is good, and, therefore, God is the source of holiness.

> "Salvation" in the New Testament is the ultimate consummation of all human desire for truth and life, freedom and love in God, the Creator and Finisher of His creation. The eternal salvific will of God takes historical shape in His acts of salvation, redemption, and liberation. Salvation is therefore not a state of human condition different from God. Rather, salvation in the universal sense is God Himself, insofar as he is present in the creaturely self-fulfillment of man as the author and goal of life.[37]

As such, the will and plan of salvation mean that the ruin of humankind and the world is not God's intention. In fact, quite the opposite is true: "Indeed, God did not send the Son into the world to condemn the world, but in order that the world might be saved through him" (John 3:17).

Social Principles and Values

The Christian concept of dignity in the context of the sanctification mandate is flanked by the social principles of the common good, personhood, solidarity, and subsidiarity. They certify enforceable rights and obligations. People are the authors of their own destinies as persons when they may live according to their natural destiny as humans. Everyone should make any subsidiary contribution they can. In the spirit of "one for all, all for one," there is at the same time an unconditional duty, to be guaranteed legally by an order, to enable every human being to realize the potential of their personhood independently and to the best of their abilities. This applies, of course, to the unborn, the disabled, or those with dementia due to old age. All humans thus have the right and the duty to develop social responsibility based on their destiny as persons. In this context, solidarity means the legally guaranteed duty to help the weak and the vulnerable who cannot help themselves. This allows for well-justified interventions (such as taxes to finance solidarity-based social transfers) in private property.[38] When people can develop their individual freedoms (creativity and imagination, industriousness and ambition, etc.) and their social nature (friendship, partnership, family, etc.), personal and social responsibility in addition to their love of God, they live according to their destinies. Once this humane goal is achieved, personhood unfolds. The materialization of human rights realizes the objectively understood personhood through defensive rights such as protection of life, freedom of religion, freedom of the press (negative freedom) as well as through socially enabling rights such as those to health, clothing, and education (positive freedom). In a welfare state, for example, *solidarity* establishes a legal relationship *in solidum* by which each member is liable for a group of debtors or the entire group is liable for each of its members. Based on such a judicial interpretation, for example, the legal principle of solidarity is distinguished from emotional brotherhood:

> Fraternity is certainly an exceedingly high moral value; however, strictly speaking, it is not the subject of a legal claim. . . . Solidarity . . . is . . . legal obligation. The exercise of this solidarity is a highly significant good for the community; its exercise is something to which every member of the community has a strictly legal claim against all others.[39]

The Christian view of humanity justifies such strict social rights and duties in the fact that the unconditional dignity of humankind is connected with the command to exercise personal responsibility (subsidiarity) whenever possible and for social responsibility to be used to help people help themselves. Wherever individuals are prevented from achieving their destinies according to their physical, mental, and spiritual abilities and possibilities, there is a violation of the "principle of the centrality of the human person."[40]

Catholic social teaching demands "social justice and social love" for the implementation of its personal idea of humanity.[41] Social love replaces both, "giving in order to acquire" as well as "giving through duty" as a habitus.[42] The insight into the common personal destiny forms a spirit that unites people and also paves the way for an emotional "unity of the human race, a fraternal communion transcending every barrier."⁴³ "Man's earthly activity, when inspired and sustained by charity, contributes to the building of the universal city of God, which is the goal of the history of the human family."⁴⁴ Social love is committed to the personalization of all people and overcomes social anonymity through emotional coexistence. Just as it responds with love, calling for an integrative or inclusive ethos, so too does it distance itself from an exclusive collectivist communal virtue.⁴⁵

Normative Humanism as a Social Program

The view of humanity, social values, and principles lend contours to the normative idea of Christian humanism today. In his encyclical CiV, Benedict XVI chose the normative humanistic postulate of a natural human condition to justify and contextually define human dignity. From this Christian perspective, inviolable human dignity is given by God and is therefore timeless, objective, and universally valid. The rights and duties of each person are derived from this independently of the individual or social benefit and collective. Human dignity thus springs from an unchallengeable objectivity. The deduction of human rights is linked to a normative foundation grounded in God (theonomic). Normative humanism is the justification of an unconditional human dignity based on an objective good and is recognizable as such by humankind. The materialization of human rights, which are merely formally guaranteed in many countries of the world (for example, in countries with despots and other dictatorships), through a "new humanist synthesis" follows a vision that does not strive to be a mere utopia.⁴⁶ "Hence a sustained commitment is needed so as to promote a person-based and community-oriented cultural process of world-wide integration that is open to transcendence."⁴⁷ The call in the CiV encyclical for a comprehensive humanistic synthesis as a socio-ethical compass is not new. Catholic social teaching fundamentally requires a normative humanistic consensus of values for the executability of its ideas of order. The social criticism of the forgetfulness of truth as the forgetfulness of humanity of our time, expressed time and again not only by Benedict XVI but also Pope Francis, is of a fundamental nature when, with the "ecology of man"⁴⁸ or "human ecology"⁴⁹ called for, both the possibilities of human self-destruction and the hubris of people to want to play the creator themselves are denounced as a consequence of culturelessness. Violations of God's plan (for example, in the disregard of social principles or a reconstruction or deconstruction of human dignity based on egoistic interests)⁵⁰ are opposed by the goal that human beings should understand themselves in their identity as persons in responsibility before themselves, before each other, and before God. This also means the orientation to the normative human nature.

SOCIO-ETHICAL EFFICACY

Mission as Identity

How does this mission take effect in the world? From a socio-ethical vantage point, for example, questions must center on how to appropriately shape peace, culture, homeland, economy, politics, law, and creation. Contexts for which these questions are relevant are also, in accordance with the missionary mandate, places of practical probation for Christians. Sanctification is understood as the mission of all those who have been baptized to act as leavening agents for the world. Even non-Christians can participate. Above all, however, Christians are called upon to question current social circumstances based on their faith and with the help of their normative toolbox. Grounded in the image of God in the human being, in God's covenant with human beings, and in God's incarnation, Christians see themselves as the responsible partners of God in this world.[51] All Christians are therefore called to understand the command to follow Jesus and continue it through their own lives. They are the agents of the sanctification of the world. As those called to holiness, all Christians are charged not only to participate in this but also to be guided by holy models. This orientation can be translated into a biblically-based individual ethic of the threefold responsibility to love outlined above.[52] It is thus a reliable compass for worship. Social interaction, for example, in society, business, or family, is morally good if it grants all who are called upon the freedom to follow their vocation to holiness. Social ethics as an instrument of sanctification also consists of enabling and favoring, in the design of rules, laws, or social norms, ways of fulfilling the vocation and thus the development of the individual ethos.

Acceptability as a Compass

Christian social ethics is part of the mission to sanctify the world. It offers people a moral compass for navigating social questions in recourse to the objective good. The content is based on the Christian idea of humanity. Applying it to decisions in dilemmas creates Christian-based legitimacy. It is not simply identical to juridical legality, technical-practical feasibility, or economic viability. Rather, the compass proves to be a purposeful concept of acceptability in a dilemma.

The concept of acceptability must first be clarified in principle before its Christian semantics can be defined. For the clarification of terms, I follow Klaus Kornwachs' essential distinction between acceptance and acceptability:

Acceptability is the result of a judgment regarding an action, its consequences, a state of affairs, a motivation, an intention—in other words, everything that can be the subject of a moral evaluation. Acceptable is that which conforms to one's own principles, values, whose priorities and adopted norms conform to such an extent that a possible conflict appears negligible. Acceptance, on the other hand, is empirically ascertainable behavior by persons or groups of persons who actually tolerate an attitude, an action, etc., i.e., do nothing about it, or consent to it (e.g., through purchase).[53]

People might voluntarily purchase consumer goods for reasons unilaterally promoted in advertising without being informed about the associated risks (for example, to the environment or their own health). Only the voluntary decision made through education or comprehensive information concerning the associated risks and opportunities can fulfill the legitimacy criterion of acceptability, provided that, in addition, the accompanying consequences can be assessed in a normatively positive way. Acceptance is shown actively or passively in measurable sales transactions or elections and other votes or, for example, in non-resistance to decisions made. Acceptability, on the other hand, only exists when all consequences are consistent with moral values. The criteria of acceptance and acceptability are thus independent of each other as long as the value basis of ethical evaluation is not simply defined as acceptance. This would be, for instance, the position of economic ethics that does not normatively question people's actions that are effective in the market.[54]

EXAMPLE 2.1

A plastic cell phone with no functionality whatsoever but with a good advertising concept might be accepted in the market from an economic standpoint. Acceptability then examines, for example, the conditions of production (consequences for the environment) and arrives at a negative normative judgment.

The content of acceptability and thus the result of a (socio-)ethical evaluation depends on the value basis of the evaluator, which must be made transparent. This comprises:

- The view of humanity and the associated understanding of human dignity (this results in an understanding of freedom and justice),
- An idea of human service and human coexistence,
- Addressees and contents of human responsibility, and
- An ideological source to be made transparent.

With the help of this set of values, other relevant values and principles can be prioritized and concrete ethical assessments can be made. Different semantics of acceptability can be derived based on different views of humanity, which are fed by alternative ideological sources. This is due to the factual plurality of existing values. This does not at all mean ethical relativism but plurality of ethically substantial (because well-founded) positioning, which is essential for a democratic culture of debate. Ethical evaluation thus occurs in three stages:

1. First-order acceptability (substantial acceptability): Within the framework of an ethics that is coherent in and of itself, a concept of acceptability is proposed from a set of values that is made transparent and conditioned by worldview, with the help of which evaluative decisions can be made in dilemmatic situations. This acceptability is a coherent and thus well-founded ethical positioning from the set of values to the specific evaluation (A_1). This independent and hence substantial positioning is a concept of first-order acceptability.
2. Second-order acceptability (procedural acceptability): In the democratic discussion of values, competing and thus contested notions of such first-order acceptability contend with each other. Insofar as the ethical understandings of people, society, coexistence, and responsibility are led to a common result of a tolerated compromise or a majority decision by means of procedures constructed in whatever way, this result can also be explained in the sense of the definition quoted above as a form of acceptability but now a different one, as long as it does not necessitate conflict. This result (A_2) itself proposes a new ethical evaluation, now inferred from the process and therefore dependent on it, with a new position of acceptability generated for it, which is tolerated even though it may differ more or less from its own original position on first-order A_1 acceptability. This does not eliminate the competition between original A_1 and inferred A_2 and other alternative ideas of acceptability. It is precisely this difference that constitutes liberal argumentation in ethics.
3. Third-order acceptability (procedural acceptability): Free debate requires an orderly procedure that does not replace first-order acceptabilities but rather can lead to democratic solutions with their help alone. This process is itself subject to ethical evaluation. A third-order acceptability (A_3) defined in this way does not directly evaluate a situation or a rule but only the process of decision-making and thus the achievement of the result in the process (the consensus, compromise, etc.).[55]

Christian semantics that can be established at the level of first-order acceptability can now be determined based on this definition of acceptability. Ethics that provide orientation necessarily presuppose first-order acceptability with transparent values and proposed solutions. The normative starting point of Christian acceptability understood in this way is the Christian view of humanity. The ultimate criterion for evaluating a rule, behavior, or idea is whether it promotes the ability of all individuals to fulfill the destiny bestowed upon them by God according to the abilities they are granted. Anything that serves this goal is to be encouraged. Anything that contradicts it must be rejected. Decisions made in dilemmas are acceptable if they, along with their consequences, better enable all people to develop the talents given to them in the context of their threefold responsibilities. In this responsibility, a Christian acceptability of the first order relies on leaving to humans those areas of individual responsibility that can be expected of them, in which they can adequately and self-determinedly fulfill their mission in this world.

NOTES

1. Cf. QA 130.
2. Cf. GS 40.
3. Cf. GS 40.2.
4. Cf. GS 43.
5. Cf. GS 36.
6. Cf. the social doctrine of the Church on this command (e.g., CA 54).
7. Cf. programmatically, for example, the encyclical DCE.
8. Such free churches, on the other hand, which seek to justify exclusive confessional or "believer's" baptism in reformative terms, must explain why the confession made there of one's own free will must now be thought of as *sola gratia*.
9. On the foundations of Catholic pneumatology, cf. G. L. Müller (2010): 390–413. The Holy Spirit, as the person of the one, triune God, is the love of God that works in the heart of man and, as love, allows reason to unfold in the sense of CiV to the "realization of Jesus Christ as the Son of the Father and the eternal mediator of the revelation." Cf. ibid.: 390. The Holy Spirit is the presence of God in man as well as the ability to know God and His will. It is thus the source and goal of the knowledge of God, gift, and task for a life of threefold responsibility (before God, oneself, and one's neighbor) out of threefold love (cf. Luke 10:27). Cf. also in this chapter below the section on the essential content of the good.
10. From a Catholic perspective, the Church embodies this eschatological tension as God's counterpart in which Christ is present as its head. Thus, Paul may call those who have been baptized "the saints" in Rom 1:7 or 1 Cor 1:2. Through this presence of Christ and the orientation toward His message, the Church, which is a sacramental organism from the Catholic point of view, can understand itself as the people of God

and *communio sanctorum*, as expressed in the Council Constitution on the Church *Lumen Gentium* (LG).

11. For characteristics of holiness in saints, etc., see the following paragraph, which focuses on the agents.

12. The question as to whether those who have not been baptized might nevertheless be destined for holiness is a separate topic that goes beyond the dogmatic scope of this discussion.

13. For the following thoughts, cf. C. Frey (1998).

14. H. Jesse (2005): 39. The highlights in the quote have been added.

15. This idea proposed by Melanchthon, as well as the attempt to build an ecumenical bridge, is likely viewed critically above all by Protestant theologians in the tradition of Friedrich Schleiermacher or Karl Barth, among others. Debates such as these make clear the need for perseverance to ensure the stability of ecumenical bridges in the field of social ethics as well. This calls for further intensive dialogue that addresses the differences and further incorporates them for the profiling of ecumenical social ethics. In this sense, the bridge proposed here is merely the beginning. A detailed hamartiological (i.e., sin-related) discussion is beyond the scope of this book. For a deeper Catholic analysis, cf. e.g., G. L. Müller (2010): 143–53. Cf. also below in this part I, in the chapter "Ecumenical Perspective," in the section on the view of humanity as a set of values, the corresponding remarks on the understanding of *natura corrupta*.

16. Cf. W. Nigg (1982).

17. H. Hümmeler (*sine anno*, ca. 1935).

18. Cf. Benedict XVI (2011). In the sense of Catholic social teaching, responsible authorities who conduct themselves in this manner belong to the "people of good will" who, for the first time in Pope John XXIII's encyclical *Pacem in Terris* (PiT) in 1963, are the addressees of a magisterial letter, alongside ministers, all Catholics, and believers in Christ. These "people of good will" might not share faith in Jesus Christ. However, by being open to the idea of transcendence and possessing reason and love (cf. encyclical CiV), they can arrive at a view of humanity that closely approximates that of the Christian and use this as a basis to assume responsibility in the world which—from a Christian standpoint—corresponds to God's will of salvation. From a Christian perspective, people of good will include all who are prepared to engage in a fair dialogue with Christian positions and their ideas about humanity and society. Accordingly, anyone who is not willing to do this is not included in this view.

19. This refers to the Christian belief that God Himself came into the world in the human form of Jesus Christ. Worshiping Jesus is therefore identical to worshiping God; the Word of Jesus is the Word of God. The very fact that God became human and incorporated human nature into divine nature (Ascension) underscores this prominent position of humans and human dignity in the plan of creation.

20. For an understanding of objectivity, cf. the chapter 1: "The Search for Good."

21. Cf. O. von Nell-Breuning (1985): 362. Human dignity is to be understood as timeless and universally valid and also objective due to the human likeness to the image of God. Thus, its claim is tied back to God, who is Himself the Absolute. The attribution as "absolute" by no means places human dignity on the same level as God.

Rather, it is intended to provide a conceptual counterpoint to a relative understanding of human dignity by which certain people might be excluded from unconditional human dignity by others for whatever reason. Because Christians believe that human dignity is given by God, it cannot be legitimately relativized. From absoluteness understood in this way it follows that, epistemologically, people must be concerned with understanding and implementing the preconceived claim and content of this human dignity. As an alternative to such an understanding of human dignity, one could assume that it is not predetermined (by God, etc.) but must be creatively constructed and determined repeatedly by human beings. Such creativity can then, for instance, make use of the egoistic interests of individuals (or inclinations), as normative individualism does. Cf. the section on normative relativism in the chapter "Ethics beyond Normative Humanism" in part II. Here, cognition based on inclinations means the absence of a connection between what is now an individualistic interpretation of good to a preconceived normativity.

22. The terms νοῦς and ὀρθός λόγος can be traced back to Aristotle. *Intellectus agens* and *ratio recta* are found in the works of Thomas Aquinas, for instance. Cf. Thomas Aquinas, STh I-II, q. 91,2.

23. In this sense, right reason cannot err. Reason can only err if it is wrongly accepted by man as right reason. By definition, it is reason that is actually successfully directed toward God. How this *ratio* can be identified as such in practical terms for humankind in relation to self-deception is in turn a problem of epistemological knowledge.

24. Analogical knowledge means that humans, even using right reason, can never approach divine reason and therefore can never fully understand divine good and *lex aeterna*. The knowledge of right reason always falls short of the divine and can only translate it into the *conditio humana* of human limitations. In consequence, there is always a need to review and possibly supplement such knowledge.

25. Cf. CiV 1 and the remarks on love as *Agape* and *Eros* in the encyclical DCE.

26. Cf. Benedict XVI (2011).

27. A hamartiological (i.e., sin-related) perspective is referred to here in part I below in the section on the view of humanity as a set of values in the chapter "Ecumenical Perspective."

28. Cf. the section on the belief in reincarnation in the chapter "Theological Humanism beyond Christianity" in part II.

29. This position, condemned by the Church as heresy, was held by the lay monk Pelagius (360–420), after whom the doctrine of Pelagianism is named.

30. CiV 1.

31. Cf. F. Böckle (1989): 155 et seq.

32. Cf. on this goal for human coexistence the encyclical QA 88.

33. Cf. on the idea and application of this principle to the topic of organ donation E. Schockenhoff (2013): 403–39, and in part III, in the chapter "Life, Work, and Death," the section on organ donation.

34. Cf. CiV 7.

35. Whether hell is empty or not and how exactly the grace of God relates to the reward for a good life are controversial dogmatic questions in ecumenical-theological

dialogue and beyond. They are not discussed further here. However, those interested in a deeper discussion of this topic from a Catholic perspective are encouraged to refer to G. L. Müller (2010): 553–68.

36. Cf. the preceding section in this chapter.

37. G. L. Müller (2010): 373. Such acts include, for example: forgiveness, mercy, eternal life after death, and so on.

38. See the section on the property system in the chapter "Economy and Economic Order" in part III below.

39. O. von Nell-Breuning (1985): 116.

40. CiV 47.

41. QA 88.

42. CiV 39.

43. CiV 34.

44. CiV 7.

45. See the section on normative relativism in the chapter "Ethics beyond Normative Humanism" in part II.

46. For the individual ethical dimension of this synthesis, cf. CiV 1; for the socio-ethical dimension, cf. ibid. 21.

47. CiV 42.

48. Benedict XVI (2012).

49. LS 5, 13, etc. See the section on the integrity of creation in part III in the chapter "Creation, Justice, and Peace."

50. See the section on normative relativism in the chapter "Ethics beyond Normative Humanism" in part II.

51. Cf. GS 11, CA 44, 2.

52. Cf. the section on the essential content of the good in the chapter "Sanctification of the World."

53. K. Kornwachs (2013): 100.

54. See the section on normative relativism in the chapter "Ethics beyond Normative Humanism" in part II and the section on the compass for the market in the chapter "Economy and Economic Order" in part III.

55. Simple majority decisions are conceivable here, or more complex processes such as discourse ethics, which is itself normatively prescriptive, or a deliberative equilibrium in the sense of John Rawls. On discourse ethics, see the section on postmodern discourse ethics in part II, in the chapter "Ethics beyond Normative Humanism."

Chapter Three

Ecumenical Perspective

For Christian social ethics to win back followers today, it is important to fully appreciate the treasures offered by different denominations along with their answers to social questions in an effort to embrace unity in diversity: for example, the emphasis on the Holy Scriptures in Protestantism, the Church Fathers in Orthodoxy, the work of the Spirit in many free churches, or tradition and the interplay of reason and faith in Catholicism. A social doctrine (as a set of magisterial pronouncements) exists only in Catholicism, systematic social ethics also in Protestantism, while a separate orthodox discipline is not systematically developed.[1] Here, I focus on the dialogue between the Catholic and Protestant positions. Different approaches to reasoning are also evident in social ethics. While these differences will receive mention in the following, they will not be the focus of attention. Instead, I propose ways to reveal a bridge built on socio-ethical systematics as an example. It makes sense to inquire as to how the Catholic position taken in this book might be enriched by Protestant thinking. First, the ecumenical profile of Christianity's view of humanity outlines in broad strokes the socio-ethical set of values. Then the basic missionary understanding of Christian social ethics can be filled in with the help of the two-regiment doctrine, before the Reformation principle of *Solus Christus* can be used as an example to present some social fields of application in which Christian thought and action can act as a leavening agent.

VIEW OF HUMANITY AS A SET OF VALUES

Ecumenical Perspective on the Good

The ecumenical-socio-ethical construction of the bridge envisaged here by no means requires a consensus to be reached in the assessment of every single political or economic issue. Moreover, in an interdenominational context, rifts remain where, for example, a final agreement in the justification controversy or in the Church's understanding of ministry (for example, on the role of women) is seen as a condition of possibility (*Möglichkeitsbedingung*) for ecumenical social ethics. Dogmatics and ethics cannot be separated. However, I do not make an agreement of the dogmatically disputed questions a precondition for further refining the picture of ecumenical social ethics. More than in other—especially such dogmatic—questions, I consider it possible and necessary for the field of social ethics to achieve a broad ecumenical consensus, which is more than a formulaic compromise of the lowest common denominator. Equally convincing and effectively communicable answers to the questions concerning the (social) justice of a social order are possible together and, in view of the challenges of secularity and (post-)modernity, of liberalism and collectivism, also necessary. Reflection on an ecumenically unifying normative basis is relevant for well-founded Christian positions on the socio-ethical issues of our time. Here we must make "the common profile of Christianity recognizable in our society."[2]

This ecumenical journey—historically speaking—does not start at zero, even if the efforts are still relatively nascent compared to corresponding dogmatic dialogues. There is ecumenical agreement on the fundamentally personal profile of unconditional human dignity, which is derived theologically from the *Imago Dei* doctrine and is found independently of theology, for example, in the United Nations Declaration of Human Rights and constitutionally, for example, in Article 1 of the Basic Law for the Federal Republic of Germany (*Grundgesetz*—GG) and the fundamental rights that follow there: "In summary, fundamental recourse to human dignity emerges as the first integrative moment of ecumenical social ethics."[3]

Catholic and Protestant theology in Germany jointly view a "human image of Christianity" as the foundation of ecumenical social ethics.[4] The profile of this view of humanity must also be sharpened with regard to controversial systematic questions. Using the unifying personal idea of humanity, an attempt will be made to bring together the various traditions into a complementary theory. Classical as well as contemporary humanists of different denominations appear as witnesses for this.

Law and Love as Bridges

The dividing line in the (socio-)ethical concepts of Catholic and Protestant provenance should not be denied. However, such tensions are not insurmountable obstacles to further sharpening the common normative basis of social ethics. In particular, two fundamental concerns of dogmatic origin must be overcome: 1.) The recognizability of a common normative foundation could fail due to the different approaches to human knowledge of divine truth; and 2.) different understandings of the role of social ethics in God's plan for the world could have irreconcilable consequences for its theological self-understanding.

- In terms of epistemology, the Protestant tradition argues primarily biblically in the sense of the *sola scriptura* principle, while Catholicism emphasizes magisterium and tradition alongside it. Natural law is applied on both sides, with the scholastic interpretation being a Catholic proprium. In the papal social encyclicals, natural law is repeatedly cited with more or less pronounced reference to Thomas Aquinas in its Aristotelian or—as in the case of Benedict XVI—also in its Platonic interpretation. The widespread suspicion that natural law is a static transposition of the divine *lex aeterna* into positive law is countered by Protestant theologian Wolfgang Maaser with reference to STh I-II, 97:2, that in the Thomasian sense "also a certain adaptation to changed living conditions promoting the general benefit is legitimate."[5] Natural law, rightly understood in this way, is by no means to be viewed statically. Martin Luther, of course, adheres to natural law as the foundation of universal norms, but he refrains from integrating these into an ontological order of being of a divine *lex aeterna*, as is the basis of Thomas. So human participation in the divine order of being, conceived in terms of substance ontology, is denied as the necessary condition of possibility and ability for the (analogous) knowledge of divine truth.[6] For Luther, the law of love (*lex charitatis*) of God in Jesus Christ is superior to the applicable natural law and natural rights derived from it. This faith-immanent bond between personal dignity and Jesus Christ is characteristic of relational ontology. However, replacing one ontology with another is not Luther's teaching. Luther regards love "as a metanorm, a norm for norms, with which the general standards of natural law are to be critically processed."[7] Natural law retains its esteem as a now contextualized justification of universal norms.[8]
- Further in dispute is how the liberation of reason is to be framed so that it can both recognize the truth of God and the given nature of humankind with its implications for the meaning of human dignity for social principles and norms. In his encyclical CiV, Pope Benedict XVI builds a bridge to

the Lutheran *lex charitatis*: "*Caritas in veritate*" is the principle around which the Church's social doctrine turns.[9] Without love—according to Benedict—no rational knowledge of truth succeeds. Only love broadens the scope of reason toward God.[10] Only when reason is assisted by an attitude of love can it lift the cloud created over humankind by the Fall and then recognize the Christian view of humanity.[11] *Lex aeterna* and *lex charitatis* must henceforth no longer be understood as an insurmountable opposition but as complementary.

- For Martin Luther, the freedom of the Christian is, at the same time, a joyfulness of the will that humans may experience themselves as instruments of God. Freedom of will detached from this is refuted.[12] Luther rejects the soteriological significance attributed by Thomasian scholasticism to human works alongside divine grace. Grace alone brings about in humans the ability to develop the humanity willed by God, which then expresses itself in an ethic of human compassion. Based on such an interpretation of the *sola grata* principle, (social) ethics is thus understood more horizontally than vertically, whereas, in the Catholic tradition, a consonance of both directions has prevailed. Philipp Melanchthon already proffered a suggestion for bridging this gap. He considered an order justifiable ontologically and under natural law to be possible since he saw the justice of God and the justice of the heart as inextricably bound to each other and therefore considered possible the thought of an order of being arising out of love.[13] In this way Melanchthon built a bridge to the concept of the social relevance of a divine idea of order as a critical instance for the evaluation of factual rules and dominions. A neo-Protestant system of ideas continues this line of thought:

> Obviously, it was the power of human sin, whose recognition compelled early Protestant thought to anchor the initially emphasized freedom of the individual Christian man in the corset of divinely authorized supraindividual orders and social structures. But what happens when the divine authorization of certain worldly orders and social structures is called into question? The answer will have to be: The corset of divine orders of creation regulating all individual ambition toward a successful life in the old Protestant understanding loses its normative meaning.[14]

In the tradition of Melanchthon, neo-Protestant thinking recognizes the necessity of an orientation toward a normative idea of order that is ultimately derived from metaphysics to shape a just social order. This metaphysical character is due to the fact that the *bios politikos*, as an expression of the world-immanent finality of humankind, is at the same time permeated by the transcendent finality of humans in their participation in God, without the perfect participation in God (the *bios theoretikos*) becoming the ethical standard of world-immanent ethics in the sense of a righteousness of works.[15] Thus, despite a denial of the direct reference to God of human ethics, a world-immanent orientation to the metaphysically founded idea of a normative supreme principle becomes logically conceivable. The relevance of a universal normative foundation for the ethical evaluation of a social order can therefore be regarded as ecumenically consensual while retaining the special property of justification theory.

This paves the way for a more detailed definition of the content of such a socio-ethical supreme principle, which will be provided in the following with the help of socially determined Christian humanism. This form of humanism can and should represent the normatively understood human being (the humanum) as the universally valid and not metaphysics-free standard for the socio-ethical legitimation of questions of our time in value context with ecumenical emphasis. At the same time, such a program provides a convincing rationale for the central idea of German Basic Law and universal human rights. What Arthur Rich formulated as a question, Christians today should understand as a concrete creation mandate: the "humanum" as a guiding concept of ecumenical social ethics.

Norm and Habitus

All humanism interprets sciences in the light of anthropology. Karl Rahner offers an exemplary way of paraphrasing this for the field of natural sciences:

> All natural sciences either directly or indirectly engage in anthropology. And they say something about man; what they say is, strictly speaking and in the final result, never a precisely divisible material knowledge about something within man himself, but determines and influences the image of the one and whole man, even where the individual natural science seeks to guard against methodological or substantive boundary transgressions.[16]

The anthropological justification of the social order in a supreme principle as a normative regulator is also (not solely) indispensable to Christian social ethics. "According to the almost unanimous opinion of believers and unbelievers alike, all things on earth should be related to man as their center and crown."[17] Humanistic social ethics starts with its personal foundation in anthropology. In a Christian sense, it questions socio-ethical arguments regarding their compatibility with God-given human beings and their dignity.

This thinking was developed into a scientific system in scholasticism. In the early twelfth century, an optimistic missionary vision in Europe stimulated the idea of a unified explanation of nature, humanity, and God. To this end, faith should be defended by understanding the divine will as rationally as possible. A human search for purpose and meaning was paired in this period with the awareness that all human knowledge is limited.[18] It felt embedded in the idea of a divinely given determination of the essence of humanity and nature. The human search for truth understood itself as perpetually incomplete, despite all systematically formulated analogous knowledge of truth. The uniform Latin language in the Occident facilitated the general intelligibility of the rationally advanced systematization. The language, method, and questions of the thinkers ultimately differed little in this foundation.[19] Unlike today, complex communication models for translating one ideologically defined form of ethics into the other were largely superfluous in this context. The great questions of Greek philosophy (for example, those of Plato and Aristotle) about the existence of things and the attempts to capture the linguistic meaning of this existence were also formative for Christian thought and science. The fallen human race thereby sought to rebuild its dignity, not against, but expressly in the context of faith and metaphysics.[20] The goal commitment of humankind, based on God's love and thus on the supernatural, was the impetus for the further development of society, the basic concern of which was a positive appreciation of humans in their friendship with God.[21] The human social nature receives an intrinsic value in God's offer of friendship. Even in the sense of St. Thomas Aquinas, the horizontal orientation toward other people and toward the shaping of society is a basic natural state of mind.

Academia's reception of contemporary Christian social ethics remains controversial in ecumenical discourse. However, the vision of a normative reorientation of human dignity based on God-given humanity substantiates the ecumenically consensual topicality of this thinking for our time. According to Oswald von Nell-Breuning, Christian social ethics must always be measured against this goal. Consequently, it is teleological by its very nature. It gains its legitimation from the idea of humanum as a pre-empirically postulated concept of the human being with normative force. The ecumenical hinge is humanism. Christian humanism discovers in human dignity the universally valid organizing principle of socio-ethical legitimacy, which Christians today can use with good reason to oppose any positivism, such as legal positivism, with which human rights might also be called into question.[22]

The Ecumenical View of Humanity

It is now possible to formulate the cornerstones of a view of humanity in Christianity that Catholic and Protestant Christians together with humanum as the supreme principle of social justice can offer and demand for socio-ethical dialogue.[23] It is not merely the ideal image of a Christian being but rather an image in which all people can recognize themselves, even if they are not prepared to share the genuinely Christian justifications in their entirety. Humans do not construct their essence themselves in a creative process of creation. Any science of humanity—and thus also social ethics—"will always have to work with presuppositions that cannot be empirically verified."[24] Whoever denies this either has a purely empirical understanding of science (but this is already a postulate) or must model ethics past the essence of humankind.[25]

The Christian occidental tradition is based on the biblical figure of Adam and recognizes the true individual (without sin) in Jesus Christ as the "human image of Christianity." Martin Luther contrasts *imitatio Christi* ethics from Christian mysticism with the doctrine of the *conformitas Christi*: "It is not we who make ourselves like Christ, but God who leads us into conformity with Christ."[26]

Consequently, the ecumenically consensual core in the idea of humanum is not in danger. Important for the common profile in current socio-ethical discourses is the agreement that the Christian understanding of humanity is not compatible with a human nature that is constantly being redefined. For the ecumenically consensual socio-ethical supreme principle of humanum, then:[27]

- Humans are personal by nature, carry their dignity within themselves, and are not the products of chance. This metaphysical foundation is linked back to the Christian convictions of creation and divine likeness.[28]
- They are dialogical social beings, ultimately founded on their dialogical relationship with the Creator and a practiced love for Jesus Christ. Self-interest and the common good are mutually dependent.
- They have consciences and—in terms of shaping their own lives—free will. Human freedom always implies the mandate of threefold responsibility (toward God, self, and neighbor) and morality (in the virtues of faith, love, and hope).
- To be human is also to be error-prone and weak, which leads to egoism (*natura corrupta*). The relationship between the Creator and His creature changed through the Fall because humankind was released from Paradise. Humans carry within them:

  > the tendency to sin and wickedness from youth (Genesis 4–11), even from the mother's womb (Psalms 51:7).[29]

In free decision and responsibility, humans become sinners by way of their thoughts and deeds. Where the human is concerned, this tendency to sin

and wickedness must be taken into account, although the theological interpretations of this remain controversial in an ecumenical context.[30]
- God calls humans to salvation. Humans transcend their respective essence.[31] The vocation creates serenity in the face of purely earthly prophecies of salvation.[32] Such an eschatological dimension brings inner freedom from transient world immanence. Human beings have purpose and may hope to hear the call of God and to realize their inherent nature.[33]

This conception of humankind describes the Christian humanum, whose presupposition Catholic as well as Protestant social ethics can explicitly oppose with the dangers of "arbitrary actions" (such as Social Darwinism, racism, etc.). "A pre-understanding is generated that gives off the framework of empirical representationality."[34] Consequently, the humanum serves as a criterion for ethical evaluations of social contexts. This results in a natural imperative: "This is a command to develop the humanum at all times and in different circumstances."[35] Thus, when opinions are articulated and decisions are made in the socio-ethical sphere, they can be examined for their humane legitimacy (as acceptability). The humanum is the ecumenically consensual, highest unconditional socio-ethical norm to which the following applies: "[A]s such, it defines the limits within which the freedom of a life design can come into its own."[36]

According to Christian understanding, the humanum with resulting criteria of Christian acceptability is neither invented nor made but discovered. The following applies to such ethics: "It is not true because it works, but it should work because it is true."[37] This humanism recognizes human nature, accessed in complementary ways, as a transcendent ethical principle. In the encyclical SRS, Pope John Paul II puts it this way: "If there is no transcendent truth, in obedience to which man achieves his full identity, then there is no sure principle for guaranteeing just relations between people."[38]

Humanum understood in this way is not just the name for the consensus on the personal foundation of ethics. Alignment with this view of humanity in Christianity provides the individual with a valid measure for ethically legitimate decisions, as well as an ideal of virtue. Beyond this, the humanum is the basis of a social idea of order.[39] Humanists such as Erasmus and Melanchthon, for example, derived social principles claiming legitimacy from the humanum as early as the sixteenth century. From this, Erasmus develops an ethical program, which he designs as an educational ideal (*Bildungsideal*). The masterminds of the social market economy base their model of society on this view of humanity, drawing on ecumenically recognized social principles.

ON THE INHERENT NATURE OF THE MISSION

To make the common profile of the Christian recognizable in our society today means to refer to the Christian humanum in socio-ethical discussions. Of course, the mission to sanctify the world is a common ecumenical concern of Christians. Christianity's view of humanity is the contextual set of values for this permeation of the world. In this section, we examine the inherent nature of this missionary mandate more closely under an ecumenical lens.

With the doctrine of the two regiments, the spiritual and the secular, which dates back to Bishop Augustine of Hippo, reformers Martin Luther and Philipp Melanchthon, in particular, offer present-day food for thought as to how the relationship between the Church, theology, and Christians and our increasingly secular world can be reconciled in contemporary society.[40] They suggest a struggle between the divine sphere (where the love of Christ, for example, through human introspection, living out the Beatitudes, etc., prevails) with the power of evil. As long as this battle is not fought out, there will be a secular regiment in between, where coercion and violence may still have legitimacy. That does not mean that everything is allowed in this in-between. Ultimately, even it must be guided by the *lex charitatis* of God. It is therefore a question of a realistically achievable yet growing permeation of the secular sphere with the spirit of Christ.[41]

The idea that such a sanctification of the world should also be sacramentally bound, for example, connects a Catholic interpretation with the founder of the deaconess movement in Lutheranism, Wilhelm Löhe, for whom all practical social welfare work (*diaconia*) in the world must start from the altar. The encounter with Christ in the sacrament of the Eucharist or the Lord's Supper[42]—according to this view—potentiates the Spirit of Christ in humans, encourages them to live in accordance with the spirit, and to use it to help shape the world. From these origins, the world should be animated with the Spirit of Christ. The encounter sets out in the world as it is and proceeds from there step by step.

Today, the Christian mandate to sanctify the world is opposed by secularist demands to suppress religion. Other confessions should provide ethical guidance. For example:

- a postmodern belief in political discourse in the sense of Jürgen Habermas;[43] or
- the belief in the inherent laws of the market or technology; or
- the belief in a rule of reason, such as that of the French Revolution, with all its consequences; or

- the belief in collectivist visions, colored red or brown, even if they quite obviously brought the opposite of peace.

Among the reformers, aspects of two-regiment doctrine can be used to counter such ideas. On the one hand, the idea of fundamentally fallen humanity is a clear warning against all consequences of godless hubris, embodied in autocratic rulers, for example. On the other hand, secular authority should ultimately be guided by the *lex charitatis* of God. From a position such as this, their inclination must be to narrow in on this, even if this will never be fully possible in the world today. At the same time, the Reformers reject political fanaticism.

For the relationship of Christians to the world today, this means:

- Theocracy is to be rejected, as is any ideology that relativizes human dignity in rules and laws;[44]
- Changing the globe in the spirit of God's love should set out realistically in the world as it is and proceed from there step by step;
- Christians should reject the idolization of the market, technology, collective, and so on. Even the religion of reason (such as that of the French Revolution) falls short of the Spirit of Christ. For, according to the Reformers, the Gospel of Christ establishes with the *ratio Christi* the idea of a reason that transcends human reason;
- Outflows of evil in the world—for the struggle mentioned by the Reformers persists today—are, moreover, to be explicitly identified, named as such, and combated in a sustained effort; and
- It is the task of theology and the Church to gradually bring the world closer to the logic of *lex charitatis*, which achieves perfection in Jesus Christ. The Christian consciousness of *ratio Christi* as a prerequisite for the sanctification of the world is incompatible with a self-understanding that makes theological argumentation dependent on an ability to connect with secular patterns of thought.

THE CHRIST PRINCIPLE IN PRACTICE

Christianity's view of humanity is the set of values upon which ecumenical Christian social ethics is built. The inherent nature of the mission is the divine spirit of love. This must become tangible in the various fields of application in the world.

Solus Christus—as an Ecumenical Principle

The Reformation principle of *Solus Christus* emphasizes, in the context of epistemology, the centrality of the Gospel and, in exegesis, the focus on the message of Christ; in the doctrine of grace, the mediation of grace and salvation exclusively through Christ.[45] Placing the Gospel and Christ at the center of knowledge, reason, and world responsibility also aligns with the necessary responsibility of Christian social ethics today. All confessional differences regarding the doctrine of justification notwithstanding, the principle of *Solus Christus* is a reminder in this respect to always keep the ultimate orientation in view despite all worldliness. From the perspective of Catholic (social) ethics, there is also much to learn about our own self-image.

On the one hand, there is the question of a Christian self-image of theology, already touched upon in the preceding section. On the other hand, there is the question of how Christians respond to the logic of an increasingly secular or at least non-Christian world. Corresponding challenges to theology and Christianity today are identified here and confronted with positions of Luther and Melanchthon, while practical orientations derived from them are proposed along these basic lines. I am guided here by assessments made by Christofer Frey.[46] Epistemology, anthropology, and ethics present themselves as productive, sometimes closely intertwined, fields of discussion for a socio-ethical perspective.

Theological Christian Identity

Attention should first be directed to some of the challenges to the contemporary self-conception of theology and Christianity.

- Epistemology: The attempt to connect to the secular world by methodological atheism or the like is widespread in socio-ethical reasoning in both Catholic and Protestant tradition. Reasoning with natural law has largely died out in German faculties. Luther and Melanchthon would likely disagree. Neither (particularly not Melanchthon) rejects natural law. Rather, revelation shows itself in natural law and in the Gospel, as both sources express the same *lex charitatis*. This is how Joseph Ratzinger emphasized it as early as 1964 and, later, as pope, provided deeper insight in his encyclical CiV.[47] Melanchthon opposed the worldly logic with the logic of Jesus in the Word of God as a rationality of its own. Theology must ultimately obtain its orientation from this reason and openly confess it. Moreover, it must explicitly allow it to unfold and introduce it into the conversation as an independent, invitational metaphysical epistemology.

- Anthropology: Particularly in the doctrine of justification, many theologians see a profile dividing Protestant and Catholic theology, including in the field of ethics. Melanchthon, who also remained open to traditional rites and sacraments, built an ecumenical bridge here as well with his idea of the *lumen naturale*.[48] In addition to the aforementioned natural law pillar of knowledge, vestiges of the goodness of humankind along with a moderate interpretation of justification are assumed, which could be compatible with a Catholic position. Even if the consequences drawn from this (possibly more strictly interpreted *sola gratia* on the Protestant side, and economy of grace on the Catholic side) each turn out differently, the views of humanity in this light nevertheless show themselves to be much more closely related than often thought. Moreover, ecumenically speaking, Christian anthropology is largely consensual anyway.[49]
- Morals: In questions of conscience, talk of a power of evil has largely given way to milder expressions today. The idea of a devil was much more tangible to the Reformers than theological thinking is today. The two-regiment doctrine implies a struggle between God and Satan. In this way, the use of force could also be justified under the requirement of the *lex charitatis*. Luther singled out the pope of his day as the anti-Christ. Today, other phenomena may come into view against which the use of force could be justified, even for a Christian, such as terrorists' contempt for humanity or the like.[50] The oft-invoked freedom of the Christian competes today with inner-theologically prescribed constraints of fact or thought, which for Catholics condemn references to natural law or the social teachings of the church—not entirely free from polemics—as pre-modern and instead identify in a postmodern paradigm the only possibility of contemporary Catholic social ethics.[51] Freedom to think differently on well-founded theological grounds should also retain a place in social ethics.

Secular Identity and Being a Christian

Now let us take a closer look at how theology and Christianity encounter ethics in the contemporary secular world.

- Epistemology: (Post-)modern epistemology emancipates itself from theology and offers reasoning that is free of metaphysics. Universalizability can be justified only by laws of reason (as in Kant or others). Outdated, hierarchically dominated truth teachings that have subjugated humankind (meaning, for example, the Church) must be overcome, with the ultimate ethical criteria of autonomy and self-determination—for instance, within the framework of contract theories, economic, or discourse-ethical ideas of ethical relativism or the like. The Reformers also wanted to overcome the existing lack of freedom, especially human arbitrariness in dealing with God's grace. For them, however, knowledge does not originate in pagan philosophy but precisely from the divine revelation in Jesus Christ. In today's terms, this means: Non-secular autonomy and self-determination are what make people free. Liberation does not happen by overcoming God. On the contrary, it arises through the internalization of His message and thus through the realization of transcendence.

- Anthropology: Explicitly secular anthropology, unlike Kant, for example, asks about being human without God. Economic ethics considers humans as egoistic utility maximizers (HO = *homo economicus*), bases its (economic) ethics on this, and explicitly emphasizes that this is not a human image but merely heuristics.[52] The distinction between the dignity of humans and that of animals runs into trouble when reason is taken as the standard of dignity because certain animals may have it while certain humans may not.[53] Discussions about the beginning and end of life are now usually conducted without reference to God but instead with reference to individual self-determination.[54] From a Christian stance, this tendency to forget God can be understood as a consequence of the more fundamental human crisis. Luther, experiencing his own fear, contemplated the human relationship to self, neighbor, and God. There we find the idea of the human being who is damaged as a whole by the Fall but who is not lost. For Luther, in particular, everything that makes humans worthy of love comes from God alone. For today's discussions, this results in an urgent admonition to modesty and a warning against human hubris in dealing with the present and future possibilities of technology, medicine, and so on. Acceptability in ethical debates must not be derived solely from the responsibility of people before themselves and others but, ultimately, a life lived in responsibility before God. Anthropology must also not be replaced by heuristics in ethics and should expressly be argued from a Christian standpoint with reference to the Bible, revelation, and—from a Catholic perspective—also to the magisterium and tradition. At the same time, the incarnation and the image of God remain, from a Christian viewpoint, non-negotiable guarantees of inviolable human dignity.[55]

- Morals: Today, for example, economic ethics, which has a tremendous influence in Germany in the wake of Karl Homann and others, warns against individual morality, at least in market-based economic decisions.[56] Higher echelons of management are home to a greater than average number of narcissists, psychopaths, and Machiavellians today—and not just in the world of business.[57] Bad leadership describes a widespread strategy of successful leadership in the absence of morals. The Reformers, on the other hand, see the salvation of people in accepting the Gospel of Christ as an inner habitus and thus explicit morality and living entirely from it. The idea is for Christ to be the reliable compass of conscience for good in responsible decision-making. For Christians, this means: Jesus' spirit wants, should, and can be the habitus of the faithful. Responsibility before God is an ingredient of Christian ethics of conviction (*Gesinnungsethik*).

Sanctification of the World Ecumenical

The mandate to sanctify the world is not a denominational peculiarity but instead a common endeavor of all Christians. This includes, above all, the awareness of knowledge with and of God as liberation, modesty before a gracious God in dealing with one's own possibilities, and a lived habitus of an internalized relationship with Christ as an individual compass of conscience. In this ecumenical spirit, an orientation to the Christian humanum with its normative social consequences for dignity, justice, freedom, responsibility, and so on can be proposed on the basis of the respective traditions of the non-Christian and especially the secular world. For Christians, Christ and *ratio Christi* are the standard for this. This set of values is, at the same time, the ecumenical foundation for an ideological dialogue with other religions and worldviews in the struggle for humanity.

NOTES

1. I limit myself here to ecumenical interlocution between Protestant and Catholic social ethics since these two are predominant in the German-speaking world. For an Orthodox contribution to this dialogue, cf., for instance, A. K. Papaderos (2005).
2. E. Schockenhoff (2008): 64.
3. G. Beestermöller (1991): 299. Cf. in this sense also H. Schlögel (1998): 19.
4. Council of the EKD and DBK (1997a): 97, 115.
5. W. Maaser (2003): 75.
6. This distinction has by no means been overcome. Cf., for instance, the delimiting emphasis on the depraved human conscience in G. Ebeling (1992): 349–51 or Karl Barth's uncompromising "No" in response to reason-based Christian ethics.
7. W. Maaser (2003): 81.
8. Cf. ibid.
9. CiV 6.
10. Cf. CiV 33.
11. For more context on this "cloud," see the notes on *natura corrupta* in this section.
12. Cf. E. Schockenhoff (2007): 193–96.

13. Cf. also in part I in the chapter "Sanctification of the World" the section on agents including remarks on the idea of the *lumen naturale* in Melanchthon and the controversial Protestant-led discussions surrounding it.

14. R. Leonhardt (2006): 137.

15. Cf. R. Leonhardt (2006).

16. K. Rahner (1980): 63.

17. GS 12.

18. German value surveys (e.g., Sinus-Milieu studies, Shell studies) also repeatedly identify a search for purpose and meaning in the present. Cf. for instance Sinus Institute (2005), *ibid.* (2018), Shell Deutschland (2006), ibid. (2010), ibid. (2015). See also the section on *Bildung* in part III in the chapter "Life, Work, and Death."

19. Cf. R. W. Southern (1997).

20. A hamartiological view is referred to later in this chapter in the section on the view of humanity as a set of values.

21. According to CA 29, 40, progress understood in this way is a revolution compared to the distance of God from humankind still advocated by Anselm of Canterbury.

22. See the section on normative relativism in the chapter "Ethics beyond Normative Humanism" in part II.

23. Cf. A. Rich (1970): 18 et seqq., K. Lehmann (2000): 59 et seqq.

24. A. Rich (1970): 17. This pre-understanding is therefore not a matter of human arbitrariness.

25. W. Röpke (1965): 18 had already seen in such experiments the danger of an "abolition of the human being."

26. U. Asendorf (1988): 106.

27. Cf. Gen 1:26–28; 2:15–17; 3:1–13, 20–24.

28. The relationship between humankind and the Creator is indispensable to the Christian justification of human dignity. Without the religious dimension there remains at least the bond to the personal humanum, which, however, leaves open the further justification of itself. See in part II in the chapter "Normative Humanism beyond Theology" the section on humanism in Amartya Sen.

29. G. L. Müller (2010): 143.

30. Cf. for an in-depth hamartiological discussion G. L. Müller (2010): 143–53. Nevertheless, God does not reject them. On the one hand, they receive garments of skins (Gen 3:21) to take with them on the journey out of Paradise. Added to this are the blessing, God's offer of the covenant, the eschatological promise, and, above all, the liberation of sinners by Jesus Christ. Christ is the new Adam and establishes a new covenant with humankind. For a corresponding Reformation position that bridges this thinking and the remaining power of knowledge of humans even after the Fall, cf. the concept of natural light (*lumen naturale*) in Melanchthon. Cf. the comments on this in the section on agents in the chapter "Sanctification of the World" in part I.

31. Cf. A. Rich (1970): 16.

32. According to T. Rendtorff (1990): 152, world-transcending hope "provides the universal consciousness of freedom by not accepting the existing world as the ultimate frame of reference for man's question about himself."

33. Non-Christians can at least share in the actuation of their being as a humane goal. This is true, for example, in the Aristotelian theory of justice of Amartya Sen, who postulates a human nature to be developed as the normative supreme principle of a just social order. See part II in the chapter "Normative Humanism beyond Theology" the section on humanism in Amartya Sen.

34. K. Demmer (1995): 31.

35. A. F. Utz (1985): 52.

36. W. Kluxen (1999): 20.

37. W. Ockenfels (1990): 72.

38. SRS 44.2.

39. Cf. E. Nass (2006).

40. Regarding the development of the "two kingdoms doctrine," see, for example, U. H. J. Körtner (2012): 384. Luther himself did not present a conclusive program for the relationship between the Kingdom of God and the world: "In Luther's own works, talk of two kingdoms or two regiments of God—namely, His world regiment through the Word in the Church and through the sword of authority in the world—has a fundamental theological function. It seeks to fundamentally describe the relationship between Christian faith and secular reality." In the confrontation with National Socialism, the idea of Christ's kingship (Karl Barth, Harald Diem, and others) presented a Christological standard for the evaluation of secular law and government, which views the Church as a prophetic existence. Cf. U. H. J. Körtner (2012): 374 et seq. Instead of two kingdoms, today, we rather speak of two ways of God's worldly relationship so that God's work is also present in the secular sphere. The goal remains, in accordance with the idea of Christ's kingship, for the Church to prophetically measure this world against Christological standards, thereby reminding humanity of its true destiny. This prophecy, then, does not leave the world to its own devices but makes orientation toward Christ its goal. In this sense, the concept of two regiments can also be fruitful today for the relationship between the law of God's love and the laws of earthly reality.

41. Without dogmatically developing the doctrine of the two regiments or even confronting the Pastoral Constitution of the Second Vatican Council "*Gaudium et Spes*" (GS) with it, it offers a helpful perspective for reconsidering Christian positioning in today's world.

42. The Catholic and Lutheran understandings of the Lord's Supper, in particular, are closely related because they believe in the direct encounter with Christ present in the host.

43. Cf. the chapter "[Post-]modern Contexts" in the introduction and the section on postmodern discourse ethics in the chapter "Ethics beyond Normative Humanism" in part II.

44. See the section on normative relativism in the chapter "Ethics beyond Normative Humanism" in part II.

45. It should be emphasized at this point that the attempt made here to build an ecumenical bridge for social ethics cannot be representative of the full spectrum of Catholic or Protestant thought. Rather, there are also strong divergent conceptions of ethics on both sides, but these are not specifically recapitulated here. As a result,

this is no more and no less than a conceivable proposal for a common foundation of ecumenical social ethics, based on the thinking and thinkers of both traditions. Opposition to this is, therefore, to be expected from both sides from those who are critical of such thinkers or such thinking of their own tradition or reject it altogether.

46. Cf. C. Frey (1998).

47. Cf. J. Ratzinger (1964).

48. Cf. in part I in the chapter "Sanctification of the World" the section on agents.

49. Cf. G. L. Müller (2010): 143–53, as well as the section on the view of humanity as a set of values earlier in this chapter.

50. See, for example, the section on just war and just peace in the chapter "Creation, Justice, and Peace" in part III.

51. Cf. F. Hengsbach, B. Emunds, and M. Möhring-Hesse (1993a).

52. Cf. for example K. Homann and F. Blome-Drees (1992). Cf. also in part III in the chapter "Economy and Economic Order" the section on the compass for the market.

53. Cf. for example in a Kantian interpretation J. Nida-Rümelin (2001) with regard to the relationship between the dignity of humans and animals, or in a utilitarian interpretation P. Singer (1979) with his inquiries into the worthiness of disabled human life. Cf. also in part II in the chapter "Ethics beyond Normative Humanism" the section on normative relativism.

54. Cf. the section on death in part III in the chapter "Life, Work, and Death."

55. Facets of this relativization are developed in more detail in part II in the chapter "Ethics beyond Normative Humanism."

56. Cf. K. Homann (1993a): 41: "The overriding task of ethics will then be to warn against morality."

57. Cf. T. Kuhn and J. Weibler (2012a).

Chapter Four

Mission in Crisis

The (missionary) mandate to sanctify the world[1] is aimed at offering people a glimpse of Christian values and buttressing this proposal with sound reasoning. This type of invitation, with a message that radiates positivity (and would help the Church regain followers), is in crisis today. The Catholic and Reformation Churches (not just in Western Europe) have been losing large numbers of their members for decades. Vocations in the clerical ministry or religious life are also declining dramatically. At least in Central Europe and America, structural debates, crises of confidence, ever-new attempts to forge ahead, and simultaneous battles of retreat overshadow the mission of the Church and Christians to be the leaven and light of this world. Whitewashing, fatalism, or even a ghettoization of elitist circles criticizing the secular world contradict the mission because Christian world service is a ministry of sanctification.

CRISIS PHENOMENA

Christian positions now play an increasingly minor role as a moral compass in our society. This is not without consequences for the self-image of Christian social ethics and aims outlined here. After confirming the mission presented thus far in part I, but before ultimately exploring the dialogue with other forms of ethics (part II) and proposing answers to the social questions of our time using a finely tuned moral compass (part III) for guidance, I will offer a realistic examination of the social sounding board already alluded to in the introduction.

My description of this crisis focuses primarily on the Catholic side of things. Countless scandals, a lack of young recruits in pastoral professions, and a steady outflow of members of the Church all influence the Church's understanding of itself and enthusiasm for pastoral discourse with the secular world and other religions. The tremendous loss of credibility, which was also self-inflicted, continues to have an impact. It is, therefore, not surprising that the Christian character of society and Christian theological values are in retreat.

EXAMPLE 4.1

- Formerly religious celebrations such as Christmas and Easter are becoming increasingly secularized. Challenges to observing Good Friday as a holy day of obligation were successful.
- Secular associations harshly criticize the church as one of society's fundamental evils.
- While tax advisors need not specifically recommend leaving the church, they would be remiss if they did at least point out the savings associated with no longer paying church tithes.
- Some even claim abortion up to the moment of birth to be a human right.
- "Marriage for everyone" at least challenges the Catholic understanding of marital unions.**

* Cf. also contemporary missionary secularism, which draws attention to itself with billboards on buses, anti-religious pamphlets, and influence on the cultural-political and ethical opinion-forming processes of our time. "There probably is no God" is one of the many, well-known slogans.
** Cf. in Part III in the chapter "Life, Work, and Death" in the section on family.

Among some Christians and in theology, we find evidence of a defensive approach to these shifts. Examples of this include the discussions concerning German bishops removing their pectoral crosses and concealing them when visiting the Temple Mount in Jerusalem in October 2016 out of consideration for Muslims, as well as the aforementioned theological attempt to connect with (post-)modernity by exercising restraint with theological arguments or through methodological atheism.[2] Fatalism also abounds.

EXAMPLE 4.2

I heard the following analogy from a learned Benedictine in 2014 during his lecture on the situation of the church: The Roman Empire was based on a founding act. There followed a rise and bloom, then the decline and decay. So it is with the church.

In a time of uncertainty, the Church's magisterium can no longer be taken for granted as a source of orientation. The ecclesiastical social doctrine of the popes is no longer the benchmark for initial orientation in Catholic social ethics.[3] This leads to ideological intermingling of Catholic positions with competing secular social ethics: sometimes with a more socialist, sometimes with a more liberal, ecosocial, or a natural law or gender perspective. This type of inner differentiation becomes a mirror of extra-theological paradigms, which thus also find their way into the inner-theological discussions of justification. The following also applies to Catholic social ethicists: "Which philosophy one chooses depends . . . on what kind of person one is; for a philosophical system is not a lifeless household item that one may discard or adopt as one pleases; rather, it is animated by the soul of the person who holds it."[4]

(Post-)modern Catholic social ethicists have been treading a path "beyond Catholic doctrine" since the early 1990s.[5] Social ethics is explicitly understood there as an ethical reflection of the political practice of faith. It questions the self-determined practice of faith by people freed from dogmatic prescriptions and critically examines its validity based on an ability to connect to (post-)modernity developed in discourse ethics.[6] The contents of religious social ethics are brought to bear under (post-)modern conditions in dialogue with the secular world, "insofar as these semantic potentials can be translated into a discourse unlocked from the ratchet effect of revelatory truth."[7]

The mystery in the sense of a religious encounter with transcendence is then to be excluded for the dialogue with secular positions. What remains of religion must then be translated into secular language in order to connect and be understood. The question of Christian orthopraxy is central there. It is answered beyond the objectively understood personal-humanistic program. A new paradigm is needed.

> The following attempt to define the concern of Christian social ethics in the tradition of Catholic doctrine thus cannot refer to any systematically developed concept of Catholic doctrine. . . . After the adoption of the neo-scholastic "rank and file," Catholic theology thus enters into an "offensive-productive confrontation with the challenges of modernity."[8]

The plurality of Christian socio-ethical positions is a boon for the scientific development of the discipline since a culture of fair disputes between different arguments on equal footing must be the logical consequence. From a Catholic point of view, the common reference for such discussions should be the social teachings of the Church. The basic orientations formulated in the social encyclicals leave room for many different socio-ethical arguments and themes. However, a unified Christian social ethics that excludes other well-founded positions from the conversation would be unscientific. This is why deconstructing the variant previously identified as the rank and file with new signs must be viewed with criticism. The validity of values that cannot be understood objectively follows the results of discourse in the sense of discourse ethics.[9] Contents and methods of ethical reasoning that are able to complete with magisterial proclamations are thus also considered.[10] Politically determined individuals and their current social questions and needs should define topics in social ethics to increase both the relevance and communicability and thus the acceptance of social ethics. This should equip people with the tools they need to better recognize concrete ethical problems in social practice and initiate the necessary social change in order to justify political engagement in helping the vulnerable as a practice of faith:[11] "Politically engaged Christians are inspired in this by the designs of meaningful life they gain from creatively re-reading their religious traditions on the foil of current experiences."[12]

The rational knowledge and transcendence of the ideal are replaced by the world of experience and practical discourse. Such a self-understanding of social ethics does not remain without consequences for the resonance of Christian argumentation in society, be it in laws, rules, role models, or the formation of opinions in the media. Niklas Luhmann, in his systems theory,[13] which is by no means uncritical from a Christian point of view, aptly recognized that politics and religion are fundamentally different issues, each with its own logic: politics is about power. Viewed with a democratic lens, compromise or consensus is part of it. Religion, on the other hand, is concerned with opening a door to transcendence for humans in their earthly existence. In doing so, it inevitably transports an idea of truth. Both strands of logic inexorably meet in a Christian socio-ethical perspective, without giving up their own proprium. But this is precisely where (post-)modern Catholic social ethics finds itself in crisis. Church defensiveness, the loss of the Christian character of society, a secular-inspired pluralization of Catholic social ethics and rejection of social doctrine as orientation lead us to ask, with a view to Luhmann, what such social ethics can give to secular society that it could not produce on its own.

RESPONSES TO CRISIS PHENOMENA

Christians should confront not only the crisis of their missionary task in all its different facets but also find sustainable responses to it. Christian ethics must face the reality of secularism without secularizing itself: "Here, a theology of secularity is concerned with the theological classification and appreciation of secularism. This is not to say that there is a secularization of theology, but rather to maintain an academic basis for the discourse of God in a secular world."[14]

I would like to present a few principles undergirding this self-understanding here for discussion at the end of part I as theses that are certainly also open to debate. This is also intended to gain some ideas from the practice beyond a scientific socio-ethical argument, as to how the order of sanctification can once again be successful with the help of social ethics.

- Courage to confess one's faith: Christians can learn from those with different beliefs.

  Example: When planning a prayer room at Wilhelm Löhe University in Fürth (a foundation of Diakonie Neuendettelsau), some of the Christian students wanted to remove a cross and a Bible from the center of the room out of consideration for the feelings of non-Christians. A Muslim woman spoke up. She didn't understand this. After all, this was a university in the Christian spirit. Surely the cross and Bible belonged there and should not be called into question.

  ○ The consequence: Christians and Christian ethics deserve a voice, and no apologies should be made even for public declarations of faith.

- Faith in transcendence: Christian faith sees in the work of the Holy Spirit an open door from the world to transcendence. Christians experience it in liturgy, prayer, sacraments, and in living from this source of strength. Christian faith gives believers comfort even in desolation, joy in the common image of God, hope even in death, meaning even in human failure, the feeling of being loved even in earthly loneliness, and joy in life and creation. Some secular thinkers, such as Charles Taylor, also appreciate this meaningful orientation of Christianity.[15] Niklas Luhmann points out that the profile-forming theme of religion is the relationship between transcendence and immanence.

  ○ The consequence: Christians and Christian ethics should address the sources of transcendence and offer them as orientation.

- Rational arguments for faith: Democratic culture thrives on the exchange of good arguments for dignity, justice, freedom, and peace. Muslims, Kantians, secularists, liberals, socialists, and others naturally also contribute their rationale in an effort to shape society. There is no reason why Christians should not do this. Once again, lessons can be learned from those with differing points of view: An avowed atheist student at my ethics institute in Fürth surprised me with his verdict on Christianity. To him, it was the most convincing religion of all. Its founder was highly credible, with its justification of unconditional human dignity unsurpassed and its teachings accessible to reason.

- ○ The consequence: Christians and Christian ethics should recognize and appreciate the solid rationale that underpins them.

- Role models: Representatives of Christianity bear responsibility for its credibility. This radiates through practiced faith, passion for and love of Christ, honest humility, strength of character, courage even to contradict, and so on. Role models include those who remained true to their faith even in times of ecclesial depression. Example: With this in mind, I surveyed a group of young adults who experienced youth ministry together in the parish. They had this to say about their faith: "For me, faith is having the good feeling that there is still someone there, and that I'm not alone in many of the situations I face in life." "Despite the early death of my mother, without it I wouldn't be the person I am today. And this experience also brought me closer to faith. It's a feeling of closeness and distance at the same time." "Sometimes those of us involved in church youth were considered rebellious, sometimes there was more of a sense of calm surrounding us. This range of emotions was part of my faith, and I still long for it at times." "Believing is hope. Hope is life." "I see many things in my life from different perspectives, I don't resent every stroke of fate, but I have to fight for my own faith in God: Doubt? Yes. Despair? No."[16]

  - ○ The consequence: Christians and Christian ethics should perceive the treasures of practiced faith in their midst today and begin here to see themselves as the leaven and light of the earth.

- Ecumenism: Unlike some other theological disciplines, Christian social ethics has a strong ecumenical set of values for its mission in the world in the "human image of Christianity." In an ecumenical spirit, it is with this concept of acceptability that we must embrace the mission of sanctifying the world.

  - ○ The consequence: Christians and Christian social ethics should approach their mission together ecumenically.

NOTES

1. Cf. the introduction to Part I and the section on the inherent nature of the mission in this chapter for more on the understanding of the mission advocated here. What is meant by mission is to practice Christianity today with a confession of faith,

reasoning, and enthusiasm and, in so doing, offer it to our contemporaries as a proposal for their own lives. A life and confession of faith such as this are understood as "animation."

2. Cf. on the perception of many such crisis phenomena in Part I in the preceding chapter "Ecumenical Perspective" the section on the Christ principle in practice. On the effect of Christian bishops concealing their crosses during a visit to the Temple Mount in Jerusalem, cf., for instance, J. H. Tück (2016). On methodological atheism, see the section on the nature of mission in the preceding chapter, "Ecumenical Perspective," in Part I, as well as R. A. Klein (2018): 308.

3. Lest I follow the concern of M. Heimbach-Steins (1994): 2–5, to regard this term as a synonym for an outdated essentialist phase in history that was overcome in 1961.

4. J. G. Fichte (1970): 195.

5. Cf. the programmatic anthology F. Hengsbach, B. Emunds, and M. Möhring-Hesse (1993a).

6. Cf. ibid. (1993): 235.

7. H.-J. Höhn (2014): 162.

8. M. Möhring-Hesse (1993): 59, 71.

9. Cf. F. Hengsbach, B. Emunds, and M. Möhring-Hesse (1993): 270.

10. Cf. ibid: 247.

11. Cf. ibid: 237.

12. Ibid: 271 et seq.

13. See the section on systems theory in the chapter "Ethics beyond Normative Humanism" in Part II.

14. M. Müller (2019): 26.

15. See C. Taylor (2009) and the introduction to this volume.

16. Cf. E. Nass (2012): 93–5.

Part II

IN DIALOGUE

The Christian idea of humanity is the starting point of Christian social ethics, whose aim is to speak to people again now with its social values and principles. It proposes a solid rationale for dignity and essential social values, thereby assuming responsibility and issuing an invitation to other forms of ethics to engage in constructive values-based dialogue about the foundations of the social order. The common struggle for human dignity as the heart of humanity to be fostered by society is today, as it has always been, the urgent task of every form of ethics and religion. After all, even if inviolable human dignity is regarded as an undisputed criterion of legitimacy for justice, at least in democratic contexts, it has one crucial flaw because there is no conclusive and generally accepted definition of dignity: "For to seek to define human dignity comprehensively would be to claim a right to dispose of it."[1]

The content can, therefore, only be plausibly justified approximately and with the help of a previously rendered, transparent view of humanity. In contrast, violations of varying degrees of human dignity are easier to identify. This is the case, for example, when people are discriminated against, persecuted, or even killed based on their race, political or religious convictions, or mental or physical infirmities. The violations of dictatorships (such as National Socialism, Communism, or Islamism), which systematically use such discrimination and violence to maintain their own power, are to be assessed as much more serious than those in progressive communities, in which violations of human dignity are more isolated. From the perspective of normative humanism, as represented by Christian social ethics, every human being possesses inalienable value simply by virtue of being human. With human dignity, this universally valid egalitarianism should absolutely exclude any arbitrary actions toward human beings. Justification for this allows for a diverse range of worldview models. In addition to the initially unsatisfactory openness to justification with the claim of universality, unconditionality demands that human dignity should be an immutable fact so that it may not be legitimately granted or denied by people or constitutions.[2]

Human dignity and human rights are vulnerable. Therefore, they must be protected.[3] The form of Christian social ethics presented here conceives of first-order acceptability for this purpose with its image of humankind and the normative humanism derived from it. With its mission, it engages in a dialogue with the non-Christian world to advocate for this protection. The main aim is to explore the extent to which other religious and secular ethics can justify unconditional human dignity as the basis of social ethics. Opinions expressed there should also be critically compared to a corresponding Christian position. This, in turn, is the reference for a dialogue that brings the values and positions of other forms of ethics into a conversation with the normative humanism of Christian social ethics. The corresponding discussions can thus reveal the proximity and distance of Christian social ethics to or from alternative models of justification for dignity and society. Such a dialogue thus also serves to probe the justification for Christian values in a pluralistic context.[4] The Christian perspective adopted for this purpose cannot and will not be denied.

First, an interfaith discussion is held from this now transparent perspective. The Islamic position takes on a broader scope in view of the urgency of Central Europe's new reality. Then several other religious takes are also discussed, without any claim to completeness. This is followed by a confrontation with some influential secular notions of ethics. Initially, models come into view that have a normative humanism in common with the Christian position from other sources of values. The discussion subsequently turns to other relevant models, which themselves do not claim to infer the meaning of human dignity from a universally valid normativity. Finally, a somewhat speculative question is posed concerning what, in view of such plurality, a normative humanistic world authority—a topic repeatedly raised by the social doctrine of the Church, for example—might look like, which would make unconditional human dignity the inviolable basis of global human coexistence.

NOTES

1. W. Huber (2001).
2. Cf. United Nations (1948/1993).
3. The protection of unconditional human rights is an indisputably Christian concept. Its derivation in the absence of God, for example, in the French Revolution, was what initially made it difficult for the Church to align itself with this tradition.
4. For a comprehensive discussion of ideological concepts of human dignity, see M.-L. Frick (2017).

Chapter Five

Theological Humanism beyond Christianity

The dialogue with religious ethics is only just beginning. This is expressly not intended to be a discussion of religious studies. Instead, this chapter is concerned with building relevant bridges which—unlike secular worldviews—contribute to the dimension of transcendence by adding a corresponding dimension of responsibility. For, in the common struggle of religions for good in the world, this responsibility also plays a central role in such a serious dialogue, which should result in a certain degree of human modesty.[1] For instance, Pope Francis also wishes to think of global citizenship in religious terms first before engaging in dialogue with the secular world.[2]

In view of the demographic reality in Germany and Central Europe, the Islamic position is of particular importance for such responsible dialogue. As in Christianity, it is not possible to speak of only one position of Islam. In addition to the numerous denominational differences, which are beyond the scope of this book, a clear distinction must be made above all between a humanist and a fundamentalist Islam. This differentiation helps to sound out where bridges to Christian social ethics are conceivable. Some other religious ideas will also be discussed later in this chapter. A potential bridge to Jewish positions is also explored, chiefly due to the common roots and unique responsibility shared. There are relatively few members of religions or views that profess reincarnation in the German-speaking world. But here, too, precisely because of the great international significance of such thinking, a search for commonalities with a personal humanism is underway. In this context, some aspects from a Buddhist perspective and from anthroposophy that are relevant to the socio-ethical concern of interest are given as examples.

ISLAM

Islamic legal doctrine, like Christian theonomy, is based on an objective natural law. Aristotelian influences—such as those of Ibn Rushd, known as Averroes in Latin—marked a historical flowering of Islamic philosophy in the Middle Ages. The Islamism of our days represents a different image of humans and society.

Legal Basis

The basis for the classical understanding of law in Islam is the religion's founder, Muhammad (570–632), who was a prophet and statesman. He also had to overcome the power of tribal law politically with a theocratic alternative while traditional customs were being renamed: for example, the existing custom of blood feud or the pagan worship of the Kaaba in Mecca. The process of creative lawmaking ended with the death of the Prophet. Subsequently, various schools of law elaborated the classical moral and legal theory of Sharia, which is still valid today and was completed as early as the ninth century. It owes its authority to the consensus of the legal scholars of the time. The ultimate goal of this right, understood as divine, is practical life guidance for believers. Five basic principles are laid down:

- The Koran is intended primarily as an ethical value system, only secondarily as a legal code. It is not a closed legal system. Therefore, other sources of law are needed.
- The Sunnah, as a collection of the Prophet's customs, serves as a quasi-standard for interpreting the Koran.
- The consensus (*Igma*) of the entire faith community must be concretely established by the representative legal scholars.
- In contrast, the analogy for the interpretation of ethical norms, which is widespread in Western law, plays a subordinate role. Free opinion in the interpretation of the law is only permissible within the limits of the Koran, Sunna, and *Igma*. Otherwise, legal analogy is rejected as illegitimate.
- As the deputy of the Prophet, the caliph is both the religious and political leader and thus the protector of all Muslims. All Muslims and all those subject to Islam are obliged to swear an oath of allegiance to him. The caliph may exercise his power only in accordance with Sharia law. He lacks creative legislative power.

Following some ups and downs with the real theocratic caliphate—for example, there was the split into Sunnis and Shiites in 661 in the wake of the violent death of Ali, the caliph's candidate—the political power of the caliphate was broken after the Mongols conquered Baghdad in 1258. Nevertheless, the caliphate remains the only legitimate state legal entity under classical Islamic law. And even though there were subsequently other caliphs by title, the original idea of the caliphate now remained as a mere legal fiction. The de facto political power passed to sultans and other rulers.

Pax Islamica versus Normative Humanism

The basic tripartite principle applies in Islam: one God, one faith, and one community. Orthodox Islam calls for a territorial body of adherents with the religious collective identity in the world-spanning ummah as a universal area of peace (*dar-al-islam*) in distinction to the war zone around it, where the Sharia is not yet in force. The following consequences result from this self-conception:

- It is assumed that the world must be divided into peace and war zones.
- The divine state, a society established according to divine will, creates earthly salvation for believers. It thus makes a universal and objective claim.[3] Its establishment is the intransigent goal.
- States are not legal entities. The open emergence of de facto states within the realm of the ummah must be understood as usurpation and *pax islamica* extended universally through war. In its natural antagonism to the territory of Islam, the war zone is defined by the fact that the laws of the so-called infidels apply in it, meaning that there is a God-given reason for war against areas where Sharia law does not apply. War thus becomes the normal legal situation.
- Non-Muslims, as members of the book religions (Jews and Christians), can submit to Islam by contract (*dhimma*):

    "Fight those who believe not in God and the Last Day and do not forbid what God and His Messenger have forbidden—such men as practice not the religion of truth, being of those who have been given the Book—until they pay the tribute out of hand and have been humbled."[4] Those who do not belong to any faith or belong to another faith (i.e., those who have not been given the book) are left with the consequence of conversion or danger to life and limb.

- Preventive strikes are not only permitted but ordained. The fundamental impairment of the *pax islamica* thus occurs in advance of material disputes through the mere existence of groups of people who do not recognize the authority of Islam or its order. The state of war is thus established.

- The legal and thus also religious regulation of external contacts of *dar-al-islam* must necessarily be "ummah-centric" and serve the interest of the Islamic community. The legitimacy of legal external contacts cannot be justified in any other way.
- The separation of *ius gentium* (as the universal natural law to which all people are entitled) and *ius civile* (as the state law positively legislated by governments) contradicts the orthodox Islamic conception of law. Sharia is considered the divine law of Muslims that corresponds to the nature of humankind. Strictly speaking, non-Muslims live in a state of lawlessness. Unless they have submitted. An equal natural right of all people in the sense of normative humanism cannot be justified in this way. Wael B. Hallaq identifies in this a basic dilemma of Islamic identity: "Modern Muslims are therefore faced with the challenge of reconciling two facts: first, the ontological fact of the state and its undeniably powerful presence, and second, the deontological fact of the necessity to bring about a form of Sharī'ah governance."[5] Fundamental incompatibilities of an orthodox Islamic legal dogma with the universal human rights idea of the UN are problematic. States are not recognized as legal entities, so that there can be no valid treaties among them and no legally valid peace order. Above all, "peace" can only be a political goal of Islam in the sense of universal Islamization. When peace is mentioned here, this concept obviously requires a great deal of explanation.

Theoretical Concept of Synthesis

A viable synthesis in the sense of normative humanism presupposes the overcoming of dogmatic barriers. Thus, from a Christian point of view, one must ask how the content and normative interpretation of human dignity can be thought of in Islam, which social values and principles can be derived from it, and how, in view of Islam's strong missionary focus, bridges between representatives of Islam and representatives of other worldviews are even conceivable.

In practice, there are some parallels to Christian thinking, such as aid to the poor (*zakat*) as a pillar of faith or the social obligation of property, while the prohibition of interest continues to apply, at least formally. More important than such helpful bridges is the fundamental question of the underlying view of humanity. Humanum is conceivable in Islam as an absolute, God-given truth revealed in the Koran. And thus, Islam seems to be a natural partner for Christian social ethics in its commitment to absolute human dignity because it also knows values that are to be understood absolutely, such as justice, equality, and freedom. Nevertheless, in Islam, there is still a perception that human dignity is added in stages in the womb until ensoulment, which is assumed to be 120 days after fertilization. According to Thomas Aquinas, male embryos became animate after forty days and female embryos after eighty days. However, the Catholic Church abandoned this view in 1869. Since then, the concept of full personhood has been applied from the moment of fertilization.

As in Christian doctrine, the unity of human persons with their individual and social nature is taught starting from Adam in Paradise. Humans, as God's creatures, carry within themselves the ultimate destiny to follow God's path. They are not understood as being created in God's image, and Jesus is not accepted as the incarnation of God. Instead, humans are God's representatives (*khalifa*) and hence moral subjects. In this sense, all people are equal before God. As in the Christian conception, there exists a destiny of humankind given by absolute divine law to follow the will of God.[6] This truth applies objectively and absolutely to everyone, whether they know it or not. Justice exists where people walk this path of truth. The freedom of humanity is to consciously choose this path. This idea of the humanum now reaches its limits in terms of finding a possible humanistic synthesis in view of those who do not choose the one way of truth and justice. "Freedom in service to God determines the value of the individual. 'Human rights' or 'dignity' of man are thus nothing more than indirect inferences."[7]

Unlike in the Christ event, in traditional Islam, humans achieve full personhood only with the right attitude toward the divine law revealed in the Koran. Egalitarian, God-given dignity replete with absolute rights and duties, therefore, awaits all Muslims. At first blush, this is a clear distinction from a relativistic human rights position. But respect for the dignity of those of other faiths is also a necessary insight for normative humanism. This is not evident in the traditional Islamic position. Accordingly, there are those who choose to have dignity and those who choose against it. They must suffer the respective consequences of their lack of belief. Absolute human rights are not simply ascribed to people as a result of their being human. They must then be justified in solely religious terms in the observance of the law of God. After all: "Defined solely by absolute transcendence, man, the servant of God, is nothing in himself, but at the same time more, existing thanks to the external intervention of God, who has mercifully and benevolently given a charter to man."[8] A mental figure such as this excludes from these rights those who do not profess the God of Islam. In this sense, universal human rights are easily justifiable for a universal Islam but not for people of other confessions in a pluralistic society. Objective human dignity is firmly anchored in Islam. The central question to be clarified, however, is how absolute dignity, even of the so-called infidels, can be justified.

The understanding of freedom also does not seem at all suitable for a global consensus at first. According to Islamic tradition, those who submit to God's law and thus to the Koran are free, meaning that freedom is the fulfillment of duty. The individual and social responsibility of humans to solve social problems, which is developed through the use of reason, is replaced here by following the precepts in the Koran. Islam has no social doctrine and no social entitlements.[9] But this does not mean that such thoughts cannot be reconciled with Islamic teachings in a complementary sense.

Oppression of women in the legal and moral sense contradicts the idea of humanum. Undoubtedly, such grievances are found in many Muslim-influenced societies and subcultures. This discrimination is not codified in the Koran. Overcoming it, then, seems to be more an educational imperative than a fundamentally dogmatic problem, as Marcel Boisard sees it, in agreement with numerous Muslim co-authors of his standard work on "Humanism in Islam." "The Muslim woman's right to social equality . . . is secured. Divine law grants it to her."[10]

Enlightenment and Reformation to Synthesis

The classical understanding of law in Islam is immutable. A secularization of law can, therefore, not be conducive to an approach to a humanistic idea of people and society. Mouhanad Khorchide, therefore, emphasizes that "change can only come from within. We don't need an enlightenment of the kind we know from European history, but perhaps a reform that focuses on the maturity and reason of humankind."[11] A modern Islamic understanding of law was successfully developed in the second half of the twentieth century at Azhar University in Cairo, a highly influential institution in the Islamic world.[12] The "reverse updating" advocated there focused on material contents of Islamic legal reality in a merely abstract tension with the still valid formal law. The caliphate then remains as a mere idealistic fiction of rapture and thus as a formula that is void of content for reality so that a space can open up for a legal order that does not follow Sharia law. The possibility of such an opening is also reflected in the fact that states have now been recognized as legal entities and that there has been at least formal recognition of the UN Charter. The Holy War can also be interpreted as an ascetic path.

A corresponding opening of Islam to such thinking would have theological and practical consequences. This includes rethinking the interpretation of the Koran as "a humanistic hermeneutic." By this, Nasr Hamid Abu Zaid, for example, means a historically critical interpretation: "My concept of a humanistic Islam is to show the truly human elements of the Koran. That is, we go back to the text to discover what else is significant for our modern times."[13]

This would also have to involve an appropriate interpretation with special appreciation of the Meccan versus the Medinan paradigm, which sets aside the rhetoric of war. Based on Islamic mysticism (Ibn Arabi) and philosophy (Ibn Rush and Averroes, respectively) of the twelfth and thirteenth centuries, Abu Zaid aims to overcome the dogmatism of Koranic interpretation that prevails today.[14] The classical dichotomy of interpretation into unambiguous and ambiguous Koranic verses, on the other hand, facilitates the semantic-fundamentalist manipulation of the Koran. Instead, a rediscovery of the multi-semantic interpretations taught by medieval Islamic mysticism and philosophy can help relate the Koran's directives to the present day and thus also overcome the demands of a literal application of Sharia law. This necessitates more than a reform of Koranic exegesis, as expressed by Elham Manea: "If we really want to enforce a reformation, then we must also consider the nature of the Koran. It is about a human nature of the sacred text. The Koranic verses were collected by people, written by people."[15]

The philosophy of Averroes, in particular, bridges the gap to the Aristotelian-Western tradition of Christian humanism, which ultimately also can be traced back to this great Islamic thinker. As a devout Muslim, for him, the Koran remains the source of divine truth. For its legitimate interpretation, he rejects the supposed unambiguities and motivates others to read the Koran itself with a sense of reason.[16] Legitimate interpretations must prove themselves before the forum of reason because reason itself, as a universal, potential intellect, shares in transcendence. As with the *ratio recta* in Aquinas, so also in Averroes does reason have the capacity to know the truth. Accordingly, the interpretation of the Koran must always allow itself to be critically questioned by this reason because reason itself has divine potency within it. This view of reason, in turn, also opens Islamic thought to enable the recognition of non-Islamic philosophies and their concepts of humanity. Now, if human reason potentially shares in transcendence, the efficacy of the divine in a non-Islamic reason would also be conceivable. This results not only in a rational-critical self-reflection of one's own religion but also in the enlightened insight that possibly even other worldviews have a share in the one divine truth, as the Second Vatican Council also emphasizes analogously in the declaration *Nostra Aetate* (NA). The universal dignity of humankind and the human rights founded in divine law can thus simply not be granted to the non-Muslims against but only in the responsibility before the divine law, as it is also demanded by Hashem Aghajari, who was sentenced to death in Iran in 2002: "People are human beings regardless of religion, even if they are not Muslims."[17] Or Muhammad Abu Zahra, former professor at Cairo's Azhar University, who wrote regarding human dignity, "that it comes to man by virtue of his being man, not because of . . . his religion, nor because he is honorable . . . ; rather, it consists in being man himself."[18] Even if there is no recognized Islamic social doctrine, a normative humanism of Islam related to social issues is easily justifiable. This requires the recollection of its own Aristotelian-philosophical or other comparable roots. But if instead classical legal dogma were to increasingly determine political and religious Muslim life, the fragile pragmatic foundation could collapse. Then the traditionally dogmatic notion of dignity, of international peace law and Islamic law, could quickly gain in importance. And the conflicts that were thought to have been overcome will—backed by their strong dogmatic legitimacy and fueled by Islamists—question the humanist idea beyond Sharia more radically than ever. A pragmatic, respectively Islamic-enlightened interpretation of the divine law and tradition enables strong positions of a common normative humanism. This will likely require not only reform but also, in relation to currently widespread thinking, a reformation that does not alienate Islam from itself but leads it back to itself and into a global community that could achieve a concept of inviolable dignity for all human beings.[19] The new theological way of thinking required for this would deprive the Islamists of their pseudo-religious legitimacy. It extends to understanding the Koran and the law.

JUDAISM

Part of the Christian self-understanding and thus also of the self-understanding of Christian social ethics is the awareness that Christian faith, vocation, and mission have their origin in Israel and Judaism. Jesus, His mother Mary, and His first disciples were Jews. Jews and Gentiles together formed the first Christian communities in Israel. For too long, however, no systematic ethical exchange of mutual learning between Jews and Christians has taken place. In the nineteenth century, for example, from the point of view of the Frankfurt rabbi Leopold Stein, of note was the attempt at a mentality that would have Christianity trump all other religions and whose universal claim was aimed at making Jewish social ethics obsolete. In contrast, it was only in the twentieth century that a serious dialogue got underway, which fortunately was taken up again after the Holocaust. For the German-speaking world, for example, the letters of Franz Rosenzweig or theological conversations between Martin Buber and Karl-Ludwig Schmidt are worth mentioning, in which they respectfully point out the fundamental difference of the perspectives of redemption in the nevertheless common search for truth.[20]

Biblical Value Basis

The divine likeness of humanity to God as witnessed in creation fundamentally connects the view of humanity and the understanding of dignity in Judaism and Christianity.[21] From this follows, according to the Jewish view, on the one hand, a strong idea of human equality before God, connected with an eschatological expectation of a messianic fulfillment.[22] On the other hand, the moral task of the human being to develop the predisposition to imitate God, which is given with His likeness, also follows from it.[23] A social order corresponding to these basic ideas must leave room for messianic fulfillment as well as for this salvific imitation on the part of humankind. On the one hand, it must therefore apply appropriate rules. On the other hand, it is associated with powerful individual virtue, which must be shown less in mere words than in practice, for example, in charity and labors of love.[24] Human morality is characterized by a threefold responsibility and love toward Creator, neighbor, and oneself. Self-love is expressed, for example, in the fact that an ascetic idea of sacrifice is not usually placed at the center of ethics. To achieve this high moral goal on earth, one must also be of sound mind and body.[25] From the strict idea of equality, one must approach others on equal footing. This also applies, for example, when others fall into hardship or poverty through no fault of their own and are unable to help themselves. In this case, assistance is obligatory: ownership entails responsibility. But this neighborly responsibility must be seen as a strict symbiosis of justice and love. Anyone in need through no fault of their own must be able to rely on the help of others in such situations.[26] This assistance must be organized by the state and privately. Ideally, however, it should never become a top-down redistribution machine of the authoritarian state. Rather, helping others help themselves in the sense of the principles of solidarity and subsidiarity aims at enabling the poor to rise from their misery so that they may once again freely reach toward that high that is God. This is why this service, on which the vulnerable must be able to depend, should not be organized solely through the anonymous redistribution of resources because to perform this work also means to satisfy a moral duty. Initially, this help is likely also motivated by a self-serving interest in reciprocity: those who serve others can also count on others coming to their aid in similar situations. And so, this help is not an altruistic gift but instead an expression of mutual solidarity. Such help, reducible to egoistic motivation, is a kind of natural morality, which, however, must always be taken together with a transcending virtue, that is, the responsibility of equals to equals before God.[27] From the love of God, then, grows love for oneself and for one another, and from this follows analogous to Christianity the threefold human responsibility.

A Strong Socio-Ethical Bridge

The close connection between the image of God and the image of human beings through the likeness, eschatology derived from this, such as equality of dignity, humankind as moral existence, and, threefold, transcendentally founded responsibility, are far-reaching areas of concordance between Jewish and Christian sets of values. It should not be concealed here that—comparable to the Islamic idea—this dignity does not begin according to Jewish views with the fusion of egg and sperm cell but—similar to what Aquinas proposed in former times—only by the animation of the embryo, forty days after fertilization. Consequently, research on supernumerary embryos from in vitro fertilization is permitted, as is preimplantation genetic diagnosis (PGD).

The same applies to the resulting demands for virtue and institutional ethics in a social order that must be legitimized accordingly. But the latter should not become an authoritarian state in which the rich give to the poor through anonymously organized mechanisms of redistribution. After all, the anonymity associated with this displaces the desired virtue of charity. This interpretation corresponds perfectly to the displacement discussions conducted by Christians between caring *Diakonie* and *Caritas* work vis-à-vis a modern welfare state operating with social entitlements. Organizing redistribution in this way would also push the concept of equality for all into the background. The idea is not to create encounters that give the impression of the higher-placed rich donating to the lowly poor, as that would diminish the dignity of those on the receiving end. On the contrary, the objective must be for these persons to meet on equal footing even in light of the help that is received. This is a very sophisticated thing to demand from a social order, which can only meet this moral imperative when such exacting social virtues are cultivated from a young age, which would undoubtedly require corresponding educational measures.

Many other parallels to Christian basic values of social ethics can be identified, of which only three important ones are outlined here as examples.

- For instance, biblical tradition has brought forth the assumption that God himself is the owner of everything on this earth. This is an initially collectivist idea, which Aquinas also used as a basis for his thought, only to relativize it later in terms of responsibility ethics.[28] Like Aquinas, Jewish social ethics also knows the important distinction between realistic *conditio humana* and utopian rapture, for example with regard to a Kingdom of Heaven to be established on earth with all selfless social beings. Instead, the Jewish notion of imitating God prompts followers to consider critically what humans, who are not God, are able to achieve on this path to imitation.[29] Later, in the Christian faith, Aquinas pragmatically justified

private property with an analogous insight, which, precisely against this background but as a result similar to Judaism and later Islam, retained its strong socially obligatory component.
- The idea of freedom plays an important role in Jewish social ethics. Likewise justified by the traditional experience of the people's bondage in Egypt and certainly not least by the atrocities in the context of the Shoa, slavery is categorically rejected.
- The Jewish religion was often suspected of representing particularly exclusive ethics limited to its own people and thus—similar to secularist collective ideologies—of presupposing an exclusionary identity. Of course, the notion of the chosen people and land of biblical origin plays a prominent role in Judaism. Nevertheless, the idea of human dignity and the image of God can also be understood in a universalistic Jewish sense. The negative experiences of tyranny and despotism that the Jewish people experienced are then exemplary of the *conditio humana*. Moreover, during the Jewish captivity in Egypt, even the Egyptians were not considered strangers but neighbors (*rea*).

The bridges between Jewish and Christian social ethics are so strong that one can only wish for an intensification of a corresponding interreligious conversation between Jews and Christians, freed from prejudices on the one hand and out of a spirit of reconciled brotherhood also in distinction from secularism and normative relativism on the other.

BELIEF IN REINCARNATION

Buddhism

The belief in reincarnation in Buddhism, as well as the concept of God, are essential differences from the monotheistic religions with their views of humanity and society. Moreover, the lack of God's grace at the end of life in Buddhism is another important difference in the understanding of the human experience. The strong reference to transcendence, on the other hand, also grounds Buddhist ethics in humankind's responsibility before this reality. Some essential aspects of this concept, which are crucial for socio-ethical dialogue, are briefly outlined here. Common ground in thinking about values and dignity is regularly explored in major Buddhist-Christian colloquia with the participation of the Pontifical Council for Interreligious Dialogue. They are the basis here for discovering a potential socio-ethical dialogue in view of a normative humanism.

The transcendent good is prescribed to humankind in Buddhism and can also be recognized and practiced by following the Buddha in life (eightfold path)[30] through meditation, prayer, non-violence, brotherhood, and reconciliation. All creatures have this responsibility and strive for liberation from the cycle in the state of nirvana. The Buddhist belief in the eternal cycle establishes the awareness of forming a family with other people and creatures. This is then not meant as a mere metaphor but healthy, sick, old, and disabled people of different ethnicities are then actually brothers and sisters to each other.[31] Practicing fraternity is considered a path to happiness and excludes, for example, the enslavement of brothers and sisters. This normatively desired empathic connectedness as social responsibility does not allow discrimination.[32] The needy are morally entitled to help, which may well justify welfare state solidarity from a motivation of long-term self-love.[33] After all, the fate of indigence can befall anyone at any time. The close, familial bond is probably not limited solely to human togetherness but also includes other living beings, whose form humans could take in a future life. An intense responsibility for creation that rejects a hybrid anthropocentrism may rise from this. After all, people are only part of the cycle of mutual dependencies. However, it is precisely because of this idea of the cycle of life that PGD or so-called "consumptive embryo research" is prohibited. Such a profound responsibility for one another and for creation also leads, according to the Buddha's model, to a virtue of non-violence freed from egoism, with which Buddhist individual virtue categorically opposes the worldly right of the strongest.[34] Thus, with an eye toward certain parallels to the Christian view of humanity, there is a responsibility toward the transcendent good, toward oneself (also in view of one's future life), toward each other and toward creation. The latter finds a stronger emphasis here, which, for example, makes it more challenging to elevate human dignity exclusively above that of other creatures.[35]

Equal human rights can be justified in terms of normative humanism. A good society, according to Buddhist conception, is linked to the idea of equality and freedom: "Buddha held that each and every man is a potential Buddha, therefore everyone must enjoy equal rights and freedom."[36]

Non-discriminatory, equal human rights can be inferred from this, which can be realized above all in a liberal society but not, for example, in totalitarian countries such as China or North Korea. However, duty and virtue are more important than law, which is not without effect on a connection between dignity and virtue: "individual rights and dignities are strongly intertwined with corresponding duties."[37] An unconditional morality given to humans thus always precedes law, from which follows the rejection of legal positivism. At the same time, at least moral gradations of dignity are conceivable, based on a person's fraternal virtue (in thought, word, and deed).[38] This logic suggests a relationship to Aristotelian thinking, according to which (public) offices should be awarded based on good character. But the Buddhist idea seems to go even further and to measure a person's dignity based on virtue. Despite all the emphasis on virtue ethics, this does not align with the Christian concept since humans do not forfeit their image in the image of God even in a state of vice.

Overall, there are significant points of contact between these forms of ethics and normative humanism interpreted in Christian terms. However, despite many socio-ethically relevant agreements (three or fourfold responsibility—including creation, non-violence, equality, freedom, solidarity, non-discrimination, duty, and virtue), it remains difficult to justify the necessity of elevating humans and their dignity, in particular considering how easy it is to relativize both on the basis of vice.

Anthroposophy

The anthroposophical view of humanity represents a strong human empowerment mission. Human beings are seen in their unique individuality as persons who are full of hidden creative potential. Mature individuality is perceived to be a desirable state of existence, through which individuals come into their own and, at the same time, are able to meet the challenges of (post-) modernity. In the sense of Rudolf Steiner, this requires a spirit of liberty that is free "from the limitations of one's own physical and mental organization (preferences, drives, instincts, etc.) on the one hand, and prescribed social values on the other."[39]

The aim is to overcome traditional patterns of thought, such as those of ecclesial or other religious institutions but not the assumption of a divine power. Rather, it is a matter of no longer allowing the content of this divine power to be dictated to us from outside but of recognizing it within ourselves: as an earthly present world of ideas that is common to all people. A respective spirituality does not feed on the imitation or orientation toward fixed (for example, Christian or other) traditions or religious authorities that prescribe morals and liturgies. Instead, individuals must come to themselves through intellectual intuition, discover in themselves the divine spirit, and through this insight become one with it and thus with humanity and the cosmos. Such an individual wholeness means overcoming an assumed split between "I" and "world."[40]

The addressee of human responsibility is the metaphysical idea of the divine. People are responsible for achieving their own self-liberation first before this idea, then before themselves. Human personality shows itself in this way: "I act only out of goals that I set for myself."[41] But this by no means translates into capriciousness or a thoughtless following of fleeting feelings or egoistic self-indulgence. Rather, the objective is always grounded in a reflective act of thought with explicit responsibility before the divine spirit in humankind. In this way, external ideas or goals can also become effective for people if they perturb their own balance of values and are subsequently discovered and adopted as their own. An essentialist cognition of things and contexts as an orientation of responsibility is not excluded, such as the question of objectivity and its answer, for example: "What is the thing considered as such?"[42] Understanding normatively understood personhood is also the object of reflection. Mature individuality with a liberated spirit is considered a semantically rich objective of good living. Such liberated persons have the (missionary) task, in responsibility before the (not personally conceived) divine idea, to empower themselves and others to attain such freedom. This process is called refinement: Starting from the idea of an earthly self-redemption that must be internalized, it is a matter of turning people into mutually inspiring evocators of the inherent creativity of the individual. Such a concept of redemption is not in line with the anthroposophical sense of the meaning of reincarnation, whose future quality in the next life people can and should help to determine by coming to themselves as far as possible now in their earthly existence. It is about personal refinement as a mission, which is goal-oriented.

For the relationship between manager and employees in a company, this might mean something to the effect of the following:[43] Employees should be empowered through good leadership to find their inner balance by discovering and developing the entrepreneurial talents already inherent within them. A culture of co-entrepreneurship built on this foundation aims at achieving a high level of identification with oneself, one's colleagues, and the company as a whole.[44] Economic success measured in monetary terms is subordinate to self-liberation. The ennoblement of every human being must not be sacrificed to it. Life (at work) is thus an integral part of a holistically humane development of virtue.

In contrast to Christian ethics, a metaphysical idea of the divine takes the place of the personal God who came into the world as a human being. The anthroposophically firmly anchored idea of a rebirth also makes a crucial difference. The same applies to the idea of human self-liberation that is associated with it. For, from a Christian point of view, the desired goal of humans at the end of earthly life is not the calculable result of accumulated virtue or achieved ennoblement. Rather, Christians see humans as being liberated by God primarily by virtue of His grace. The social homogenization (e.g., in a group, community, company, society, etc.) also harbors the danger of paternalism, which leaves little room for anything else. What about people who do not want to and/or cannot take on refined co-responsibility themselves?

What of those who, due to personal setbacks, are unable to strike the desired balance and are sometimes less motivated or even overwhelmed? Must they only be called forth until inner balance is achieved again? Or should a social culture with such high personal aspirations not leave space and time for these fragilities without direct intervention? From the point of view of Christian ethics, there is at least the concern that too much desired homogeneity may obscure the view of the individual and so again externally it is too paternalistic to pretend what the individual has to recognize in order to be free in the given sense of anthroposophy.

Nevertheless, considering such differences, very practical examples of bridging this anthroposophical view to Christian social ethics can be seen in partnerships with respective educational institutions (Walldorf) or corporations (dm). Anthroposophy represents a holistic mission of human service, which can apparently be successfully implemented in education and economics. The success of an individual, a group, or a society cannot be verified in monetary terms alone. First and foremost, success has existential human undertones. Social ethics needs virtuous people and makes the development of virtue in responsibility before a given metaphysical instance of the divine a missionary goal. These assumptions of a given objectivity, its recognizability along with its consequences for practical social ethics are—despite all their differences from Christianity—undoubtedly also essential commonalities.

BRIDGES IN THEOLOGICAL HUMANISM

Normative humanism in Christianity and Islam can meet in some socio-ethical positions, for example, in questions regarding the protection of life, in the understanding of marriage and family, for adequate social welfare for the poor, for the relativization of a normativity of business, technology, and success, for special responsibility toward creation, for the future of religious education, for God's participation in morally important decisions, for example, including through a culture of prayer, and so on.[45] Jewish and Christian social ethics are even more closely related in many areas. From the common idea of the image of God follow remarkably similar notions of dignity, responsibility, and concepts of social order and coexistence. Islam, Judaism, and Christianity have in common the idea of the social obligation that ownership entails.

Several bridges to Christian social ethics could also be identified for Buddhism with its belief in reincarnation, although a strong emphasis is placed on virtue and responsibility toward creation here.[46] Regarding the consequences for the dignity of the unborn, the Christian position is closer to the Buddhist position than to those of the other two monotheistic religions.

Nevertheless, in the understanding of unconditional human dignity, some essential tensions remain here, which anthroposophy alleviates by singling out the human being. It is not possible to speak of normative humanism if it is not possible to justify an elevated dignity of the human in relation to other living beings. However, in light of the different views of humanity and the ideas of transcendence represented, the socio-ethically relevant bridges of the monotheistic religions to each other that have been pointed out prove to be more enduring in contrast.

NOTES

1. See, for example, T. Michel (2008): 85 et seq.
2. Cf. on this in the introduction to this volume in the chapter "Substantive Positioning in Dialogue" the corresponding quote from Pope Francis, Address to Representatives of Various Religions, quoted by D. M. Mitchell (2018): 73.
3. Cf. M. Boisard (1982): 122.
4. Koran: IX, 29.
5. W. B. Hallaq (2013): x.
6. Cf. M. Boisard (1982): 53, 59, 61.
7. Ibid.: 93. Cf. also ibid.: 87–90.
8. Ibid.: 94. Cf. ibid.: 125: "Lawless toward God and the law, man can, however, demand the rights that the Koran assures him of toward others and the (Islamic; added by E. N.) community."
9. Cf. ibid.: 55, 123.
10. Ibid.: 105.
11. M. Khorchide (2012).
12. This tradition has largely broken down in our century.
13. N. H. Abu Zaid, quoted by C. Modehn (2010).
14. Cf. N. H. Abu Zaid (2008): 167–73.
15. E. Manea, as cited in C. Modehn (2010). Cf. also, for example, the approaches to Koranic exegesis by Mustafa Öztürk. On this, see F. Körner (2008).
16. H. Aghajari (2002) calls for such maturity in Iran to free people from their bondage to the mullahs. Cf. for instance also such an interpretation of reason by Muhammad Abdus more than a century ago.
17. H. Aghajari (2002).
18. R. Wielandt (1993): 191.
19. In the same vein, H. Aghajari (2002) recalls the idea of an "Islamic Protestantism" as developed twenty-five years earlier by the murdered Ali Shariati.
20. Cf. V. Lenzen (2013): 204 et seq. with references to F. Rosenzweig (1935) and M. Buber and K. L. Schmidt (1933): 265.
21. Cf. L. Baeck (1913).
22. Cf. L. Baeck (1914): 11.
23. Cf. M. Buber (1964): 1061, M. Brocke (1976): 78 et seq.

24. Cf. M. Brocke (1976): 76.
25. Cf. J. Sacks (1992): 24.
26. Cf. S. Lauer (1995).
27. Cf. J. Sacks (1992): 16.
28. See the section on the property system in the chapter "Economy and Economic Order" in part III.
29. Cf. M. Brocke (1976): 78.
30. These include as virtues Right Understanding, Right Thought, Right Speech, Right Action, Right Livelihood, Right Effort, Right Mindfulness, and Right Concentration.
31. Cf. S. Huifeng (2015).
32. Cf. S. Dorji (2015): 206.
33. Cf. L. N. Sharstri (2015).
34. See R.-S. Her (2018) and E. Fernando (2018).
35. On the now stronger emphasis on Christian responsibility before creation, see the section on creation in part III in the chapter "Creation, Justice, and Peace."
36. S. Dorji (2015): 206.
37. Ibid.
38. Cf. ibid.: 204.
39. K.-M. Dietz (2008): 26 with reference to R. Steiner (1995): 167 et seq.
40. Cf. K.-M. Dietz (2008): 20–9.
41. Ibid.: 29.
42. Ibid.: 23.
43. Such an idea of people and coexistence underlies, for example, the corporate culture of the drugstore chain (dm) founded by Götz Werner in 1973.
44. In this way, anthroposophy can become a partner for economic success for a discussion on leadership ethics in the sense of a stewardship model. For principles of Christian leadership ethics, see the section on the compass of good leadership in part III in the chapter "Leadership and Organizational Culture."
45. Above all, they share the conviction that morality should be based on responsibility to God. Cf. on this from an Islamic perspective, for example, A. Izetbegović (2014): 209: "The fact remains that atheism has no means whatsoever to preserve or protect the principle of morality itself."
46. Empirical studies also suggest that the sustained practice of Buddhist meditation is difficult to reconcile with Christian identity. Cf. A. Meuthrath (2014). Therefore, despite all the similarities discussed here, it must be pointed out once again that there are essential incompatibilities between Christianity and Buddhism in the understanding of life and transcendence.

Chapter Six

Normative Humanism beyond Theology

It seems obvious to simply distinguish between religious and secular concepts in ethical and socio-ethical discussions. This overlooks the fact that there are central ethical concepts that, on the one hand, appear secular since they do not presuppose a knowledge of God for their view of humanity and society. Yet, on the other hand, they assume—in contrast to (post-)modern models—an objectivity given to humans or a recognizable human nature, from which a concept of inviolable human dignity can easily be justified. This does not expressly exclude the idea of God. This applies, for example, to Immanuel Kant's ethics of reason, Amartya Sen's neo-Aristotelian approach to empowerment, Adam Smith's economic anthropology, and phenomenological humanism, which are briefly presented here in light of this frequently neglected background alone and introduced into the conversation with Christian social ethics. Such approaches are not united by a creed but instead by a universalistic conception of well-founded inviolable human dignity (i.e., normative humanism).

HUMANISM IN IMMANUEL KANT

Dignity and God

Kant develops an ethics of reason as an ethics of duty. For the justification of human dignity, a self-knowledge of reason takes the place of a theonomic view of being—in comparison to religious ideas. Understanding reason with its objective laws is the task of metaphysics as a transcendental science. Transcendental knowledge is the knowledge of the logical necessities of reason (*Denknotwendigkeiten der Vernunft*). Any use of reason, it is assumed, presupposes these conditions. These include, above all, ethical laws and principles. They embody the good, which humans—unlike in secular (post-) modern thinking—neither construct nor negotiate communicatively themselves but discover and recognize instead. The good is represented by moral law: "Act only according to that maxim by which you can at the same time will that it should become a universal law."[1] As the supreme logical necessity of reason, it establishes absolute ethical norms with categorical imperatives. For example, an unconditional concept of dignity can be formulated as a categorical imperative: "So act that you use humanity, whether in your own person or in the person of any other, always at the same time as an end, never merely as a means."[2] This and other unconditional principles apply universally, objectively, and have timeless validity. Kant supports normative humanism with this concept of human dignity because this imperative of unconditional dignity forbids the pure instrumentalization of any one person by any other person. It is considered a logical necessity of reason. To abide by it is morally good; to violate it is morally bad. Thus, it is not a transcendentally derived nature of humankind that is the basis for interpreting absolute human dignity here but instead the laws of reason in which that which *ought* to be is immanent. Since they claim objective validity, they are equally immune to subjective interpretation by individual inclination. Here, inclination refers above all to a heteronomous desire of humanity, which contradicts autonomy and impedes the knowledge of reason.[3] This understanding of the knowledge of good is briefly explained in the following.

What morally and objectively obligates humankind are the objective conditions of practical reason.[4] Humankind is not bound to a goal given to reason but only to the observance of the laws of reason. In the determination of the laws of reason, practical reason already follows these laws, thereby giving itself its own *ought*, by proceeding according to its own logical necessities. Normative rules are categorical because they are necessary for reason if they follow autonomous reason and thus correspond to the moral law underlying practical reason. Autonomy in the sense of self-legislation exists when individuals give themselves their laws without any inclination (i.e., without egoism) according to categorical imperatives.[5] Individual egoistic inclinations, on the other hand, destroy autonomy. The absoluteness of ethical norms follows from this formal universalizability of the will so that the moral law and the autonomous reason oriented to it are supreme principles of morality. Beyond autonomy, only hypothetical imperatives can be formulated. The autonomous (i.e., inclination-free use of practical reason) enables people to have transcendental knowledge of good (i.e., insight into moral law and categorical imperatives and thus into well-reasoned unconditional human dignity). People who, incapable of such insight, should at least accept the categorical imperatives and the social rules derived from them as duties so that even a nation of unreasonable people (or of devils, for that matter) could be led according to the laws of reason.[6]

The humanum in Kant, with its categorical imperative of human dignity, of course, includes all people (i.e., also the unborn), severely disabled, or dying. Nevertheless, in this normative humanism, there is at the same time a tension that could call into question precisely this unconditionality. Autonomy in the sense of reason free of inclination is the foundation of dignity for Kant and is, therefore, its prerequisite. On the other hand, it also seems conceivable outside of the humanum, namely in the non-human reasonable nature: "Autonomy is therefore the ground of the dignity of human nature and of every rational nature."[7]

But what is this non-human rational nature that possesses dignity by virtue of autonomy? And then what dignity has human nature, which has no autonomy? It seems conceivable that rational, non-human beings also possess an unconditional dignity equal to the autonomous human being, while at the same time, there are human beings who lack this autonomy and thus dignity. So, what about rational animals? And what about non-autonomous people? The former German Minister of State for Culture, Julian Nida-Rümelin, for example, called for fluid transitions between human and animal rights on explicitly Kantian grounds.[8] This is where unconditional human dignity begins to falter. At least here, besides the categorical concept of dignity, there remains at the same time a certain ambiguity in the Kantian understanding of normative humanism.

Although transcendental knowledge cannot say anything substantive about God in the recognition of good, God nevertheless plays a central role, at least as a regulative idea that is logically necessary. This is because the categorical imperatives again presuppose the ideas (soul, world, and just God) as logical necessities. The ideas are "an indispensable standard of reason"[9] for the knowledge not of an essential reality but instead of a logical necessity. Because they are conditions of the possibility of reasonable knowledge that are logically necessary, the ideas have "real" reality in the sense of logical principles. This also implies a transcendental idea of God:

> If, then, we are asked the question (with reference to a transcendental theology): whether there is something different from the world, containing the ground of the order of the world and of its connection according to general laws? Our answer is, *Certainly there is*. For the world is a sum of phenomena, and there must, therefore, be some transcendental ground of it, that is, a ground to be thought by the pure understanding only.[10]

This implicit concept of God from a transcendental absolute ends the regress in questions of legitimacy. It is true that humans cannot recognize anything of God. Thus, the good as the universally valid reference of ethics is not the result of a knowledge of God. But God is a logically necessary idea of this good, which is given substance in the moral law and the categorical imperatives derived from it. But if this idea, which is necessary for thought, did not correspond to reality, then the universal claim of this good would also collapse because it would no longer be possible to think meaningfully about a logical necessity. Thus, Kant's normative humanism is by no means godless.

Virtue and Responsibility

In their actions, human beings are morally responsible before themselves and toward others first to moral law and the universal principles derived from it (the categorical imperatives). Moral role models, in particular, must be less egoistic in order to be autonomous in the sense of Kant and to recognize these principles, act accordingly, and enable other people to achieve liberating autonomy. Their example "must be done from the appropriate moral motive."[11] The categorical imperatives are meant to define specifically how people coexist. All human beings ultimately have a moral obligation to attain autonomy themselves and to enable others to do so, in other words, to recognize that which is good selflessly and to act accordingly: "One has both a duty of perfection to oneself and a duty to promote the happiness of others."[12]

This establishes an unconditional human responsibility of each individual to cultivate a social spirit of autonomy. This duty also has priority over, for example, economic goals, since financial success should ultimately always serve the transcendental human goal. This ethics of duty has the missionary aim of liberating people from egoism and bringing them to autonomy by effectively influencing rules, individuals, and relationships. Its goal is always also the individual virtue of the agents.

Personality is realized on the one hand in negative freedom: A necessary condition for a culture of autonomous-personal freedom is the unconditional duty to guarantee an "ability to act independently of determination by alien causes."[13] Coercion and deception must therefore be avoided at all costs.[14] But Kantian personhood is realized not only in negative but also in positive freedom: personal development as normatively required autonomy means the ability "to be a law unto themselves."[15] This, in turn, is rooted in another categorical imperative:

> A rational being belongs as a member to the kingdom of ends when he gives universal laws in it but is also himself subject to these laws. He belongs to it as sovereign when, as lawgiving, he is not subject to the will of any other. A

rational being must always regard himself as lawgiving in a kingdom of ends possible through freedom of the will, whether as a member or as sovereign.[16]

Thus, as far as possible, all people must be supported so that they may develop the highest degree of human freedom as personhood, according to Kant.

Principle Ethical Acceptability

Kantian objectivity is the godfather of countless (social-)ethical positions today. It offers good justification for first-order acceptability. Examples of this achievement can be found in some current approaches.

This applies, in particular, in the field of medical ethics, for example, the principles approach of Tom Beauchamp and James Childress.[17] This concept, known as "principlism," assumes (instead of moral law) a "common morality," from which the evidence of four prima facie principles of equal rank is derived, which for ethical judgments (for example on the use of medical technology) with their respective results must always be dialogically weighed against each other in order to arrive at an overall judgment regarding acceptability. These quasi-categorical imperatives are the following:

1. Autonomy in the sense of self-determination is first understood as patient autonomy. This implies the need for well-informed consent to essential (medical) interventions as well as respect for privacy.
2. Damage avoidance corresponds to the '*Nihil nocere*' principle. This also includes, for example, the unconditional prohibition of mental mortification or (legally unenforced) incapacitation.
3. The transitions to the positive principle of doing good are fluid. It is essential to protect the rights of the elderly and disabled, for instance. These people must receive support in their everyday lives, for example, through technical assistance systems, so that they may participate in normal life to the greatest extent possible. Active intervention is necessary as help in case of danger.
4. Justice as equality formally requires things that are alike to be treated alike, while things that are unlike are to be treated unlike. In material terms, the need for a legal framework for fair distribution, which should guarantee equal basic provisions for all people, follows from such a deontological interpretation. An unconditional social obligation can then be derived from this: "Therefore, a society has an obligation to provide healthcare to people whose functional capacity is impaired to remedy or compensate for such deficits."[18]

With these four (universally valid) categorical imperatives, the ethics of principles presents semantically rich criteria for first-order acceptability, which, on the basis of this setting, allows for comparison with other, likewise conceivable normative criteria. In concrete moral decision-making, the four principles serve as benchmarks for deliberative normative analyses that result in substantive evaluations of moral dilemmas.

Despite the attempt to define their content, however, the principles are kept so general that a practical application for the evaluation of moral dilemmas (for example, at the beginning of life, at the end of life, or for the use of medical technology, etc.) still proves difficult. For what does it mean in concrete terms to "be just" or "do good"? Differentiated interpretations and a tenable set of values with a view of humanity and society are needed: But the basis for these values is missing. While the principles approach offers a substantive concept of acceptability, it is easily vulnerable to attack in an evaluative, democratically held debate because "dispensing with a profound moral substantiation or justification of principles, however, must be viewed critically,"[19] according to Anna Linke.

The four principles are in limbo in terms of justification theory, especially since the "common morality" argument calls universality into question. The four principles are, in the end, mere postulates that may or may not be shared. But it is theoretically possible to assert them transcendentally as Kantian necessities of reason. The complex weighing and weighting discussions could find a resolution in that acceptability offers a viable ultimate principle to which the other values and principles must be subordinated. Methodologically, this would mean crystallizing ethics of principles into a supreme principle.

HUMANISM IN AMARTYA SEN

The socio-political program of the neo-Aristotelian capability approach, as it has been systematically developed from a contemporary secular point of view, in particular by Amartya Sen,[20] likewise constitutes a normative humanism whose kinship to a corresponding Christian vision also derives from a unifying Aristotelian root. Here as well, social ethics develops from the normative idea of the human being with substantive concepts of justice, equality, and freedom.[21]

Sen assumes that human beings, by their very nature, not only egoistically pursue their own interests but, due to their natural social disposition, also strive for communal action.[22] He goes one step further, speaking of an added, deontological rationality, which even makes it possible for people to make beneficial decisions out of a sense of duty.[23] An idea of humanity is the starting point for socio-ethical systematics. Sen, for example, is concerned with answering the pressing question of humanely justifiable equality. And this informs his prepositive inference of the fundamental right to the development of basic capabilities such as health, creativity, personal responsibility, or social integration—the very qualities that lend personhood to humans in the first place.[24] These basic capabilities are an expression of freedom, and they correspond to the standard of quality of life to which all people are entitled. To produce such an objective quality of life, individuals must be empowered to actually live out the long-lasting freedom that is in tune with nature. Reference to this legitimacy is postulated as objectively given. Self-determination is conceived as a decision sphere, to which all persons are entitled in order to strengthen their own personal responsibility. Freedom presupposes the development of individual responsibility. It is understood as personal space to weigh options related to responsible decision-making that enables appropriate choices among multiple alternatives. Empowering egalitarianism ties the legitimacy of rights to the creation of an individual sphere of freedom as a sphere of responsibility. Justice in this sense demands that individuals be liberated to such positive, empowering freedom by having the state remove obstacles that would stand in the way of freedom of choice. The aim is not to equalize the basic functions that are actually obtained but instead to equalize the ability to obtain such basic functions. Social rights thus oblige governments to provide all individuals with the choices to develop basic functions with appropriate educational and health facilities. This requires universal access to a minimum standard of choice.[25] The provision of choice alone only optimizes the sphere of responsibility when individuals themselves are able to make independent decisions. Consequently, the task of the state must be to enable individuals to be responsible for their nature. Since the decision for the specific development of these basic abilities lies with the individuals, this poses a challenge to the concept of personal responsibility. So how individuals accept the education offered by the school system or whether the sick use the hospitals that are open to them lies within their own personal responsibility. The ability to use the sphere of freedom is a basic prerequisite of positive freedom understood in this way. The desired positive freedom of self-determination as an empowering space demands and enables a responsibility toward the weaker members of the community, which is aligned with human nature and therefore counteracts the absence of freedom. The right to empowerment is a fundamental social right to which everyone is entitled. If, for example, the socially disadvantaged are prevented from developing their basic functions through no fault of their own, this deficiency entitles them to the resources required for empowerment, provided these resources can be publicly financed. The natural claim to empowerment is categorical, but the right derived from it to interfere with the free disposition and discretion of others is contingent. This Aristotelian-based objectivity is now considered a standard of legitimate distribution.[26]

An idea in Christian social ethics aligns with the capability approach not only in its rationale but also in the many consequences for socio-ethical principles.[27] Two important differences for corresponding implementation in the welfare state should be noted here: 1.) From a Christian point of view, it is necessary to ensure a justified minimum standard not only but especially for those who can barely or no longer be enabled to assume their own responsibility (i.e., for whom the space to weigh the various options can no longer open up positive freedom). People with intellectual disabilities, for example, must be empowered so that they may assume a level of responsibility commensurate with their abilities. And if even this form of empowerment is no longer possible, these individuals are still entitled to the absolute protection of their right to live a dignified existence. 2.) A Christian socio-ethical concept of threefold responsibility replaces the mere postulate of the natural basic functions and the dignity derived from them by the idea of a God-givenness and God-likeness of humans.

HUMANISM IN ADAM SMITH

More than virtually anyone else, Adam Smith is cited as the mastermind behind economic liberalism. After all, he understands the common good in the liberal sense as the satisfaction of egoistic individual interests.[28] A more careful examination of his idea of freedom, however, shows how closely he ties it to an imagined human nature, including God in this equation. According to Walter Eckstein, Smith, for all his criticism of the prevailing church faith of his time, represents "the conviction of the existence of an omnipotent and benevolent deity, whose action is most clearly expressed in the purposefulness and order of the world."[29] According to this assessment, there can be no question of direct divine intervention in Smith's case. Here, he follows the basic understanding of the so-called deism.

Now, how is this coexistence of God, nature, and freedom to be thought of in Smith? In his *Theory of Moral Sentiments*, he is concerned with a psychological-ethical interpretation of human nature with the normative claim to direct it toward the development of the God-given destiny. For Smith, nature is the given condition of possibility for responsible human action. This responsibility is the normative claim—based on created and free human nature.[30] "Adam Smith's writings cannot be adequately understood without considering theological issues like natural law."[31] Smith assumes a given human nature that is not subject to discursive processes of self-definition.[32] This human nature consists of positive as well as normative components, which determine the motivation of humans and their souls. Humans also have a sympathetic disposition alongside their egoistic motivation for action.

> How selfish soever man may be supposed, there are evidently some principles in his nature, which interest him in the fortune of others, and render their happiness necessary to him, though he derives nothing from it except the pleasure of seeing it. Of this kind is pity or compassion, the emotion which we feel for the misery of others, when we either see it, or are made to conceive it in a very lively manner. That we often derive sorrow from the sorrow of others, is a matter of fact too obvious to require any instances to prove it.[33]

He maintains that this sympathetic ability to put oneself in another's shoes, solely for the sake of the other, is a social motivation of one's own. It is not intended as a derivative of egoistic motives but instead as an independent motivation. The two tendencies are neither interwoven nor do they cancel each other out. Morality comes into play in the individual weighing of competing motivations with the soul instructing humans with the help of reason.[34] For Smith, there are three distinct parts of the soul in human nature: reason is considered to be the principle over the irascible part of human nature and over the concupiscible. The virtue of justice stands for a harmony between the three faculties of the soul. According to Smith, following Plato's image of the charioteer, it is then present "when each of those three faculties of the mind confined itself to its proper office . . . when reason directed and passion obeyed."[35]

According to this, the soul is the normative force in human nature. The ability to reason, which is implanted in the *conditio humana*, is not itself the norm but instead the given instrument for endowing the soul with the virtue of justice. This instrument is to be understood as a prerequisite of practical ethics.

How can the soul guide people toward justice? To this end, Smith designs a quasi-personal normative instance as a model. Humans struggling for a sense of orientation in their decision-making cannot avoid an inherent conflict between egoistic and sympathetic dispositions. Social responsibility is also constituted by specific decisions, each of which is preceded by an inner dialogue of motivations. First, humans must consult the judge within (conscience) for this purpose. But such subjectivity is not sufficient for rendering a good decision. It requires—as in Christian and other religious thinking in the law of God or with Kant in the moral law—an objective normative instance, which lies before the human will. Thus, even for Smith, knowledge of good is neither a creative construct nor a communicative negotiation process of heteronomous interests. According to Smith, the moral goodness of human decision is judged by the impartial observer he conceived of in this way. He brings in an intersubjective position, which has value-realistic features.

It is true that Smith does not—like Kant, for example—present an elaborate justification of inviolable human dignity. Thus, we cannot speak here of an elaborated normative humanism. His normative anthropology, however, is based on God's act of creation, which grants people an ontological normativity and potentiality for the good inherent in their souls and the resulting ability to see the objective good. According to Smith, self-interested egoistic and sympathetic social motivation determine individual decision-making. God-given nature enables humankind to be free. It gives people an intersubjectively personal orientation in the soul, which is normatively articulated in the idea of an impartial observer. This is undoubtedly a normative anthropology with a liberal normative humanistic thought, which—apart from the missing explicitly theological references—has much in common with Christianity's view of humanity.

PHENOMENOLOGICAL HUMANISM

Phenomenological anthropology—if one can speak of it at all in view of the complexity of this school of thought (with Martin Heidegger, Edmund Husserl, Karl Jaspers, and many others)—also postulates a kind of essentiality and its recognizability in view of humanity and human dignity. On the one hand, it is possible to come to sociological conclusions in the field of social research based on this. On the other hand, it is also possible to infer potential normative consequences for human dignity. The essentialist anthropology of phenomenology is a worthwhile interlocutor for Christian social ethics.

From a phenomenological perspective, humans are both physical and social beings with a culturally embedded sense of "being-in-the-world" (*Dasein*). In the field of social research, it follows that phenomenological sociology "ought to examine how people themselves experience their social reality; how do social agents themselves navigate in and explain the order of the reality in which they live?"[36]

Phenomena are the appearances of objects (or human beings and other living things) themselves. They are, at the same time, a world-immanent revelation of being. The objective being is there in the phenomenon (*Dasein*), it shows itself in the *there*. Therefore, phenomenology is an essentialist philosophy of facticity:

Phenomenology is the study of essences, and it holds that all problems amount to defining essences, such as the essence of perception or the essence of consciousness. And yet phenomenology is also a philosophy that places essences back within existence and thinks that the only way to understand man and the world is by beginning from their "facticity." It is the goal of a philosophy that aspires to be an 'exact science,' but it is also an account of "lived" space, "lived" time, and the "lived" world.[37]

It examines the conditions of possibility of the subjective experience of this objective being in reality. To this end, phenomenology is a transcendental inquiry into the relationship between the world (revealed being in things, living beings, and contexts) and the subject. Realization happens in the immediate perception. Researchers must set aside or bracket the natural trust of humankind in an external (not in that which is experienceable in things, living beings, and contexts) reality or dogmatics (including mathematical laws). This so-called basic attitude of epoche opens the view to the being, the essence, to the "things themselves." The question concerns the conditions of possibility for the manifestation of being. Objects are thereby endowed with a self-transcendence. The way from the fact to the being lets the human being marvel in view of the world and in being human, which comes into being in actual human beings themselves. "*Dasein* is a state of being whose existence is characterized by openness—and this openness transcends the boundary of the self."[38]

For example, every human subject experiences a counterpart G differently depending on the subject's own experiences. The subjects S1 and S2 (cf. figure 6.1) are aware that the other subject is objectivizing them. That is, through the limits of empathy, I also perceive the other subject initially only as a counterpart (object) and not as a subject. The awareness of one's own objectivization by another, of one's own objectivization of another and

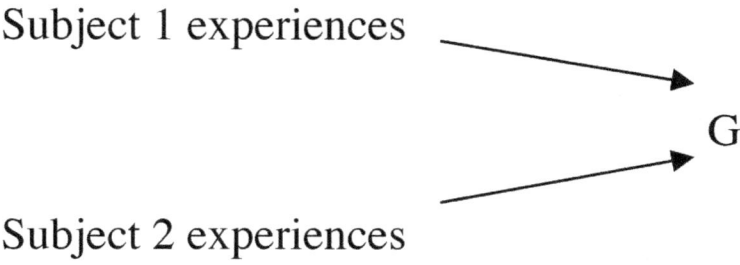

Figure 6.1. Phenomenological Transcendental Revelation. *Source*: Author.

of one's own subjecthood, makes it possible to experience the other person as a subject as well. I realize that G is the object of a subjective experience transcending my own self. And thus, the perception of G is transcendent. Transcendence, in this sense, is the experienced diversity of existence. At the same time, I experience the essential being of the counterpart, in both its revealing and elusive nature.[39]

This presupposes an essence of the human being that is at the same time revealing and elusive. This essence can be recognized not by an observing subject alone in its entirety but instead perspectively in the visible phenomena. Because there are different perspectives of a specific human being, for instance, there are also different insights into the nature of this human being. Here one could superficially assume a relativism, according to which everyone indifferently defines the essence. But this would not constitute phenomenological thinking. Because here, it is not about construction of truth but instead about cognition of a given. This idea meets with a Christian idea, according to which the good should not and cannot be constructed by oneself but instead should be recognized as given. Heidegger connects this recognition of essence with an idea of human dignity and humanism. The goal is "for man to become free to accept his humanness and to find within it his dignity."[40] And this idea of human dignity in freedom is not the fruit of heteronomy; rather, its genesis is an essentiality that precedes the actual human being. This is because "every humanism is either grounded in some form of metaphysics or makes itself the ground of some form of metaphysics."[41]

Distancing himself from postmodern secularism, Canadian philosopher Charles Taylor has taken up phenomenological thinking to welcome back religion and its ethics in the context of a secular world.[42] His sights are primarily set on Christianity. It is true that a dominance of secularism is maintained here and that a traditional religion with universal ethical claims is rejected. However, on the basis of phenomenological openness to transcendence, it is conceded that religion enables people to have important experiences of the senses and, with its morality, its idea of good, and its view of humanity, it can provide well-founded answers to the essential human longing for self-transcendence. The good justification of human dignity and of being loved by God as a basis for social love are the precise characteristics that are recognized as special strengths of religion, which the secular world is unable to produce on its own. Without accepting the religious confession itself, religion is at least placed at the service of the (dominantly secular) society.[43]

Phenomenological essentialism meets with a substantive normative humanism of Christian ethics, despite the presence of tension between the two. Because Jesus is God Himself from the Christian point of view, at least Jesus can know the essence of things as a whole so that His knowledge goes beyond the phenomenological perspectivity of humankind. Jesus Christ recognizes being (*Sein*) and the whole from all sides as that which is true. But this cannot exist in phenomenology in this way. Transcendence from a Christian theological perspective, moreover, is more than the experienced diversity of existence. Theology dares to look beyond things. Transcendence refers to God's reality, which comes into being in the being of things. Objectivity is given from a Christian point of view and not a mere, subjective perception. Because it reveals itself, it can be recognized by analogy and with a corresponding basic attitude. Recognition from reason and love enables purposeful amazement as access to the revelation.[44]

BRIDGES IN NORMATIVE HUMANISM

A commonality between Christian social ethics and the core values of ethics according to Kant and Smith is that God is essentially included in the concept of what is good. Even if these non-theological ethics are not concerned with the knowledge of God, as has been shown here, God nevertheless plays a role in them. Both concepts also assume an objectivity of the good, which must be recognized and applied in specific decisions or in the design of rules and coexistence. Therefore, people can and must recognize what is objectively good and it is neither a construction of meaning nor a deliberatively agreed consensus. On this point, the views of Kant and Smith meet with normative humanism in Amartya Sen and with phenomenological essentialism. Sen's neo-Aristotelian social ethics, with its concept of capability, comes very close to the Christian ideas of personhood, solidarity, and subsidiarity.

The four concepts briefly outlined in this chapter are objectivist. Kant can provide solid rationale for unconditional human dignity as a categorical imperative in his ethics of reason. Although this figure of thought leaves a certain ambiguity in view of the concept of autonomy, it comes very close to a Christian ethic with such normative humanistic core values. Beauchamp and Childress's Kantian-inspired principle ethics expressly offers first-order acceptability and is widely used mainly in the field of medical ethics. If, however, the transcendental level of justification is neglected, this type of substantive ethics loses plausibility. This form of ethics of principles, therefore, requires a sharpening of the level of justification to strengthen its plausibility. Sen can at least assert human dignity without explicit reference to transcendence with references to Aristotle. Smith does not grant inviolable dignity to humanity with the God-given soul and potential for normative objectivity. However, the impartial observer would likely have little trouble adding this as normative content of the theory. Phenomenological essentialism sees human dignity as metaphysically grounded in transcendence and thus as an axiomatic positing. Taylor, in this tradition, places (Christian) religion at the service of a secular society. This welcome is desirable from a Christian point of view, especially in contrast to a (post-)modernity so critical of religion. Overall, in addition to the religious core values discussed in the previous chapter, the basic ideas of humanity espoused by Kant, Sen, Smith, and phenomenology can also be considered normative humanisms. This fundamentally connects them with the Christian social ethics represented here, despite all their differences.

NOTES

1. I. Kant AK V, 30: *Critique of Practical Reason*. Cf. the parallel version: "Act only in accordance with that maxim through which you can at the same time will that it become a universal law" (I. Kant AK IV, 421: *Groundwork for the Metaphysics of Morals*).

2. I. Kant AK IV, 429: *Groundwork for the Metaphysics of Morals*.

3. Cf. I. Kant AK V, 33: *Critique of Practical Reason,* ibid. AK IV, 426: *Groundwork for the Metaphysics of Morals*.

4. First, in the *Groundwork for the Metaphysics of Morals*, Kant assumed that categorical imperatives must be inferred from the logical necessities of theoretical reason. In the *Critique of Practical Reason*, he considers such a conclusion inadmissible so that categorical imperatives are held to be unfathomable as mere facts of practical reason.

5. Cf. J. Heinle (2017). According to Kant, then, it is not an expression of autonomy to do what one pleases "but that you also set certain limits for yourself (= self-legislation)."

6. Cf. I. Kant AK VIII, 366: *Toward Perpetual Peace*: "The problem of establishing a state, no matter how hard it may sound, is soluble even for a nation of devils (if only they have understanding) and goes like this: 'Given a multitude of rational beings all of whom need universal laws for their preservation but each of whom is inclined covertly to exempt himself from [these laws], so to order this multitude and establish their constitution that, although in their private dispositions they strive against one another, these yet so check one another that in their public conduct the result is the same as if they had no such evil dispositions.'"

7. I. Kant AK IV, 436: *Groundwork for the Metaphysics of Morals*.

8. Cf. J. Nida-Rümelin (2001).

9. I. Kant AK III, 384: *Critique of Pure Reason*.

10. I. Kant AK III, 457: *Critique of Pure Reason*.

11. N. Bowie (1999): 66.

12. N. Bowie and P. Werhane (2005): 64.

13. N. Bowie (1998): 1085.

14. Cf. C. Korsgaard (1996): 113. Practically speaking, this basically means: Termination of employment for operational reasons within an organization can be

legitimized by the fact that the employees have previously agreed to this potential risk in a voluntary labor contract. Cf. N. Bowie (1999): 48–53.

15. N. Bowie (1999): 63.

16. I. Kant AK IV, 433 et seq.: *Groundwork for the Metaphysics of Morals*.

17. Cf. T. L. Beauchamp and J. F. Childress (2001): 3 and the section on digitalization in the chapter "Future Issues" in part III.

18. A. Linke (2013): 50.

19. Ibid.: 51.

20. In addition to Amartya Sen, Martha Nussbaum is also considered to be an authoritative representative of this capability approach.

21. Cf. in detail E. Nass (2006): 195 et seqq. on this systematic bridge between Christian social ethics and Sen's capability approach.

22. Cf. A. Sen (2002).

23. On deontological rationality, cf. A. Sen (2003): 9.

24. Cf. A. Sen (1993): 31.

25. Cf. A. Sen (2003): 36.

26. Thus, given the scarcity of resources, the capability approach offers a rationing criterion that takes individual responsibility seriously. The causative principle is therefore applied, not only to avoid moral hazard but also as early as the decision to make scarce resources available to the public.

27. See, for example, the sections on the compass for the market and on the social market economy in the chapter "Economy and Economic Order" in part III.

28. Cf. A. Smith (1789/2007): 16.

29. W. Eckstein (1994): LI Note 1.

30. Nature and freedom, which should not be confused with arbitrariness, are not antipodes in Smith. O. Höffe (1981): 31, for example, describes freedom as distinct from arbitrariness without Christian justification: "Man is free insofar as he can develop from within himself ideas of the goals and paths of his life and attempt to act in accordance with these ideas." Accordingly, freedom is understood as the ability to take responsibility for one's own life.

31. P. Oslington and K. Hawtrey (1996): 84.

32. St. Gallen-based business ethicist Peter Ulrich, on the other hand, takes more of a Kantian discourse-ethical view in his Smith interpretation and implies that Smith assumes an unconditional rule of reason, omitting God and rejecting a normatively understood nature. Cf. P. Ulrich (1998): 16 et seq. The conditionality of reason recedes in this interpretation: "The liberal worldview of Smith, like that of Immanuel Kant, is founded in the philosophical primacy of the 'realm of freedom' (to be determined critically-rationally by the 'moral law') over the 'realm of nature' (determined empirically-mechanistically by laws of nature), including the inner nature of man." When Ulrich cuts the root of Smith's contingent conception of nature in God and replaces it with a process of self-definition (of man, environment, and norms) under the postulated primacy of deliberative reason, nature itself now requires a new guideline, which in Ulrich's sense can be conceived of as a kind of freedom of discourse. Nature, then, is not interpreted as the Smithian basis of freedom. Freedom itself shapes nature

by defining it. Such a reading turns away from Smith's assumption of an objective anthropological backbone to ethical reasoning.

33. A. Smith (1790/2006): 4.
34. Cf. ibid.: 6 et seq.
35. Ibid.: 246.
36. D. Zahavi (2007): 94.
37. M. Merleau-Ponty (1966): Preface.
38. D. Zahavi (2007): 49.
39. Cf. H.-G. Heimbrock (2007): 55.
40. M. Heidegger (2000): 321.
41. Ibid.
42. Cf. especially C. Taylor (2009) and corresponding interpretations by M. Kühnlein (2018) and ibid. (2018a).
43. To regard Christian ethics as an answer to this invitation as a narrative that is helpful to society and has a peacemaking effect is a potential response. Moreover, it must always be borne in mind that Christian social ethics is more than an instrument of the secular.
44. Cf. in part I in the chapter "Sanctification of the World" the section on the objective good and its realization.

Chapter Seven

Ethics beyond Normative Humanism

Normative humanistic social ethics, whether founded in Christianity, religion, or the secular world, encounters a widespread understanding of ethics that denies the recognizability of an objective truth and was, therefore, criticized by Pope Benedict XVI as relativism. In doing so, Benedict was consistent with his predecessor John Paul II, who, especially in his social encyclicals, repeatedly tied the question of the legitimacy of rules and social order back to a transcendent absoluteness. In the following chapter, the basic paradigm of normative relativism, postmodern discourse ethics, and the socio-ethically relevant features of systems theory will be presented as several influential currents of this thinking of ethics beyond normative humanism and critically discussed from the perspective of Christian social ethics.

NORMATIVE RELATIVISM

Basic Concept

Normative relativism has many faces, including individualistic and collectivistic variants. Before briefly presenting these two interpretations, this section outlines the basic unifying normative idea behind these otherwise very different ethics. Normative relativism denies the existence of truths beyond their physical explicability as well as the recognizability of a nature of humankind from which normative conclusions for the enforcement of human dignity and corresponding rights and duties can be drawn. Instead, the individual and the collective are the ultimate instances for the justification and recognizability of human dignity and a legitimate community oriented toward it.[1] The realization and substantive determination of dignity are then created. Then it is not valid to epistemologically acknowledge a truth of human dignity given (by God, reason, or others). Instead, the content of this dignity must or may be determined by individuals or collectives themselves.

Normative relativism rejects the objectivity and universalizability of values, as well as transcendental and transcendence cognition.[2] Such thinking is in the tradition of Auguste Comte's law of three stages. According to this law, there are three successive stages in the intellectual history of humankind. The first (and most primitive) is a mythological-theological one, in which humans make their cognition dependent on the will of higher powers (such as religious ethics). The second metaphysical stage is characterized by the replacement of the humanized deities by abstract beings. But here, too, it is still a mere fabrication. Only in the third positive stage does one recognize the actual task of science in the restriction to positive presupposition. People should abandon the assumption of an absolute normative reference of good once and for all and instead settle for a relative view of things. Now a brief outline of individualist and collectivist varieties of such secularism can follow.

Normative Individualism

In normative individualism, ethical objectivity is replaced by hypothetical norms derived from different egoistic inclinations of individuals.[3] A legitimate order can thus be legitimized by various expressions of the will of egoistic individuals who create a hypothetically defined human dignity in the social contract. Normative individualism has its roots in a heteronomous interpretation of contractualism. The content of what human beings and human dignity are results from a contract that balances different egoistic interests of the parties involved. Many social-contract theories—but not those of Immanuel Kant—declare the specific individual to be the instance for the justification and determination of the content of human dignity and of a community oriented to it. Goals and criteria for determining the purpose and task of order can then be derived solely from the rational (egoistic) evaluations of the individuals concerned. The legitimacy of rules follows the freely expressed will (the preferences of the individuals concerned) and is thus contingent: "normative individualism is a meta-normative device for a 'proper' evaluative judgment on social states. In such context, normative judgments about social states have to be derived from the judgments of the 'relevant' individuals."[4] There is no given law from which principles of order can be deduced. In particular, empiricism, as the logical progression of David Hume, radically breaks with all forms of objective knowledge. Such a consistently executed heteronomous strategy for defining human dignity is content with hypothetical norms. The legitimacy of human rights, human duty, and human dignity in the tradition of Humean empiricism remains relegated to evolving, egoistically inclined norms. The binding nature of human dignity does not follow an absolute standard. Social conditions, rights, and duties are legitimate and thus in accordance with human dignity to the extent that they are found to be legitimate by the real people who are affected by them based on their rational utilitarian considerations. Otherwise, they are illegitimate.

Human rights are relegated to the interest-based interpretation of human dignity in normative individualism. The discussion about a commentary on Article 1, Paragraph 1 of the Basic Law for the Federal Republic of Germany in 2003 makes clear the relativistic character of this normativity. For Ernst-Wolfgang Böckenförde, human dignity is an objective-legal norm with an absolute claim, "an axiomatic perpetuity decision in favor of the value content of fundamental rights given to the Constitution."[5] It is an inviolable absolute that is given to the founding and shaping of the community and whose interpretation is beyond the reach of changing social values. Matthias Herdegen, on the other hand, denies such absoluteness in normative individualistic terms. Human dignity and human rights must also be open to new semantics that are subject to changes in social values. Herdegen justifies dignity without recourse to objective norms and leaves its substantive codification to a balancing of social interests: "Despite the categorical claim of all human beings to dignity, the nature and degree of dignity protection are certainly open to differentiations that take into account specific circumstances."[6] Accordingly, the content of human dignity is to be derived from a balancing of competing human interests and is therefore not bound to a predetermined view of humanity, normative nature, or reason. The interpretation of human dignity is then relative because it is not based on an absolute standard. Goals and criteria for determining any legitimacy are gleaned from individual preferences. This is the paradigm of normative individualism[7] and should replace the axiomatic interpretation of human dignity in normative individualist terms.

Legitimacy is thus grounded in the hypothetical validities established by individuals. No absolute human rights and obligations can be conclusively established. This applies, for example, to the securing of a publicly provided subsistence minimum, which Friedrich A. von Hayek only postulates beyond the normative individualistic paradigm. A justification of social transfers to the needy arising from egoistic motives can at best succeed if these are seen as mere "tolerance premiums" (*Duldungsprämien*) to reduce the "social threat potential."[8] The needy receive their alms only so that they do not endanger the social peace of others, who in turn benefit from this peace. But that means the following: Strictly speaking, those who would never come up with the idea of resorting to violence or are not (or no longer) capable of using force to secure their own existence would have to remain excluded from such social transfers (e.g., people with severe disabilities, the unborn, pacifists, people with dementia, and those on their deathbeds).

Such a normatively individualistic interpretation is nevertheless logically predicated by a categorical claim with the unconditional demand that legitimacy be bound to utility, without this claim itself being heteronomously inferable. It is argued that a legitimate interpretation of human dignity precludes commitment to a normative absolute. After all: "Precisely stated, the central thesis of normative individualism is: 'All political and legal decisions find their ultimate justification solely in relation to all individuals affected by the particular decision.'"[9] This postulated exclusivity is an absoluteness that is not further substantiated. Because normative individualism permits the formulation of hypothetical imperatives alone, but its normative foundation itself makes a categorical claim with the unconditional utility commitment of legitimate human dignity, a fundamental coherence problem emerges here. Normative individualism cannot itself be justified normatively individualistically. It is based on an ideologically conditioned postulate that can be shared or rejected.

Normative Collectivism

A hitherto underestimated parallelism exists between the views of humanity of normative individualism and normative collectivism. The socialist model of materialistic humans, for example, thinks of dignity not from the individual but from the collective: "The masses do not simply place their strength at the disposal of the socialist state. By appropriating the policies of the party and the state, they thereby increasingly gain the power and ability to represent their own interests."[10] Freedom, according to such a view, is what the ruling party defines it to be. From this perspective, any healthy person who wished to leave the former GDR, for example, violated the freedom of the collective. And that is why the *Republikflüchtlinge* (deserters from the republic) were treated as fair game. Following systematic dechristianization, it was necessary and possible to determine anew what human dignity is. The resulting *Sinnvakuum* (vacuum of meaning) had to be filled with an alternative worldview. The value and dignity of the human being are then measured by the materially countable performance for the collective. This is why retired persons were allowed to leave the GDR.

The party has the power to decide who is a human subject and what that subject is entitled to: "The progressive part of the intelligentsia which passes to the positions of the working class becomes the subject of politics, while such members of this stratum as are unable to make this transition remain 'objects' of the politics of the working class."[11] This subjectivizes and desubjectivizes people. Individuals and their talents do not belong to themselves but instead to the collective. And this—represented by the party—assigns to individuals their mission in service to the collective. In normative collectivism such as this, the value of dignity is again measured by a benefit, which is now that for the collective. The unconditionality of dignity is lifted. Parallels can be found in the racial ideologies of fascism or in religious fundamentalism, which now deny and grant dignity to people not according to class but according to race or religion.

Consequences for Human Dignity

The consequences of normative relativism for human dignity can be outlined using how the weakest link in the chain of society is dealt with as an example. For it is in the consequences for the disabled, the ailing, the dying, the losers, and so on that the very fabric of the underlying concept of dignity is revealed. First, I present as the most radical variant of normative relativism a Darwinian position, which, in its unadulterated form, certainly does not find acceptance today, but in its fundamental idea, it nevertheless resonates in some (still) accepted judgments. This is followed by responses of normative individualism and collectivism.

- Darwinism: Darwinian ethics may distinguish different levels of human worthiness or define some humans as non-humans. Those who fall outside such a definition then possess inferior (or no) human dignity and may be treated or mistreated accordingly. In ancient times, it was customary in Sparta, for example, for only the strong to survive so that only the good genes would reproduce in the small, defensive Greek city-state. The weak were thrown to the wolves as children. Charles Darwin, too, not only analyzed the laws of evolution but also normatively demanded the survival of the fittest, which later led to Social Darwinism.[12] The thinking behind this is as follows: A life of sickness is worth less than a life of health. Its spread is harmful to the human race and, therefore, should not be endowed with the same rights. Racial ideologies such as National Socialism explicitly embraced Social Darwinism and implemented it—in relation to people with disabilities—in the cruelest way, for example, with the "euthanasia program." As different as these individual models of thought with their respective pseudo-"values" may be, they are united—each with different consequences and each at a different level of radicality—by the basic notion of inferior human lifeforms. Christianity is not the only viewpoint that rejects ideologies such as these.

- Economized dignity: Less radical is an economic ethics in the sense of normative individualism. The needy are entitled only to a tolerance premium derived from the egoistic benefit of others. Nevertheless, it should be noted that, strictly speaking, defenseless people on their deathbeds and people with disabilities or dementia are left behind. Human dignity is violable in this sense, insofar as it is no longer justified as an absolute value but only as a mere derivation of the egoistic benefit of the healthy and strong.
- Collectivized dignity: In secular normative collectivism, peoples' dignity is consistently made dependent on their membership in a particular class or race. The "brown" variant openly embraced Social Darwinism in the past. In the "red" variant, dignity is awarded and denied by the party. So here, too, it is violable by the ruling party that arbitrarily seizes it.

As different as the areas of application and the ideological roots of the ethics only briefly outlined here may be, with their views of humanity and the relativizations or even elimination of human dignity derived from them, they are united by an essential common basic idea: the strongest in a society elevate themselves above the weak and judge their dignity with different arguments. There are some practical examples of this today with implications for the right to life: In Belgium, parents can have their seriously ill newborn infants killed under certain circumstances.[13] The number of people born with disabilities in Germany is declining.[14] Australian sociologist Peter Singer asks the following: Why should healthy monkeys have fewer rights than severely disabled people?[15] Wouldn't it be better for some people with disabilities not to have been born? American sociologist Martha Nussbaum opines "that certain severely handicapped children are not human beings, even if they are descended from human parents."[16] Here, the talk of an "inferior" or "unworthy" human life shines through, even if those representing such positions and ideologies may categorically reject this.

POSTMODERN DISCOURSE ETHICS

Basic Concept

Discourse ethics also establishes values beyond the axiomatics assumed by Böckenförde. Its normative relativism makes a strictly democratic claim and enjoys great popularity as a secular procedural model of postmodernism in opinion-forming processes as well as in the scientific disciplines of ethics. It explicitly abandons the modern idea of semantically rich universal concepts of truth.[17] Expressly postmodern, it advocates an ethics of plurality. In the meantime, a wide variety of secular and theological concepts of social ethics have followed this paradigm shift from metaphysics to deliberative evolution, which trusts human beings to define for themselves what they are and should be. The basic idea and fundamental questions of discourse ethics are presented in this chapter from the perspective of Christian social ethics represented here.

Discourse ethics is a form of procedural ethics that, based on normative postulates, demands a set of instruments for democratic decision-making processes and, alongside modern ethics, a fortiori seeks to replace pre-modern ethics.[18] The framework conditions of the procedure are primarily normative here. The results of the procedure (the concrete semantics of values, for example) should intentionally be left open. Discourse ethics thus aims to overcome dogmatism and, as a democratic form of procedural ethics, claims to shift the paradigm from metaphysical justification to communicatively developed legitimacy. Contents of values and norms are not discovered, as in transcendental or transcendence models. They are creatively negotiated by individuals. Discourse is the only legitimate way to do this. Those who argue reasonably assume that they will be heard. With discourse comes the perlocutionary assumption of mutual respect. Jürgen Habermas subsumes this logic under what he calls the principle of universalization ("U"), according to which every valid norm can be accepted with all its consequences by all those concerned if it is generally followed.[19] Under the condition of freedom from domination (i.e., without exercising power over others), all those affected by the decision should discuss the relevant problem with rational arguments until all are convinced of a common solution as a consensus. The corresponding substantive result is then legitimate because it has gone through the legitimate procedure. Specifying the content of discourse outcomes in the sense of normative axioms is prohibited. Applying "U" in a community thus also enables an open-ended discussion on how to interpret human rights because their validity is not normatively set: "However well-grounded human rights are, they may not be paternalistically foisted, as it were, on a sovereign. Indeed, the idea of citizens' legal autonomy demands that the addressees of law be able to understand themselves at the same time as its authors."[20]

The outcome of the discourse is negotiated in the process and remains valid until the discourse community revisits the subject. Metaphysics-free justification of ethical judgments should thus succeed in evolutionary conversation processes under given rules.

Karl-Otto Apel goes one step further by adding—unlike Habermas—the supplementary principle "E" with "Part B" of applied discourse ethics. Ideally postulated conditions of communication, because of their difference from the historically given, non-ideal reality of the actual conditions of discourse, necessitate a teleological process toward the ideal procedure. If these "unavoidable" conditions of communication are fulfilled, legitimacy results from the execution of the discourse.[21] Here as well, good reasons guarantee legitimacy. Thus, wholly in line with Apel's "postulate of self-collection,"[22] the correspondence of the theoretical result of discourse ethics with the execution of its argumentation steps must be verified: Apel assumes in principle "E" the realization of ideal conditions of communication as a non-hypothetical ought for legitimation processes in "open society." From this, he concludes "that man must necessarily be ahead of himself in order to be man."[23] The formal procedural imperative is thus projected onto the essence—the being—of man.

There are also theological continuations of this line of thought. Bernhard Preusche, for example, aptly depicts the reality of present-day political-democratic opinion-shaping by adding fragments of John Rawls' theory of justice.[24] According to this, in discourse, before an argument is articulated, it is first necessary to arrive at a balance of considerations in a kind of inner dialogue. This means that it must first be weighed what other (possibly conflicting) arguments there might also be on this question or that. In this kind of discursive meta-communication, all discussants should first consider all possible objections themselves, thereby relativizing their original positioning before it is introduced into the field of democratic debate. This discussion is then a finalization of the consensually prepared positions that must be controlled in a communicative way. In practical terms, only those ideas that would likely stand up to the scrutiny of such a forum should be introduced.

Idea of Acceptability

As an example of the consequences of communicative procedural ethics for normative orientation, in this section, the focus shifts to the current discussion concerning the legitimate use of new technologies in the healthcare system. Arne Manzeschke, Karsten Weber et al.[25] have proposed a postmodern, procedural conception of ethical evaluation based on discourse ethics for such assessments. Their Model for Ethical Evaluation of Socio-Technical Arrangements (MEESTAR) is widely recognized, at least in Germany. In this model, acceptability is procedurally tied back to a consensus developed in discourse ethics that currently concerns seven basic values and principles. However, it ultimately remains open to a virtually unlimited number of changing catalogs and semantics. This ethical evaluation of technologies is three-dimensional. Temporarily valid ethical criteria are postulated that evaluate technical assistance systems under three observer perspectives (individual, organizational, and social) with four levels of ethical sensitivity (from "completely harmless" to "should be refused"). Subsequently, an overall assessment is made from the respective individual evaluations. The following values and principles are proposed:

- Care in the avoidance of negative paternalism,
- Autonomy in the sense of independent self-determination,
- Social participation,
- Safety, first as objectively and then as subjectively perceived damage prevention,
- Privacy as negative freedom with special reference to people with cognitive impairment,
- A more egalitarian understanding of justice in the sense of a set of values that is always being discursively redefined, and
- Self-perception as the user's attitude toward aging and dying.

These seven values and principles are revisable hypotheses in discourse that must remain valid both semantically and nominally.

The ethical evaluation of concrete socio-technical arrangements is also carried out in terms of discourse ethics: "the ethically relevant questions . . . should be discussed in public to make good decisions in this sensitive and relevant field of Res publica before the normativity claims the de facto."[26] Participation here is the legitimation criterion of ethical judgment. Politicians, users, the social environment, researchers, and providers take part in this discourse, which is open in terms of content, in order to lead it—in the sense of the "U" principle—by consensus to normatively acceptable (because accepted) judgments with temporal validity, using reasonable arguments and preserving freedom of control. The view of humanity and, ultimately, also the concept of freedom and justice remain deliberately vague in terms of content as a set of values since their semantics must remain open to potentially changing catalogs of criteria for ethical evaluation. The selection of ethical values and principles must always take place anew in a consensual discourse among those concerned. Once it is available, at least a step-by-step ethical evaluation can take place by using MEESTAR to identify the concrete use of technology as more or less just, safe, and so on to arrive at a balanced decision taking into account the seven preliminary ethical evaluation criteria with regard to the three perspectives mentioned.

This model has proved itself in practice. At the same time, some questions arise.[27] MEESTAR is a normatively set procedural tool for determining a notion of acceptability. A semantically meaningful evaluation of such acceptability can only be made

- in the medium or long term by those participating in the discourses who, with their own substantive value concepts, constantly reprioritize the ethical criteria, and

- in the short term by the evaluators who apply the instrument and, thus, themselves, on the basis of their substantive value concepts, in turn weigh the criteria to arrive at an ethical judgment (about legitimacy).

Seen in this light, MEESTAR is a technical tool of normative reflection whose utility depends on the existence of substantive notions of acceptability vis-à-vis itself, fed by notions of dignity made transparent in meaningful sets of values.[28] Such a tool does not and cannot present its own concept of first-order acceptability for ethical evaluation. Discourse is presented as legitimate in terms of third-order acceptability, with the help of which second-order acceptabilities can be generated. The concrete results obtained in the process are inferred concepts of ethical evaluation, dependent on first-order acceptabilities, such as a Christian socio-ethical position.

Criticism and View of Humanity

Several fundamental questions for discourse ethics are summarized here:

- Quasi-metaphysically, humankind is assumed to have a discursive nature because the "E" principle is postulated as an axiom, at least by Apel. From this follows the normative determination of how humans must be, namely discursive. So, *ought* is inferred from *being*. The assumption of a discursive human nature on which the theory is based contradicts its own thesis of asserted metaphysical freedom.
- The "U" principle is also a prediscursive postulate. People who put ruthless enforcement of their own interests in place of "U" communicate clearly without speaking a word through the silent use of force (e.g., in terrorist attacks such as those committed on September 11, 2001). The principle of force thus competes with "U." Accordingly, to ensure respect for mutual human dignity, a meta-principle is required that helps people sort out violence in order to assess legitimate choices and provides a good rationale for the choice of "U."
- The execution of the open discourse must clarify who is allowed to join in the discussion and who sets the topics. Which arguments are considered reasonable and, therefore, legitimate? And which ones are sorted out as illegitimate beforehand? The exclusion of discourse results that establish a metaphysical or transcendental objectivity contradicts the requirement of open discourse. Also, the procedure of discourse itself could be suspended in discourse.
- If all those affected by the question under discussion have a say, what arguments are there against weighty interference by those who place their own

power and intolerance above respect for the other party? Then there would be no other means against people like Hitler, Stalin, or Bin Laden than discourse. The law of the strongest would thus prevail. But if totalitarian currents or even ideological lobbyists are to be kept out of the decision-making process, then conditions of access to the discourse are needed. Only then can those who disavow discourse be excluded with good reason. This exclusion then serves to protect humanely liberal discourse.
- To actually lead all those concerned in a discourse to a consensus, this utopia of Habermas could—in my opinion—be replaced by representative democratic majority processes without major losses in stringency.

From the point of view of normative humanism, further issues and questions arise:

- The explicit relativizability of human rights is problematic.
- Discourse as a communicative procedure aims to take the place of substantive ethics, but with its prediscursive conditions, it is itself a normative postulate.
- The concrete procedure is preceded by normative preliminary decisions. Who has the power here to exclude the legitimate and non-legitimate ex-ante (i.e., prediscursively)?
- With the inner pre-selection of arguments called for by Preusche, discourse can become a balancing mediation without contentious positions. In such an understanding of democracy, who defines the corridor here as to what may and may not be "legitimately" said?
- The content of the exemplary second- and third-order acceptability represented in MEESTAR depends on other worldview-based and, thus, substantive first-order acceptabilities that are brought together in discourse. This form of postmodern procedural ethics does not provide any orientation itself; it neither wants to nor can. It remains reliant on first-order acceptabilities to offer a compass for navigating these issues.

SYSTEMIC ETHICS

Basic Concept

Systems theory criticizes discourse ethics for its justification of legitimacy from the communication process and is based instead on self-controlling processes that, as constructivism, impute the construction of reality to the individual.[29] There, communication, in turn, plays a central role in a corresponding understanding of humanity and normativity. As in discourse ethics, there is no objective normativity to be discerned in systemic ethics. Rather, systems produce values and norms from within themselves. This approach to understanding social reality and ethics also enjoys great popularity, especially in application areas of education or the theory and practice of leadership and management and this, in turn, in Christian contexts. The basic ideas of the theory and the underlying constructivism, as well as the associated view of humanity, are discussed in this section.

Systems theory, which dates back to Niklas Luhmann in particular, sees itself as a sociological meta-science that, in the sense of an epistemological methodology, aims at being logically upstream of ethical systematics. As sociology, it attempts to explain society as a whole and classifies religion, for example, as one subsystem among others. Constitution, communication, and language games of essential social areas and sciences (besides religion and theology, for example, economy, law, etc.) are a central topic. Systems theory is not itself a system but stands above systems epistemologically because it identifies and classifies them. The role of ethics in the normative management of the St. Gallen Management Model, developed on the basis of systems theory, is, for example, as a "blank canvas for meaning,"[30] a placeholder for semantically substantive ethics. By its own claim, systems theory does not aim to be ethics in its own right. It aims to be theoretically and practically compatible for diverse forms of ethics.[31] Is it really so universally adaptable, or does it not imply its own ethical paradigm? This is the subject of the discussion that follows.

Systems theory basically considers the rules of social behavior to be changing outcomes of complex subjective interactions. These are then carried out by people in entities separated by their own language games. These are the so-called systems. As a basic principle, whenever a system (such as a human group, a social milieu, a company, etc.) finds itself in an internal imbalance, it strives for balance. Different types of systems can be distinguished. What are known as autopoietic living systems are relevant for the management of people. Humberto Maturana defines it this way:

> There is a class of mechanistic systems in which each member of the class is a dynamic system defined as a unity by relations that constitute it as a network of processes of production of components which: (a) recursively participate through their interactions in the generation and realization of the network of processes of production of components which produced them; and (b) constitute this network of processes of production of components as a unity in the space in which they (the components) exist by realizing its boundaries. Such systems I call autopoietic systems . . . an autopoietic system that exists in the physical space is a living system.[32]

Autopoietic self-referential systems are made up of people (e.g., in school classrooms, technical departments, the board of directors of a company, etc.). These systems produce new things from themselves following disruptions (e.g., through external or internal changes) in their internal balance. Social systems function much like a thermostat. A change in the outside temperature affects a disturbance of the present equilibrium. This disturbance is replaced by a new equilibrium, and the temperature adapts once again. Today's social systems are perturbed by events (information) from their environments (by other systems); in other words, their equilibrium is disturbed and challenged. They are distinguished from each other by their own binary codes. For comparison:

- Economics follows the code of efficiency/inefficiency,
- while politics follows the code of power/powerlessness,
- religion follows the code of code immanence/transcendence,
- and law follows the code of right/wrong, and so on.

The goal of systems is always to achieve a new state of equilibrium with the help of and within the limits of their own language games and thus to ensure the survival of the system. Mutual interactions between the systems are facilitated by translations. Only the information that can be decoded into one's own language is admitted. Therefore, there is no trivial understanding, no direct transmission of information: "For this systems theory there are no transgressive inputs and outputs."[33] In an autopoietic system, there is a kind of collective harmony. New things only emerge from within the system itself. Direct external intervention aimed at influencing a desired result is therefore impossible.[34] The complexity of the causes can at best be reduced, albeit without simple cause-effect relationships.

Constructivism

The disruption of a familiar working atmosphere in an organization, for example, has a perturbing effect on the team working there. In this case, the consequence of the malfunction—in contrast to the thermostat—is not clearly predictable. Systems theory explains that which is constructivist. Constructivism assumes that

> individual worldviews are shaped and actively constructed through a history of interactions that an individual experiences with his or her physical and social environment. In this context, construction . . . is to be understood . . . as an unconscious process in which experiences are ordered and related to one another more or less consistently.[35]

It follows that "our cognitions are cognitions of a self-organizing system, the brain, bound to its possibilities and limits of cognition. These, in principle, do not allow statements about the actual, the 'true' nature of the world."[36] Accordingly, the brain as a self-contained system has no direct access to the world. It ascribes identity to objects by calculating a reality and putting it into an order (i.e., by constructing it). Supposed identity of objects is based on repeated arithmetic operations in the brain. These are then the object of epistemological research.

> ### EXAMPLE 7.1
>
> For example, an employee may be expected to present an idea on the topic of discussion during a meeting. If the employee remains silent and waits, information is encoded that is not immediately understood by the others. The others see this behavior as perturbing their expectations. Using their own language, they transform this disturbance into information that applies to them (e.g., the employee is poorly prepared) but which may possibly conflict with the actual intended message of the silent employee. Perhaps the employee's silence is a kind of ritual preparation leading up to the presentation of an ingenious idea or the like.

Constructivism rejects straightforward assignments of behavioral interpretations into "true" or "right" and "false" or "wrong." Circular explanations of behavior (such as students in the classroom or employees in the organization) assume recursive feedback between cause and effect: cause is effect and vice versa. Thus, neither objective knowledge can be achieved, nor can if-then correlations be determined as social laws (as in critical rationalism with Karl Popper, Hans Albert, or others). This is because the simple cause-effect logic is replaced by a circular explanation. The simple "if-then!" is replaced by the contingency-conscious "if-then?"[37] A simple formalization will help grasp this idea: the complex behavior of the human being depends on internal states "z." Humans are thus non-trivial machines. In a simple model, this might mean:

- x is the external impetus,
- z is the inner state of the human being or another living being (such as feelings, fears, hopes, moods, etc.), and
- a, b . . . are further internal and external influencing factors.
- Behavior y is past-dependent (for example, because people are adaptive) and unpredictable.[38]

- The behavior of humans as non-trivial machines in a social context (such as a school class or work team) then follows the simple equation:
  - $y = f(x,z)$ or
  - more complex dependencies: $y = f(x,a,b,c \ldots)$.

EXAMPLE 7.2

When during a meeting an employee throws a pen across the room out of anger over a decision made by a manager present, the mood of the thrower, the manager present, and the other employees in the room change after the pen is thrown. The location of the pen in the room also changes, among other things. The altered mood of the manager (and so on) affects the mood of the employees present and the atmosphere in the room. And their reaction, in turn, changes the mind of the person who threw the pen, which further affects the environment, and so on. What will happen now? This cannot be predicted. This may be followed by a second throw with another writing implement or perhaps an apology. Why this or that happens depends on the overall structure of relationships, the rules of interaction and communication, and so on. Why, for example, does an apology follow? Perhaps because the other employees criticize the thrower? Perhaps because the manager gave the thrower a stern look? Perhaps because the thrower suddenly had a guilty conscience or similar.

Thus, there is no clear basic attribution for social references. Equal causes do not have equal effects. Similar causes do not always have similar effects. Therefore, according to the systemic view, social situations are neither reproducible nor predictable. No clear cause for an observed effect can be determined because of the complex feedback loops.

Criticism and View of Humanity

Based on the basic ideas behind systems theory and constructivism, we can now examine the view of humanity that is decisive for social ethics. The systemic approach presupposes a view of humanity that has three essential facets. According to this, the human being is understood as a non-trivial machine, as apersonal, and as desubjectivizable:

- Human behavior is not easily controllable by incentives from a systems theory perspective. Humans are thus taken seriously as non-trivial machines in their complexity with their inner states of mind. This essentially means simply memorizing rules or instructions is not enough to change

people. The goal is internalization through successful perturbations. From a systemic point of view, this does not essentially distinguish humans from dogs or trees or other living creatures.
- The systems theory research program advocates an apersonal approach and thus an identifiable concept of humanity. Living beings (and thus also humans) are not considered to be autopoietic systems themselves. The person as a subject does not play a role in the sociological interest of systems theory: "But social things cannot be understood from the subject."[39] For Luhmann, the human being as a subject only comes into view in the different perspectives of social subsystems:

> The unity of the subject is the paradox of self-observation, the unity of the distinction necessary for it. And the unfolding of this paradox can take different paths depending on what the subject distinguishes itself from so that it may designate its own identity. This means, however, that there is no guarantee that all subjects will take the same approach, nor is there a guarantee that a subject will not change from situation to situation the distinctions that identify it—sometimes its wife, sometimes its subordinates, sometimes its body, sometimes others who are morally inferior and possibly even God at times. The subject would then be the distinction, to be updated in each case, between self-reference and hetero-reference, each with different determinations.[40]

This social concept of subject does not correspond to the continuity of a personal identity, but the subject is then merely the result of different perspectives. Humans participate more or less intensively in various autopoietic systems. A human individual can be involved in practical life without any problems sometimes in the social system economy, sometimes in the social system religion, and so on, even if these systems are separated from each other with their own language games, provided the individual uses the appropriate code. The focus is on the human being not in the continuity of personal individuality but instead as part of a different system with its own codes. The people involved are understood in their roles corresponding to the respective system with the corresponding expectations but not holistically in their life history as identified persons with corresponding responsibilities. Roles change in relational shifts (for example, the chair of a sports club board oversees a meeting, while in the office, the same person is a subordinate clerk). Teachers and students, managers and employees are then as "reception of their individuality by the system" merely the environment of communication. The communication with the corresponding codes, on the other hand, is the subject.[41]

- The apersonal view is flanked by an implicit desubjectivization of people. In human interpretations, the construction of meaning happens in the constructivist understanding. There is no intersubjectively valid but only hypothetically selected sense of actions, human life, the economy, or others. A reduction of complexity made in the attribution of meaning by selection is revisable. It thus lives in the context of permanent contingency of that which is not chosen: "One must . . . start from a world-constituting field of meaningful experience and action, in which personalities and social systems first identify themselves as differently structured contexts of selected experience and action."[42]

  People who are not able to constitute meaning in this way are then, strictly speaking, not subjects. For this reason, people now explicitly exist who are not subjects.

- The human individual is composed of various coevolutionary systems: The biological system—including organs such as the stomach and kidney—produces life, the mental system produces consciousness, and the social system produces communication.[43] The individual is split into different systems. These are subject to biological and psychological laws, which in turn make use of atoms. Then who is the "I"? Where do consciousness, responsibility, conscience, or even the soul have a place?[44]

That is: The systemic model is based on its own ideological postulates, including its own view of humanity.[45] It establishes a normative theory that opposes Christian ethics. Responsibility would then have to be thought of apersonally. In each case, it concerns communication within the framework of one system, which, however, does not evaluate the communication of the same person in another system. People are responsible in the various segments (systems, sections, etc.) of their lives, for example, in the family system, sports club, trade union, church community, as a child, young person, adult, retiree, and so on. System-wide responsibility of people, for example for earlier behavior in other own life contexts, seems difficult to justify here: for further example, the assumption of responsibility of a former GDR border guard for his shots at the wall in front of a court of law later on in unified Germany. The shooting happened in the context of system A, and the court decided in the context of system B. A fortiori, the assumption of responsibility for one's entire life, which, according to the Christian view, is expected of every human being before God after earthly death, cannot be made systemically plausible.

Furthermore, there is no recognizable objectivity in system-theoretical thinking that ethics could use for orientation. Once constructed, realities can be repeatedly revised without harm. Those who are continuously reconstructing a relative view of themselves and the environment then—above all, apersonally— are continuously recreating their lives. The focus on the continuity of being a person and thus on the responsibility for individual actions in the past is easily lost. Subjects of responsibility are not persons but systems: communication, relationships, rules, and so on. Their counterpart is not a law of reason or God, nor efficiency, but instead the appropriate construction of reality promoted by them. Responsibility is fulfilled when the reduction of complexity succeeds and systemic habitus spreads as a mentality. To rephrase this in individual ethical terms: "Always act in a way that increases the number of choices you have."[46] The apersonal view of humanity is an essential difference between this and Christianity's view of humanity. Ferdinand Rohrhirsch even says in view of systems theory: "In a sophisticated, rationally convincing way, personhood . . . is made to disappear in systems thought."[47]

Finally, there are also some theological and scientific-theoretical concerns.

- First, the theological view: From a Christian vantage point, systems logic breaks down with the incarnation of God because the dialectics of immanence and transcendence, which is supposedly essential for religion, become one. A religious worldview presupposes a notion of good as being something that must be discovered and also seeks to be understood. Without such understanding, which denies a systemic view, religions lose their orienting effect and raison d'être.
- There is also a scientific-theoretical perspective that complicates the compatibility of Christian ethics and systemic thinking. From a systemic point of view, the autopoietic system religion and with it metaphysical thinking has the pragmatic sense of overcoming contingency, which is afflicted with a high probability of error, by making the unavailable, such as death or suffering, interpretable through symbols and rites as placeholders or through a return to God. Transcendence merely explains the immanently inexplicable. From a systemic point of view, it makes it possible to talk about meaning without knowing it, in reference to revelation and mystery. Religion thus imposes a permanent openness on people. Metaphysical systems then communicate about something that is at the same time elusive. According to the systemic view, society is constantly forming new, functional religions. Since there is no true and no false, religion and metaphysics are relative in every respect. Thus, for constructivism, they are not a discussion partner in questions of cognition but instead one variable among many in the context of their own systemic theory. This makes it difficult to imagine a dialogue on equal footing.

Consequently, a systemic perspective is not seamlessly compatible with a Christian one. However, individual systemic insights can be incorporated into Christian social ethics once essential incompatibilities have been overcome, for example in leadership ethics.[48]

ASPECTS OF CONSTRUCTIVE OPPOSITION

Social ethics beyond normative humanism sees in human dignity a set of values to be creatively constructed by human beings. This basic conviction also unites otherwise ideologically competing positions, such as postmodern and normative individualist economic ethics. For example, Peter Ulrich and the St. Gallen Institute for Business Ethics understand "every human image as a human self-design" and conclude that "man 'is' what he makes or tries to make of himself in the human community as a social, cultural, and historical being."[49] The normative individualist school, which Ulrich explicitly opposes, employs the same logic. Karl Homann and his numerous students believe that, in the spirit of freedom, it must be people themselves "who first define in each case what their world, their interests, their preferences, and their costs are."[50] Similar positions are held by Friedrich August von Hayek, Günther Patzig, Karl Raimund Popper, and many more. Apparently, with all the differences in such secular arguments or intentions, there is nevertheless a broad common sense regarding the legitimacy of evolutionary value definition processes.

It rejects an axiomatic substantive specification, which is to be recognized as normative humanism and subsequently implemented as the measure of a good design of society. Normative relativism, discourse ethics, or systemic ethics, in their various facets, thus cannot establish a normative unconditionality of values and dignity. The various forms of ethics beyond normative humanism, as in their ethical interpretation, forego the assumption of an objective good, whether grounded in religious transcendence or transcendentally in the form of reason. People themselves are the authors of good, which they creatively define either out of considerations of utility, in communicative processes, or as constructions of meaning and which they repeatedly put up for disposition.

In the context of social philosophy, concerns about such a development can be found in the secular world, for example, in the theory of justice invoking Kant in John Rawls or the neo-Aristotelian capability approach of Amartya Sen or Martha Nussbaum discussed previously in this chapter.[51] Such shifts toward an argument that requires normative axiomatics remain in the widespread dictum of freedom from metaphysics. Thus, Rawls embeds the legitimation of his concept of justice in a contractualist construct of the state of nature and, in his later works, relativizes the original Kantian objective claim.[52] Although Nussbaum invokes Aristotle in her justification of basic human rights, she uses constructivist features in her interpretation of them (in relation to children with severe disabilities).[53] According to such an interpretation, the definition of dignity itself is then only hypothetical. For Sen, in turn, objective human dignity is based on an ideologically neutral postulate. However, one searches in vain for terms such as natural law or the law of nature in Nussbaum and Sen.

A value and dignity constructivism—in whatever form—establishes ethics beyond normative humanism. Such a postulate, common to the approaches discussed in this section, is itself an axiom and constitutes the fundamental difference between the religious or secular humanisms discussed earlier. Associated with this, explicit (or also implicit) freedom from metaphysics is a legitimate, further postulate, which Christian social ethics beyond methodological atheism cannot share.

NOTES

1. Cf. J. Ratzinger (2005): 14.
2. It should be noted here that proponents of normative individualism, such as D. von der Pfordten (2005), also wish to place Kantian ethics in this category since there, too, the ethical legitimacy of rules and order is derived only from recourse to individuals. I follow the view according to which Kant's ethics starts with the individuals in terms of cognition, but the legitimacy of rules and orders is not the result of their egoistic expressions of will but the autonomous cognition of the necessities of reason in moral law and categorical imperatives freed from egoism. Such ethics then, at best, fall into a methodological individualism (approach to the individual) but not into a normative one because the source of normativity with the moral law precisely claims universal objectivity for itself.
3. Cf., for example, W. Kersting (2002): 19.
4. V. Vanberg (1986): 114.
5. E.-W. Böckenförde (2003).
6. M. Herdegen (2003).
7. Cf. V. Vanberg (1986): 114.
8. Cf. K. Homann / I. Pies (1996): 220.
9. D. von der Pfordten (2005): 1069. The highlights in the original quote have been deleted. Cf. also C. Müller (2013).
10. U. Huar (1978): 142.
11. Ibid.: 146.
12. Cf. J. Bauer (2009) and the section on the family in part III in the chapter "Life, Work, and Death."

13. Cf. R. Reingold / L. Mora (2020).
14. Cf. Statista (2022b): From 2001 to 2013, the number of births to people with disabilities in Germany dropped from 312,400 to 298,400; from 2013 to 2019, the number dropped much more sharply to 258,000 in a much shorter period.
15. Cf. P. Singer (1979).
16. M. Nussbaum (1993/1999): 199. With this interpretation, Nussbaum moves away from Amartya Sen's anthropological statements in her interpretation of the capability approach.
17. Cf. in the introduction the remarks on the distinction between modernity and postmodernity.
18. Cf. the introduction to this volume.
19. Cf. e.g., J. Habermas (1984): 212.
20. J. Habermas (1996): 301.
21. Cf. K.-O. Apel (1986).
22. K.-O. Apel (1996): 21. The highlights in the original quote have been deleted.
23. K.-O. Apel (1997): 101. The highlights in the original quote have been deleted.
24. Cf. B. Preusche (2017).
25. Cf. A. Manzeschke, K. Weber et al. (2013). See the section on digitalization in the chapter "Future Issues" in part III.
26. A. Manzeschke (2011): 106.
27. Thus, the model lacks a mature long-term perspective that accounts for the complex consequences of technological networking, including its indirect consequences (e.g., on the view of humanity and coexistence).
28. In the field of corporate management, for example, this assignment corresponds to the goal of normative management in the systemic St. Gallen model. The task of the latter is to integrate the values of society into the company's own corporate culture, thereby taking account of changing values. Normative management handles and depends on substantive value concepts, as does MEESTAR. Cf. the presentation of the St. Gallen Management Model in E. Nass (2018): 123–29.
29. Cf. fundamentally N. Luhmann (1971): 53, on autopoiesis ibid. (1999): 325.
30. H. Höver (2016): 211.
31. Cf. E. Nass (2018): 109–29.
32. H. Maturana (1999): 153 et seq. The bracket is found like this in the original.
33. N. Luhmann (1999): 334.
34. An addressee must first translate a sender's intervention into the language code of the addressee's own system. Then it may have an impact, but the impact may be different than that envisaged by the intervening sender. For example, an ethicist can demand justice from an economist. The economist translates justice into the economic language of efficiency and concludes that justice exists where efficiency prevails (for example, in the sense of a tolerance premium for the needy). However, the ethicist may have intended something else when speaking of justice in an economic context, such as ensuring a minimum standard of survival based on the inviolable dignity of every human being.
35. F. B. Simon (2007): 68.
36. W. Meinefeld (1995): 100.

37. Cf. F. M. Orthey (2013): 6 et seq., 33.

38. On the logic of the behavior of living beings as non-trivial machines, see in detail H. von Foerster (1988).

39. N. Luhmann (1997): 1030.

40. N. Luhmann (1994): 46.

41. Cf. F. M. Orthey (2013): 8.

42. N. Luhmann (1985): 53.

43. Cf. N. Luhmann (1998): 48 and ibid. (1988): 266.

44. W. Korff (1977): 47 criticizes this approach as "humanity without a soul." See also T. Rendtorff (1990) for this assessment: 173.

45. The view of humanity identified here is not explicitly articulated as such by Luhmann since he sees in views of humanity the danger of ideological seduction. Nevertheless, a systemic idea of the human being is the fundamental value basis of the theory.

46. F. M. Orthey (2013): 8 based on H. von Foerster.

47. F. Rohrhirsch (2013): 18 et seq. then also immediately proposes, following Martin Heidegger, an overcoming of the systemic via a phenomenological approach, which is undoubtedly worth discussing.

48. Cf. E. Nass (2018): 193–226 and ibid.: 227 the corresponding overview.

49. P. Ulrich (1998): 70, 25. However, it seems that the human being is subordinate to this. See also Ulrich (1998): 207 (teleological being) and ibid. (1995): 89 (social being).

50. K. Homann (1988): 164.

51. See J. Rawls (1971/1999), M. Nussbaum (1988/1999), A. Sen (2002), and the corresponding section in part II in the chapter "Normative Humanism beyond Theology."

52. See, for example, J. Rawls (1993/2005).

53. Cf. M. Nussbaum (1990/1999): 199.

Chapter Eight

World Authority for Unconditional Human Dignity

NECESSARY MATERIALIZATION

Christian social ethics represents a normative humanism as a value basis for establishing unconditional human dignity and social values and principles derived from it. It aims to—and can—build bridges to other theological or secular ethics on this basis. The discussion in the preceding chapters revealed some examples of closeness and distance.

Finally, part II will now examine whether such bridges could potentially lead to an approach that spans multiple worldviews to ensure that unconditional human dignity receives solid international support. Merely formally guaranteed human rights, which are not sufficiently materialized in large parts of the world, are unacceptable.[1] Could an institutionalized world authority for values counteract this skewed state of affairs? In view of the ongoing violations of violable human dignity and global economic and ecological challenges, the idea of strengthening international institutions that could or should help enforce humane values worldwide with moral and legal pressure is not new. The United Nations and other institutions are obviously overwhelmed with such a task. Similarly, the Catholic Church has recently issued repeated calls for such an international world authority (e.g., Pope Francis and his predecessors Benedict XVI or John XXIII).[2] An objectively based, universally valid constitutional idea that also includes a basis for legal sanctions against violations (by governments, for example) would need to be formally established at the international level and implemented with resolute political support.

The Universal Declaration of Human Rights formally codifies a catalog of inalienable rights that are necessarily vested in every human being and require no further legitimation other than their direct derivation from human dignity. Any person anywhere may invoke these rights at any time, even if they are not codified in the respectively applicable constitution of that person's country. Ongoing violations of this are, for example, when dictatorships discriminate, persecute, disenfranchise, criminalize, and so on people on the basis of race, political or religious convictions, mental or physical infirmities, and so on. This is because human dignity precludes arbitrary behavior toward human beings. Human rights have validity independent of positive law. In legal terms, human dignity is reflected in fundamental rights, which are based on human rights and are intended to translate them into the respective constitution as positive law. In contrast to human rights, fundamental rights are therefore positively granted rights. Human rights, to which people are legitimately entitled based on their dignity, regardless of their codification, are represented in the respective constitution by legally enforceable fundamental rights. A constitution can therefore deny certain human rights to its citizens and thus declare them illegal. But then their abbreviated catalog of granted fundamental rights violates human dignity and the illegitimacy of such constitutional loopholes is proved.

The Charter of Human Rights is considered customary international law throughout the world. However, violations of this are par for the course.[3] It remains controversial under which conditions, in the name of human dignity, states may curtail the sovereignty of third countries by imposing outside sanctions. There is no universally recognized world authority whose decisions are absolutely binding and whose sanctioning options promise lasting success. Such an institution is necessary if the Charter of Human Rights is not to have a merely appellative character. At the same time, it seems to be a fiction because it can only fulfill its mission if it can refer to a normative synthesis of the world community that legitimizes it. A first step out of the dilemma is the search for such a synthesis. Justified concerns about potential paths of gradual implementation must not prevent the formulation of the necessary goal in advance. The ethical basis must be an understanding not only of concepts such as human dignity, justice, or freedom but also a semantic clarification and thus a substantive positioning with which grievances may be clearly identified and sanctioned.

The legitimacy of international interventions to enforce human rights is determined by the view of humanity as the basis of normative dignity. Based on a previously formulated integrating consensus on human dignity, a strong political world authority would have to be able to clearly state its contents, apply criteria for intervention, and enforce sanctions against violations. The synthesis necessary for this in the sense of the United Nations Charter of Human Rights does not demand the universal commitment to a particular religion or worldview but rather the commitment to the semantically substantive and universal value of dignity, which is not merely formal but also is enforced materially.

Religions and secular worldviews think differently about the justification of dignity. Depending on the tradition, more individual or more collective accents come into play. As a proposed, normative humanistic condition, the well-founded, unconditional individual right of every human being is assumed here, which also cannot be legitimately granted or denied by a collective. If the enforcement of this inviolable human dignity is the goal of the global community, then the different views of humanity and concepts of dignity derived from them cannot simply be juxtaposed with their ethics. They must be normatively measured against the objective claim of such material human rights and dignity. Incompatibilities with certain views of humanity can and must then be clearly stated.

VISIONARY CONTOURS OF AUTHORITY

A normative humanistic idea as a basis for a world authority of human rights seems like a utopian fiction in a world of differing *Weltanschauungen*. However, global integration presupposes an overarching understanding of human dignity, including its content, before a political institution can make itself its guardian. Possible steps on the way to such a synthesis are—at least speculatively—suggested based on the discussions in this part. It has become clear how challenging it is to identify a common substantive set of values for human dignity. At the same time, however, many hopeful bridges between religious and secular ideas have come to light, which do not discredit the undertaking of such a global moral set of values as mere utopian thinking. So, what humanistic synthesis as a set of values could such a world authority be armed with? And by what means might it be found?

Different views of humanity are conceivable that could be used to justify an integrating synthesis for the enforcement of human rights for a political world authority. World religions, including Christianity, must carry out important preparatory work so that the universal constitutional donors can agree on a global idea of normative humanism that is acceptable and enforceable. Anton Rauscher is cautiously optimistic here:

> Orientation to the essence of man is a great opportunity for people and peoples to learn to respect and understand each other in a world that is growing together. These opportunities must be seized. In the longer term, a common code of values can prevail that ensures cooperation and peace. Considering how much the circle of states that have embraced the 1948 United Nations Declaration of

Human Rights in one way or another has grown, this is an encouraging sign in a world where the blanket of humanity is still thin.[4]

The path to such a humanistic synthesis requires a communicative procedure, at the end of which is a third-order acceptability.[5] Getting there requires a constructive struggle of various first-order acceptabilities. The competing positions do not have to throw their conceptions of humanity and their justifications overboard. Otherwise, these core values would remain mere hypotheses. In contrast, substantive positions in particular (i.e., well-founded and controversial positions) should reach a binding result in a communicative procedure (second-order acceptability). Even after such an agreement, they should not give up their own figure of justification but instead keep it present for the time being for their own plausibility and further dialogue on questions of justification. That is: third-order acceptability (a common humanistic synthesis) presupposes first-order acceptabilities (such as Christian social ethics). Once the synthesis is found, the dialogue on the competing justifications for this humanistic content continues, and these would then be, for example, Christian, Islamic, Jewish, or secular views of humanity. When religions and worldviews communicate with each other in this way, they value both each other and that which is foreign by engaging in such an open exchange of good reasoning on equal footing. This idea of acceptability is the alternative to secularism and saves the idea of human dignity from possibly being ignored or relativized as a postulate.

The idea of universal human rights is normatively humanistic, be it theonomic, Kantian-autonomic, or something else. Thus, for the determination of a normative basis of the integrating world authority, limits are drawn, albeit within wide boundaries. The UN peace order, which would now have to be served by a political world authority, was originally a Western idea, born of a Christian, and later also a Western, sense of superiority in Europe and North America. It was inspired by Christian and secular humanist ideas. In contrast, Islam's political and religious opposition to this makes it fundamentally difficult to accept such Western humanism. One cannot simply expect Islam to adopt the Western tradition and certainly not to abandon its own declared beliefs. My conviction from a Christian perspective is that the Islamic world can and should bring its own idea of humanism into such a synthesis. This could include the connection to Averroes' conception of humanity and ethics or to the "reverse actualization" of legal tradition or the like. Under such conditions, Islam could also recognize a political world authority based on normative humanism. Part II hinted at individual aspects for these and further possible bridges to a humanistic synthesis. Not to be underestimated are the permanent obstacles that make it necessary to turn away from familiar paths in such understandings. The dialogue with other religions and worldviews is no less demanding: for example, with Buddhism, whose conception of humankind cannot be regarded as normative humanism without restrictions but whose view of humanity is nevertheless connected with its basic concerns through many parallels in content. But other religions and worldviews must also be considered: for example, Hinduism, Confucianism, nature religions, and secular variants of normative humanism.

The world community is by no means starting from scratch in terms of successfully installing a powerful world political authority on a humanist foundation. The Human Rights Charter is the normative basis. The next step will be to push for its enforcement, with reference to the Charter, to achieve a universal synthesis that legitimizes a strong world authority. Once this has been installed and equipped with the appropriate sanctioning and intervention options, the contents of the Charter may materialize. If states subsequently resist the judgment of this body, this refusal confirms their disregard for objective human rights. This unmasking is followed by appropriate sanctions previously agreed upon by the community of states in the internationally applicable, legally effective synthesis. The common idea of human dignity must be so specific that violations of it can be identified by neutral courts with authority. It must be broad enough to accommodate cultural differences of interpretation as appropriate. It must be universally valid and, for this very reason, translated in a culture-dependent manner.

World authority should thus be able to effectively enforce interventions in sovereign states on the normative-humanist basis, according to the position advocated here. If, on the other hand, the international community of states respects popular sovereignty absolutely, the materialization of human rights would fall by the wayside. Outside intervention would be prohibited. There would then be no mandate to intervene in dictatorships from the outside. The primacy of popular sovereignty relies instead on the self-awareness of sovereigns to grant themselves human rights as fundamental rights out of insight. But human rights will then quickly become victims of absolutized cultural differences and national identities. This contradicts the claim of their universal materialization. If, in the spirit of normative humanism, an objective understanding of human rights is applied to popular sovereign constitutions as a yardstick for their legitimacy by the global authority, external intervention can be justified. Respecting popular sovereignty under the primacy of human rights to be materialized reveals the objective lack of freedom that can now be ascertained and justifies the mandate of intervention. Only a universal synthesis of human rights legitimizes this solidarity mandate of intervention. Criteria for necessary sanctions and interventions can be derived from the timeless human rights and obligations that must be protected at all costs: defensive rights such as protection of life, freedom of religion, and freedom of the press in the sense of negative freedom on the one hand, and social-enabling rights to health, clothing, and education beyond mere tolerance premiums[6] in the sense of positive freedom on the other. According to Article 28 of the Universal Declaration of Human Rights, there exists an entitlement "to a social and international order in which the rights and freedoms set forth in this Declaration can be fully realized."[7]

Only when a normative humanistic understanding determines international constitutional law, to which every human being worldwide can refer, will every human being also be materially entitled to human rights vis-à-vis the universal world order.

The thought-provoking ideas for an integrating world authority outlined in this concluding chapter of the dialogue section point in an undoubtedly visionary direction as to how human dignity and human rights could be brought to bear worldwide as a third-order acceptability. They replace the lethargy of a mere fiction.

NOTES

1. See, for example, Amnesty International (2018).
2. Cf. CiV 67: This world authority should "be universally recognized and . . . vested with the effective power to ensure security for all, regard for justice, and respect for rights." See also, for example, LS 175.
3. On this contradiction between theory and practice, for example, in Iran, see H. Aghajari (2002). Numerous other countries can be mentioned here. See, for example, Amnesty International (2018).
4. A. Rauscher (2008a): IX.
5. Cf. in Part I in the chapter "Sanctification of the World" the section on socio-ethical efficacy.
6. Cf. K. Homann and I. Pies (1996): 220.
7. United Nations (1948/1993).

Part III

APPLICATION

Christian social ethics aimed at winning back followers today proposes the basic contents of the view of humanity and society it represents as a moral compass to help charter the rough waters of the myriad dilemmas faced in a pluralistic reality. These contents and their respective lines of reasoning were first outlined in part I. In its approach, it explores similarities and boundaries with alternative socio-ethical positions that not only offer comparable orientation frameworks but also aim to do so. Part II provided examples of proximity and distance to the Christian compass and debated them in a constructive discussion. This dialogical orientation of Christian social ethics does not contradict its own profile, with which it differs from other ethics of this kind both in terms of content and, above all, justifications. Its profile as a defined first-order acceptability is regarded precisely as an important condition for democratic value dialogues in a pluralistic society, at both the national and international levels.

Part III follows up by proposing Christian orientations for concrete socio-ethical fields of application. The basis for this compass, which is now being used in a variety of ways, is the value profile of the Christian mission in the world, which was touched upon in part I and further explored in the dialogue in part II. This compass must be comprehensible in its reasoning and therefore prove to be a practical aid for decision-making with good justifications when confronted with socio-ethical conundrums. Some of these topics will be discussed as examples. Answers from Christian social ethics are given, for example, to social questions concerning how to deal with creation and justice, life, work and death, the economy and society, and leadership and organizational culture, as well as the challenges of digitalization. Emotionally charged topics, such as the fair distribution of scarce goods, the question of the legitimate use of violence, the beginning and end of life, the position of the family, the culture of living charity, the opportunities and limits of digital technology, and so on are examined and sometimes lead to contentious positions. These are clearly summarized under "Consequence and Compass" at the end of each section.

Chapter Nine

Creation, Justice, and Peace

Owing to the headings of the ecumenical, conciliar process, common Christian responsibilities surrounding creation, justice, and peace are explored here first as areas of application. For corresponding positions on these topics, each is provided with an orientation compass guided by the Christian social ethics presented here.[1]

PRESERVING CREATION

Undoubtedly, responsibility for creation is one of the most urgent issues facing humanity. Many Christian movements and initiatives are active in this area. In 2015, Pope Francis placed this topic on the agenda of the Church's social teaching with his encyclical *Laudato Si* (LS). The fundamental ideas behind this piece offer important Christian orientations that are presented and discussed with their associated justifications, theses, and provocations at the beginning of this section on application. Clearly, Pope Francis does not discuss the issue in isolation but rather places the question of preservation of creation in the context of further issues of justice. This introduction to the various areas of application already affords a number of diverse perspectives.

New Focal Point of the Church's Social Doctrine

Pope Francis presented the idea of new wineskins for new wine with this creation encyclical not only thematically but also stylistically and systematically. Emphasizing environmental protection as a theme of a social encyclical is new. It is true that the concept of ecology is broadly extended here, for example, to include interpersonal relationships. Nevertheless, the understanding of the common house (οἶκος) encompasses, besides humankind, above all the relations with the earth and thus with what surrounds the human being as creation. Stylistically, the encyclical is not—like its predecessors—a scientifically structured treatise. Images of the Bible, mysticism, and prayers, not least including those of St. Francis of Assisi, make the text a spiritually infused sermon with captivating passion and emotion. This vitality, wholly novel for an encyclical, convincingly radiates the message of Pope Francis, who is so authentically human. His life he puts into words: gestures, signs, images, spiritual practice, and so on. The natural law justification of ethics represented in the social teachings of the Church up to and including Pope Benedict XVI is no longer systematically applied.[2] The fundamental ethical questions of justification, which are always found in encyclicals, are now replaced by a radical orientation toward application with concrete proposals for good human behavior and thought. However, the manner in which they are derived is not left to chance. It is primarily addressed with recourse to Franciscan theology and mysticism (e.g., Bonaventure). Models of the liberation theology long rejected by the Church are also used to analyze the economy. Nevertheless, these should not be interpreted as a continuation of the theology of Benedict XVI.

It is true that the numerous references—as is usual for an encyclical—to preceding Church teaching documents show that Francis sees himself squarely in the tradition of social doctrine (LS 15).[3] This corresponds to the papal self-understanding. But it is undeniable that he does not simply continue the thoughts of others. Francis does not follow the well-worn paths of the Church's social doctrine. In this way, he does justice above all to criticism from outside the Church, which identifies the sluggishness and antiquatedness of the Church in its path dependency. Francis is striking the chords of a new paradigm whose forward-thinking power has yet to be proved. What is new about this paradigm in the field of theological systematics is not the term itself but instead the semantics of human ecology (LS 5, 13) associated with it, which he presents as the key to a socio-ethical evaluation of contemporary problems.[4] This understanding of ecological humanism cannot simply be leveled into the previous doctrinal tradition. This would deprive the encyclical of the innovative explosive power it contains. It will be shown here to what extent *Laudato Si*, with its new focus on the integrity of creation, is less an evolutionary than a revolutionary Church document before this challenging message is then critically acknowledged.

Analysis: Culture of Human Self-Destruction

Like any normative humanism, the ecological variant profiled by Francis starts with the human being. His holistic human ecology normatively considers humans in the context of their relationship to God, their neighbors, and the environment (LS 27). God has given humans this responsibility in the order of creation. Observing it leads to good while disregarding it leads to evil for the individual and—through the consequences aggregated in rules and incentives—for humankind as a whole. Such a theological perspective attests to a current human ecological crisis manifested in many self-destructive phenomena (LS 79). According to the pope, the reason for this stunted threefold culture of relationships is a fundamental crisis in the economy.

First, a look at the concretely addressed crisis phenomena that dehumanize people today. As already mentioned in the apostolic exhortation *Evangelii Gaudium* (EG), from a privileged view of the poor, what is condemned most is the social and economic exclusion of people in urban slums, for instance, who are basically seen as expendable because they are not useful to a society focused on consumption and profit.[5] The value of human beings today is largely limited to their economic utility, which can be measured in terms of monetary value. Humans, forgetting God, attempt to take God's place by using economic logic to define who is human in the full sense of the word and who is not. This perverts the inviolability of human dignity, which Christians infer from the image of God (LS 84). Anyone who has no apparent use is thus no longer human in the full sense of the word. This view of humanity contradicts holistic human ecology. It flies in the face of the essential dimensions of human responsibility.

- First and foremost, this affects the human relationship with God since, from the Christian point of view, it is tantamount to the self-destruction of the humanum. It corresponds to the even more radical extension of ethics of so-called economic imperialism developed by Nobel Laureate in economics Gary Becker, which can also be found in a less potent form in some current forms of economic ethics. Normative economics sees itself as a continuation of ethics by economical means in all areas of life. Following such logic, good action is oriented toward consumption and efficiency. The pope views this as a breeding ground for exploitation (LS 5). However, this type of economic ethics can be used to justify a destructive anthropocentrism, which nevertheless excludes a large part of society. This is paradoxical because large swaths of humanity are denied dignity in the name of ethical focus. This exclusion is identified as a fundamental evil of our time. According to this, the ethics of *Homo economicus* also leads to the global uniformity of humankind with a throwaway mentality, characterized by fear on the one hand and greed on the other (LS 59, 105, 203).
- Such a culture also contradicts holistic human ecology because it corrodes the Christian aspiration of people cohabitating as a human family and thus

their responsibility toward their neighbors. People become mere functioning cogs in the gears of economy, understood as just one humane resource among others serving short-term profit. When consumerism and efficiency rule the "good" human condition, human security (LS 48) and social integration (LS 46) lose their value. There is a normative individualization (LS 208) with social coldness in the sense of a merely anonymous coexistence in society, which, for example, is propagated by US Nobel Laureate in economics James Buchanan as a "moral order" people should strive for.[6] For Francis, these are the consequences of such incentive logics, which displace cultural social treasures, such as those of the indigenous peoples (LS 145), as well as individual morality, against which, for example, in the sense of the liberal economic ethicist Karl Homann and his school of thought, precisely such economic ethics must warn.[7] After all, an individual virtue that emphasizes security, inclusion, or cultural diversity may interfere with the predictability of economic allocations. Ways out of a worldwide social injustice (LS 48 et seqq.) are complicated by interdependencies in international debt (LS 52), thereby perpetuating the exclusionary logic of human self-destruction.

- In addition to this myopic focus on economic calculation, the pope continues, society has lost sight of its symbiotic relationship with the environment, which the plan of creation ascribes to humans as the addressees of this responsibility. This is the third violation of the requirement of holistic human ecology. Global warming (LS 167), the lack of clean water (LS 185), mountains of waste, and air pollution are cited as examples. Other issues include migration (LS 25), social tensions, and wars (LS 14, 142) as logical consequences of the lack of responsibility of the rich minority to the poor, excluded majority in the world. The intrinsic value of created beings has also been forgotten under the regiment of anthropocentric economics. This is identified as a betrayal of the divine creation mandate (LS 69). Pope Francis programmatically speaks out on behalf of the poor and Sister Earth (LS 49) alike. The admonishing voice of creation experiences an unprecedented revaluation in the social teachings of the Church with this equality.

The human ecological crisis can thus be put into focus: Forsaking God, social indifference, and a reckless attitude toward creation are understood as a triple breach of the human contract toward God, opening the door to the technical hubris of feasibility without responsibility toward God, creation, and social culture.

Francis sees this self-destruction of humankind as inseparably coupled with a correspondingly destructive regiment of moral-free power, made possible by a shoulder-to-shoulder relationship between the powerful market and technology (LS 102). Human virtue atrophies in the name of freedom, with humans now paradoxically elevating egoism to morality and shaping human relations following this normative logic (LS 105). The basic evil here is the displacement of political control by unbridled market power (LS 196). Following an assumed utilitarian pragmatism (LS 205), the globalized financial system (LS 54, 144), normative economic view of humanity, market logic focused on short-term profit (LS 32, 54), private property system detached from social obligation (LS 93 et seq.), and technology-dependent market system as a whole lead to uncompensated external environmental effects for the poorest (LS 36), to their massification and enslavement (LS 105) as well as to a displacement of the real economy (LS 110). Corruption and political pressure from financial dependencies are accompanying consequences. From this perspective, the technological-economic paradigm destroys human ecology by decomposing the three dimensions of responsibility in terms of individual and social ethics, to the detriment of peace with God, the world, and people among themselves (LS 229).

Systematics: New Order Through New People

For Pope Francis, holistic human ecology is the normative instance of the divine plan with human beings (LS 5, 13) and is thus among the normative conditions that a community cannot produce on its own. While other encyclicals discuss social and economic issues, the ecological question is not only addressed here as a field of application of a previously defined ethical system, although this alone would be innovative. More importantly, it is placed before the brackets of every Christian-ethical legitimacy as an ingredient of the divine plan and thereby defined as a value compass with first-order priority. The concept of nature is frequently used to justify this normative objectivity, but here it is not understood normatively in the scientific-theoretical sense in such a way that absolute (human) rights and obligations can be derived from it with the help of human reason. Francis sees nature more in a commonly understood sense as creation, whose normativity is now derived not (in terms of natural law) from an objective being but rather from humankind's relationship to creation (LS 6, 115, 120). Instead of natural law, biblical or mystical-theological sources serve as evidence-based justification of such objectivity in view of human ecological catastrophes. The starting point is the logic of love of the divine plan (LS 77), which is more spiritual than rational, and which permeates the three human relationships of responsibility. Thus armed with a different justification of values than classical social doctrine, Francis distances himself from normative relativism, which his predecessor had also identified as an opponent of Christian humanism, thereby preserving the universal claim of ethics. In contrast to his predecessors, however, the pope has allowed the classical level of reasoning to recede into the background.

The primary value compass of human ecology aims to replace the power of the market with a primacy of politics (LS 196): a thesis that can also be found, for example, in current discourse-ethical approaches to economics (e.g., in the work of the St. Gallen business ethicist Peter Ulrich).[8] Human-ecological orientation to the common good should replace egocentric self-interest in laws and virtues (LS 42). Such an aspired shift in the system leads to a new normative concept of progress, which can rein in technology and market power with a politically consistent revitalization of the Christian principle of the general purpose of valuable goods (LS 42, 67). For the time being, this new synthesis has nothing to do with a third path of "sustainable growth" driven by the social market economy because this is seen as a false compromise that, at best, shrouds the evil of market logic (LS 191). But according to Francis, there is no time for such self-deception. Rather, the answer lies in radically transforming the system to create a new economy under a politically organized ecological primacy (LS 12). A fundamentally false order with its constraints and path dependencies should be transformed into a new Jesuan-inspired order (LS 82). The dialectic of technological-economic paradigm and exclusion is to be overcome by a new holistic synthesis of human ecology, which cultivates spaces of empowerment for every human being, thus allowing the three levels of responsibility foreseen in the divine plan to unfold.

This requires a new, virtuous human being who fulfills this responsibility and thus revolutionizes the human ecological order.

Implementation: International Regiment of Virtue

Virtue education with the displacement of consumerism and egoism (LS 192), small or larger ecological gestures made by every human being, political primacy over market power (LS 203), community ideals instead of individualism (LS 208), and a common good orientation within the framework of a strictly socially obligatory definition of property (LS 93) are the political consequences of a new ecological world order with new people.

Such a cultural change requires a socio-ethical concept of order and an individual-ethical cultural program. Socio-ethical universalism, in the sense of the traditional Catholic vision of a human family (LS 13, 52), is now, above all, to inspire the international solidarity of the poorest (LS 14, 142). The authority for the internationally effective enforcement of human rights discussed in the previous chapter and called for by Benedict XVI as a political world authority (LS 175) is now conceived as an international leadership under the premise of the option for the poor. This body should see itself as the guardian of a continuity of human ecological culture even beyond national changes of government (LS 181). The implementation of the idea of a human family is more concretely linked to a universal political cultural regiment for the enforcement of a universal ecological consciousness (LS 207). Business must be understood as a serving part of this culture, which is not itself at the mercy of the market's inherent order.

The aim is to permanently change people with the help of the new political regime. This new lifestyle requires a comprehensive educational program, especially for exploiters and egoists who are driven by consumption. Then—according to this visionary idea—they will also change the global conditions and the global order. The pope develops an impressive program of Franciscan ecological spirituality to this end, which is unique in its synopsis of the Church's social teaching. It calls for an individual and communal ecological conversion that should be prophetic and contemplative at the same time (LS 216). An ideal of how humans should live together aligned with God's plan is sketched in mystic, Trinitarian, and eucharistic terms by which actual coexistence must be measured. According to a Jesuan model (LS 221 et seqq.), this includes a charism-oriented culture of gratitude, charitability, simplicity, a sense of connection with the environment, moderation, humility, wonder, serenity (LS 224), mindfulness (LS 231), harmony, justice, fraternity (LS 82), and tenderness (LS 91). Pope Francis considers the individual and communal conversion to the universally conceived cultural model to be feasible (LS 205). In this way, he brings the Christian virtue of hope, which offers encouraging arguments that conversion is worthwhile for everyone, even though it may be late but not too late.

The socio-ethical demand for such an international human-ecological cultural authority and the individual-ethical demand for a rethinking on the part of the individual correspond with each other. The goals are the repression of egoism and, as a result, a new freedom before God. The appropriate shaping of the threefold ecological responsibility into rules and virtues is the key to this. Bertold Brecht's question of whether for such a new social synthesis first the people or the conditions must be changed thus remains open in this logic—and likely rightly so.

Consequence and Compass

The innovative effect of the environmental encyclical in the context of Catholic doctrinal proclamation can hardly be overestimated. One of the great achievements undoubtedly lies in making spiritual theology a fertile ground for the questions of social ethics with unprecedented passion. Establishing the ecological question in the context of threefold human responsibility as an essential component of the primary value basis of Christian social ethics is a necessary and courageous step forward in view of the comprehensive ecological challenges that face humankind. Questions that beset people today are vividly illustrated with concrete images so that the message can reach many people who otherwise tend to close their minds to a systematic theological approach. The affectionate language, especially toward the poor, makes the text sympathetic especially to these disadvantaged people, something that is well suited to Christian social ethics and is certainly a major boon to its reception in many countries of the world. Francis is also harshly critical of the failure to apply to humans the same principles seen in ecology, where there is a demand to protect the environment without protecting human life (LS 136).

For a fruitful discussion of the impact of the encyclical, several critical observations can be made in conclusion.

- The threefold responsibility of human ecology derived from the divine plan, places humans' responsibility to themselves second, although Jesus Christ emphasizes this in the Golden Rule in place of the earth as an equal addressee alongside social responsibility, which in turn is derived from responsibility to God. Despite this aspect being found elsewhere in the encyclical (LS 155), this new hierarchy could overshadow the equally important personal aspects of self-love and responsibility inferred from it. Neglecting to love oneself is certainly not the pope's intention, considering the growing number of people (including young individuals) suffering from mental illness and the stresses experienced by many (for example, in their careers). The revaluation of the earth must not lead to a devaluation of the human's own self-love; rather, it is about achieving a mutually appreciative relationship between the two.
- The idealistic view of humanity, which seeks to displace egoism, does not seize on the realism of St. Thomas Aquinas, who already turns away from such a wishful thinking of an ideal form of communism in the justification of his doctrine of property. The truth is that humans are not only altruistic and selfless. Taking this into account is incumbent upon the organizations responsible for shaping the social order in all its facets. Thus, for example, according to the teaching of St. Thomas, private property as a secondary natural right always remains only the next-best solution. However, it does justice to the sinful nature of humans and is thus justified and commanded in Christianity in a corresponding private property system as a form of responsibility ethics.[9] Instead, the encyclical favors an ecologically utopian idea of humanity. Secular communism was not the only model to fail in pursuit of this utopia; even the model of the corporativist professional or-

der, which was presented as a Christian market alternative in the *Quadragesimo Anno* encyclical, struggled with it as early as 1931.
- The fact that ethics is not based on natural law does not detract from the topicality and practicality of the encyclical. However, the universal claim of unconditional human responsibility and dignity loses plausibility as a result. Using God's plan, the Bible, and mysticism as references make it difficult to defend these arguments in fundamental discussions with secular or non-Christian religious ethics, which are characterized by arguments of reason. That Franciscan tradition can be well reconciled with natural law was demonstrated, for example, by the late scholastics of the School of Salamanca. Rediscovering such a symbiosis, instead of sacrificing natural law, seems consistent, innovative, and worthwhile to represent the substantive message of the encyclical in a clear and well-reasoned manner.
- The systematic dialectic with some class-struggle motifs seems confusing but is likely to be understood as a residuum of the influence of liberation theology. A substantive discussion of free-market economic theories is expressly rejected (LS 46). Rather, the focus must be on the true development of people. Attitudes like this only harden the fronts between the church and liberal economics. While connectivity to secular theories is otherwise sought in many modern and postmodern theologies, this categorical refusal to seek any such connection at all is rather surprising. However, I believe that dialogue on equal footing such as this is necessary to bridge the chasm and re-establish a culture of business philosophy that combines economic and ethical rationality. This is the task of future-oriented economic ethics, which recognizes both the positive and negative ethical aspects of the market.[10] Market logic should thus be viewed in a more nuanced way, with its own equity potential to avoid wasting scarce resources. What exactly is meant by condemned utilitarian pragmatism? Utilitarianism has many faces. The implied equation of the market with economic imperialism paints a distorted picture of a free economy. Gary Becker's ideology is undoubtedly incompatible with the Christian notion of justice. But the social market economy, for example, shows in its humanistic program another face of social justice borrowed from Christianity, which has nothing to do with economic imperialism yet adheres to market principles. From a Christian point of view, this third path seems more promising than a planned economic transition, which Pope Francis himself later admitted at the award ceremony for the Charlemagne Prize of Aachen.[11] He put his radical critique of the market into perspective there and built bridges to the field of economic science. These bridges notwithstanding, it is still insufficiently clear what Francis means precisely by the term "social market economy." Semantic clarity, however, is crucial if the relationship between

market and order is to be discussed in any meaningful way. It remains to be determined in a dialog with the economic sciences how exactly the relationship between the market and the economic sciences and the Christian concept of humanity, which was mentioned by the pope in the encyclical and which was initially seen as very distant, should now be structured in a new evaluation without relativizing the ecological thrust.

- Depending on its concrete form, the visionary international regiment of virtue harbors the danger of statist paternalism. Who sets the content of such large-scale education? What is meant by a social reversal (LS 216)? The conversion of an individual is educationally and spiritually conceivable. If this is meant as a collective consciousness that is to be moved to conversion, there is a danger of sacrificing the view of the individual to that of a collective. This would be problematic from the perspective of the Christian view of humanity. So, what does Francis mean by this new awareness? Such unresolved questions leave room for misunderstandings that, from a liberal perspective, could primarily fuel concerns about ideological re-education or a collectivist order. Francis, however, specifically highlights individual responsibility (i.e., he has the individual and his personal responsibility very much in mind and, therefore, has good reasons to oppose such concerns about a collectivism advocated by the Church). Further clarification would be helpful here.

SOCIAL JUSTICE

Pope Francis' cross-contextual approach in his environmental encyclical places the question of the integrity of creation in close relation to issues of justice, economics, technology, and so on. The focus on social justice plays a special role. This will be the focus of a separate section, as there is some controversy surrounding the actual meaning of this elusive term.

In social ethics, social justice must distinguish between social value and social virtue. Before asking for a semantically substantial concept of social justice as a value, we must remember the important distinction from the virtue of a just human being already established in part I: As a social virtue, it relates to the attitude of individuals; as a social value, it is an intended objective in the shaping of society. This section now deals with social value, which is concretized in the coexistence of society and corresponding rules, such as laws, and, from a Christian perspective, ideally paired with the social virtue of social love.

Between Weasel Words, Consensus, and Dissent

The term "social justice" shares the same fate as positive terms such as human dignity or social market economy of being identified as a "weasel word" (Friedrich A. von Hayek), "a phrase from which all meaning has been siphoned, like an egg sucked dry by a weasel, with nothing remaining but an empty shell."[12] The importance of clearly explaining conceptual semantics as they relate to human dignity has already been emphasized in detail.[13] Such central value concepts can only be discussed in a meaningful way if they are used to convey a semantically substantive position (in the case of human dignity, for instance, the underlying view of humanity with rights and duties derived from it).

Social justice is more or less undisputed as a value that should shape social coexistence. If this positive assessment is largely consensual, political parties, trade unions, churches, associations, and so on are interested in others perceiving them and the positions they represent as socially just. Why is social justice held in such high esteem? Apparently, it is based on a broad moral consensus of our society, which, in Germany, after all, gives itself an order as a social federal and constitutional state (GG Art 20, 28). What could be more natural than to declare social justice to be the guarantor of this constitutional self-understanding today? What the law prescribes positively, it redeems normatively. Then it always stands for something good. The roots of its goodness reach from antiquity to the present: Classical Greek philosophers, such as Plato, Aristotle, and others, were already concerned with justice as a goal of the state, but the Enlightenment (Leibnitz, Kant), modern social philosophy (John Rawls, Amartya Sen),[14] and the churches in their tradition as well as in current pronouncements held and continue to hold it up as an undisputed value. The variety of social justice that Luigi Taparelli (1840) and Antonio Rosmini (1848) first spoke of under the impact of the worsening social question of their time, and that was magisterially recognized as a value in Catholic social doctrine in the encyclical *Quadragesimo Anno* (QA) in 1931, enjoys an arguably even broader popularity. Because the insertion of "social" also suggests the addition of moral goodness. It resonates with an idea of equality, the extent and content of which, however, is not yet expressed by the term "social justice" alone. Here we find a paradox: Social justice is broadly a socially consensual good, but there is no consensus on its semantics. Thus, it is a fallacy to think that social justice simply means more social transfers, more redistribution of income, wealth, or even public debt.[15] Rather, it is in keeping with the democratic principle of using competing arguments and content to wrestle with existing content of essential social values (such as human dignity, freedom, and, indeed, social justice), which our polity cannot produce on its own. A semantic discussion of the term is also warranted from a socio-philosophical perspective. The first fundamental question we must ask is: What denotes social justice at all, beyond political or ideological interpretations?

From the perspective of order ethics, justice is the right corresponding to human dignity, while as social justice, it is derived from the distribution law corresponding to human dignity. This makes it a socio-ethical standard for assessing positive law as it relates to social distribution issues and the social fight against hardship and poverty. The content of social justice is tied back to its conformity with the underlying understanding of human dignity. Thus, there may be a different understanding of social justice depending on how human dignity is defined. It is, therefore, not—as Hayek said—merely the universal justice related to society. Rather, it is the subfield that questions the legitimate (re)distribution of scarce resources, such as tax rates and entitlement rights. Because there are competing versions of human dignity, there are also various interpretations of a just distribution law. As a result, those wishing to discuss social justice in a politically or socio-ethically meaningful way must communicate their understanding of human dignity and use it as the basis for coherent rules on the distribution of scarce resources.

Order-Ethical Contexts of Social Justice

The concepts presented in Parts I and II on both sides of normative humanism can be considered as authoritative ideas of human dignity for the determination of social justice, which are being discussed today. These can now be greatly simplified and assigned to four basic societal models, which set out the framework for different basic ideas of social justice. The ideas of social order are distinguished based on the concept of human dignity and social cohesion. The following synopsis provides a broad overview of fundamentally different normative conceptions of social order for a rough but helpful distinction according to two main criteria:

- The idea of human dignity is the answer to the fundamental question of normative ethics concerning the content and rationale for the most important core values.
- The idea of social cohesion is the answer to the fundamental question of virtue ethics concerning the values of people who shape actual cooperation.

These two perspectives (normative ethics and virtue ethics) can each be assigned two contrasting positions for the simple synopsis:

- Normative ethics: A distinction is made between a normative humanistic response, which can establish unconditional dignity, and a normative relativistic response, which cannot.
- Virtue ethics: A distinction is made between the idea of affective cooperation, which presupposes a sense of social belonging, and the idea of anonymous coexistence, which can manage without such ambitious goals.

Four basic normative models of social order can thus be distinguished in such a system:

1. Normative humanism with anonymous coexistence as an adequate idea of living together,
2. Normative humanism with the goal of affective social cohesion,
3. Normative relativism with anonymous coexistence as an adequate idea of living together, and
4. Normative relativism with the goal of affective social cohesion.

These four models can now be assigned to the different schools of social ethics discussed in this volume in Parts I and II.

1. An idea of Kantian autonomy fits model 1 (autonomous duty). Normative humanism is easily justified here, whereby cohabitation need not be affective. Ultimately, mere performance of duty is sufficient. No sense of belonging or insight into the contents of the normative idea of humankind is required.[16]
2. For instance, a Christian-humanist idea would fit well with model 2 (personal social love). Here, too, normative humanism is easily justified in the idea of personhood but is now flanked by the ideal of social love (i.e., also affective social cohesion).[17]
3. A normative individualistic idea (normative individualistic "moral order") derives what is now conditional human dignity from egoistic interests so that there is no normative humanism. An anonymous coexistence is sufficient for cohabitation, as affective cooperation is considered unrealistic. Following the classification of James Buchanan, this way of living together is called moral order.[18]
4. A normative collectivist idea (normative collectivist "moral community") derives conditional dignity from the collective interest and power of the ruling vanguard (e.g., party). Cohabitation is characterized by a strong affective cohesion that constitutes the dominant identity (for example, as race, class, or religion). Following the classification of James Buchanan, this cohabitation is called a moral community.[19]

The following simplified synopsis of models of social order emerges from this classification, depending on ideas about human dignity and social cohabitation.

Table 9.1. Four order-ethical contexts of social justice

Social virtue / Human dignity	Absolute	Conditional
Anonymous	1. Autonomous duty	3. Normative individualistic "moral order"
Affective	2. Personal social love	4. Normative collectivist "moral community"

A socio-ethical idea of social justice is itself part of such order ethics. The assignments are not always clear, but this system helps with appropriate categorizations. Different understandings of social justice can thus be presented, taking this contextuality into account.

Responses Beyond Normative Humanism

Focus is first placed on responses that go beyond normative humanism. These are based on the conceptions of humanity of normative collectivism, discourse ethics, and normative individualism as presented in part II in the chapter "Ethics beyond Normative Humanism."[20] These views of humanity are expressly referred to again here.

The positions on the content of social justice selected here as examples have a profound influence on modern debates of justice. Even if normative collectivism, for example, does not meet with broad approval, its ideas nevertheless shape political debate. The interpretations of these three influential basic positions selected here will be compared with their basic ideas and consequences in a synoptically simplified way: starting from the view of humanity all the way to the rules of distribution derived from it.

- Normative collectivism—generally on an atheistic basis—views people first as a collective entity. People have the task of being as intrinsically motivated as possible to implement the given idea of community with all the talents available to them as individuals. Social justice is realized in the ideal of a community property system. Interventions in this common property must be justified. Individual development serves the progress of the collective. It always has a service character and no intrinsic value. Thus, solidarity clearly takes center stage, but strictly speaking, it ends with respect to those who do not want to or cannot serve the collective goal. If such a position is implemented politically, as in a communist or fascist dictatorship, this can be used as a basis for legitimizing tangible consequences for cohabitation and distribution. Here are a few examples: Political persecution or the deportation or elimination of elderly or disabled people could be justified in this way. Living together presupposes a sense of community freed from egoism, excluding supposed enemies in class or racial struggle. Human dignity is made dependent upon how the human being benefits the collective. And the ruling party is totalitarian in whether it grants or denies human dignity.

- In postmodern discourse ethics, the human being is recognized as an individual who, in the forum of discourse itself, determines the nature and content of humanity and dignity. Social cohabitation must not be determined by racial or class struggle but instead by discourse that is free of domination. At the same time, however, there remains a skepticism toward ruling elites, which could become a breeding ground for discussions about envy. In discourse (about the content of dignity and social justice), no axiomatic eternal decisions are allowed, because human rights are also negotiable. Social rights, for example, of the unborn, people with dementia or mental disabilities, or the dying, cannot necessarily be safeguarded by potentially relativized human dignity. These people also do not benefit from the fact that social justice should also mean the situation of the least advantaged people in society should be optimized, possibly 1.) through the highest possible social transfers (John Rawls)[21] or 2.) for example, through an independent, universal basic income (Philippe Van Parijs).[22] This is done by either 1.) forcing high performers to pay the highest possible taxes or 2.) destroying egoism by means of the appropriate education so that people selflessly earn as little as possible for themselves instead of the community. This idea of social justice has not fully overcome the utopia of a selfless collective human and an idea of competition between rich and poor, and it prefers a strong welfare state that provides for its people over private-sector initiative. Welfare losses could be unwelcome side effects. However, social justice determined by discourse ethics on the one hand and the market and private property on the other are not fundamentally mutually exclusive. Individual responsibility, subsidiarity, performance, tradition, and freedom tend to take second place.
- Social justice can also be filled with content in normative individualism, even if the use of this term may be rather unusual in liberal circles, for example. In fact, normative individualistic social justice also undoubtedly exists. It has many varied facets, now liberal or libertarian in nature. Basically, focus is first placed on egoistically conceived human beings with

their own responsibility. Human dignity is conditional because it is derived from egoistic utility calculations on the market (for instance, with the idea of a "tolerance premium"). An anonymous coexistence of competitors in the market is sufficient for cohabitation. Social justice demands the avoidance of coercion and, therefore, the lowest possible taxes. This is because income taxes—brought to their logical conclusion in libertarian terms with Robert Nozick—for instance, are ultimately regarded as a justification for forced labor.[23] Subsidiarity takes precedence over solidarity in this case because unconditional social rights cannot, strictly speaking, be justified. Social transfers are conditional "tolerance premiums" designed to mitigate "threat potential."[24] The weakest, who do not pose a threat to social peace, are quickly left behind.

These three concepts of social justice can now be clearly compared:

Table 9.2. Concepts of social justice beyond normative humanism

Social justice in the idea	of normative collectivism	of postmodern discourse ethics	of normative individualism
of humankind	collective	precedence of the collective over the free being (*Freiheitswesen*)	egoistic free being
of human dignity	granted or denied by the ruling party	agreed or disagreed upon in discourse	determined by utility calculations in the market
of responsibility	selfless social responsibility	priority of social responsibility (precautionary social state)	performance and personal responsibility
of community	e.g., class struggle and class consciousness dialectically take the place of bourgeois order	opposite the rich and poor; new forms of human coexistence are created in discourse	anonymous coexistence is sufficient; overcoming classic social ties through laissez-faire
of economy	planned economy	market with strong regulations	free market
of (re)distribution	collective ownership	private property with strong social obligation (high taxes)	private property, non-coercive social transfers, and tolerance premiums

None of these three positions is more socially just than the other. And there are numerous other alternatives: for example, social justice in Islamic, Social Darwinian, Kantian, utilitarian, anthroposophical, and other thought. Each interpretation uses its own view of humanity and society to derive rules of distribution, which, from its point of view, are considered humane and thus define social justice as either more socialist, liberal, and so on. From the respectively chosen and idealistically defined understanding of humans and human dignity always follows a semantically rich concept of good and social justice, which is concretely reflected in humans' self-understanding and in the design of relationships, rules, and entire orders. The three examples beyond normative humanism discussed here show the following: Variants of social justice can either reduce achievement, personal development, and prosperity and/or allow the most vulnerable to fall through the social safety net in the absence of an all-encompassing anthropology and thus a balance of solidarity and subsidiarity.

Response of Normative Humanism

Christian social ethics infers unconditional human dignity from the image of God. Dignity—as in Kantian ethics—cannot be legitimately granted or denied. All persons have been commissioned by God to develop their given talents as fully as possible in order to build the Kingdom of God on earth. This requires a high degree of personal responsibility based on one's own abilities. At the same time, every human being has the task of helping those who are weaker and shaping social relationships in the sense of the threefold love (toward God, oneself, and one's neighbor—and with Pope Francis also toward creation). Thus, social responsibility is also an essential consequence of Christian ethics. Socially just are those laws and rules that enable all humans, as far as possible, to develop the threefold responsibility that God has entrusted to them.[25] This then involves weighing up a good measure of solidarity and subsidiarity.

Since social justice in this Christian sense sets objective standards, the same applies to the poverty it seeks to alleviate. This refers to involuntary and thus socially enforced poverty that deprives the needy of what is necessary for the development of their human dignity. From the point of view of Christian social ethics, poverty means the forced prevention of the development of personhood. This includes, first of all, obvious material need. But the exclusion from education, health services, or religious development is an additional facet of this coercion. Poverty understood in this way is then an objective and not a relative value. If, on the other hand, it is a relative value, as is usual in the calculation of national poverty limits, calculated from the comparison with the income or wealth ratios in this society, there will always be a high proportion of poverty defined in this way, no matter how high the standards of living of the poorest people in this country are.[26] Conversely, if the term is tied to the ability to develop personhood, it is actually possible to eradicate poverty entirely. Viewing it in this way is more meaningful in terms of evaluating the reduction of poverty than the relative version.

Consequence and Compass

This section presents a compass on social justice with consequences from the perspective of Christian social ethics:

- Christian social justice means the greatest possible development of personal and social responsibility in equal measure for all human beings. Social transfers as mere "tolerance premiums" are clearly incompatible with this. After all, this justification would leave the poorest among us without an unconditional right to assistance. They would only receive an allowance if they endangered social peace. Negative freedom, which protects against having something arbitrarily taken away from one's possession, is not enough, as it does nothing to help those who have no possessions. A Christian conception of social justice, on the other hand, is based precisely on the idea of objective rights of entitlement and positive freedom. Regardless of the benefits for society, any person in need of assistance has an unconditional right to community support.
- The Christian interpretation of social justice is grounded in the equal dignity of human beings as persons but not in an idea of equality that implies unconditional egalitarian redistribution. Despite having equal dignity, people are not equal. The evil of poverty can be identified as an objective state based on the concept of a person. Poverty can be defeated when it is understood in this way. This should be the aim of Christian social ethics. Thus, in order to eradicate poverty, unconditional entitlement rights of the most vulnerable (as sufficiency and as empowerment in the sense of positive freedom) must be redeemed, to which unconditional obligations of solidarity correspond. This then also applies to equal access opportunities in the areas of health and education. Once these spaces for empowerment options have been created, the individual responsibility of using these spaces takes hold. Social justice, therefore, on the one hand, provides support for those who cannot use these spheres of freedom. On the other hand, it is not a regressive form of compensation; rather, it is a progressive form of empowerment for the good and thus a liberation program.

- So social assistance must go so far as to help people help themselves using their own strengths. The fight against poverty does not mean material equalization but rather the ability to be free in the sense of everyone being at liberty to develop independently the talents and gifts given to them: from a socio-political point of view for the service of the common good but beyond this from a Christian point of view as personal development in the sense of the human mission through God.
- This idea of empowerment focuses above all on the most vulnerable, who are not able to contribute to the common good themselves (through their own work, for example). For them, the social system must ensure care that also enables the disabled or elderly, for example, to develop based on their potential.[27] Measures that merely immobilize people, deport them, or even deactivate them (such as certain assistance systems in old age) contradict this idea of freedom and thus the Christian concept of personhood.[28] Christian social justice is a society that opens up such positive freedom to everyone so that everyone can answer responsibly to God's offer of love to the best of their capabilities. Where this positive freedom does not exist because of poverty, where constraints prevent people from developing their personhood, poverty exists as a social injustice that must be remedied. This conclusion follows directly from Christian anthropology.

JUST WAR–JUST PEACE

Between War and Peace

There is no doubt that apart from the preservation of creation and social justice, (military) peace is a precious commodity, which must be preserved to the greatest extent possible. Everyone who has experienced war with all of its horrors first-hand will emphatically confirm this. Nevertheless, there are always discussions about whether and, if so, under which conditions this precious commodity may possibly be violated in favor of another one, in the sense of a "just war" (*bellum iustum*). The legitimacy of military intervention is a highly topical issue, particularly in view of military interventions in the recent past, but also looking ahead to various trouble spots throughout the world. This now also includes the question of how to deal with a form of international terrorism that had presented itself as a state-like entity in an Islamic form known as the Islamic State (IS). In the face of such phenomena, the question of whether military interventions can be legitimized was and still remains an issue.

Catholic bishops in Germany have attempted to avoid the term *bellum iustum*, which is certainly also misleading, at least since their writing of "Just

Peace" in 2000.[29] Speaking of a just peace seems less misleading. In this document by the bishops, the concept of peace is not illuminated in all its possible areas of application (to also include internal peace, social peace, etc., for example). The change in terms does not take the socio-ethical questions that still demand answers off the table. Can state-imposed military force be used legitimately? And if so, under what conditions?

A Christian socio-ethical orientation in such a dilemma is offered in this section, exemplified by the fight (including German participation) against the IS in Iraq and Syria (ISIS). The jihadists want(ed) to bring peace to the world from their point of view. For them, peace is only where people unite as a community of right-wing Islamic believers (*umma*) under the caliphate and Sharia. Beyond this community is a war zone.[30] Salafists, ISIS, and their allies around the world had not reinvented an Islam that was prepared for violence and terror. Their ideas are in the theological tradition of Wahhabism, which is the state religion in Saudi Arabia.[31] Germany and other Western countries also participated in the military fight against ISIS. Was this intervention legitimate? A Christian answer to this question is by no means trivial, but it is necessary in order to navigate the ethics of peace.

Evaluation Criteria

First, the classical evaluation criteria of the *bellum iustum* theory are presented, then they are critically discussed and applied to the selected example.

It is important to note that war should be viewed as fundamentally evil by all Christians. The "*iustum*" in the idea of *bellum iustum* does not insinuate that war is something to strive for. It is always merely a matter of justifying evil. Nor is it a continuation of politics by other means. As an ultima ratio, nothing more can ever be considered than its justification, which is necessary in the truest sense. Strict criteria must be met for this. Both the Catechism and the Compendium of the Social Doctrine of the Catholic Church formulate the relevant criteria for transparent examination. According to this, such legitimacy is not ruled out, but it is subject to conditions: "The strict conditions for legitimate defense by military force require rigorous consideration. The gravity of such a decision makes it subject to rigorous conditions of moral legitimacy. At one and the same time:

- the damage inflicted by the aggressor on the nation or community of nations must be lasting, grave, and certain;
- all other means of putting an end to it must have been shown to be impractical or ineffective;

- there must be serious prospects of success; and
- the use of arms must not produce evils and disorders graver than the evil to be eliminated. The power of modern means of destruction weighs very heavily in evaluating this condition.

These are the traditional elements enumerated in what is called the 'just war' doctrine. The evaluation of these conditions for moral legitimacy belongs to the prudential judgment of those who have responsibility for the common good."[32]

The basic principles *legitima auctoritas, intentio recta, iusta causa, ultima ratio*, and *minus malum* are applied.[33] The reason, ends, and means must be just. For the legitimate right to war, it thus follows: 1.) The aggression to be fought is conflict directed against the fundamental rights of innocent people. That is the just reason. 2.) The intervention promises success in establishing peace by eliminating aggression. That is the just ends. 3.) All other means of eliminating aggression have been exhausted beforehand. Therefore, war is the last resort available. 4.) The use is limited to the defense against aggression. 5.) It is ordered by a legitimate authority. 6.) The means of war used is commensurate with the threat: The harm caused by the alternatives of either engaging in war or avoiding it must be weighed. Finally, the legitimate right in war demands 7.) the protection of innocent bystanders and a controlled, exclusively military use of weapons in compliance with martial law.

These criteria can be used to discuss whether, from a Catholic perspective, the military deployment against ISIS was a just war in the sense of the classical criteria or not. Clarifying this is a necessary step but only the first one toward a socio-ethical assessment, as this type of discussion will not satisfy pacifists. This is why Christian pacifists and ethicists also criticized John Paul II for reintroducing "the principle of just war, of defensive war" in the context of the Bosnian war, citing Augustine and Thomas Aquinas to justify military acts of violence.[34] The pacifist inquiry into the Christian legitimacy of such a doctrine is fundamental in nature. And it remains current. Finally, the history of Christendom shows an abundance of shameful abuses of this justification for war. Furthermore, following some very sobering experiences with ostensibly preventive wars in recent years, including the conflict in Ukraine, it seems even more obvious to question the category of a just war (not only) from a Christian socio-ethical perspective.[35] The more fundamental second question of orientation is thus that of a possible Christian legitimization of a military operation (against ISIS) beyond the doctrine of *bellum iustum*. I will begin with the first question, the question of application.

Two Questions

First, I will examine the specific question of whether the military intervention in question is justified in terms of current Catholic doctrine. Of course, such assessments are also subjectively colored and should be viewed with skepticism, depending on the perspective.

The just cause 1.) can be seen in the unprecedented barbarism of terror against the innocent and defenseless:

> **EXAMPLE 9.1**
>
> A few years ago, a SVD missionary told me about a confrere who saw a road in Syria that led to Turkey and was dominated by ISIS. The road was flanked with impaled heads as far as the eye could see. And he added: "It's far worse there than we could ever imagine: It's hell on earth!"

In my opinion, there was a just goal 2.) from a Christian perspective, given the atrocities that had to be ended. But the success of lasting peace requires a clearer strategy than the one pursued following the most recent wars in Afghanistan or Iraq, for example. Regarding just means, it is obvious that 3.) it was not possible to negotiate peacefully with ISIS terrorists. Of course, the original combat mission, which is now considered to have been successfully completed, is not enough on its own. Accompanying measures must be taken, such as eliminating sources of income for terrorists. In addition, a humanistic interpretation of Islam should be promoted throughout schools and universities around the world. This interpretation is buttressed by the great tradition of Averroes, for example, and breaks the spell of fundamentalism within its own theology.[36] Humanization takes time, however. In my view, there were no promising alternatives to warfare in sight at the time for containing aggression in the medium term. It seems to me that history has proved that it was not a war of aggression or a "pre-emptive strike," even in the face of countless terrorist attacks worldwide in the aftermath of the military victory over ISIS 4.). The lack of a clear UN mandate likely raised some doubts as to the just principle 5.). But the UN Security Council identified ISIS as a threat to world peace in its resolution of November 20, 2015. This allowed the right to collective self-defense (Article 51 of the UN Charter) to come into play. Those who do not share this legal interpretation are referred to the EU mutual defense clause (Article 42, 7 of the TFEU in conjunction with Article 87 GG). To question the legitimacy of such a mandate would be to fundamentally bury the European idea. In terms of weighing the different evils 6.), the question remains as to which more egregious evils would otherwise need to be identified. To ultimately comply with the law in war 7.), the military deployment against ISIS obviously needed to be weighed against this. Operations such as this, which endanger otherwise uninvolved parties, are evils that must always be strictly avoided. After all, one war crime cannot simply be justified with that of the others, even if it is clear that ISIS is the actual perpetrator of such war crimes (for example, in the abuse of civilians by using them as living shields). In summary, the military operation against ISIS can be regarded as legitimate in the sense of the doctrine of *bellum iustum*, taking into account the above-mentioned constraints and the current state of knowledge.

Now to the more fundamental question, which must also be answered regardless of the specific context: Why not renounce this doctrine of a just war in Christian social ethics as a matter of principle since Jesus preached peace and not war? Anyone who affirms such a renunciation as a Christian leaves the territory of Catholic dogmatics at the very least. Similarly, Martin Luther does not advocate strict pacifism in his doctrine of the two regiments. Nevertheless, Christian pacifists may believe themselves to be in the right beyond Catholic doctrine and Luther by referring exclusively to the words of Jesus in Scripture. Above all, the Fifth Commandment and the Sermon on the Mount, with the command to "Love your enemies," were adduced as reasons for such a deconstruction of the *bellum iustum* doctrine. These then replace the doctrine of just war as criteria for an appropriate Christian evaluation of the legitimacy of war and violence. In order to do justice to this view, the question of the justification of the military operation against ISIS (again, only by way of example) must now be addressed beyond the doctrine of just war.

According to the Hebrew text, the Fifth Commandment strictly prohibits murder. This puts an end to the objection that killing is fundamentally forbidden. Otherwise, the killing of animals would also have to be forbidden, and Jesus' Passover meal would have been in violation of this. The Fifth Commandment also does not forbid the killing of people, as long as it is not murder. This does not rule out justifiable homicide in self-defense, for example. Those who acknowledge this can continue to argue that the military action against ISIS is not an act of self-defense but rather—like many bad examples of the past—appeals to baser instincts such as financial or other power interests. In ethics of responsibility, the answer to this doubt can be evidence of the growing threat situation worldwide at the time (and to this day). Anyone who continues to object that intervention increases the risk of terrorism in this country or in neighboring countries is unlikely to be contradicted. However, anyone who had used this as grounds for rejecting the war effort against ISIS would have put themselves in a quandary. Whether terror would then have diminished in Europe is doubtful. Conversely, the killing and oppression would have continued in the expanding ISIS territory. ISIS declared its long-term objective to be the destruction not only of Christianity but also of the secular Western world at large. The supposed security would thus be dearly bought with the increasingly likely global threat of terrorist militias uniting in the name of their false "peace." This spread of misery was fought with military might. For those who accept this argument, a final objection remains: the murder of uninvolved bystanders, which is inevitable in war, is forbidden. While this may be a justified objection, it does not offer anything new. It finds its answer analogously in the *bellum iustum* criterion of law in war 7.). Consequently, military action against ISIS cannot conclusively be prohibited with respect to the Fifth Commandment.

For Christians, the unconditional prohibition of the direct (planned and intended) killing of innocent people applies.[37] The soldier (even in such a "just war") has no general authority to kill. The question of a legitimate use of force is directed solely at the behavior toward combatants on the side of the aggressor. This must always be about protecting one's own troops and the civilian population. There can also be objections to such a justified use of force, with which justification even in the case of self-defense then one's own life is valued higher than the life of the aggressor. Ultimately, this pits one life against another. The moral justification of self-defense is rooted in asymmetry: The aggressor (e.g., ISIS, a group that wanted to use force to wipe Western civilization from the face of the earth) is attacking a fundamental human value that must be protected. This is why

> the right of self-defense cannot be denied to the one being attacked . . . while the aggressor is about to commit a grave injustice. The party being attacked, who legitimately possesses a fundamental resource, must have the moral ability to defend against an unjustified attack, because the right to this resource would otherwise have no reliable basis in human relationships.[38]

From the vantage point of social ethics, this self-defense ordered by state power is therefore justified in order to protect the fundamental resource that is endangered because without such self-defense terror would take hold, replace legitimate state power, and bring disaster upon the people. This is a defensive right but not a positive right or a moral duty to defend oneself by any means.[39]

Finally, a strong pacifist argument is the reference to Jesus' commandment to "Love your enemies," which breaks the spiral of violence through non-retaliation and even love to achieve reconciliation (*Entfeindungsliebe*), following the example of Mahatma Gandhi.[40] From a Christian ethics standpoint, God is love; Benedict XVI also clearly referred to this basic principle of Christian ethics, for example, in his encyclical CiV.[41] For humans, the answer to this is the threefold commandment of love of God, love of self, and love of neighbor and with it love of one's enemies. There is no legitimate relativization to this because, for Christians, love is an anchor in the ethics of conviction. This is why war against one's enemies is intrinsically bad behavior. The balancing of evils already applied in the *bellum iustum* theory is no more than the answer to a dilemma within the commandment to love. The goal of the commandment to love one's enemies is precisely to break the cycle of violence and counter-violence. The use of force against enemies contradicts this goal. On the other hand, in a self-defense situation involving an acute threat, the goal of reconciliation cannot be achieved by renouncing violence. Jesus says, "If anyone strikes you on the right cheek" (Matthew 5:39) as an example of refusing to retaliate but not the threat to one's own life. In the first case, the goal of reconciliation can be achieved; in the second case (if I am killed by my attacker), it cannot. This is a significant qualitative difference.

> The aim of loving one's enemy is . . . reconciliation with the other. . . . However, in an acute threat situation, which requires instantaneous action, there is no chance that love for one's enemy will achieve the intended aim. . . . As long as there is no obligation to renounce self-defense from the commandment of love (even in the radical form that Jesus provides through the involvement of the other person), the attacker may still engage in self-defense—a potential reaction that is not morally prohibited.[42]

Violence legitimized in this way can only ever be a reaction to which there is no alternative. If, in such a tragic situation, there is now no choice but to violate the fundamental principle of love, then, whether one likes it or not, the *minus malum* must be chosen.

Consequence and Compass

Now I will propose some Christian socio-ethical guidelines on the basis of these discussions.

- The Christian mission is a culture of peace that understands all people of good will as a human family under the commandment of love[43] because they are all made in God's image. This vision of peace is in fundamental contradiction to such ideologies of peace and community that claim human rights exclusively for themselves as a privilege of a race, a class, or a religion and forcibly exclude, humiliate, or murder others who are defenseless.
- From a Christian vantage point, this is opposed by an inclusive ideal of a pluralistic coexistence with equal dignity for all. For this, under the

strictest conditions, it is worth accepting even the evil of war for the sake of the Kingdom of God. Christians are called upon to build this kingdom.
- The talk of just peace seeks to avoid the misunderstandings surrounding the *bellum iustum* theory. Clearly, the use of military force and threats of such force are always an evil from a Christian perspective. Nevertheless, Christian social ethics must deal with the question of a legitimate use of military force under these strict conditions.[44] In this case, it would be better to speak of a justified rather than a just war.
- Based on current knowledge, the military intervention against ISIS fulfilled the conditions of the *bellum iustum* theory.
- Even the commandment to love one's enemies does not naturally lead to pacifism. If, for example, an Islamist holds a knife to a Christian's throat and demands that he renounce his faith, then there are only two alternatives, both of which contradict love. Claus von Stauffenberg and other conspirators who attempted to assassinate Adolf Hitler on July 20, 1944, also considered what it meant to kill another human being—as did the Allied forces in World War II—perhaps even more so. These were also dilemmas. Thus, the legitimate Christian decision cannot simply perform a utilitarian calculation that pits one life against another. That would go against the spirit of Jesus. Nor can it simply be derived from a directive from Jesus to engage in war since there is no such thing. Instead, it requires an examination of conscience, for which those responsible for it, according to Christian faith, give account once before God.
  - In the first example given, a choice must be made between love of God and love of oneself. Since love of God is the origin of self-love, the decision to martyrdom here is a legitimate one. But not everyone will be able to make this choice.
  - In the other cases, it is a matter of balancing violations within the commandment to love one's neighbor. The enemies to be loved here are the tyrant, the armed forces of a dictatorial system, or even ISIS. Other neighbors are the defenseless, who can be helped by violence or war. Pacifism would leave the defenseless to die. On the other hand, violence and war against the tyrant or tyranny do not merely strike just any opponent in the sense of the commandment to love one's enemies but, to put it in missionary terms, the powers of evil. Resisting them and destroying their power, on the other hand, is expressly permitted by Holy Scripture (cf., for example, 1 Peter 5:9, 1 John 3:8).

An attitude of strict Christian pacifism arrives at results different from those presented in this compass. Personally, I also think it is a legitimate Christian position—albeit one that I probably would not share.

NOTES

1. Due to the urgency of the subject of creation currently under discussion, this topic is placed first in the triad here, without any intention of relativizing the central role of the question of justice and peace.

2. The article by J. Ratzinger (1964), which is occasionally cited against it, does not adopt natural law either but instead warns against its ideologization. Cf. on his application of natural law as pope, for example, the address delivered to the German Bundestag: Benedict XVI (2011), as well as the encyclical CiV.

3. For the sake of reader-friendliness, references to the encyclical LS are indicated in this section by naming the respective chapter in the encyclical text using a text-immanent approach.

4. Cf., by analogy, Benedict XVI's (2012) speech on the "Ecology of Man."

5. Cf. EG 53.

6. Cf. J. Buchanan (2001).

7. Cf. K. Homann (1993a): 41, as well as the section on normative individualism in the chapter "Ethics beyond Normative Humanism" in Part II.

8. Cf. section on the compass for the economy in the chapter "Economy and Economic Order" in Part III.

9. Cf. the section on the property system in the chapter "Economy and Economic Order" in Part III. For a hamartiological discussion on the nature of the sinful human being, cf. in Part I in the chapter "Sanctification of the world" the section on agents and the section on the view of humanity as a set of values in the chapter "Ecumenical Perspective."

10. Cf. the chapter "Economy and Economic Order" in Part III.

11. Cf. Pope Francis (2016). E. Mack (2015) already argued for a milder interpretation of the market critique such as this. A corresponding attitude is also clearly underlined by the economic ethics statement of the Congregation for the Doctrine of the Faith et al. (2018).

12. R. Wagner (2008).

13. Cf., for example, the chapter "The Search for Good" in Part I.

14. Cf. J. Rawls (1971/1999), ibid. (1993/2005), A. Sen (1993), ibid. (2003).

15. For a broad congruence of social justice and redistribution, cf. for example, F. Hengsbach (2011).

16. Cf. Part II in the chapter "Normative Humanism" in the section on Immanuel Kant as well as I. Kant AK VIII, 366: *Toward Perpetual Peace*.

17. Cf. Part I in the chapter "Sanctification of the World" in the section on essential content of the good. This idea of personal social love is roughly in the tradition of Catholic doctrine, which Pope Paul VI called a "complete humanism" (PP 42). Benedict XVI understands this form of social ethics as a new humanism (PP 66, CiV 19). With its openness to transcendence made possible by reason in love, ethics can reopen itself to an objective truth: "The greatest service to development, then, is a Christian humanism that enkindles charity and takes its lead from truth" (CiV 78).

18. Cf. J. Buchanan (2001).

19. Cf. ibid.

20. Reference is also made to the corresponding remarks in Part II on the schools of thought beyond normative humanism. Normative individualism corresponds to order-ethical context 3 in table 9.2, normative collectivism to context 4. Discourse ethics cannot simply be assigned to a category here.

21. Cf. J. Rawls (1971/1999), ibid. (1993/2005).

22. Cf. P. Van Parijs (1998).

23. Cf. J. Wolff (1991).

24. Cf. K. Homann and I. Pies (1996): 220.

25. Cf. in Part I in the chapter "Sanctification of the World" the section on the essential content of the good.

26. Cf. on the relativity of the concept of poverty in the calculation of national poverty lines *sine nomine* (2008): "In Europe and Germany the national poverty limits are calculated based on a percentage of the median income. 60% of the national median income is considered the poverty risk threshold. 50% of the national median income is considered the poverty line. If the median income is 1,500 euros per month, the poverty risk threshold is 900 euros and the poverty line is 750 euros." This relativity results from such a definition and is independent of a country comparison on income or cost of living.

27. On this addition to the capability approach, see in Part II in the chapter "Normative Humanism beyond Theology" the section on humanism in Amartya Sen.

28. See the section on digitalization in the chapter "Future Issues" in Part III.

29. Cf. DBK (2013/2000).

30. Cf. in Part II the corresponding chapter "Theological Humanism beyond Christianity" with the section on Islam.

31. It should be noted that Saudi Arabia applies Sharia law on the one hand while claiming to be an Islamic, democratic nation-state on the other, which W. B. Hallaq (2013): XI sees as self-contradictory.

32. CCC: 2309.

33. Cf., for example, G. Beestermüller (2003): 46 et seq. and on the foundation of the principles STh II–II, 40 a 1.

34. Cf. A. Cowell (1994).

35. Cf., for example, G. Beestermüller (2003).

36. Cf. in Part II the corresponding chapter "Theological Humanism beyond Christianity" with the section on Islam.

37. Cf. E. Schockenhoff (2013): 256–70.

38. Ibid.: 264.

39. Cf. ibid.

40. Cf. M. Vogt and R. Husman (2019) with reference to "*Entfeindungsliebe*" as a core idea in the work of P. Lapide (1984).

41. Cf. CiV 2, 6, as well as Part I in the chapter "Sanctification of the World" in the section on the objective good and its realization.

42. E. Schockenhoff (2013): 265. Cf. also M. Chiodi (2006): 297.

43. For the Catholic understanding of "people of good will," see the corresponding explanation in Part I in the chapter "Sanctification of the World" in the section on the agents. This includes people of very different religions and worldviews, including

people who do not believe in God. According to this, people of goodwill include all those who are ready to engage in a fair dialogue with the positions of the Catholic Church and its ideas of humanity and society, and who, with a sense of love, assume responsibility in their lives in the form of unconditional human dignity.

44. Cf. M. Honecker (2005): 235.

Chapter Ten

Life, Work, and Death

Changing ideas about family, work, education, life, and death and the associated images of people and society have a decisive influence on culture and coexistence in Germany. Christian social ethics must face this change—including with the help of moral-theological insights—and examine what it means here to recognize the signs of the times and, at the same time, to strengthen its own proprium in its mission to sanctify the world. Some likely very contentious orientational guidelines will be proposed in this chapter for these sensitive areas.

FAMILY

Good, Tradition, and Ideal

The family is not a discontinued model. According to Shell Youth Studies, it is still highly rated by young people (aged twelve to twenty-five) in Germany—despite high divorce rates and low birth rates. The desire to have children of their own rose steadily among young people until 2010.[1] This trend has since declined somewhat, although this is not attributed to a fundamental rejection of having children of one's own but rather to fears of compatibility with one's career. The 2015 study states the following: "There is strong evidence that concern about the difficulty of reconciling work and home life is having an impact on the wish to have children. Overall, at present, only 64 percent of all young people want to have children; in 2010, the figure was 69 percent."[2]

The Sinus Milieu Study says this of value consciousness in 2018 in Germany:

On the one hand performance and efficiency, pragmatism and a utilitarian orientation, multioptionality and multitasking; on the other hand "Regrounding," trying to regain a foothold and find emotional stability and security, promoting sustainability and deceleration, reinterpreting traditional values, combining old values to form new ones, engaging in selective idealism.[3]

Despite all the pragmatism, there is still a longing for a reliable compass that may require reinterpretation. The search for constants in life has been a trend since 2002, according to all the Shell studies conducted since then. The family is an asset that should not be sacrificed in the process. As such an anchor, it continues to play the decisive role:

> As ever, young people value their own families highly. The vast majority of young people find the necessary backing from their families and gain positive emotional support on the way to adult life. Over 90 per cent of young people have good relations with their parents. Nearly three-quarters would bring up their own children in approximately, or exactly, the same way as they were brought up themselves. This figure has increased steadily since 2002.[4]

The family, therefore, continues to be held in high esteem as a valued asset. Marriage and family in Germany are also under the special legal protection of the constitution (GG Article 6). But what does that mean today? This is highly controversial. A distinction is made between modern and traditional families, whereby in the Christian-influenced Western cultural sphere, the addition "traditional" can be understood to mean a monogamous marital and thus lifelong cohabitation of husband and wife with their own or adopted children, filled with mutual love.[5] This "traditional" form of family, which, from a Christian point of view, is still considered the ideal,[6] must today, in view of a great variety of lifestyles (such as a temporary partnership legalized in France, patchwork constellations, single parents, non-marital cohabitation with and without children, same-sex partnerships with the right to adopt, polygamous unions, etc.) and phenomena going beyond this, such as a partnership with virtual figures, and so on,[7] face the question of whether it can and should still be considered an ideal to strive for. The socio-ethical question is not what the family actually is today but what the family should be today and in the future. Different patterns of interpretation can also be found at the theoretical level.

Responses of Normative Relativism

Secular positions beyond normative humanism also have a strong claim to define what family should be. Some of these are briefly presented here.

Consider first the Darwinian conception. It articulates a clear idea of the normatively good with reference to the family. The Darwinian theory of evolution, with its random principle for the origin and development of the species, denies the idea of a divine plan as the standard of good. For the determination of a semantics of family, a reasonable recourse to the plan of God is thus obsolete. Charles Darwin draws inspiration for his statements on the family from the early capitalist economist Thomas R. Malthus. The latter assumed a necessary selection of the capable because of a geometric population growth compared to merely linear food production growth. Darwin writes: "I now had a theory, finally, with which I could work."[8] His biological ethics thus consistently lead to Social Darwinism:

> Both sexes ought to refrain from marriage if in any marked degree inferior in body or mind. . . . All do good service who aid toward this end . . . if the prudent avoid marriage, whilst the reckless many, the inferior members will tend to supplant the better members of society. Man, like every other animal, has no doubt advanced to his present high condition through a struggle for existence consequent on his rapid multiplication; and if he is to advance still higher he must remain subject to a severe struggle. . . . There should be open competition for all men; and the most able should not be prevented by laws or customs from succeeding best and rearing the largest number of offspring. (II. XXI. 403)[9]

Following such logic, the family has no self-value but merely a service value for the biological refinement of the human race. Thus, it is subordinate to a more important good and is itself a second-class good. It is instrumentalized by biological normativity (as, for example, was cruelly practiced under National Socialism). Then what is supposed to be family must subordinate itself to the target parameters of the now supposedly higher biologistic good. Social Darwinism is not openly advocated today.

Other contemporary secular ethics reject at least an axiomatic fixation of the family as a valuable good. For discourse ethics and normative individualism, the family is initially an empty formula whose content is constructed by people, depending on the consensus result in discourse or in the derivation from utility calculations. The determination of the content of what family should be follows the responsibility of humans before the discursive or egoistic self-determination of humankind. This always results in new, relative, and equally valid semantics. This, in turn, makes, for example, in discourse the rational, in normative individualism above all the assertive egoistic people themselves authors of the meaning of family as a valuable good. An idea of the family given as objective cannot be thought of as a relevant orientation. A metaphysics-free concept of family beyond transcendental cognition or transcendence cognition remains open-ended and can potentially semantically endogenize all possible contents. Restrictions on content, such as those in normative humanisms, are excluded here because it is prohibited to ban thinking, provided that only the rules of legitimization are observed. Normative individualism is closely connected with the idea of moral order for human coexistence: The anonymous coexistence of egoistic utility maximizers is sufficient here, but according to the value studies, this apparently does not reflect what young people are feeling today. Economic imperialism, in its extreme form, makes a normative demand for instrumental action in egoism even in the selection of life partners and the decision for offspring.[10]

Thus, discourse ethics and normative individualism can determine ever-new, changing semantics of what family is and what it should be. The discussion about its content as a normative reference cannot be continued at this point either because in such ethics this is consistently incumbent on the forum of discourse or the reconciliation of egoistic interests.

The Traditional Christian View of Family

According to its understanding of acceptability, Christian social ethics can formulate and discuss the normative content of family.[11] According to its idea of what is good, this ideal is not the result of discourse and the egoistic balancing of interests.[12] It is far from the normative ideas of Social Darwinism, and it also cannot follow purely egoistic explanations of family in terms of economic imperialism.[13] The Christian ideal defines normative criteria as characteristics of family that offer a compass to distinguish the value of family from other forms of life. From a Christian point of view, family can be justified as value that is objectively given to humans, whose semantics are withdrawn from arbitrariness and human agreement, and brings with it a binding responsibility toward the objective (the law of God). A substantive determination of the nature of family can, therefore, not be open-ended. Its semantics can be derived theologically from humankind's responsibility before God and from humankind's moral nature. Facticities or majorities are not a sufficient criterion for semantic determination of the family as a good to be acceptable.[14]

In the following, the nature of the family in the Christian sense, in accordance with tradition, with its socio-ethically relevant justifications, is defined in more detail to clarify this content before the relationship to other forms of human coexistence is questioned. The addition "traditional" is now dispensed with in order to avoid the associated premature suggestion of its antiquated nature.[15] Instead, this passage covers the "classical" Christian image of the family, which is then also put to the test in the confrontation with other current Christian interpretations.

There is no clear normative definition in the Bible that could simply be adopted as a foil for an evidence test of an appropriate concept of family for the present and the future. The *Familiaris Consortio* encyclical is a worthwhile read for guidance on determining the content. Here, Pope John Paul II systematically emphasized the nature of marriage and the family and their particular importance for society:[16]

> The family finds in the plan of God the Creator and Redeemer not only its "identity," what it "is," but also its "mission," what it can and should "do." The role that God calls the family to perform in history derives from what the family is; its role represents the dynamic and existential development of what it is. Each family finds within itself a summons that cannot be ignored, and that specifies both its dignity and its responsibility: Family, "become" what you "are"![17]

From the Catholic point of view, on the one hand, an essence of family is assumed here (what family is at its core and therefore should be in concrete terms), which results from God's plan. On the other hand, this requirement is contrasted with the mandate that specific families should approach this way of being dynamically (by becoming similar to the being itself). Despite a necessary analysis of the changing situation of family in society, normativity of the factual is thus not assumed, which regards as family that which lives under the name at this moment. Thus, there is acknowledgment of the sociological evolution of forms of human cohabitation and the broad use of the concept of family.[18] But the normative concept of family that John Paul II brought into focus goes beyond what family should do or has (become) in practice. The basic question for determining the classical image of family remains what makes it a normative good in the sense of salvation history (*Heilsgeschichte*).

The classical family in the Christian sense corresponds to the ideal mentioned previously: a monogamous marriage filled with mutual love between a man and woman who live together their whole lives with their own or adopted children. God Himself is love (1 John 4:8) and emerges from Himself with the creation of the world and humankind.[19] According to the Genesis creation narrative, this love prompts God to create human beings as the man Adam and the woman Eve. Man and woman commit to each other in a monogamous, permanent relationship. This singled-out and exclusive love between man and woman corresponds to "a deeper anthropological need for acceptance and security," akin to an inner desire for permanency[20] and goes beyond the commandment of charity. The procreation of one's own offspring and thus the founding of a family is a reflection of the divine act of creation and is meant to be an image of God's eternal and unconditional love.[21] Based on the classical understanding, this is only conceivable if both partners are totally committed to each other, which presupposes exclusivity and permanence of the covenant for this love.[22] The exemplary covenant of the man Adam with the woman Eve marks the basic anthropological statements of the classical understanding of marriage and family: "the personhood of both partners, based on the divine likeness of man and woman, the prominent significance of the dual sexuality of humans, and the wholeness of body and soul in their daily lives."[23]

This also refers to the embedding of human sexuality in such a "protective and developmental space" of mutual reliability, which—according to the ideal—in monogamous and lifelong marriage makes the practice of total devotion and unconditional security possible in the first place.[24] This classical Christian understanding of family (beyond discussions about its sacramentality or other dogmatic issues) is based on biblical anthropology and gains its content through analogies to God's love and creation, taking into account deeper human longings and needs. The *human condition* and divine destiny are, therefore, deeply intertwined. In addition to the direct characteristics of the classic family image, this results in a number of other consequences with a socio-ethical significance:

- Giving rise to new birth: Giving rise to new birth from mutually devoted love is essential to the future of any society.[25]
- Role awareness: In the family, people get to know themselves in natural roles and are trained to shape such understandings of their respective roles with their corresponding boundaries and responsibilities for social interaction in society as well. Parents are given "the opportunity to assume a basic form of moral responsibility in being a mother and a father as a shared existence for the child."[26]
- Communicating values and virtues: The family is the nucleus of social cohesion and the place of learning not only of faith and love[27] but also of other essential values and virtues (such as mutual responsibility, sacrifice, justice, advocacy for the weak, willingness to share and forgive, fidelity and trust, caring for the sick, sharing in joy, showing compassion, wisely dividing up subsidiary tasks, etc.).[28] The family is a "kind of school of deeper humanity."[29] Pope Francis has expressly underscored this special importance of the family as a place where values are conveyed.[30]
  - This includes, for example, educating children to be independent and responsible adults. This duty follows the analogy with the creation narrative, according to which God also created humans and helped them to live as beings in the world.[31]
  - This also includes loving, responsible cooperation between generations: "This happens where there is care and love for the little ones, the sick,

the aged; where there is mutual service every day; when there is a sharing of goods, of joys and of sorrows."[32]

Rethinking the Christian Family?

The classical image of the family is not without controversy, even from a theological standpoint. There are numerous attempts to understand the Christian family in a different way today. Thus, the declaration of the Central Committee of German Catholics on the 2015 Synod on the Family includes a broad concept that makes practiced responsibility one of the normative anchors of the family: "By family we also mean non-marital forms of binding partnership and generational responsibility, which make a major contribution to social cohesion and must be treated fairly."[33]

In contrast, the current policy statement promulgated by the Christian Democratic Workers Association (CDA) of 2015 in Germany formulates something closer to the classical ideal:

> The concept of family is practiced in different ways—in marriage, in partnership or as a single parent; but many siblings, relatives and friends also live as close-knit communities for long periods. For us, a family is present in particular in cases where parents take on permanent responsibility for children and vice-versa.[34]

Unquestionably, this definition can also result in a variety of constellations, although transitions are still discernible in the special emphasis placed on the parent-child relationship. There are no profound theological justifications in these two exemplary positions, nor should they be expected for policy statements such as these. Their postulates most likely reflect the need to broaden the classical concept of family.

A theological gender perspective also views such a necessity—now not only with a detailed justification but also other substantive consequences. Marianne Heimbach-Steins is its main Catholic representative in Germany. With consequences for the understanding of the roles of men and women as well as the understanding of the family, she is not concerned with a critique of the difference in biological sex but instead in social sex (gender), in other words, the cultural embedding of human beings in socially predetermined gender roles.[35] Here one sees a considerable deficit of justice that must be destigmatized to raise humanity's awareness of identity beyond dogmatism and paternalism. This is because gender has so far been associated with social roles and behaviors (in the family, for example) that must still be overcome. This can refer to education, clothing, choice of profession, language, or virtues acquired through upbringing that rob people of their freedom. The assumed feminine crisis of identity is focused on social gender and decoupled from biological corporeality. Based on this, feminine identity is understood in the context of biological difference, while social gender is supposed to emancipate itself from mere otherness or even a deficiency compared to masculine identity.[36] Conventions that are perceived as constraints must be overcome here. This social dimension of sexuality thus takes into account ethical gender theology, which also affects the ideal of the family.[37]

Gender theology (i.e., theological questions concerning social gender) explicitly seeks to deconstruct a natural law rationale and sees its normative rationale as closely related to discourse ethics and systemic constructivism.[38] The discourse paradigm is not simply adopted but subjected to a reconstruction. According to Heimbach-Steins, following G. Marschütz, gender is "primarily a consequence of discursive practice and hence a cultural construct."[39]

Following discourse-ethical logic, this means that justice of the gender order must constantly be renegotiated in a societal discourse by all people concerned. People should—somewhat analogously to the understanding of human rights in Jürgen Habermas—become the authors of their own human existence. After all, that is what makes them autonomous.[40] Heimbach-Steins puts it this way: "The core of the matter is to recognize autonomy of the (also) gender-defined subjects as actors in their own (life) stories."[41] The theological gender perspective supplements Habermas' criteria of legitimate discourse with an essential restriction and goes beyond this paradigm with this new construct:[42] Based on this, discourse on determining the content of social gender is a liberated search to define the "truth" of gender justice with the previously (prediscursively) adopted gender perspective.[43] This introduces a prescribed objectivity. The gender perspective itself is no longer the subject of discourse. Rather, is it systematically positioned before the bracket of creative norms and thus elevated into the circle of Habermas' objectively presupposed procedural rules. That means the following: The theological gender perspective becomes an objective condition for legitimate socio-ethical discourse as it is necessary for the thought process.

Heimbach-Steins seeks to justify this capability to connect in Biblical terms by referring to Galatians 3:26 and Mark 3:31–36. Apostle Paul's call: "There is neither . . . male nor female," is interpreted as gender perspective. The same applies to Jesus' emphasis on personal choice over lineage: "Whoever does the will of God is my brother and sister and mother." Thus, Jesus Himself—according to the interpretation—abolishes the (social) gender, thereby introducing the gender perspective. In addition, in the spirit of the Second Vatican Council, it is a sign of our times challenging the Church to open its doors for it.[44]

Both this perspective and its reasoning strategy have consequences for the understanding of marriage and the family. The close interconnectedness of biological and social gender is rejected, and with it, the biological-social unity of the person.[45] In the Book of Genesis, we read that God created humankind as man and woman—Adam and Eve.[46] There, the difference between man and woman is linked to the normative mandate to give life to offspring if possible. Considering the laws of the old and new covenants, spouses in the family should assume the role of mother and father in loving fidelity to each other. These roles are undoubtedly part of social gender and are constantly being reinterpreted. It could now be concluded that, alongside the patriarchally determined differences of social gender from the gender perspective, the undoubtedly socially determined parental roles should also be deconstructed. This could result in the recommendation to remain childless to avoid the socially normed roles of father and mother. The following passage does not pursue this line of thought. This would import the theoretical problems in the justification of discourse ethics and systems theory and would also be hostile to life.[47] Theological attempts at justification do not change this skepticism. The biblical statements of Jesus and Paul cited for this purpose (Galatians 3:26–28 and Mark 3:31–36) focus not on the question of gender but instead on humanity's path to salvation. This path is not affected by gender or lineage. The primary aim is for all people to come together in confessing their belief in Christ: This establishes the Church as a new form of family. This emphasis on determination for Christ as the way to salvation is the essential message in the biblical passages cited here.

Consequence and Compass

The objective reference for determining the content of the good of family, as presented by the classical understanding, raises suspicions of a paternalistic dogmatism from the ivory tower that has become alienated from the realities of family life in practice. So, it is essential to constantly review whether the content of the good recognized as objective actually corresponds to God's law.[48] As a result, there is still marked room for interpretation of the substantive definition of family, which must be explored within the framework of theonomy in order to arrive at a nuanced conclusion on this path. The aim of semantics developed in this way is to provide a sustainable Christian orientation that builds on this foundation that considers the hallmarks of our time in its concept of family beyond dogmatism and nominalism. From the point of view of Christian social ethics, it can be determined which normative semantics of family are essential for a convincing orientation today. In his letter *Amoris Laetitia*, Pope Francis criticized the Church for too long for advocating abstract ideals of the family that are incomprehensible to many.[49] For a compass on what the family should be from a Christian perspective, it is, therefore, not enough to refer to mere postulates from dogmatics and tradition. Social realities and Christian attempts to redefine the concept of family must also be taken seriously. For such search movements and dialog with the non-Christian world, it is all the more necessary to have a family concept, which, as a compass, defines the limits and ranges for such orientation. The solution is a transparent profile that corresponds to God's mission and is articulated in a comprehensible way with sound reasoning instead of postulates. The consequences are as follows:

- Based on the concept of family as a valuable good that is intended by God and worthy of protection, God has an idea of what family should be. People can and should recognize this idea as a framework for the existence of family in concrete terms.[50] This knowledge must be questioned critically again and again, for example, with biblical arguments or sources of revelation, from insights gleaned from church proclamation, theology, and Christianity in practice. It remains a dynamic process of discovery. A constant further development of the semantics of family is not only conceivable but also necessary in the sense of the principle *ecclesia semper reformanda*. However, it must consist—considered from the perspective of God—of a justified expansion of knowledge with regard to the given objective good.
- The reference for such knowledge is the classical understanding of marriage and family, where marriage is considered to be a prerequisite to family.[51] Family is, therefore, a monogamous marriage filled with love between a man and woman who live together their whole lives with their own or adopted children. Non-marital unions with or without children, permanent same-sex partnerships, and single parents each have important similarities along with significant differences with this classical concept of family and are, therefore, not families according to this understanding.[52] This is not meant to disparage people who practice these ways of life. Rather, it is a way of distinguishing these unions from family in the classical sense.[53] Other terms should be found for such ways of life similar to the family to help defuse the confusion between the concepts. This will help achieve clarity without discriminating against people. Eberhard Schockenhoff, referring to a decision of the German Federal Constitutional Court in 1987, sums up the essential difference thus: "The fact that, in addition, there may also be incomplete families in which similar educational and support services are provided through the cohabitation of parents and children does not conflict with the guiding principle of a 'complete' family and the 'best possible' realization of these tasks."[54]

- From a Christian point of view, expressly temporary connections held on a trial basis, polygamous connections, and connections between a human being and virtual beings or robots or the like are not only conceptually alien to the family but should also be morally rejected. They either contradict (due to their temporary or polygamous nature) the idea of love and absolute devotion[55] or deconstruct (by means of a virtual or other artificially created partners) the essence of human love.
- The classical ideal, for example, is also contrasted by painful experiences of failure. Regardless of the fact of a failed family, charitable groups such as *Caritas* and *Diakonie* in Germany, among others, naturally step in to alleviate hardship and assist those affected (especially children).
- Children make our society rich. Deconstructing the role of father and mother would contradict God's plan of salvation in light of His love for children and the life-giving mission with which He has entrusted humankind.
- There is public debate about giving special incentives to educated couples to encourage them to have children because, statistically, their children would raise the standard of living in our future society. Apart from the questionability of the correctness of this quality hypothesis, this obviously applies an economic yardstick to the value of children, which is unacceptable from a Christian vantage point.
- Families are the first learning space of binding mutual responsibility between generations. The family is a place where the personal search for meaning and a good life can prove itself in a special way when the focus is on shared social responsibility rather than material success. From here, social values and virtues have a living effect on society. The socio-ethical task is to advocate in society for rules that strengthen families as spaces of trust, where children are fundamentally understood as a treasure and a blessing.
- From a Christian perspective, it is self-evident that man and woman and those who cannot be assigned to either of these genders have equal dignity, for all human beings are made in God's image. Gender justice means equal dignity even without deconstructing social difference.[56] The sexes are called upon and enabled by social rules and virtues to develop their talents freely and to live up to their moral claim to God with personal and social responsibility. There must be no social preference or disadvantage in terms of such a salvific ability.

WORK

Sanctification in the world also happens in active work, be it gainful employment or volunteer work. The question of the value of work is gaining great social significance in view of the imminent upheavals in the labor market (e.g., crowd work, Industry 4.0, etc.)[57], including the associated consequences for families, which challenge not only sociological and political but also Christian socio-ethical competence. According to theological tradition, human work always means gainful employment. Volunteer work, the fine arts, or familial and friendly education and care services also count as work. Such activities presuppose motivation independent of wages and, in the spirit of the principle of subsidiarity, decisively shape the foundation of values in a society, which is why they are especially appreciated from the Christian understanding of humans as persons. Pope John Paul II dedicated his 1981 Encyclical *Laborem exercens* (LE) to the topic of "Human Work," which outlines the meaning and significance of the work from the perspective of Catholic social doctrine. The rich treasure of this programmatic doctrinal writing is opened up through an interpretation of the mission of creation and the redemptive work of Jesus Christ in relation to the bona fide realities of the modern world of work. John Paul II knew that, based on the individual perspective, work may be a burden to some and a source of fulfillment to others. The encyclical counters a relative evaluation with timelessly valid standards on the meaning and significance of work. A correct reading of the primacy of labor over capital therefore forbids one-sided ideological alienations that would seek to interpret the papal circular as a call to class struggle or Swing Riots.

Personal Service Value

A distinction must be made between the objective and subjective meaning of work.[58] The changing framework conditions, such as technical progress and political or cultural influences, are considered objective. Subjective meaning focuses on the personal dimension. Human dignity in the sense of the principle of personhood demands the development of the God-given natural destiny of humans with their individual and social nature: "If we want to express in one word that for man his selfhood as an individual being and his social nature are equally essential, then we say: he is a person; individualitas and socialitas together make up his personalitas."[59] Humankind's active interaction with technology and nature creates differentiated relationships. In the objective sense, the technical means, which are themselves the result of creative human labor, make it possible to experience the social interdependence in society based on the division of labor. "The mechanized course of action can only work with the finest interaction between all the participants."[60] Knowledge of this, therefore, establishes the mutual appreciation of various work achievements, stimulates creativity, and reminds us that people always depend on the cooperation of others in their work. This motivational view leads to a social identity of mutual appreciation. When humans cultivate natural resources with their minds and/or bodies, they directly encounter God's works of creation in them. The objective conditions must be examined to determine the extent to which they correspond to the normativity of the subjective dimension. Above all, activities with and centered around people must be examined to see what scope they create for the development of the individuality and sociality of those involved.

In accordance with its subjective significance, the value of work is not measured primarily in terms of market price or economically countable output but instead in terms of service value for the development of the person.

> However true it may be that man is destined for work and called to it, in the first place work is "for man" and not man "for work." In fact, in the final analysis it is always man who is the purpose of the work, whatever work it is that is done by man—even if the common scale of values rates it as the merest "service," as the most monotonous, even the most alienating work.[61]

The wage paid on the labor market for gainful employment is therefore not a reliable gauge of the subjective value of work. Family services (education, care, etc.), for example, often generate high value added in the sense of personhood without earning a wage. They deserve special appreciation as a service to the development of the human being as a person with both personal and social responsibility, encompassing both the individual and the social dimension. This quality is based on the development of the personalities of the inactive people themselves, as well as on their contribution to the development of the personalities of the people positively affected by their work.

The prerequisite for a positive evaluation of the work is the non-coercive choice of the corresponding activity. Self-determined work enables people's potential to unfold toward their God-given destinies and thus sets them free. It must be distinguished from externally determined work. While self-determination liberates, heteronomy dehumanizes the human being as a means to an end. When individual and social responsibility die off with work, when wages and leisure time are so scarce that they have no liberating effect, and when *individualitas* and/or *socialitas* are suppressed, humans are prevented from realizing their full potential. Non-self-determined work alienates people from themselves, from each other, and from God. Then it does not let them be "more" but less "human."[62] This applies not only to all forms of forced labor but also to the exploitation of health, education, and the family forced by work. Such phenomena need not be relegated to the past (like the industrial revolution). They are also a new face reflecting the zeitgeist of anonymized labor relations of the present, when the utilitarian functionality of so-called "human capital" is replacing personhood as an overriding goal. With this violation of the principle of personhood, such work must be criticized above all from a socio-ethical point of view. In the long run, it also leads to a loss of work motivation and economic efficiency.

Human work has its first model in God's act of creation, assigning social responsibility to humans in the process.[63] It is also a culturally creative communal work of charity that brings out the social nature in people.[64] It enables the provision of spiritual and material goods in service to the community and to the weaker members in order to enable them to live out their human destinies. Work is thus solidary because it creates the conditions of possibility for personal development. Solidarity, according to its origin, refers to a certain legal relationship between debtors, according to which everyone is responsible for everyone else. Solidarity is practiced on the one hand by everyone who is integrated into the process of division of labor and on the other hand by everyone who vouches for the liability of a co-debtor who is unable to perform. What is required and appreciated is the performance of each capable member based on the division of labor. Above all, work is valued whose fruits, in turn, enable people to fulfill their destiny, not the consumerist waste of scarce resources for the benefit of privileged societies and classes at the expense of hunger and war in the poorest regions of the world.[65] This social dimension can be experienced above all in the experience of serving one another and working together.[66] According to the Pauline understanding of the ideal community as a body with many members and with Christ as the head, everyone is co-responsible in the sense of subsidiarity to make their contribution and contribute the talents they have been given to the collective good. This results in mutual appreciation of simple work and the social responsibility to perform for and stand by each other in a sense of solidarity.[67]

Personhood presupposes the (not merely formal, but) material right and, in the same sense, the material duty of humankind to assume responsibility and to exploit human creative potential. The social identity of the one body, which human social nature urges to unfold, goes beyond mere duty. It gives people the freedom to embrace their destinies while using the talents that have been given to them. It is also filled with a spirit of togetherness that is nourished by a common love for the Head, Jesus Christ.[68] In such a spirit, the work duties of subsidiarity and solidarity are also transformed into acts of social love. This enables the different groups of societies based on the division of labor to have an "Awareness of their belonging together as members of one great family, as children of one and the same heavenly Father."[69]

The work endowed with intrinsic value by the relationship with God and by the social love derived from it serves the development of the natural destiny given to humans by God, thereby realizing the principle of personhood in a normative, humanistic way. After all, self-determined and thus liberating work brings both *individualitas* and *socialitas* to fruition.

Christian Significance

The work is often also a toil, the meaning of which is not immediately apparent.

> All work . . . is inevitably linked with toil. The Book of Genesis expresses it in a truly penetrating manner: The original blessing of work contained in the very mystery of creation and connected with man's elevation as the image of God is contrasted with the curse that sin brought with it: "Cursed is the ground because of you; in toil you shall eat of it all the days of your life."[70]

But from a Christian point of view, work is by no means the curse of original sin because work explicitly participates in the divine labor of human redemption.[71] The hardship is nevertheless a consequence of human hubris. Even before reaching for the apple from the tree of knowledge in Paradise, work belonged to humankind. It was not until later that God's curse followed. However, the curse was not over work but instead over the soil of the field, which is the source of humans' food through laborious work.[72] This realistic consciousness opposes, for example, the Marxist utopia of a classless society in which everyone would perform their work with unadulterated joy, completely selflessly and out of pure love for society. A true, unadulterated experience of toil has healing properties. It reminds people to be creatures and not the creator. In doing so, it urges people not to play God themselves. Toil also allows people to participate in Christ's work of redemption, which frees them from the cycle of sin: "By enduring the toil of work in union with Christ crucified for us, man in a way collaborates with the Son of God for the redemption of humanity."[73] Through the cross of Christ, humankind is redeemed, and the guilt of Adam is atoned for. Enduring toil is a consciously experienced liberation from the cycle of sin.[74] It is not a curse but rather the spell of that curse. And thus, even the toil of self-determined work gives a freedom in the sense of personhood. Being freed from the cycle of sin helps us consciously reconcile with God. It encourages humans to experience themselves as God's beloved despite Adam's guilt and therefore not only to accept their own existence as such but also come to love it. This encourages respect for oneself and increases readiness to engage in creative pursuits and performance. Workers who recognize or sense this spiritual meaning feel absolutely committed to the plan given by God and understand themselves only from the horizon of consciousness of being included in this plan and fulfilling a God-given task as a part of it. The insight into the spiritual meaning of the effort connected with the work as well as the understanding of humans in their destinies as persons are inseparable.

The reward of gainful employment is not an end in itself. Rather, its use is also committed to the mission of creation and thus to the threefold commandment of love.[75] The earned wage creates a space of freedom for the development of personal and social responsibility. Without wages, workers would remain at the mercy of the propertied classes and dependent on handouts or social transfers. Material independence protects against this. The acquisition of wages creates the space for independent decision-making and for creativity, thereby fostering the development of the *individualitas*. As recognition, it also strengthens self-confidence and self-love. It motivates people to perform in line with their personality, which, in turn, benefits the public. The freedom of decision and personal responsibility given with such independence also challenges social responsibility in dealing with wages. Like the other material or spiritual fruits of labor, wages are also a condition of material solidarity. Wages provide workers with material resources that enable them to fulfill duties of solidarity toward the weak.[76] They also create a space for tangible acts of charity, such as voluntary welfare that goes beyond the duty of solidarity.[77] Above all, wages create the material basis for subsidiary educational and childcare services provided within the family. "Work constitutes a foundation for the formation of family life, which is a natural right and something that man is called to. In a way, work is a condition for making it possible to found a family, since the family requires the means of subsistence which man normally gains through work."[78]

Because wages also reduce the overriding concern for physical subsistence, they allow for leisure time that is not dominated by gainful employment, leaving time for important family tasks, unpaid cultural education, and creation or other volunteer activities. If humans are no longer heteronomous slaves to gainful employment, they also have more freedom to cultivate their relationship with God without any specific purpose. In this sense, the material good of wages also improves the conditions for Christians to develop the immaterial good of their love for God.

Non-paid labor, such as volunteering, homemaking, parenting, and childcare, lacks recognition in the form of wages. However, it is not the scarcity on the market that primarily determines the moral value of work but instead its contribution to the development of humans in their personal and social responsibility before God and humanity and, thus, also their contribution to the shaping of a social order that creates the appropriate framework for the development of their God-given destiny.

In view of increasing labor productivity, there is sometimes a demand for a move away from labor-driven society. According to the social philosopher Philippe Van Parijs, for example, an egalitarian basic income independent of performance fulfills desirable sociopolitical steering functions.[79] This is intended to create free space for raising children. Voluntary work and cultural activities, such as the humanities, theater, sculpture, and so on, are also receiving a boost. From a socio-ethical point of view, it can undoubtedly be a welcome goal to expand the scope for culture and family. From the perspective of Catholic social doctrine, however, this type of basic income, with its negative performance incentives, is an unsuitable means of achieving these ends. It also fails to recognize the meaningful nature of self-determined gainful employment. This is why it is much more important to strengthen the status of inactive work in the context of labor-driven society and in the sense of subsidiary support and demands.

In principle, Catholic social teaching is based on the idea of performance and combines it with a commitment to a liberating work ethic. God's own Son was a carpenter. He does not preach laziness and instead challenges people to develop their own abilities with courage and responsibility.[80] This is why Thomas Aquinas counts sloth among the seven deadly sins.[81] Therefore, in the case of deliberate waste of the talents entrusted to humans by God, to the detriment of the person and society, the following applies: "Anyone unwilling to work should not eat."[82] Those who are lazy and do not work—despite being capable of doing so—violate the commandment of personhood as if they were violating a God-given duty. On the one hand, they punish themselves with voluntary bondage. On the other hand, they deserve to be sanctioned by their community. However, through self-determined work, humans develop personhood and become free to pursue their God-given destiny.

Consequence and Compass

Work is always a commitment of humans to themselves, to society, and to God:

> Man must work, both because the Creator has commanded it and because of his own humanity, which requires work in order to be maintained and developed. Man must work out of regard for others . . . and the whole human family of which he is a member: Since he is the heir to the work of generations and at the same time a sharer in building the future of those who will come after him in the succession of history. All this constitutes the moral obligation of work.[83]

- From a Christian socio-ethical perspective, the theological contexts of meaning and significance of work enrich the often ideological discussions on the relationship between work and capital by reconnecting to the transcendentally founded personal principle.
- Meaningful work gives freedom. If personhood (understood as the maxim of self-determination directed toward the fulfillment of God-given destiny) is realized as the meaning of work, then this gives humans more self-respect in their activities, brings them closer to their neighbors, creates an identity of values out of a spirit of social love, makes God's nearness tangible even in everyday work, encourages performance, and gives meaning even to hardship. Such a basic attitude prevents people from being blinded by the illusory sense of the work fetish or consumerism.
- Meaningful work is also an act of self-love that lets an individual's nature unfold. Moreover, creativity and a willingness to innovate are not merely ends in themselves, as they correlate closely with social responsibility. The self-determined work also has a liberating effect in the joy of being allowed to share responsibility for the talents given by God and the responsible handling of the entrusted creation.[84]
- Work that is liberating and fruitful in this sense gives meaning to individual self-development because people grow into the challenge they accept. "Work is a good thing for man—a good thing for his humanity—because through work man not only transforms nature, adapting it to his own needs, but he also achieves fulfilment as a human being and indeed, in a sense, becomes 'more a human being.'"[85]

The individual and social dimensions are inseparable from humans' involvement in their God-given destiny. Based on this perspective, questions about the consequences of work for individuals, culture, and society as well as for creation, therefore, cannot be posed in separate discussions.

- Work also has a gratuitous intrinsic value. From its understanding of personhood and family, the Catholic tradition assigns a special value to non-gainful employment in this regard, partly because it is performed without remuneration and, therefore, presupposes a motivation of virtue or love.
- Labor-driven society is not being adopted but shaped. Work and wages provide opportunities to use skills for personal fulfillment and social good. Incentive structure and education create the framework for this. From a Christian perspective, the motivation to perform serves the greater purpose of developing one's destiny. In this context, the performance principle is a normatively humane demand on work motivation because it challenges individual performance resources in the service of personhood, society, creation, and, thus, the kingdom of God.

BILDUNG

From a Christian standpoint, good work is always based on an internalization of values and virtues paired with a corresponding framework of rules, which makes the development of personhood as part of the threefold responsibility possible. *Bildung*, in the sense of the German tradition of education, personal edification, self-cultivation, and lifelong learning, is the foundation on which such a culture of responsibility is built. A basic understanding of *Bildung* is outlined for this purpose. If this is done from a socio-ethical perspective, it cannot and should not open up pedagogical discussion forums. Rather, it is about the fundamental relationship of education to ethics and the resulting consequences for socio-ethically relevant topics in the present and future. This primarily concerns questions about fundamental educational goals but also about concrete contexts, such as how to deal with inclusion. Since the concept of education today—contrary to its original roots—is now largely secular, a Christian perspective on it also offers a good testing ground for building bridges between Christian socio-ethical positions and the world of today.[86]

Bildung and Ethics

The concept of *Bildung* enjoys broad social approval. At times, one might even be hard-pressed to find anyone who expressly opposes it, similar to concepts such as human dignity, social justice, or the social market economy. And just as with these concepts of consensus, unanimity quickly falls apart when its precise content must be defined in more detail. Thus, the concept of *Bildung*, much like the elusive values or goals or ideals mentioned previously, is in danger of becoming a weasel word that has lost all meaning.[87] In contrast, an attempt will be made here to establish a semantically substantial positioning, which is at the same time a socio-ethically relevant orientation compass.

The origin of the concept of *Bildung*, which is unique in German compared to other languages, is biblical since it is based on the idea of the image of humankind in the image of God in the Book of Genesis (Gen 1:26 et seqq.).[88] In mysticism (Meister Eckhart), the term finds the following religious meaning beyond craft in the sense of nobleness of heart: Humans are created in God's image. The human soul would now have to relinquish its form (*entbilden*) to allow God to imprint (*einbilden*) on it. Overcoming egoistic and other human motives frees the human soul to God, who then animates humankind. Those who experience this ensoulment have thus been formed (*gebildet*). According to this, humans becoming subjects is the result of God dwelling within them. This is the way to salvation, to the knowledge of goodness, and to freedom in God. The references of this concept of education to the Christian mission of salvation are unmistakable. They can be found, for example, in the epistemology of Thomas Aquinas.[89] This originally religious meaning of the term has been largely lost today but continues to have an effect on some basic features of its usage.

The present concept of *Bildung* has numerous, sometimes mutually contradictory, but at least dialectical, facets.[90] Materially, it stands for a canon of knowledge to be imparted, formally for the active promotion of talent, functionally for improved skills in the world of life and work, idealistically for the orientation toward a purposeless ideal with corresponding consequences for virtue and ethics. Secularly, "*Bildung* is understood as empowerment for reasonable self-determination."[91] The term has individual features when it comes to becoming a subject and forming a personality. The social side refers to the embedding in a certain social culture or its further development. On the one hand, it works in a way that enables people to conceptualize an existing life context and shape their lives within this framework. But it should also have an educational effect by enabling people to question the existing culture and to develop it further, oriented toward an appropriate ideal. This means not only education and learning but also cultural understanding and design. In this respect, *Bildung* is the encounter of humankind with self-transcendence, with an ideal that is also normatively effective.[92] This ideal is now the compass for the person who has had the benefit of *Bildung* to question existing social and life contexts, to reinforce them or to change them. *Bildung*, in this perspective, thus presupposes a recognizable idea of what is good. For example, in the sense of Plato's Allegory of the Cave, it makes the difference between appearance and reality (*Schein und Sein*) and thus enables humans to experience self-transcendence and an orientation toward an ethical ideal or law.

Thus, *Bildung*—this can be stated even without in-depth discussions of educational theory—remains in its origins and in a broad sense closely related to ethics even today, provided that the idealistic aspect and associated idea of holistic personality development are not abandoned. This background enables us to identify some contemporary challenges that arise from such an understanding or that seek to fundamentally challenge precisely this understanding.

Several Challenges

The socially desirable link between *Bildung* and ideals can lead to temptation or salvation (healing). Abuse is conceivable: In such a case, false (i.e., morally bad) *Bildung* is instrumentalized for a dehumanizing ideology by prescribing to people pseudo-religious goals as supposedly objective ideals and orientations.[93] This form of temptation is well known from historical contexts, for example, in the service of fascism and communism. The "postmodernization of *Bildung*"[94] seeks to protect against such abuse. It points to the fact that, strictly speaking, it (as well as dignity, justice, etc.) can only be spoken of in the plural. The concept of an educational ideal (*Bildungsideal*) guided by a comprehensive objective notion of what is good and could establish a universal claim is then abandoned. A (post-)modern understanding of education can—even beyond religious reference—make itself the standard of good things. The prerequisite for this is a secular narrative of what is good. This raises the question of a corrective to distinguish between spirits and ward off ideological abuse.[95] The term can then be interpreted and instrumentalized politically or ideologically with very different contents with purely specific meanings. Thus, in a postmodern way, it loses the character of an objective good for society.[96] In this way, the dissemination of a belief in the laws of the market or technology could also be thought of as *Bildung*.

Bildung always faces the danger of being an exclusive good that excludes certain people. If *Bildung* is linked to the ideal of human dignity, however, an egalitarian claim must be derived from it.[97] Inclusion and education are then inextricably linked and fundamentally concern all people (i.e., people with and without disabilities, of different origins, young and old, and so on). However, the question remains as to what exactly is meant by this inclusion, how equality is to be understood, and how it can be implemented in the educational system, for example.

It is possible to reduce the concept of education to economically useful skills, such as learning methods and tools for success, of functionalized factual justice without ethical reflection. Personality formation associated with this could either dispense with ethics altogether and even promote Machiavellianism or narcissism.[98] According to the results of the Shell Youth Studies, such a development has shaped the value consciousness of young people in Germany for several years. Such thinking had a major impact until 2012. However, there are signs of a reversal in the trend from 2015 onwards. Various basic attitudes of egoism subsequently gave way to a new idealism for environmental and social ideals so that, in 2015, there was talk of a young "generation on the move" and, in 2019, of a generation that had returned to idealism and a desire to speak up.[99]

Excursus: Economized Context of *Bildung* in Transition

One of the main reasons for the development up to the reversal of the trend in 2015 will have been the influence on society of a way of thinking that uses the HO as a model and thus has a normative effect on people's real behavior. From such an economic point of view, it has "proved to be eminently sensible, at least when one wants to theoretically model behavior in markets, to assume that market participants behave as if they were pursuing egoistic interests."[100]

This economic fiction influenced the incentive structure and value consciousness of our society. The model assumption of the HO sets incentives in such a way that people actually behave egoistically or at least instrumentally (*zweckrational*). Pragmatism in various forms thus determined the decisions of young people in Germany. A spirit of "ego tactics" prevailed—according to the 2002 Shell Study[101]: "Ego tacticians . . . are interested in a high quality of social coexistence. However, they also want to see their own wishes and ideas fulfilled in the process. They are constantly asking: How does behaving or engaging in a certain way benefit me? What does it do for me, what is the result for me?"[102]

The 2010 Shell Study dubs it "psychoeconomics, . . . justifying the benefits of social investments": "One might suspect that it is precisely those idealistic attitudes that contribute positively to satisfaction . . . that can be understood at least in a broad sense as 'investive.'"[103]

Based on this, the basic instrumental attitude was marked by "valuing performance and enjoyment equally."[104] According to the 2002 study, the "intensive search for personal and social identity" was guided by opportunism, convenience, and the exploitation of opportunities. The 2010 Shell Study speaks somewhat differently of an attitude of "hedonism"[105] with a high regard for achievement as the gateway to enjoyment in the near future.[106] "Psycho-economics" is responsible for a relatively low altruistic inclination, for example, to help the socially disadvantaged.[107] The assumption of a strong influence of normative individualistic ethics on such feelings with its recommendations on guiding the ego tactical choice of partner, family planning, social commitment, institutional design of the healthcare system, and so on solely based on utility calculations is then obvious.[108] An economy with the claim of replacing ethics and making individual morality superfluous also conveys to humans, as a belief in themselves and the market, its own dimension of meaning, which does not go beyond the conventional stage of value development. According to such an understanding, there is no place for ethics that cannot be translated into the utility language of economics. An economized society that unilaterally assumed self-interest maximization as a decision-making motivation led to personality-forming incentives to act

- that underestimate people's social motivations (and hence their capacity to contribute to the economic value creation process),

- that promote a lack of solidarity, and
- that consequently impede holistic personality formation.

The economic model could thus serve the purpose of confirming itself in a circular way without orienting itself to the personal development of humankind based on a view of humanity. In this way, value concepts could be unilaterally determined within the framework of economization and transformed into pragmatism. Such stimulus-induced personality deformations often happen insidiously. Many people were and are confronted with this in a material way today. Where people are understood and evaluated solely in terms of economic benefit, for example, essential characteristics of human personality are ignored.[109] This view leads to ethically and economically deficient results. "All of the families of our company's executives have split up in recent years."

This statement from a senior executive at a marketing firm was probably not an isolated incident. If, for example, professional activity is seen as the primary space for work, life, and meaning, this is often at the expense of family and the psychological balance of employees. If humans alone are a factor of production, the development of social virtues or the consideration of social values for the development of humans as persons has no intrinsic value. It is then only ever in the service of optimizing the sum of economic output. Individuals may well be sacrificed in this way.

Admittedly, employees in the workplace may be granted their social motives. However, they are not meant to be incorporated into their day-to-day work routine but instead into their lives beyond this context. In one's career, however, it should be possible to rely on the fact that potential ethical concerns and arguments would already lead to good by the rules designed according to economic regularities, as Karl Homann's economic ethics provides, for example.[110] Tearing them apart into separate spheres (professional versus personal life) does not do justice to human nature. This thinking paves the way to a potential schizophrenia that decouples what belongs together or—as economic imperialism suggests even more radically—the path to finally overcoming motives driven by instrumental action in all situations of life that do not follow a utility calculation. Neither long-term optimized economic benefit nor human satisfaction nor mature ethical judgment can be expected from people shaped in this way.

The search for meaning, fears, dreams, and emotions, together with social-empathic motivations, are just as much a part of human beings and their decisions, not only from a Christian perspective but also as an inner need to ensure one's own benefit from the survival of the fittest. The former dimensions of the human being are excluded in the economic model of ethics. At the same time, people in a social climate characterized by this are basically expected to make a difficult decision. They should define for themselves what humanity and the environment mean. These decision-making processes, in turn, do not follow any objective ethical principle or humane ideal given to economics. The definition must lead to a kind of HO as a human image because no other point of view is allowed. Social goals, which, according to the latest Shell Studies, are quite widespread among young people in Germany, are sidelined so that young people merely endure the deplorable state of economization but do not adopt a convinced HO attitude as an adapted way out. However, this phase of social shaping seems to have been overcome since 2015.

Christian Humanism

According to Ulrich Kropač, good education in a liberal understanding (also in the sense of Jean-Jacques Rousseau) is guided by the nature of humans and serves their freedom. It must serve no other purpose than this freedom and excludes a mere collectivization of the subject.[111] This concept of *Bildung* is obviously based on a view of humanity. It is closely connected with a normative humanism similar to the one Christian humanists, who were also pedagogues, held up as a mirror to their time. Erasmus of Rotterdam, Philipp Melanchthon, and others were not only concerned with a knowledge of faith but also with an understanding of faith, with an individual maturity in faith, as it was strongly demanded by the Reformation.[112] To this end, these Christian humanists advocate ethics with the goal of "humanitas," the noble formation of mind and heart, which, at the same time, should shape humanity. Jesus Christ is the model and more important than saints or scholars. He is the criterion par excellence for all ethically legitimate decisions. This also applies to the *Bildung* of rulers and the cultural shaping of the social order. The secondary values and principles derived from this in Erasmus, for example, were progressive for the time:[113]

- Christian *Bildung* of those in power,
- Justice for all,
- Solidarity of Christian people,
- Extension of freedom of expression, and
- Raising awareness before rushing to war.

These values and principles outline a European peace program that proscribes war among Christians. The common good, solidarity, peace, freedom, justice, and the idea of Europe are founded by Erasmus in human nature, which is, therefore, declared to be the measure of ethical *Bildung* because

God Himself became human. Christian-humanistic ethics is based on the human being, who is dignified by Jesus Christ.[114]

Classical Christian humanists thus arrive at social principles and an educational ideal by a different route than the scholastic one. The results are largely the same. In his encyclical CiV, Benedict XVI calls for a new humanistic synthesis, expressed in a habitual spirit of love to be rediscovered. Ecumenical social ethics stands in the humanistic tradition with its call for a positive formation of consciousness: "The contribution of the Christian faith is to create confidence in life by trusting in the grace of God. 'Faith wants to encourage life.'"[115]

Consequence and Compass

Now, based on the challenges for a Christian concept of education outlined in this section and with the Christian view of humanity identified in part I, I put forward for discussion some consequences concerning the concept and practice of *Bildung* from a Christian socio-ethical perspective.

- *Bildung*, in the Christian sense, is a holistic concept. It describes the virtuous rise of the human subject in freedom and responsibility before God. It enables people to understand the real contexts of life in the light of the Gospel and possibly to form them as leaven in the sense of the *lex charitatis*. It thus gives humankind a transcendentally based compass for shaping the world on the one hand and for questioning worldly ideals and goals in the light of the objectively good on the other.[116] *Bildung* understood in this way always has a God-given objective and, in its permanent orientation to this ideal, brings about the eschatological as well as ethical self-transcendence of the human being.
- This basic understanding is incompatible with a mere economic, political, or other means of using *Bildung* to serve. At the same time, with the Christian ideal made transparent as a normative reference, it offers good grounds for unmasking inhuman ideologies with their educational programs.
- Christian humanism as the basis of *Bildung* forbids limiting it to mere functionality and factual justice. Otherwise, it would only serve to instrumentalize humankind, pushing the goal of becoming a subject aside.[117] In contrast to this is the normative humanistic ideal, according to which humans must be enabled by education and remain open to the pursuit of ultimate questions (of meaning, truth, the good, etc.) and thereby to transcendence.
- In the awareness that secularized education could fall prey to a false ideal, if thought oriented toward it is ultimately unable to conclusively justify

such a humane meta-compass, (Christian) religion with its reference to transcendence could also be taken from a basic secular understanding to help provide solid reasoning for a secular concept of *Bildung*.[118] Then religion fulfills a desired purpose for stabilizing secularism but must always hold itself accountable for not losing sight of its actual mission.[119]

- One-sided promotion of STEM subjects (science, technology, engineering, and mathematics) in schools and purely functional skills in vocational qualification programs guts the holistic concept of *Bildung*. Virtue, ethics, transcendence, and philosophy then play either no or, at best, a subordinate role. Findings from recent Shell Studies suggest that interest in these topics (beyond STEM subjects) is on the rise again.
- More and more students in Germany are graduating from high school with university entry qualifications (*Abitur*). Lower secondary school (*Hauptschule*) diplomas are becoming increasingly rare, and these schools are dying out. Apprenticeship positions remain unfilled, and the number of trainees is declining.[120] While this rise in higher-level education is encouraging, the death of the *Hauptschule* also marks the death of schools focused on fostering practical and technical skills that were effective in preparing people for skilled trades, for example. It would appear that such professions are no longer chosen or appreciated today. This development is regrettable from a Christian perspective. Theoretical, practical, and manual skills are just as valuable and should be promoted just as intensely. The increasing disregard for practical training contradicts the Christian idea of the diversity of people (and their talents) with equal dignity. Different talents make up the individuality of a person. An increasing number of *Abitur* students is far from proof that the German school system is successfully promoting this level of diversity. It would be in line with the Christian mission of salvation to recognize the diversity of people and their talents and to strengthen them through appropriate forms of schooling.
- Inclusion in the educational system is a lofty goal that does justice to valuing diversity (in health, background, age, etc.). Inclusion should not only affect people with disabilities but instead all people. For the school sector, this means, for example, a reduction in special needs schools because children who previously attended school there must now attend regular schools under appropriate supervision. From a Christian socio-ethical point of view, the promise of a comprehensive "inclusion for all" always reaches its limits when it is demanded as a means of leveling the playing field, for example, for people with various disabilities, and cannot be fulfilled in terms of human and financial resources, for instance, due to a lack of pedagogical, psychological, or special educational staff. Special schools are a learning space worth preserving for those who have better odds of

thriving there based on their individual needs. Reasons for this can include the following: atypical psycho-social development (e.g., autism), highly specialized support (e.g., for deaf people), the need for a sense of achievement, for security among people with comparable disabilities, and more.

ORGAN DONATION

Illness has a way of reminding people of their physical limits. In many ways, death is the final frontier. Medical care offers help. A dilemma arises when sick people die who could have been saved by donor organs from other people. Neither doctors nor drugs nor the latest technologies can help.

Ethical Dilemma

In Germany, around 8,460 people were on the waiting list for a donor organ in late 2021.[121] Of these, about 6,600 people were waiting for a donor kidney. The waiting period for organs in Germany is about six years. Every year, about 1,000 people on the waiting list in Germany die. The development of technical substitutes has not been able to remedy the situation thus far. Rather, medicine relies on postmortem or living organ donations (especially kidneys). For example, in 2021, 475 kidneys were transferred from living donations and 794 from postmortem donations. Germany was and is a recipient country of donor organs in the association of countries united in the Eurotransplant Foundation.[122] Although there is strong support for organ donation among the German population, the number of donors has continued to fall steadily from an already low level in 2010 (donor rate of 15.5/1 million population) to its lowest point to date in 2017 (donor rate of 9.3).[123] How can we explain the shortage of donor organs and further decline? This could be due to the following reasons:

- Brain death as a prerequisite for postmortem organ removal can rarely be clearly established.[124] The idea of having organs removed from one's body while still alive is just as daunting as the thought of being kept alive artificially after brain death has been diagnosed in order to keep the organs that are being considered for removal fresh.
- In general, postmortem donations raise the fundamental question: When is a human being dead? Those who do not consider a person to be dead after what is known as brain death will have trouble explaining why they advocate for the removal of organs from these people who are then considered to be dying. After all, this would be tantamount to killing.

- In many cases, relatives consider the mutilation of their loved one's remains to be an unreasonable imposition.
- Time and again in the past, there have been scandals at transplant centers that gave the impression that doctors or lobby groups were systematically more concerned with their own business than with the welfare of patients. This was reflected in the drop in donor numbers through 2017. Since then, there has been a renewed increase in the willingness to donate: The rate rose to 11.3 in 2018 and fell again to 10.8 in 2021.[125]

Altruistically motivated organ donations have so far been insufficient to end the deadly dilemma in Germany. The plight of the sick waiting for an organ is so great that there are incentives for a thriving black market due to international shortages and long waiting times (such as on the Eurotransplant list).[126] This is exacerbated by great social needs, especially in poor countries. Live kidney harvesting for a small fee so that one's own children do not have to prostitute themselves, forced kidney harvesting from prisoners, postmortem kidney harvesting after euthanasia without certain determination of death or after executions of politically persecuted persons, for example, in China, are (or were) sources of this criminal black market.[127] While the donor of a kidney—with poor medical care and usually inadequate aftercare—receives about €3,000 for the organ, recipients on the black market must pay up to €160,000 for it.[128] With criminal energy, illegal traffickers exploit the hardships of the people to do business with fear, exploitation, and murder. The goal must be to dry up these markets by making enough transplants legally available. The overarching task is to find a way out of the vicious circle of exploited hardship. The social debate about how the permanent shortage of donor organs in Germany can be remedied must go beyond day-to-day political discussions (keyword: opt-in versus opt-out policy) and address multiple fundamental socio-ethical questions if it does not want to result in overly simplified or purely intuitive and emotional solutions. This chapter first examines the legal situation prevailing in 2019. It then presents criteria for Christian socio-ethical acceptability, which can be used to evaluate various models that are assumed to increase postmortem or live donations.

The Evolving German Legal Situation

Awareness of the consequences of this vicious circle has led to a change in legal assessment in Germany. This development brought more legal certainty and was always aimed at bringing together freedom of the person and a higher volume of donations. In the new German states, the regulations of the GDR "Ordinance on the Performance of Organ Transplantations" (July 4, 1975) continued to apply as state law until the Federal Transplantation Act (*Transplantationsgesetz* [TPG]) was passed in 1997. This mandated an opt-out policy, excluded material consideration for transplants, and provided primarily for postmortem harvesting with a high chance of success and without mere use for research. In the former federal states, the regulations of the German Criminal Code (StGB) were applied until 1997, which resulted in some legal uncertainty. Living donation of vital organs after consent was prosecuted as manslaughter (*Totschlag*) (§ 212 StGB) or "killing upon request" (*Tötung auf Verlangen*) (§ 216 StGB). The live removal of organs that were not essential to life was considered bodily injury under §§ 223, 230 StGB and, since there was no intention to heal on the part of the physician, also a violation of the principle of *nihil nocere* (principle of no harm). Such harvesting was only permitted with the express consent of the well-informed donor, provided that this did not constitute a violation of morality (§ 226 StGB).[129] A monetary gratuity for the donor was not considered immoral per se, but organ trafficking for pure profit was. Postmortem donation initially meant disturbing the peace of the dead (§ 168 StGB). It was allowed after the explicit consent of individual donors during their own lifetime. Relatives' right to care for the deceased came into play when no injunction was available.

In 1997, the German Transplantation Act introduced the extended opt-in policy nationwide, which built on the rules of the former states. While a narrow opt-in policy only permits postmortem organ harvesting if the deceased have consented to organ harvesting during their own lifetime (e.g., by means of an organ donor card, in the case of the extended opt-in policy, if there is no corresponding consent), relatives can decide on organ removal, whereby the basis for the decision must be the known or presumed will of the deceased. Two physicians must have independently determined brain death. Then artificial respiration and tumor and infection testing are performed. The data is forwarded to Eurotransplant, where the waiting lists are kept. This is followed by retrieval, shipment of the transplants, and burial of the donor. All other things being equal, the allocation is made to those on the waiting list who are most in danger of dying. Living donations are considered a last resort and may only be given by adults to close relatives or particularly close people without any foreseeable health risk and only in transplant centers designated for this purpose, whereby the recipient's health insurance company must cover the costs of the procedures as well as pre-transplant and post-transplant care. There is a strict ban on commercialization, which is punishable by up to five years in prison.

The Raise Awareness of Transplantation Donation Act (*Gesetz zur Regelung der Entscheidungslösung im Transplantationsgesetz*) has been in force in Germany since November 1, 2012.[130] The principle of voluntary decision, which underlies the opt-in policy, is retained. In addition, it also introduces mandates for health insurers to regularly inform and survey people over sixteen years of age, the results of which must be kept open. A discussion was scheduled in 2019 to discuss the pros and cons of an opt-out policy in light of the still low numbers of donors. The government hopes that a corresponding paradigm shift will help resolve the shortage problem.

Path to a Christian Set of Values

Current, day-to-day political discussion and the search for an ethically justified solution to the dilemma must always remain cognizant of the tension between impaired individual freedom of choice, higher donation expectations, and other ethical criteria. Exclusive rationing models such as the "club policy" are also being discussed, at least in scientific circles. The same applies to the repeated attempts to legalize organ trade, which is currently punishable by law but that, according to its representatives, would seem to offer a good solution. Do these proposals deliver what they promise? All proposals must always stand up to health economist Peter Oberender's provocation: "Ultimately, it is a value judgment: Can you argue in good conscience that it is acceptable for people to die every year because they have no chance of receiving a donor organ?"[131]

An ideology-free evaluation of the various solution models is needed and is approached here from the perspective of Christian social ethics. A four-dimensional view for evaluation is first proposed using criteria by Michael Sandel:

- D1: Solution expertise to increase the number of legally and morally legitimate transplants taken and to dry up the black markets
- D2: Rules for equitable distribution of transplants
- D3: Consequences for human self-understanding (in relation to human dignity and the human environment)
- D4: Consequences for the culture of human coexistence[132]

What is still missing here is an ethical foundation in a view of humanity, which is offered here in the sense of Christian social ethics. Humankind's primary responsibility before God demands the unconditional protection of the life of every human being, who is dignified as having been created in God's image. Moral action as a grateful response to what ought to be in human existence presupposes voluntary self-determination. This also applies to organ donation, if it is to be understood as a moral act. In their responsibility before themselves as God's creatures, having been made in His image, the

Catholic Church initially rejected organ removal in principle as an intervention in the personal integrity of the individual and as something that was intrinsically bad (*intrinsece malum*). This view was revised by Pope Pius XII. In the Christian view, people do not own their bodies like commodities. Instead, they *are* their bodies. Consequently, according to Christian belief, the individual parts of the body have no legitimate price and cannot be traded.[133] From the Christian point of view, the conscious and, therefore, morally responsible violation of personal integrity is only possible by weighing moral goods with equal value. If love for the gift of one's own body competes with the commanded love of one's neighbor, such self-injury is morally legitimate because the love of Christ restores personal integrity according to Galatians 2:20: "and it is no longer I who live, but it is Christ who lives in me." A sacrifice understood in this way (which goes beyond human duty) is only conceivable as an unpaid and voluntary act.[134] There must never be any coercion or pressure with respect to the willingness to donate. That is because no one has a legitimate claim to another person's organs. For Christians, one's own body is not only not a saleable private good, but it is also not a collective good. Organ donation is an altruistic sacrifice (that must never be made under pressure or coercion). For the spirit of coexistence addressed by Sandel, this means: What needs to be strengthened is a social spirit of helping, even without anything in return.

Charity in the sense of the Parable of the Good Samaritan assumes a natural willingness to donate organs.[135] On the other hand, following the principle of "*ultra posse nemo posse tenetur*"[136] in the sense of Schockenhoff, there can also be good ethical and justifiable Christian reasons against organ donation, so that it is not always morally necessary.[137] This section will now discuss and assess models for increasing postmortem donations and, finally, economic models (especially for living donations) from the perspective of Christian ethics against this background of Christian evaluation.

Models for Increasing Postmortem Donations

As alternatives to the opt-in policy valid in Germany (in 2019), the main options to be discussed with regard to postmortem donations are the opt-out policy and the club policy.

Opt-out policy: In contrast to the consent or opt-in policy, the opt-out policy practiced in most European countries (and in the new German states until 1997) basically presupposes, in the spirit of the solidarity principle, a legally enforceable obligation on the part of all persons to be willing to donate postmortem. Only an express objection by the individuals concerned during their lifetime or, in the absence of a corresponding declaration, by relatives at the time of death, can then safely prevent the removal of organs. As a result, those who suppress the issue during their lifetime usually then become potential organ donors once brain death has been declared. People's tendency to avoid the decision because they see it as a hassle or inconvenience is often said to result in an increase in transplants at the expense of a conscious decision. An information policy in which relatives are merely informed of plans to harvest organs—only if there is no contradictory expression of the will of the deceased—and a compulsory government regulation could further strengthen this trend.[138] Many countries already deem the opt-out policy to be a viable compromise in increasing the number of transplants without the need to take immediate coercive measures. A comparison shows that countries with an opt-out policy are generally far ahead in terms of the number of transplants performed. Nevertheless, some countries with an opt-out policy (such as Bulgaria) still rank far behind, while the United States (with an opt-in, first-person consent system) is far ahead. The opt-out policy alone is not an unchallenged guarantor for a solution to the shortage of transplants. Confidence in technology and honesty in transplant centers, as well as economic incentive systems for affected physicians, are also essential prerequisites that would need to be further developed or created by law. Nonetheless, even according to critics of the opt-out policy, there is basically a positive correlation between this regulation and the number of transplants performed.

The ethical evaluation now takes up the four dimensions with a Christian focus. It seems likely that, other things being equal, more transplants will be available with the opt-out policy so that an improvement over the current situation in Germany can be assumed (D1). However, statistics suggest that this does not adequately address the shortage. The distribution of organs is organized publicly, as is already the case, so that no ethical deterioration can be assumed in this area as a result of the introduction of an opt-out policy (D2). The body is fundamentally understood as a collective good. Objections to collective use must be specifically justified (D3). This fosters a social spirit of publicly organized mutual performance of duty (D4). This social spirit certainly corresponds to the Christian understanding of Franz Böckle and Martin Lintner but contradicts the position of Schockenhoff and the above-mentioned public statements of the churches and their representatives. The addition of the Christian set of values results in some fundamentally critical assessments.

- People's tendency to avoid the decision because they see it as a hassle or inconvenience may lead to an increase in transplants at the expense of a conscious decision. Undoubtedly, moral pressure is rising on those who do not wish to be donors. There are also good reasons for such a refusal

(criticism of the brain death criterion, etc.). Such concerns are morally discredited by the opt-out policy.
- The expected increase in transplants will be achieved mainly through people's unwillingness to consciously deal with the issue so that the process cannot be described as voluntarism, altruism, or a donation. Organ donation loses its moral value. This is of particular importance with this kind of gift (of one's own body), especially if, as religious people do, one sees the body as a gift from God.
- Because of personal integrity, no one has a legitimate claim to another person's organs. Not only is the body not a private good that can be sold, but it is also not a collective good. However, the opt-out policy introduces precisely this type of collectivism.
- There is a danger of a dam breaking and a culture of social coercion taking hold. An information policy and, to an even greater degree, a compulsory state regulation all the way to compulsory living donation are examples of steps that would tighten up the process, to which the introduction of an opt-out policy would at least open the door.

Club model: Liberal schools around Hartmut Kliemt, Friedrich Breyer, Manfred Tietzel, and others introduced the club model as deliberately distinct from the opt-out policy.[139] Basic assumptions are:

- the strictly selfish behavior of people in the sense of HO,
- the justice principle of reciprocity,
- a priority of individual personal responsibility over the common good,
- the organs are considered as available private property of the individuals, and
- replacement of the principle of need by the utilitarian Quality Adjusted Life Year (QALY) criterion—subordinate to the strong priority of an allocation to club members[140]—for an allocation of transplants.

The central idea here is as follows: "As organ recipients, priority should be given to those patients who themselves—when their organs were still healthy—declared their willingness to donate their organs. In all other respects, the consent solution applies."[141] Those willing to donate will join together in a club of organ donors in order to relieve the state of costly bureaucracy on the one hand and to realize solidarity of the solidary on the other hand. All those who make their organ donation conditional on a non-quid pro quo basis are treated as club members so these altruists have no disadvantage. Club members transfer ownership of their organs to the club. The predicted outcome, due to strict reciprocity under conditions of individual self-benefit maximization, is an increase in the number of postmortem transplants while preserving individual freedom of choice. Entry into the club is characterized by the spirit of ensuring one's own survival rather than a depressing reflection on one's own death. The utilitarian distribution tends to favor younger sick patients, serving to increase the likelihood of success of the operations. Although the organization in private clubs offers greater freedom of decision (e.g., in the design of the statutes), the preferential admission of young members who possibly also practice a high-risk sport leads, in addition to the problem of fragmentation into units that are too small, to a risk of discrimination, which, at the same time, is associated with negative incentives with regard to health responsibility (i.e., it is better to avoid such dangerous pastimes out of a sense of responsibility). The result is the proposal of a public-law club policy, in which, for example, the general local health insurance funds or others manage the corresponding data register. If the club policy were introduced, a cut-off date would have to be set by which any responsible citizen could enter, whether healthy or sick, old, or young. Parents decide for their children. After the cut-off date, only healthy individuals can then enter to prevent moral hazard. For children who are not registered and who become seriously ill, Kliemt and Breyer concede that separate regulations still need to be supplemented.

In this model, too, the volume of transplants is expected to increase (D1). With the reciprocity criterion, public distribution takes leave of the principle of need as well as of the principle of equal access to health care services for all (D2). As in an options transaction on the stock exchange, one's own organs are used as a commodity to gain preferential access to transplants, even in the case of one's own need (D3). Coexistence is characterized by a utilitarian spirit of reciprocity (D4). In connection with the Christian set of values, some critical evaluations arise in this regard as well.

- The conditional distribution of health benefits need not necessarily be rejected as unfair. Thus, in the Christian sense of personal responsibility, one may consider introducing the causative principle for rationing health care services. However, the question of the chances of allocating transplants to people with disabilities, for example, remains unresolved, especially in view of the utilitarian QALY criterion.
- The transfer of the human body into individual and tradable private or club property is unacceptable. The same is true of the counterfactual reduction of human beings to the heuristic fiction of the HO, which causes moral human nature to be lost from view.
- Altruistic motivation is neither diminished nor enhanced because it is irrelevant in the organ donor club. The looming threat of being excluded from

life-saving measures if they are not taken builds pressure. The culture of voluntarism is damaged as a result.
- Coexistence is now characterized by a culture of "*do ut des,*" which is at least morally overcome with the teachings of Jesus.
- The design or interpretation of charity plays no role in the club model.

Market Models

There is also a need to discuss market models that contemplate regulated organ trade, particularly living donation (especially kidneys). After all, representatives of such models expect a sufficient increase in kidney transplants from commercialization while preserving human self-determination. The prioritization of living donation is justified by advantages in organ quality, improved minimally invasive techniques, and reduced susceptibility to misuse.[142] The ethical basis is the so-called liberal conception of humanity, from which the tradability of paired organs is removed while the donor is alive is justified with the freedom of humanity as self-determination over one's own body. A normative claim is derived from this:

> As has been explained in detail, a ban on commercial organ donation significantly restricts the liberties of individuals because they are no longer free to decide how to use their own organs. Thus, against the background of a liberal-democratic view of humanity, it is not the abolition of the organ trade ban that requires justification, but its introduction.[143]

The free right of disposal of human beings over their organs is assumed to be a fundamental right: "It is a fundamental right of man to be informed of the market value of the goods and resources available to him by nature, and also to be able to offer them under his own responsibility."[144]

Economic imperialism and the idea of "rewarded gifting" are to be distinguished as market models. In a discussion that is as free of taboos as possible, these proposals are to be exposed to critical questions:

- What are the consequences when (for example) kidneys become market commodities?
- Will the number of transplants thus increase sufficiently in a legal way?
- Will this solve the black market problem?
- And what are the consequences from a Christian ethical point of view?

Gary Becker's proposed solution to the monetization of organ donation is embedded in his strictly liberal model of economic imperialism.[145] In terms of normative individualism, ethical judgments cannot be justified by collective interests or state pressure and coercion but solely by the selfish interests of self-interest maximizers. The unjust dependence of sick people on networks of altruistic persons willing to make living donations should be replaced by a fair distribution via a regulated market. If potential organ donors are allowed to expect monetary compensation for their opportunity costs, the supply of transplants on the market will be completely elastic, and the shortage situation will dissipate. "We estimate the value of price of an organ from living donors by computing how much additional income or market consumption an individual will require in order to be indifferent between selling an organ or not."[146] In accordance with the laws of the market, this price would also apply to organs donated postmortem (especially kidneys). The completely inelastic supply of altruistic living donation would thus become obsolete. The price for the living donation of a kidney is then the sum of surgical costs and opportunity costs:

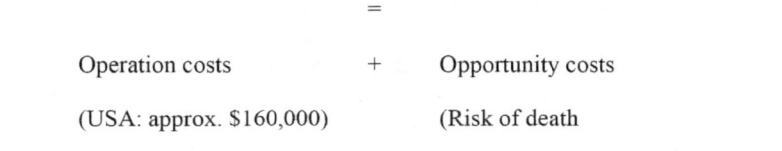

Figure 10.1. Just Price for a Kidney in Economic Imperialism. *Source*: Author.

Mortality risk is calculated as the average lifetime value of a young person (measured in dollars) multiplied by the surgery-related mortality rate of one per thousand. Since Becker, using 2004 as an example, puts the "value of statistical life" of a young person in the United States at $5 million, he arrives at a $5,000 premium for the risk of death.[147] Assuming an average annual income of $35,000, the premium for four weeks of lost work is $2,700. The cost of potentially diminished quality of life due to kidney loss is estimated at $7,500, thus putting the price of a kidney at $15,200, the price at which the average young US citizen would donate a kidney since they are compensated for the opportunity cost they incur. The actual price of a kidney still legally sold in India in the 1990s was about $1,200 in 2005 prices. Since the cost-of-living ratio between India and the United States was about 1:15 during this period, this gives a trade price for a kidney in the United States of $17,000, which Becker interprets as approximate confirmation of his estimated calculations.

Becker does not consider altruistic donors for his model. The higher a purchase price is set for the organ, the more the assumed number of transplants now available on the market increases. Once the opportunity cost equilibrium is reached at $15,200, an absolute elasticity of supply is assumed from then on. There are then enough organs available. All recipients willing to pay this price will benefit from a transplant, or so the theory goes. Since health insurance funds are also conceivable buyers, this institutionalization is intended to close the corresponding equity gap in distribution.

A liberal variation on Becker's model is the idea of the transplant as a gratified gift (rewarded gifting). Peter Oberender et al. share essential basic assumptions of economic imperialism, such as normative individualism, a supply-side approach to scarcity conditions and private ownership of bodies and organs as potential commodities. However, in the alternative approach, the focus is no longer on an orientation to the profit motive but instead first on increasing the supply of transplants. The now increased cost pressure is also expected to provide positive incentives for the faltering substitution research, especially since a decreasing number of dialyses releases corresponding financial and personnel potential. Taken seriously here, in contrast to Becker, are the dangers of so-called "health imperialism" that exploits poor countries and people for the benefit of the rich.[148] The criterion for the allocation to be made by the health insurance funds must, therefore, not first be the willingness to pay: Trading on an organ exchange may only take place under strict supervision of the trading partners and in compliance with standards to be defined publicly. These include the following rules: The health insurance companies as customers represent the potential recipients of transplants. The organ donors turn to brokers, who in turn can act on stock exchanges under the supervision of the health authorities. Participation in international trade is restricted to representatives from countries where adequate quality standards of care, operation, and follow-up are respected and where such social systems are effective that prevent the sale of organs from pressure (especially from social distress).[149] In addition to safeguarding medical standards, such conditions are also intended to prevent health insurers or brokers from acting like merchant rings and exploiting their market power. Any surpluses generated are to be passed on immediately by the health insurance funds for appropriate research purposes. This should make the allocation of transplants transparent, legitimate, and qualified. However, this does not mean that the price of a live transplant is the same everywhere in international comparison. People in poorer countries receive less money for their organs of the same quality. However, this is not to be understood as injustice but—similar to Becker's model—is due to the different price levels of the countries. The danger of a "race to the bottom" of the health and social systems is prevented overall, on the one hand, by the appropriately set standards and, on the other hand, by the self-healing powers of the markets, which force inferior (health) quality out of the market at excessive prices.

Another shortcoming of an economically imperialistic organ trade is seen by the representatives of rewarded gifting in the fact that altruism does not play a role as a motivation there. Kenneth Arrow, like Oberender, was already arguing for its rehabilitation. Altruism should not be displaced by monetization: "I do not want to rely too heavily on substituting ethics for self interest. I think it best on the whole that the requirement of ethical behavior be confined to those circumstances where the price system breaks down. . . . We do not wish to use up recklessly the scarce resources of altruistic motivation."[150]

Now, the basic idea of rewarded gifting is precisely that even with a market solution, this motivation should remain as an important pillar of willingness to donate: "The best answer is by creating a market arrangement to exist in parallel with altruistic giving."[151]

As with donating blood, for example, there should also be a reward for the living donation of a kidney that does not diminish the positive feeling of helping to save lives. In this use of remaining altruistic with added financially motivated provision of kidney transplants, the hitherto prevailing shortage could be efficiently solved without mercantilizing the social spirit. Thus, in contrast to economic imperialism, the quantity of traded organs increases. As a consequence, the ineffectiveness of a crowding-out effect (displacement of altruism by trade) is then postulated. Possible feelings of guilt on the part of recipients could also be mitigated by appropriate payment.

An ethical evaluation can now be made again, first in principle, and then with reference to the Christian set of values:

Whether there will actually be more transplants in terms of economic imperialism is uncertain not only because this assertion is a mere prediction but also because, moreover, the altruistic motivation to donate is suppressed (D1). The trade of organs on the market is intended to benefit lonely people without altruistic networks. Insured persons whose health insurers cannot cover the costs, especially in poor countries, are left out (D2). Bodies and lives are seen as commodities measurable in dollars. Body parts thus receive the price achievable by the market. The price for this is derived from the average value added by people. This would allow the monetarization not only of individual organs but also of life as a whole, which is fundamentally at odds with a liberal view of human beings (D3).[152] A social spirit of altruistic voluntarism is replaced by a commercial logic according to which everything can be monetized (D4).

The idea of rewarded gifting, on the other hand, offers a more mature system. Whether here—as hoped—with the introduction of this market for transplants from living donors regulated in this way, the number of transplants will increase, however, is by no means certain, despite the idea of gratified altruism. Michael Sandel, for example, explicitly disputes the positive effects. As an example, he points to the negative incentives of a gratuity offered to Swiss citizens for agreeing to the siting of a nuclear repository near their homes.[153] Before an announced monetary reward, approval of this camp was greater than afterward. This crowding-out effect shows that there are moral values and motives that are destroyed by self-interested financial incentives. This applies, for example, to (Nobel) prizes, friendship, children, or even the altruistic motivation for living kidney donation. Altruism, he said, is precisely an increase in utility that, by definition, cannot be monetized. If financial gratification comes into play, this destroys altruism, so that, as a result, the motivation problem of the economic imperialist model cannot be solved.[154] Until the market model of rewarded gifting is tested, such forecasts remain mere speculation. At the very least, the potential power of the crowding-out effect nevertheless calls into question, with some justification, the efficiency and thus the problem-solving competence of even rewarded gifting. Even the supposed push for substitution research is by no means evident. The current immense cost of dialysis is already building considerable pressure to seek alternatives, which would be unlikely to be sustained by the introduction of exchange trading (with supposedly lower overall dialysis costs) (D1). In terms of access conditions to the international market, many countries are eliminated because their health and social systems are far from meeting the requirements. If, for example, a kidney is fifteen times cheaper in one country than in another, the dangers of exploiting market power against people in health and social need also remain. If the question of the social status quo is added, it must be asked how, for example, poor people from poor countries who do not meet the standards could benefit from donor organs at all. There are no answers to the dilemma of such a two-class supply (D2). Humanity's self-image corresponds to that of economic imperialism (D3). If the suppression effect yields results, there would also be no difference in terms of the consequences for the social spirit compared to the consequences of implementing the kidney market in the sense of economic imperialism. The idea may be that "Such actions are intended to remunerate the donor in a subsidiary way, not to serve as the original motivation." But this is where the various motivations become blurred. "In the case of commercially motivated consent, to speak of a donation ... is misguided if that motivation is not altruistic."[155] The fear of the economic displacement of social consciousness thus remains (D4): The "commercialization of blood and donor relationships represses the expression of altruism ... [and] erodes the sense of community!"[156]

The addition of the Christian set of values complements the critical inquiries already outlined here.

- The liberal view of humanity assumed in the economic approaches, according to which humans' bodies belong to them like any ordinary commodity, and the monetarization and tradability of organs thereby inferred fundamentally contradicts the Christian idea of creation. The rewarded gifting approach also competes with the Christian view of humanity, even if, for example, professing Christian Peter Oberender was first concerned with saving human lives. Moreover, to interpret compensation as justifying a good sense of guilt reduction contradicts the view that there can be no price for organs and altruism.
- Becker objects that, from an ethical perspective, organs should not be commodities in return for payment, arguing that this is precisely what has long been practiced in professional armies.[157] So there can be no question of breaking a taboo. Apart from the fact that a taboo that has already been broken cannot be a convincing argument for the breaking of another taboo, it must be countered here that the volunteer soldiers receive pay for their occupational risk and not, for example, as a "mutilation bonus." Otherwise, soldiers would receive piecework pay for each limb they have lost. Instead, soldiers will rescue comrades in danger under enemy fire, for example, not to gain the highest possible bounty for injured body parts but instead to save their comrades' lives. This is a major difference with which Becker's argument must be rejected.
- The supposed strengthening of the protection of life through an increase in kidney transplants is highly questionable due to the deliberate repression of altruism in economic imperialism. A logic of monetization diminishes the spirit of voluntary motivation as moral responsibility before God and before one another. It also has negative consequences for many subsidiary tasks in the areas of social infrastructure (such as care, family, school, etc.).

Consequence and Compass

The compass that follows begins with the question of brain death and offers an evaluation of different models for regulating organ donation. This compass can provide orientation, but there is no ideal solution to the dilemma described by Oberender for drying up the black markets.

- First of all, even from a Christian point of view, the very question of when a person is dead is controversial. According to a definition proposed by Harvard Medical School in 1968, a person is considered dead when there is an irreversible cessation of all functions of the entire brain and an incapacity of the body to holistically organize itself (so-called brain death criterion).[158] On the one hand, there are strong arguments for this definition in the Christian faith. Schockenhoff and Nikolaus Knoepffler, for example, see human personhood as irreversibly lost in brain death.[159] However, it should also be noted that brain-dead mothers have given birth to children (as was the case with the "Erlangen baby").[160] Body temperature regulation continues to function, as does the body's defense against infections. According to neurologist D. Alan Shewmon, for example, the assumption of brain death as a definite indication of human death merely simplifies the legalization of organ removal at the expense of a clean definition of death.[161] Various representatives from medical ethics besides Shewmon adamantly reject such legalistic pragmatics as a criterion of ethical legitimacy because, according to this view, life is killed at the expense of life. A potential rejection of brain death as a safe criterion for human death would need to be followed by a rejection of the now legalized definition of post-mortem organ donation, which would certainly be controversial in view of the already low number of organ transplants in Germany.[162] Physician Axel W. Bauer thus demands:

> The finding that brain death is not the death of the whole human being makes it necessary to inform the citizens comprehensively and not in a manner guided by certain interests. People must be informed of the fact that a "brain dead" person's organs are actually the living organs of a person who is not dead, but only dying—until the organs are removed by surgery, thereby causing the donor's death.[163]

Those who share this view see in the brain death criterion a disregard for the dignity of the human being in death. Whether one accepts or rejects the brain death criterion, in both cases, the question of the moral evaluation of active euthanasia arises in equal measure.
- Opt-out policy: Christians may judge the opt-out policy both positively and negatively. The spirit of social love, as demanded by the churches for coexistence, following Josef Cardinal Höffner, for example, corresponds to a cultivation of recognition for the sacrifice more than that of a mere fulfillment of duty.[164] Loss of freedom and collectivization of the human body weaken the arguments for the opt-out model for followers of the Christian faith. The all-important alleviation of human hardship is likely being bought at a high price. However, a good cause does not justify any means necessary. Moreover, the opt-out policy would in no way solve the shortage of transplants in Germany.

- Club model: A presumed increase in transplants is also dearly bought here. The idea of the body as a collective good is replaced by a private law interpretation, which is not an improvement from a Christian perspective. The consequences for the social spirit fundamentally contradict a Christian idea of coexistence.
- Market models: With the fundamental contradiction to the Christian view of humanity, the trade-off is huge from a Christian vantage point. Therefore, as long as not even the predicted increase in transplants can be demonstrably expected, the Christian judgment must be negative. No ideal solution to the problem could be shown here. The only cause for hope over the long term can be medical progress that renders transplants unnecessary. This is no source of comfort today, and so the discussion is far from over. The goal must be to eliminate the continuing violation of human dignity in the future, even without the price of other violations of dignity. An increase in postmortem unpaid kidney donations can succeed through further intensified education and consistent practice of social virtues in upbringing and education. The basic idea of the opt-in policy, therefore, seems the least evil: Education is the liberal basis for a voluntary, conscious decision to donate organs and stands in opposition to a mentality of suppression. As a result, organ donation is and remains a conscious and socially recognized donation arising from altruistic motivation without financial or similar compensation in this model.

DEATH

After discussing exemplary areas of life and an initial confrontation with the physical limitations of life based on the subject of organ donation, we now turn our attention to the treatment of death and dying in our society. The culture associated with it is meaningful for the prevailing understanding of life as a whole and for the corresponding understanding of human dignity and coexistence. This discussion with the concluding compass is, therefore, a special mirror of good life from the perspective of Christian social ethics.

Human dignity is particularly vulnerable when it comes to the weak, the sick, the needy, and the dying. The majority of people in Germany are in favor of an even further liberalization of so-called euthanasia and thus also of its active variant.[165] Professions of consensual words (such as dignity, justice, etc.) alone or social majorities for certain opinions are not a sufficient criterion for an ethically plausible position. The question of dignity in dying is the subject of a highly emotional debate in society. Dying often means suffering. It always means life. The discussion surrounding a suitable approach to dying was and is being conducted precisely in the dispute about the gradual legalization of euthanasia at the end of life. Media reports show many individual fates that demand the right to self-determination even in death and thus a liberalization of policies concerning euthanasia. This would eliminate the elaborate process of relocating to other countries where active euthanasia is permitted (e.g., Switzerland), which would also make many things much easier. An appropriate Christian response to this challenge is the subject of this section.

Emotions and the Right Measure

Media encounters with personal stories of terminally ill people touch us and challenge us to think about how to concretize the unconditional dignity of humankind in death. Two practical examples will be used to demonstrate this conflict of feelings and develop it into a perspective of responsibility within a Christian-ethical framework. Familiar ethical models can then be discussed to help answer what it means for humans to die with dignity and who can legitimately measure it against what.

First, then, two practical conundrums that may stir and thus challenge emotions.

EXAMPLE 10.1

Here, I think back very personally to an emotional encounter for me from my chaplaincy in the Lower Rhine region of Germany. As a fairly young priest about twenty years ago, I was called to a home visit to anoint a sick patient. The patient's relatives led me into the bedroom. Here, I looked into the eyes of a person who was tied to the bed: His outwardly proliferating cancerous ulcers were covered with cloths. Every few seconds, he moaned loudly. Certainly, it would be possible to help someone in a similar situation today with more effective pain medications. This would undoubtedly be called for. But it was not yet so at the time. And, to this day, I cannot forget these sights, the looks on patients' faces, and their cries. I instantly thought: "Dear God, please save this person from his suffering!" And remembering this encounter, I understand people who think or say: "This cannot be the will of God. Let us put an end to this suffering. We must also actively aid the process if necessary." As a possible Christian reason, charity would come to mind to enable this person to fall asleep peacefully as quickly as possible through the active support of others. That is a strong argument. And I admit that I understand people who have such thoughts out of honest concern and with an honest conscience. . . . And yet, ultimately, I come to a different conclusion in this dilemma.

> **EXAMPLE 10.2**
>
> It was precisely during the contentious phase surrounding the revision of § 217 StGB (concerning assisted suicide) that the personal story of then EKD Council President Nikolaus Schneider was brought to the attention of the general public. The latter had said that he was fundamentally opposed to active euthanasia. However, he would support his wife, who had been diagnosed with cancer, in dying if she—unlike himself—decided to take the step of euthanasia. This statement has earned him a lot of personal recognition. It was used by advocates of the most liberal legislation possible in favor of their demands, but this was not Schneider's intention. Nevertheless, this discussion also caused some Christians to doubt whether, for reasons of freedom or mercy, individuals should decide for themselves when and how they want to die, whether with or without outside assistance.

What might at first touch the heart and sway one to the side of the liberalization proponents with arguments such as charity, mercy, or self-determination is not the only decision-making compass. There must be added reflection on the reasonable grounds for the evaluation and its consequences (for example, for coexistence, etc.). Former constitutional lawyer Ernst-Wolfgang Böckenförde reminded us that the social value compass should always include values given to humans (by God, reason, etc.), in addition to sentiment and majority opinion.[166] For the free, secular state lives on preconditions that it cannot guarantee itself.[167] Such values, which are unavailable to humans and also to democratic majorities, are above all human rights and even more so the justifications of human dignity, which make them an axiomatic decision of eternity and, therefore, do not leave their interpretation to changing majorities.[168] The question of the ethical evaluation of active euthanasia requires an examination of acceptability in addition to acceptance arguments.

Responses of Normative Relativism

(Possible) answers that correspond to the figures of thought of normative relativism first come into view here.[169] Dignity is not an absolute value beyond higher purposes in this case but finds its content and its limits in the respective principle of utility, from which arguments of common good or self-determination can be extrapolated. The question of a culture of dying is also embedded in the context of other right-to-life issues (such as that of the dignity of the unborn, people with disabilities, and others).

The normative individualistic logic of the acquiescence premium can be readily extended to the dying. The costs to be spent on these people could—

from an economic point of view—be invested more efficiently in the healthy or the only temporarily ill. In the case of liberal legislation, social pressure could be built up with reference to the then-existing law to have one's life ended, be it to use the money thus saved for other, supposedly more promising purposes or in order not to steal time from other people and not to be a burden to them.[170]

Consequently, in normative collectivism, people on their deathbeds could also be subjectivized or de-subjectivized, depending on their political sentiments on the one hand and their supposed social usefulness for the collective on the other. It is, therefore, not surprising that the society of the utopians in Thomas More's collectivist order left its aged people to themselves because they supposedly no longer contributed anything (materially) to the collective.[171] The same is found in some early Eskimo cultures.[172]

Human life in the throes of death could be seen with appropriate reasons as less worth living in normative individualist or collectivist perspectives. Normative relativism can thus legitimize a culture of dying that elevates the healthy members of a society above its most vulnerable members and ascribes more dignity to the strong than to the weak. Contemplation of an "inferior" or "unworthy" human life, which was already shown in part II in the basic notion of normative relativism, continues in the view of the culture of dying. The positioning of normative humanism stands in opposition to this.

Response of Normative Humanism

Our view is first directed to Kantian ethics, which provides sound justification for inviolable human dignity. To this end, Kant formulates his categorical imperative, according to which people should neither regard themselves nor any other person solely as a means to an end but always as an end in itself. Autonomy, for Kant, is the highest expression of human freedom to which all people should aspire. However, this is by no means to be confused with the state in which people are able to follow their will (arbitrariness, egoism, inclinations, heteronomy, etc.) without restriction.[173] This kind of freedom, which is nowadays often confused with self-determination, is not what Kant means by freedom. The truly free (autonomous) human being does not simply follow his will but binds himself with his will to the categorical imperatives as an orientation in life and becomes free when "want" and "ought" align in this way. Humans who are free want to do what they ought to do. However, "ought" is not humankind's own creation. It is normatively given to humans through the law of reason. Accordingly, a human expression of will that contradicts the moral law and thus reason cannot be autonomous. In this sense, for example, when evaluating the decision to die, the expressed will of the person concerned may not simply be regarded as legitimate per se. First of all, it must be determined whether this statement was not made under duress, fear, addiction, depression, or the like. In such cases, the demand would not be morally permissible anyway. If none of these restrictions is fulfilled, it is still necessary to distinguish between self-determined decisions that must be considered autonomous (legitimate) and non-autonomous (illegitimate). For humans are not the measure of good in their responsibility for themselves alone but only in their responsible behavior before moral law. This is precisely what constitutes our freedom, which is bound by the moral laws of reason. However, this also means that all humans have a duty to do what the law of reason expects of them, if necessary, also against their own personal interests. Based on his categorical imperative on humankind's end in itself, Kant rejects suicide in principle because it destroys human autonomy.[174]

Kantian logic also facilitates the evaluation of the "Causa Schneider" described in the example. Kant considers a decision legitimate and good if its basic idea could be raised in society to a universal law that is valid for all. Based on this, it is certainly legitimate for people to accompany their spouses in love until the end, even if they make decisions that I myself would not. Such a culture is easily conceivable as a measure of our society. But this does not at all apply to the consequence that a certain form of human life is no longer considered worth living. After all, if I made this logic a general principle, the dam would break. More discussions would likely follow about what type of life is worth living and what type of life is not.

Christian dignity: From a Christian point of view, the dignity of the human being is based on the image of God in every human being, independent of ideas and laws of reason. It is underlined by the incarnation of God in Jesus Christ. Violating this dignity is thus prohibited in principle. From a Christian perspective, this is true from the fusion of the egg and sperm until death.[175] Life is given by God. He is the Lord of life and death.[176] In their responsibility before God, human beings must not arbitrarily destroy the gift of life.[177] Therefore, Christians cannot simply agree with the individualist who says: "What I want is good. And if I want to die, it is therefore good to help me to do so." Those who argue in this way understand freedom as self-determination with no normative objective reference (such as God). Human desire would be the criterion of legitimacy.[178] There is no instance there other than my unbound will when I ask for orientation in my life. This logic of a quasi-sacrosanct self-determination must have been clearly contradicted, not only with Kant but also from a Christian point of view as well. After all, Christians always also share responsibility toward God, the Creator of Jesus Christ. Aware of my responsibility before Him, I question the Bible and tradition: Nowhere here do I find a reference that calls for killing people who are suffering. On the contrary, Jesus gives new life and hope in suffering. Every human being is the image of God: from the beggar to the successful entrepreneur, from the disabled to the able-bodied, from athletes in their prime to those suffering in agony. Nowhere in these Christian sources is there a direct legitimation to extinguish the image of God in a human being. Eberhard Jüngel justifies the clear rejection of any form of active euthanasia resulting from this as follows: "Whoever cannot endure injury to human life cannot, in truth, endure the dignity that man irrevocably has even in the most miserable circumstances of life."[179] If Christians internalize this attitude, then talk of a supposedly undignified life becomes unthinkable, and it leaves the slippery slope of questioning the equal dignity of the lives of people with disabilities, those with serious illnesses, of the unborn, and of the dying. With Jüngel's words in mind, I wholeheartedly agree with the example I mentioned at the beginning of this chapter from my time as a chaplain—despite or precisely because of the suffering that became apparent in the process—and I am glad that today, through hospices and palliative medicine, the physical and psychological suffering inherent to dying can be significantly alleviated compared to back then.

It should also be borne in mind that people may have an important mission when they are dying, which they should not abandon prematurely. One of my experiences clearly illustrates this: In a survey of young adult Christians (ages twenty-five to thirty-five), I wanted to find out what led them to remain true to their faith, despite many inquiries and even though being a Christian was not always popular among their peers.[180] In addition to many expected responses, it was noticeable that several cited their encounters with Christians who were close to them nearing the end of their life, such as their mother, father, or grandmother, as an important reason for doing so. In this most radical of situations, these loved ones who faced death apparently remained firmly committed to their faith, which had a profoundly convincing effect on the young people I surveyed. Because dying is life, people of faith also have a mission in dying. And they often have important information to share.

Consequence and Compass

The discussion here concerning a positive culture of dying exposes the views of humanity and understandings of dignity that are often obscured in expressions of opinion. The slippery slope that can lead toward thoughts and discussions concerning life that is supposedly no longer worth living must be exposed here. A compass for charting the waters of Christian responsibility then offers the following guidance:

- Rejection of any form of active euthanasia.
- Within the historical framework and the Christian understanding of dignity, there must be opposition whenever the strong attempt to raise discretionary power and control over the dignity of others is made, thus making it possible to contemplate human life being unworthy of living in the first place.
- Self-determination of humans must be understood in Christian responsibility before God or in Kantian terms before an obligatory concept of reason. Otherwise, it cannot justify legitimate laws or decisions in terms of such ethics. Self-determination alone, therefore, is not the ultimate measure of good in this sense of normative humanism, nor is it sufficient legitimation for active euthanasia.
- The process of dying should be a celebration of life (for example, in hospices) that facilitates reconciliation with one's own existence, with others, and, if possible, conscious preparation for one's own death in a caring and loving environment.
- An open visiting culture should be a welcome part of everyday life for people in hospice care. Hospice patients should also be able to talk with others about their life and death. Whether family members or medical professionals, the spirit of those who are there to love and care for the sick can spread.
- A culture of love toward the dying (and others in need) radiates out into society and can help counter the progression of anonymity and increasing egoism. This service can be performed by normative humanists with or without any religious confession. Christians cannot simply brush away such behavior without losing their credibility because this would betray their faith and, consequently, the message of Jesus.

NOTES

1. Cf. Shell Deutschland (2010): 18.
2. M. Albert, K. Hurrelmann, G. Quenzel, and TNS Infratest Social Research (2015).
3. Sinus Institute (2018): 20.
4. M. Albert, K. Hurrelmann, G. Quenzel, and TNS Infratest Social Research (2015). According to the survey, 72 percent of young people find it particularly important to live a good family life.
5. On this content, understood as the essence of family, cf., for example, E. Schockenhoff (2008) or the encyclical FC. For an explicit appreciation of a family in which spouses assume responsibility for children who are not their own, reference should be made, for example, to the encyclical FC 15: "However, we must not forget that conjugal life does not lose its value even when the procreation of new life is not

possible. Bodily infertility can be the occasion for spouses to engage in other important services to human life, such as adoption, various forms of educational activity, assistance to other families, to poor or disabled children." On the ideal of permanence and reliability, see also Council of the EKD (2013): 62 (no. 46).

6. It is worth noting in this preference a difference between Catholic and Protestant interpretation that goes beyond the dogmatic question of sacramentality. From the Protestant point of view, this difference consists in the fact that marriage, as a prerequisite of family, claims "sole validity" for Catholics, whereas it claims "maximum validity" for Protestants. Cf. E. Schockenhoff (2008): 294 with reference to W. Pannenberg (1996): 124–31. The Protestant Church does not consider marriage with regard to permanent cohabitation to be the only "good gift of God" but instead one of many. Cf. Council of the EKD (2013): 13, 54. Cf. also ibid.: 60 (no. 44). "The New Testament makes it clear: Cohabitation in marriage and family is important, but it is not the only possible way of life." Analogous to this difference between Catholic and Protestant views is the evaluation of a voluntary (not medically induced) decision by married couples to refrain from having children of their own. In the Catholic view, marriage is not valid if such a decision is made (cf. CIC Can 1096). M. Marquart (1995): 299 arguably replaces this exclusivity with an encouragement to parenthood from an evangelical perspective: "Even if the co-creative mission of the spouses is part of the entelechy of marriage, there may nevertheless be good reasons . . . for deciding not to have (one's own) children in a specific case. Christian-based ethics will usually encourage parenting." The dogmatic discussion about the sacramentality of marriage, which goes far beyond this, is beyond the scope of this chapter. While Catholic dogmatics affirms this, Martin Luther rejected it in his writing "On the Babylonian Captivity of the Church" because it lacked the necessary Words of Institution by Jesus. According to this, marriage is divine institution but of natural order. Cf. on this dogmatic discussion from a Catholic perspective, for example, G. Müller (2010): 757–68, here especially 765 et seq.

7. For an overview of such forms of human cohabitation, see, for instance, E. Schockenhoff (2008): 306–10; for recent questions about marriage between humans and virtual figures, among others, see, for instance, E. Jozuka (2018).

8. T. R. Malthus (1789). For the quotation from Darwin's autobiography, see J. Bauer (2009): 5.

9. C. Darwin (1871): II. XXI. 403.

10. Cf. G. Becker (1981).

11. For a fundamental understanding of acceptability as the basis of normative argumentation, cf. in Part I in the chapter "Sanctification of the World" in the section on socio-ethical efficacy. Precisely because of dogmatic differences on the understanding of marriage, it should be noted that this section primarily takes a Catholic position. Comparisons with the Protestant understanding shall nevertheless be included in these considerations.

12. Cf. in Part I in the chapter "The Search for Good," as well as for discussions with discourse ethics and normative individualism in Part II in the chapter "Ethics beyond Normative Humanism" the sections on normative relativism and on postmodern discourse ethics.

13. In such individualistic justifications, which make egoistic benefit the criterion for the union, a danger is seen precisely to the permanence and reliability which marriage and family are supposed to offer partners and not least their children. Cf. AL 33 et seq.

14. The procedure of such a normative humanistic determination could also be reconstructed secularly—under a premise *"etsi deus non daretur"*—for instance, as Kantian necessity of thinking of reason or as a new-Aristotelian basic human function in the normative humanistic sense along the lines of Amartya Sen, for instance.

15. Cf. S. Belardinelli (2007). Cf. also A. Polaino-Lorente (2007): "Once the term 'traditional family' is sanctioned by the use of language, it becomes much easier to label this type of family as obsolete, as socially meaningless."

16. In his letter AL 58–88, Pope Francis recalls essential principles of the Church's teaching on marriage and the family, highlighting the importance of the encyclical FC in AL 69.

17. FC 17.

18. This could be reconstructed descriptively in a micro-macro model based on J. Coleman (1986), with which a semantic change of social macro phenomena, such as family, can be traced back to changes in individual life practices and their subsequent aggregation.

19. Cf. in detail Part I of the encyclical DCE under the heading "The Unity of Love in Creation and in Salvation History."

20. Cf. E. Schockenhoff (2008): 295.

21. According to AL 11, love in the family is the Holy Spirit. A similar idea can be found in Protestantism. Cf., for example, Council of the EKD (2013): 59 (no. 43). "For the Reformers, too, marriage and family were characterized above all by divine love."

22. Cf. FC 11 with regard to the union of man and woman as a reflection of God's loving act of creation: "This fertility is directed to the generation of a human being, and so by its nature it surpasses the purely biological order and involves a whole series of personal values. For the harmonious growth of these values a persevering and unified contribution by both parents is necessary. The only 'place' in which this self-giving in its whole truth is made possible is marriage, the covenant of conjugal love freely and consciously chosen, whereby man and woman accept the intimate community of life and love willed by God Himself which only in this light manifests its true meaning."

23. E. Schockenhoff (2008): 293. The highlights in the original quote have been deleted. See also AL 13.

24. Cf. ibid.

25. Cf. AL 13. Cf. also on the definition of family—with simultaneous appreciation of a decision to be childless—Council of the EKD (2013): 13: "Its mission is to preserve and transmit life in the many ways it cares for others across generations."

26. E. Schockenhoff (2008): 295. Cf. also FC 15: "In matrimony and in the family a complex of interpersonal relationships is set up—married life, fatherhood and motherhood, filiation and fraternity—through which each human person is introduced into the 'human family' and into the 'family of God,' which is the Church."

27. Members of the classical family should strengthen one another in faith, even in times of doubt. At the same time, the family acts as missionary of love within society. Cf., for example, FC 17: "Hence the family has the mission to guard, reveal and communicate love, and this is a living reflection of and a real sharing in God's love for humanity."

28. Cf., for example, CCC 2207 et seqq. and LS 214. Cf. also FC 42: "The family has vital and organic links with society, since it is its foundation and nourishes it continually through its role of service to life: It is from the family that citizens come to birth and it is within the family that they find the first school of the social virtues that are the animating principle of the existence and development of society itself." Cf. also AL 52: "No one can think that the weakening of the family as that natural society founded on marriage will prove beneficial to society as a whole. The contrary is true: It poses a threat to the mature growth of individuals, the cultivation of community values and the moral progress of cities and countries."

29. Cf. GS 52, FC 21.

30. Cf. LS 214.

31. Cf. AL 17 and FC 36: "The task of giving education is rooted in the primary vocation of married couples to participate in God's creative activity: By begetting in love and for love a new person who has within himself or herself the vocation to growth and development, parents by that very fact take on the task of helping that person effectively to live a fully human life."

32. FC 21.

33. Central Committee of German Catholics (2015).

34. *Chistlich Demokratische Arbeitnehmerschaft* (CDA) (2015): 13.

35. Cf. M. Heimbach-Steins (2015). This perspective is not aimed at questioning biological gender as a mere social construct. This distinguishes this feminist gender theology from radical deconstruction theories, such as that proposed by J. Butler (1990), where biological gender is also deconstructed, thus further hampering a feminist line of argument. S. Vaaßen (2010): 9 cites the GenderKompetenzZentrum in 2006 in this regard, noting, however, that the following quote has since been deleted from the respective Internet source: "Humans are born with biological traits that fall along a spectrum between male and female. . . . After birth, people are divided into two categories on this basis: girls or boys. This in some ways arbitrary determination of 'biological gender' (sex) also determines social behavior expectations in most societies."

36. Cf. the discussion of identity in French feminism. For a concise yet insightful overview, see C. Breger (2013): 62–65. From a theological standpoint, Aurelius Augustinus had already refuted this view in his City of God Chapter XXII, 17. Cf. Aurelius Augustinus (ed. 2008).

37. One ethological perspective concerns behavioral research.

38. Cf. on the attempted deconstruction of natural law M. Heimbach-Steins (2015): 12.

39. M. Heimbach-Steins (2015): 7 citing G. Marschütz (2014): 432.

40. Cf. the section on postmodern discourse ethics in the chapter "Ethics beyond Normative Humanism" in Part II.

41. M. Heimbach-Steins (2015): 13.

42. C. Breger (2013): 73 calls this "the partially analogous rejection of postmodern discourse theory."

43. Cf. M. Heimbach-Steins (2015): 14.

44. Cf. ibid.: 14 et seq.

45. See, for example, AL 56 with references to synodal passages of *Relatio finalis* 2015: "Yet another challenge is posed by the various forms of an ideology of gender that 'denies the difference and reciprocity in nature of a man and a woman and envisages a society without sexual differences, thereby eliminating the anthropological basis of the family.' It is a source of concern that some ideologies of this sort, which seek to respond to what are at times understandable aspirations, manage to assert themselves as absolute and unquestionable, even dictating how children should be raised. It needs to be emphasized that 'biological sex and the socio-cultural role of sex (gender) can be distinguished but not separated.'" Pope Francis goes even further in his critique. During an address in Tbilisi, he is quoted by Vatican Radio as follows: "A great enemy of marriage today is the theory of gender. Today, there is a global war trying to destroy marriage, not with weapons, but with ideas. This is why we have to defend ourselves from ideological colonization." Cf. *sine nomine* (2016). By marriage, Francis is referring to the sacramental covenant between a man and a woman in the classical sense. Cf. ibid.: "'Marriage is the most beautiful thing that God has created.' According to Genesis, in marriage, man and woman become one flesh, 'the image of God.'"

46. In the 2016 *Einheitsübersetzung*, a German translation of the Bible for liturgical use in Roman Catholic worship, "male" and "female" are translated more grammatically precisely according to the Hebrew text without prejudice to Adam having been created as a man and Eve having been created as a woman.

47. Cf. Congregation for Catholic Education (2019). Based on this, gender perspective is an ideology that "denies the difference and reciprocity in nature of a man and a woman and envisages a society without sexual differences, thereby eliminating the anthropological basis of the family."

48. Cf. in Part I in the chapter "Sanctification of the World" in the section on the objective good and its realization.

49. Cf. AL 36.

50. Cf. in Part I in the chapter "Sanctification of the World" in the section on the objective good and its realization.

51. Once again, the difference in denominational understanding should be pointed out. According to the classical Catholic view, marriage is the sole condition for the family; according to the Protestant view, it is the best condition.

52. Where today, for example, the Church or theology refer to homosexual partnerships with adopted children as families, the classical understanding has, therefore, been replaced by a new one.

53. Conversely, in an evaluative comparison of life forms, even in concrete practice, problematic classical families may not be compared with exemplary non-classical forms in order to infer superiority of non-classical forms.

54. E. Schockenhoff (2008): 305 with reference to Federal Constitutional Court decision (*BVerfGE*) 76, 1 (51).
55. Cf. AL 53.
56. The broad agreement of such gender with gender justice, which does not reject social difference, can still be found, for example, in P. Herre (2003). See, for instance, S. Vaaßen (2010): 16: "However, rigorously ignoring the biological perspective on men and women, in view of the fact that invoking physiognomic differences has been used in the past to justify social hierarchies in the gender order, does not necessarily promote the creation of equality or the abolition of role stereotype, because ultimately any other mechanisms can be used to stage and legitimize the oppression of one gender."
57. See the section on digitalization in the chapter "Future Issues" further in Part III.
58. Cf. Compendium: 207 et seqq.
59. O. von Nell-Breuning (1985): 36.
60. J. Höffner (1962/1997): 159.
61. LE 6.
62. Cf. LE 9.
63. Cf. LE 4, 25.
64. Cf. preface to LE.
65. Cf. GS 34.
66. Cf. J. Höffner (1962/1997): 144.
67. Cf. O. von Nell-Breuning (1985): 54 et seqq. and 1 Cor 12:12–27.
68. Cf. Col 3:17.
69. QA 137.
70. LE 27. Cf. Gen 3:17b.
71. Cf. J. Höffner (1962/1997): 147 et seq., Compendium: 263.
72. See, for example, J. Höffner (1962/1997): 130: "It is misleading to read the third chapter of Genesis as a curse on labor, misleading to such a high degree that even speaking this way should be avoided; for the curse did not affect the labor of humans, but the soil on which they toiled. Hardship is not a curse but an atonement. Christians who bear afflictions may repeat the words of Paul: 'I am now rejoicing in my sufferings for your sake, and in my flesh I am completing what is lacking in Christ's afflictions for the sake of His body, that is, the Church' (Col 1:24)."
73. LE 27. For the ecumenical discussion on the relevance of human activity for salvation, see the corresponding chapter in Part I.
74. Cf. Rom 8:21.
75. Cf. Compendium: 202.
76. Cf. ibid.: 204.
77. Cf. Eph 4:28.
78. LE 10.
79. Cf. P. Van Parijs (2001).
80. Cf. Mt 13:55; 25:14 et seqq.
81. Cf. STh II–II, 35,1.
82. 2 Thess 3:10.
83. LE 16.

84. Cf. LE 10, 25.
85. LE 9. Cf. Lk 9:25.
86. Cf. U. Kropač (2019): 15.
87. See, for example, in Part III, in the chapter "Creation, Justice, and Peace," the section on social justice, and, in the chapter "Economy and Economic Order," the section on the social market economy.
88. Cf. U. Kropač (2019): 202–5.
89. Cf. the chapter "The Search for Good" in Part I. Kant's concept of autonomy as a prerequisite for the transcendental knowledge of the objective good is also related to this. For there, too, overcoming egoism opens up autonomous knowledge of the categorical imperatives as necessities of reason. Cf. in Part I in the chapter "Normative Humanism beyond Theology" in the section on Immanuel Kant.
90. Cf. U. Kropač (2019): 202, 216.
91. W. Klafki (2007): 19 et seq.
92. Cf. U. Kropač (2019): 206.
93. Cf. U. Kropač (2019): 209.
94. R. Englert (2003): 22 et seq.
95. Cf. U. Kropač (2019): 219 et seq., 226.
96. Cf. ibid.: 215 et seq.
97. Cf. ibid.: 205.
98. Apparently, these personality traits often lead to success. Cf. T. Kuhn and J. Weibler (2012a), U. Kropač (2019): 214, and further in Part III in the chapter "Leadership and Organizational Culture" in the section on the compass of good leadership.
99. Cf. Shell Deutschland (2019).
100. J. Weimann (2001): 40. Cf. on the idea of normative economics based on this in Part II, in the chapter "Ethics beyond Normative Humanism," in the section on normative relativism. For the controversial discussion about the also normative HO assumption and its evaluation from the perspective of Christian social ethics, cf. further in Part III in the chapter "Economy and Economic Order" in the section on rethinking economic ethics.
101. Cf. Shell Deutschland (2002): 31 et seq.
102. K. Hurrelmann (2001).
103. T. Gensicke (2010): 224.
104. Ibid.: 198.
105. Shell Deutschland (2010).
106. Cf. T. Gensicke (2010): 196–202 (cited here: 198).
107. Cf. ibid.: 210, 222–26.
108. Cf. in Part II in the chapter "Ethics beyond Normative Humanism" in the section on normative relativism as well as further in Part III in the chapter "Economy and Economic Order" in the section on the compass for the market.
109. Cf. a corresponding application in leadership ethics in the section on the compass of good leadership in Part III in the chapter "Leadership and Organizational Culture."

110. Cf. in Part II in the chapter "Ethics beyond Normative Humanism" in the section on normative relativism.
111. Cf. U. Kropač (2019): 209.
112. Cf. ibid.: 206, 227.
113. Cf. W. P. Eckert (1967).
114. Cf. ibid.
115. H. Schlögel (1998) with reference to: Council of the EKD and DBK (1997): 21.
116. Cf. R. Englert (2003): 24, 27.
117. Cf. Ibid.: 23.
118. Cf. U. Kropač (2019): 222.
119. Cf. the approach of C. Taylor (2009) and the comments on it in Part II in the chapter "Normative Humanism beyond Theology" in the section on phenomenological humanism.
120. Cf. Statista (2022), ibid. (2022a).
121. Cf. Eurotransplant (2022).
122. This includes the following countries: Croatia, Slovenia, Hungary, Austria, Germany, and Benelux. The allocation of postmortem donor organs in this network is carried out with a transparent points system according to the criteria of need and the expectation that the donor organ will be accepted by the recipient's body.
123. Cf. Eurotransplant (2022).
124. On the brain death criterion, see the section on death in this chapter.
125. Cf. Eurotransplant (2022).
126. Cf. G. S. Becker and J. J. Elias (2006): 3–24.
127. Such transactions with euthanasia "could occur for example when, in order to increase the availability of organs for transplants, organs are removed without respecting objective and adequate criteria which verify the death of the donor," John Paul II wrote in his encyclical EV: 15. Cf. also Benedict XVI (2008). On the death requirement for legitimate organ donation, cf. Compendium: 476. On the crimes against detainees, which were only legally condemned by the Chinese government in August 2013, see IGFM (2012). According to the 2012 WHO report, by then, the international black market was supplied with about 10,000 transplants from live harvests annually, mainly from China.
128. Cf. *sine nomine* (2012). Paid, live organ harvesting is only legal in Iran.
129. Accordingly, even with consent, interventions that led to mutilation, paralysis, and so on, such as the removal of eyes, were prohibited.
130. The Amendment to the Law on Transplantation (*Gesetz zur Änderung des Transplantationsgesetzes*) has also been in force since November 1, 2012. In addition to the legally prescribed compliance with EU quality standards, it also requires the relevant centers to hire transplant officers.
131. C. Schmergal (2011) citing Peter Oberender.
132. Cf. M. J. Sandel (2012). "D" stands for dimension.
133. Beyond an explicitly Christian argument, as an analogous objection J. Beckmann (2012): 127 postulated: "The being of the body is detached from its

subject-boundness, it becomes a pure thing over which the subject can then freely dispose as with personal property."

134. Cf. E. Schockenhoff (2013): 425.

135. Cf. M. Lintner (2007): 73, F. Böckle (1989): 155 et seq. along with the explanations on this in Part I in the chapter "Sanctification of the World" in the section on the essential content of the good.

136. Cf., for instance, a parallel in Islamic thought, which A. Izetbegović (2014): 296 does not see in this way when, with recourse to Sura 2:286, he asserts this idea in contrast to Christianity as a special characteristic of Islam: "Humans cannot be Christians because 'God does not impose on any soul more than it is capable of.'"

137. Cf. E. Schockenhoff (2013): 403–39.

138. The information policy deems the absence of an objection by the deceased to be passive consent.

139. Cf. F. Breyer and H. Kliemt (1995), M. Tietzel (2001): 159–71.

140. According to the QALY criterion, the quality of life still to be expected is compared (in years and the degree of quality).

141. F. Breyer and H. Kliemt (1995): 137.

142. Cf. M. Lintner (2007). Such regulations have only been legalized in Iran but no longer in India and Pakistan.

143. P. Oberender and T. Rudolf (2003): 24.

144. M. Beutin (2013): 199.

145. Cf. G. S. Becker and J. J. Elias (2006).

146. G. S. Becker and J. J. Elias (2006): 3.

147. Cf. G. S. Becker and J. J. Elias (2006): 12, which, for this calculation, follows the model of W. K. Viscusi and J. E. Aldy (2003): 18–24.

148. Cf. M. Beutin (2013): 192–200.

149. P. Oberender and T. Rudolf (2003): 13 points out that about 80 percent of donors of live removals for money legally performed in India in the 1990s regret their decision. The reason for this, he said, is not the payment received but primarily the lack of medical follow-up care. A paucity of information takes care of the rest.

150. K. Arrow (1972): 355.

151. S. Satel (2006).

152. This unsolved problem of modern market economies is recognized even by representatives of economic ethics like K. Homann (1993): 1294 in that "in modern market economies, more and more social relations are being transformed into monetized market relations, which erodes the emotional core of society, which is indispensable."

153. The study by B. Frey and R. Jegen (2001): 590 is used as the basis for this.

154. Cf. B. Broumand (1997): 9.

155. D. Witschen (2005): 285.

156. R. Titmuss (1971): 277.

157. Cf. G. Becker and J. Elias (2006).

158. Found in N. Knoepffler (2018): 10.

159. See, for example, E. Schockenhoff (2013): 405–23, N. Knoepffler (2018): 23.

160. In contrast to the case in Erlangen (Germany) in 1992, it has now been possible on several occasions for the child not only to survive in the womb of the brain-dead mother but also to be born alive. See, for example, C. Berndt (2013).

161. Cf. D. A. Shewmon (2009).

162. This is the conclusion drawn by P. A. Byrne, C. G. Coimbra, R. Spaemann, and M. A. Wilson (2005) in a statement signed by fifteen participants of a meeting of the Pontifical Academy of Sciences. Thesis 13 reads: "The termination of one innocent life in pursuit of saving another, as in the case of the transplantation of unpaired vital organs, does not mitigate the evil of taking an innocent human life. Evil may not be done that good might come of it."

163. A. W. Bauer (2012): 15.

164. Cf. D. Witschen (2005).

165. Cf., for example, Statista (2017). Being a euphemism, the term euthanasia is not without controversy.

166. For a discussion of such normative axiomatics in the sense of Böckenförde, see in Part I the section on ethics beyond normative humanism.

167. Cf. E.-W. Böckenförde (1992).

168. See also E.-W. Böckenförde (2003).

169. See the section on normative relativism in the chapter "Ethics beyond Normative Humanism" in Part II.

170. On euthanasia on-demand in the Netherlands after the liberalization of the law in 2001 and an exploration of possible motives for the desire to kill on demand, see M. Alsheimer and B. Augustyn (2006): 8. According to this study, the concern of being a burden on others was still a reason for 13 percent of those who wanted to be euthanized on demand. Ingo Habenicht warns that such an attitude could also be attributed to social pressure.

171. Cf. T. More (2006).

172. Cf. *sine nomine* (2004).

173. Cf. I. Kant AK V, 33: *Critique of Practical Reason*, ibid. AK IV, 426: *Groundwork for the Metaphysics of Morals*, as well as the remarks on the autonomous knowledge of reason in the categorical imperatives in Part II in the chapter "Normative Humanism beyond Theology" in the section on Immanuel Kant.

174. See, for example, J. Heinle (2017): "Thus it becomes clear why suicide is a problem in terms of Kant's ethics. For with the act of suicide man destroys that which makes him a self-determined being of reason, namely his autonomy, which enables him to conceive of himself as a being of freedom and to act out of this freedom. But precisely these actions borne out of freedom mean, according to Kant, that man cannot simply do as he pleases, but must also impose certain limits on his own actions (self-legislation)."

175. In the field of theology, the discussion about the question of the beginning and end of life is not the subject of social ethics but primarily of moral theology. Thomas Aquinas still assumed that one could only speak of a human being in the womb after ensoulment. This view is outdated. The Catholic Church assumes the moment of fusion of egg and sperm cell as the beginning of human life. This not uncontroversial moral-theological position is not simply asserted dogmatically but is

justified with biological arguments on both the Catholic and Protestant sides. Cf. for this M. Hollerbach (2011): Eberhard Schockenhoff thus views the topic with regard to the embryo in this way: "[The embryo] is human, and with the completion of fertilization develops in its own way. It does not develop gradually but is given with the fusion of the maternal and paternal gametes. . . . If one were to describe this in today's terms, one would note that the Catholic Church does not bind its doctrinal proclamation to philosophical concepts, but rather it says that from the very beginning the human embryo is owed the same respect given to human beings per se, that a gradation of the fundamental rights of being human is therefore not permissible." This position is criticized for reducing personhood to the mere presence of genes. Friedrich Hauschildt counters from a Protestant perspective: "Now the difficult problem emerges: Is there a transition from one stage to another that justifies saying: Before this moment there is no human life, after this moment there is human life. If you look at the stages of development, then you come to the realization that the really clear moment of delineation is fertilization." Cf. also on this subject M. Hollerbach (2011). The discussion about when a person is dead is controversial even among Christians. The brain death criterion, as briefly touched upon earlier in this chapter in the preceding section on organ donation, is a possible but also criticized definition.

176. See, for example, Pope John Paul II in his encyclical EV 53: "God proclaims that He is absolute Lord of the life of man, who is formed in His image and likeness (cf. Gen 1:26–28)." This close relationship highlights that human life deserves special protection on its own merits.

177. Self-defense in exceptional situations is a special case in this regard, which was discussed in the example of the so-called just war in the chapter "Creation, Justice, and Peace" in the section "Just War—Just Peace." Criteria were mentioned there that, under very strict conditions, can also morally permit violence and possibly even killing in self-defense or in defensive warfare, even if killing another human being always remains evil. Two major differences should be mentioned here as to why there are different moral evaluations of suicide (or assisted suicide) on the one hand and such instances of killing in self-defense on the other: 1.) Violent acts committed in self-defense in exceptional situations under such strict conditions are directed against someone who is guilty and who is considered to be a danger (possibly for an entire order). E. Schockenhoff (2013): 270 explains it this way: "Invariably, we are dealing with threat scenarios in which an individual or an adversarial collective poses a mortal danger to others that they do not have to simply accept without responding." One may assume that cases of assisted suicide do not pose such a threat. 2.) Giving permission to kill in the sense of an assisted suicide opens the door to discussions on a life not worth living. This is not the case in instances of self-defense because committing violence against or even killing an aggressor does not simply allow such a conclusion. The act of killing remains a *malum* even in this case because even the life of the aggressor does not lose its value.

178. E. Schockenhoff (2013): 49 points out that the introduction of necessary consent as a decisive criterion of legitimacy has led to a fundamental upending of the content of ethical principles. The principle of non-violence against innocent people is now interpreted in such a way that a disregard for free will is to be understood as

violence and is therefore forbidden. The consequence contradicts what was originally intended: "Prohibiting violence . . . now equally secures unfettered access to mind-altering drugs and pornography as it does the free right to abortion, suicide and euthanasia for all citizens."

179. E. Jüngel (1997): 34.

180. Cf. E. Nass (2012): 63 et seqq. as well as some of the quotes in Part I in the chapter "Mission in Crisis" in the section on responses to crisis phenomena.

Chapter Eleven

Economy and Economic Order

In society, the main area of application of social ethics is the economy. Here, for example, the economic behavior of individuals (micro level), of companies (meso level), and the choice and design of the economic order, including the associated rules, are viewed through an ethical lens. In the discussion needed to address this subject, Christian social ethics does not claim to take the place of business administrators, economists, or economic policymakers themselves. However, with its values, it offers a compass for navigating some fundamental economic decisions, concrete dilemmas, and economic debates related to questions surrounding topics such as dignity, creation, justice, and freedom. The Christian economic ethics perspective presented in this chapter concerns itself with providing such guidance. Following a brief outline of the systematics of economic ethics, compasses on the choice of property and economic systems (fundamental issues), on the monetary and financial crisis (concrete dilemma), and, finally, on recent challenges in behavioral economics (science) are selected for this purpose.

COMPASS FOR THE MARKET

Economic Ethics as Communication

As a dialog-driven communication program, economic ethics synthesizes the language games of ethics and economics. Applying economic ethics thus enables us to make decisions after understanding and weighing the arguments of both sides. Different forms of market economy are practiced in Western culture. With this in mind, the following section assumes a market economy context when introducing a system of economic ethics. In the course of this chapter, however, we will question such positing, with a view toward property and economic systems, for instance.

So, the first question concerns the profile of economic ethics in the context of the market: When, for example, questions concerning efficient research funding or a fair income tax rate are discussed in socio-ethical terms, the economist and the (social) ethicist, as protagonists of their respective disciplines, must communicate with each other in a way that facilitates mutual understanding and ultimately arrive at an economically appropriate normative judgment. That is: Economic ethics makes it possible to address economic issues by ethical means and to address ethical issues by economic means. A theory of economic ethics must then clarify, in a mutually comprehensible way, what is meant by efficiency, justice, or human dignity for the macro, meso, and micro levels of the economy so that the disciplines do not talk at cross purposes. Economic ethics brings ethics and economics together in an understanding way. The content of this communication interest is revealed by a fundamental comparison of the two language games. Ethics is thus fundamentally concerned with the question of the good, as presented at the beginning of part I. The basic economic perspective must now be outlined in order to extract the corresponding economic ethics communication program from it.

So now, let us look at the basic economic concern in the context of a market economy: "Economics is the science of the use of scarce resources by society to produce valuable economic goods and of the distribution of those goods among its members."[1] Three market-based perspectives are briefly presented here: Pareto efficiency, price mechanism, and the HO heuristic.

- Economic logic is fundamentally about (Pareto) efficiency and thus about the appropriate allocation of scarce goods. The use of scarce resources is considered pareto-superior[2] and thus normatively desirable if the transition from one state of distribution of scarce resources (labor, machinery, land, capital, etc.) to another makes at least one member of society better off without making any other member worse off. Starting from any status quo of allocations, there are usually countless uniquely efficient or inefficient states vis-à-vis this state.[3] A state is pareto-optimal if there is no efficient distribution with respect to it (as status quo). According to the logic of efficiency, a pareto-superior allocation is always preferable. This avoids wasting scarce resources and is an ethically desirable result—an ethics of efficiency, so to speak. Misallocations waste scarce resources and are immoral.
- Economic logic offers other ethically relevant aspects: From a market economy perspective, the price basically ensures that the market is cleared and interventions in the distribution results of the market must be well

justified by the welfare state. The market can be understood as a game with clear rules and with arbitrators (such as the antitrust office) who are entrusted with ensuring that the market functions properly. Unprofitable businesses disappear from the market. Competition motivates market operators to offer better quality at a lower price. Consumers benefit from this. These improvements would then make up the consumer surplus. Reallocations are designed to serve the market, to external effects, for example. Perfect competition is an ideal model in this context. Functioning competition increases consumer surplus compared to a monopoly economy. These welfare effects are also undoubtedly ethically desirable outcomes.
- The market economy assumes that market players will behave as egoistic utility maximizers. All other things being equal, from an economically rational standpoint, a state with more money in one's pocket is always preferred. This is the simple logic of *Homo economicus* (HO). As a rule, HO should not be understood as an economic conception of humankind but rather as a heuristic that is far removed from reality. Human behavior in the market can be more easily analyzed and predicted with the heuristic HO assumption. The more consistently people in the market behave in accordance with this logic, the more accurate the economic forecasts of supply and demand behavior will be, for example, in relation to the consequences of price changes, interest rate policy, and so on. As from an invisible hand, the aggregated individual decisions of the many HOs should result in the satisfaction of the collective preference of society. Aggregated egoism thus enhances the common good, according to another ethically based liberal assumption. The assumption of the HO is initially a description without normative content. It does not necessarily always correspond to the real behavior of the people in the market. Because in the concrete reality of life, preferences other than economically rational ones are always incorporated into human decision-making, even in the market. Taking these into account in economic models and forecasts would make them more realistic but also more complex.[4] The dilemma between the simplicity of the model and its lack of realism may lead to the conclusion that the pragmatic instrument of the HO should be used as a normative tool to demand that people actually behave as rational HOs in the market in order to improve the accuracy of forecasts and to be able to (re)act with prices, incentives, and other market instruments with the aim of achieving desired allocations. But this would already be the step from economic science to economic ethics, which can be found, for instance, in the normative individualism discussed in part II. It can, therefore, be stated as the following: Economics in the context of a market economy considers the efficiency achieved by the form of order, rules, and individual and aggregated human behavior of selfish utility

maximizers under market conditions. From both a business and an economic perspective, the goal of economic efficiency demands that everyone involved and, as a result, the rules they set conform to market requirements provided that economic rationality is achieved with normatively desirable consequences for allocation, prosperity, and the common good.

Bringing together the concerns and language games of ethics and economics is the declared goal of economic ethics. This combines the search for good and the search for efficiency in the field of economics. To this end, a corresponding approach to economic ethics (as a position of acceptability) must first disclose its value basis with the concept of human dignity and responsibility in a semantically rich way. Within a communication program, it must answer the question on this basis as to what (possibly hierarchical) relationship there is between the goals of service to humanity and economic efficiency that is understandable for the essential language games of ethics and economics alike.[5] The fundamental response of economic ethics to the coexistence of these two essential goals should be applied to concrete normative questions in the context of a market economy:

- at the macro level, for example, to the question of a just and efficient economic order,
- at the meso level, for example, to the question of fair and efficient pay for managers in the company, and
- at the micro level, for example, to the question of fair and efficient individual consumption behavior.

Any economic ethics in a market economy context must deal with the laws and ethical consequences of efficiency. Economic ethics thus places economic findings in a normative framework that measures the ethical legitimacy of economic efficiency by the extent to which it can increase the well-being of those concerned. This assessment is based on a conception of humans and their well-being that is controversial in an ideologically pluralistic society. This is why different approaches to economic ethics compete with each other.

Systematics of Economic Ethics

Three schools of economic ethics are based on three different ethical concepts, which differ fundamentally in terms of values.[6] The economic approach (Karl Homann et al.) argues in a normatively individualistic way: According to this, what is legitimate is what is derived from the selfish interests of individuals. The integrative approach (Peter Ulrich et al.) provides a discourse ethics framework with a hint of Kantianism. According to this, what is legitimate is what is well-founded based on human duties toward the outcomes of discourse. The metaphysical approach, to which the Christian positioning represented here belongs, argues theonomically (i.e., in responsibility before God). According to this—as was pointed out in part I—what is legitimate is what can be derived from a transcendental divine command. Here the doctrine founded in Jesus Christ is at the beginning of ethics. In other religions, these are different sources with reference to transcendence.[7]

Integrative and metaphysical approaches to economic ethics differ fundamentally in their evaluation of economics. This is already evident in the hierarchical relationship between economy and service to humanity. In the words of Peter Ulrich, "doing business means creating value." He calls for imbuing business with a sense of service for the benefit of morally determined goods.[8] This is because the values he is referring to cannot be measured in monetary terms. Swiss-Dominican Arthur F. Utz went even further in this respect, arguing that he believes economy is "the totality of those acts by which man utilizes material goods to meet his needs for life and culture."[9] Compared to Ulrich, the goods in the service of which economic activity should be directed are even more concretely oriented toward the goal of human development. Economic efficiency is understood as a benefit earned from service to humanity. According to this view, the economy and the market as an instrument are part of the social culture, which is designed to serve people in developing a holistic destiny, which Christian metaphysicists believe to be ordained by God. Here one might fear a paternalism of ethics over the economy. So Homann and his students offer a different argument. In their understanding of economic ethics, they are fundamentally concerned with practicing ethics under the conditions of the economy and translating their values into the language of economics, upending the hierarchy in the process. In the market context, service to humanity should be the consequence of economic efficiency.

Depending on the approach of economic ethics, the concept of humanity and human dignity is also associated with a social idea of human coexistence. In the economic approach, the moral order of anonymous coexistence is proposed, in the integrative approach, a politically dominated discourse community.[10] In the Christian approach, this is the ideal of affective cooperation. Application references are, for example, also questions regarding the just and efficient market, which should, therefore, be humane and economical. This includes the justification of state social transfers, the semantics of social justice already discussed above, but also the question of why, whether, and in which places individual virtue is desired in the market:[11] in the rules, in individual moves, or the like? The following economic ethics system can now be presented based on such considerations regarding the connection between values and concretization:

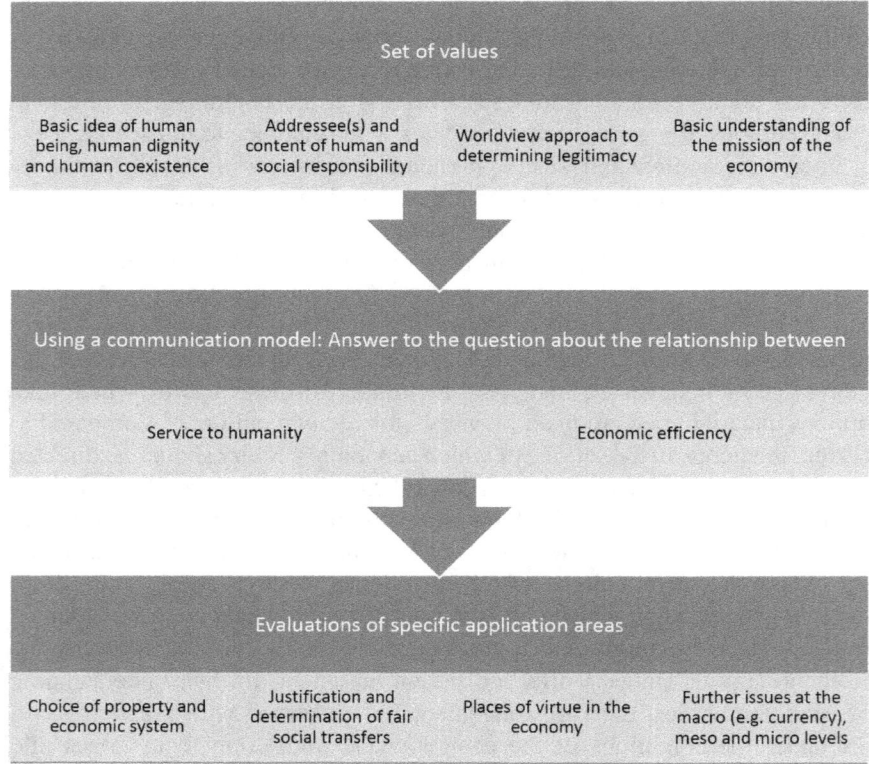

Figure 11.1. Economic Ethics System. *Source*: E. Nass (2018), *Handbuch Führungsethik, Vol. I: Systematik und maßgebliche Denkrichtungen* (Stuttgart: Kohlhammer), 71.

Main Features of Christian Economic Ethics

There has been no coherent approach to Christian economic ethics so far that one might consider representative. Too many heterogeneous attempts and approaches exist. Depending on preference, reasoning can have more neo-socialist or discourse-ethical, sometimes Kantian, sometimes biblical or natural law-Aristotelian, or even liberal leanings. This diversity analogously reflects the heterogeneity in the landscape of secular ethics. Many of the approaches are not primarily shaped by their core area, the theological foundation, and teachings of Jesus Christ but rather by their compelling references to external secular models.[12] In contrast, the present volume attempts to offer a substantial positioning to outline the metaphysically based economic ethics explicitly rooted in Christianity, thereby providing a recognizable alternative to the influential metaphysics-free models of liberal or discourse ethics. The approaches of Christian social ethics that are alien to theology are thus put aside to find an anchor in an ecumenically consensual idea of normative humanism and thus of service to humanity understood in this way.

What is appropriately presupposed for this in the sense of the Christian mission in the world (part I): Christian economic ethics—like its alternatives—should disclose its ethical rationale, which, in the approach advocated here, ultimately derives from the biblical teachings of Jesus Christ. Thus, it is metaphysically transcendent. As normative humanism, it is based in theonomy and, therefore, on the assumption that the good and the just have their origin in God. The normative starting point of Christian economic ethics understood in this way is the anthropology of the Christian view of humanity outlined in part I. There is a solid rationale for the unconditional rights of every human being to develop in a spirit of creativity and community not as the result of human self-designs, discourse, or construction but instead based on the equal dignity of every human being as a person in the image and incarnation of God. This should absolutely frame the logic of the market. Personhood understood in this way determines the Christian humanum as a normative prediscursive criterion, which—to say it again in the sense of Ernst-Wolfgang Böckenförde—even democratic society cannot produce from itself.[13]

This form of Christian economic ethics is initially to be thought of in a similar way to the integrative approach on an anthropological level with the aim of returning to an economic philosophy in line with Adam Smith.[14] The discourse is not the objectified instrument for a postmodern creative shaping of social values and principles. Rather, a metaphysically based idea of humankind—the humanum—in God—must be presupposed in order to avoid possible relativizations of human dignity in the results of the discourse.[15] Arthur Rich, for example, translates this humanum as a normative regulative of the economic-ethical dialog of the disciplines of ethics and economics into the criteria of relationality, participation, and co-humanity.[16] Rich demands defining the content of human justice (or the humanum) as a relationship between freedom and solidarity[17] as a "pre-scientific-prescriptive" or prediscursive benchmark for an economically legitimized decision. Consequently, where in discourse the substance of humanity is violated, its results are illegitimate. The humanum, as the substantive framework of the legitimate dialogue between the disciplines of ethics and economics, confronts the assumed dangers of mere procedural ethics, freedom from random valuation, and market Darwinism. The unconditionality of this transcendental rationale for a (humane and) just society and thus the primacy of this idea of service to humanity is ecumenical consensus.[18]

As in Ulrich's integrative approach, the HO heuristic is replaced by an anthropological presupposition that—like Smith—assumes a complex dualism of human rationalities. The ethical counterpart of the economically egoistic rationality for the inner-human dialogue is anthropologically justified. The inner HO need not be killed. In fact, HO represents the economic ratio even with certain ethical relevance because efficiency prevents the immoral waste of scarce resources. This is now countered by an independent ethical reason—as was anticipated in the sympathy of Smith and developed further by Ulrich. What is meant by this is an inner human spirit of social love as an affective social-moral basic attitude, which is based on and includes being loved by God. This means more than mere altruism, perhaps even an action that lessens one's own benefit, as Amartya Sen argues.[19] That is: Unlike in economic imperialism and in economic ethics, rational decisions of humans in the market that may even reduce utility are conceivable and ethically permissible.

EXAMPLE 11.1

A bakery that must survive in the marketplace makes good profits. Let us assume that a potential unskilled employee, who would otherwise have no chance of success in the labor market due to his mental capacity, submits an unsolicited application. When based purely on egoistic rational considerations, it is unlikely that the bakery will hire him because the applicant will cost the bakery more than he brings in. This would unnecessarily lower the profit. Even if the manager has no altruistic motives, according to Sen, it might still be rational for her to hire the applicant out of a mere sense of duty that imposes on her inwardly to help the vulnerable. Then this decision is not to be reinterpreted in an altruistic way because the manager's actions after the decision are not based on the consideration of the candidate's well-being but solely on the fact that she is fulfilling a duty. Such a deontological motivation enables legitimate decisions beyond egoism and altruism because the responsibility toward a duty is the guiding principle.

Sens's consideration is compatible with both Kantian and Christian economic ethics. Social love, feelings, and duty are to be considered as non-economically reducible motives of rational decision. The communication with the economic-egoistic rationality of humankind is possible because both rationalities originate from a—God-given—human nature. This presupposes the primacy of ethical reason.[20] At the end of the inner dialogue—in analogy to Kant and Smith—the final safeguard of economic-ethical legitimacy is the substantive review of the decision by an objective authority. This is the Christian humanum understood here. Theoretically, however, this test could even be omitted under an ideally realized primacy of ethical reason. The Bible and history teach, however, that this is not how people are.

If people understand themselves collectively as God's creatures, according to the metaphysical ideal, they coexist differently in the context of the economy—independent of what is merely legally enforceable—than if they considered themselves to be interchangeable random products of evolution. From a Christian point of view, people are, at the same time, by their nature, moral beings who assume responsibility for themselves and others to the extent they are able. Morality and virtue are thus essential characteristics of human existence. Therefore, they are by no means postulated naturalistically. Speaking in Christian terms, the responsibility of moral humanity exists above all before God because all human beings have received a mandate from God to do good, for the fulfillment of which they should be responsible according to their own unique abilities. In this responsibility, Christian economic ethics cannot be satisfied with mere rule-based ethics, which warns against individual morality with the economic approach within the framework of rules ultimately determined again by economic logic of use. This would be tantamount to depersonalization since the development of individual virtue in all areas of life is such an essential task of personal growth. Both the design of rules and strategies in the economy (and in business) and the concrete moves in their context are systematic areas of morality and virtue. The normative individualistic moral freedom in the moves of the economy demanded, for instance, by Homann et al., must, therefore, be rejected from a Christian standpoint because it corresponds to the individual mandate of people to act morally in all areas of life, including the market.[21]

Consequence and Compass

Now a Christian compass for economic ethics may be sketched to offer a set of tools that provides orientation even for concrete questions of evaluation. Thus, from this perspective, economic ethics is the normative framing of positive economic laws by the Christian humanum as meta-ethics.

- Considerations of HO, as well as the results of the discourse, are never legitimate by themselves. They must always be examined for their compatibility with humanity as the fundamental legal authority of the primary service to humanity. The HO assumption is helpful, but in itself—as with

Smith—it is not a normative authority. Even discourse free of domination is not considered normative, as the results could contradict the humanum. This means turning away from linking economic legitimacy to interests, consensus, and majorities. Christian economic ethics, which argues metaphysically with a moral determination of humanity given by God, brings—anthropologically based—economic and ethical rationality into a dialogue of economic philosophy. Legitimacy of economic decision follows neither from economic rationality alone nor from the procedure of discourse but instead from the comparison with the metaphysically given goal of humanity. The economy is a necessary but not sufficient benefit for the development of the given human being.

- Economic efficiency and all understandings of human service put forward for whatever ethical reason must ultimately be measured by whether they are in line with a metaphysically determined idea of the humanum given to humans. The communication of ethical and economic arguments succeeds in the sense of an economic philosophy.
- Humans are considered to be created in God's image. From this follow unconditional moral rights and duties in business at all levels and the threefold Christian responsibility. Self-love is therefore expressly permitted—as it is in Judaism, for example. Also, developing such virtue within the economy is an essential goal of personal fulfillment and, thus, of freedom. Correspondingly, killing is not a goal. Order, rules, and relationships are just when they enable individuals to live out their God-given destinies and develop the talents bestowed upon them for this purpose.
- According to the Christian interpretation, the legal principles of solidarity and subsidiarity demand from the economic order a concept of rules, virtues, and empowerment strategies, ideally with a high degree of affective unity. Anonymous coexistence held together solely by a common bond with economic principles does not fulfill this condition. The mere nominalism of values and principles translated into economic terms is also rejected. This is because the values and principles that frame the laws of the market themselves are not immune to market laws. They are absolutely attached to the Christian humanum as an independent moral point of view.
- The undisputed demand for the development of the human being as a person in the economy includes, for example, cultural needs that cannot simply be translated into utility calculations, as well as existential questions about the meaning and purpose (*Sinnfrage*) of economic activity. Responsibility understood in Christian terms is compatible with a principle of freedom that fits within it. Freedom of contract and protection of private property stand not only for a rejection of collectivism but also for the avoidance of coercion—in Friedrich A. von Hayek's sense—a basic evil of

a liberal order.[22] They establish a demand for negative freedom as a right of defense and for positive freedom as a future-related entitlement derived from social responsibility.

PROPERTY SYSTEM

Consequences for the economic order can now be derived from the economic-ethical compass. The fundamental basis of the economic order is the property system. Competing conceptions of humankind, society, and social justice each suggest different models. I present a Christian derivation along with a corresponding compass here.

Christian social ethics revolves around two questions regarding the social order: 1.) What rules create justice (i.e., the law oriented toward human dignity)? and 2.) In the context of such rules, how can people develop virtues so that they may lead good lives before God? Order ethics and virtue ethics cannot be separated. This was systematically developed by Thomas Aquinas in his *Summa Theologica* (STh) with a clarity that has never been surpassed. In his treatises on social ethics, there is a chapter in which Thomas explores the question of how to respond to theft and robbery with law and virtue. In this context, his justification and limitation develop the Christian understanding of private property, which remains authoritative today for all Christians—not just Catholics.[23]

Between Human and Divine Law

The theologically motivated thoughts of Thomas place private property in a field of tension between the right to freedom and social obligation, which is reflected in contemporary German jurisprudence:

1. Property and the right of inheritance shall be guaranteed.
2. Property entails obligations. Its use shall also serve the public good.[24]

In this context, the concept of ownership must be legally distinguished from possession: "Possession of a thing is acquired by obtaining actual control of the thing."[25] This means that a tenant or even a jewelry thief can be in possession of something. Ownership of property, on the other hand, denotes the spiritual "right of disposal over material goods and pecuniary claims."[26] This distinction presupposes that humans as spiritual beings can legally make things their own, thus giving them the right to sell said things or manage them independently of any physical power over them: "The owner of a thing may, to the extent that a statute or third-party rights do not conflict with this, deal with the thing at his discretion and exclude others from every influence."[27] This right to freedom is fundamentally tied to an idea of performance equity: "To this extent, the guarantee of ownership complements the freedom to act and to create by recognizing for the individual, above all, the stock of assets acquired through one's own work and performance."[28] The normative justification for this fundamental legal position goes back to Thomas but is by no means evident in his theological system. There is no systematic doctrine of property in the Scriptures.[29] Nevertheless, from a Christian perspective, the question of property must be approached based on the order of creation. According to this, it is assumed that God is the sole owner of the earth: "God intended the earth and everything in it for the use of all human beings and peoples. . . . All other rights, whatever they may be, including the rights of property and free trade, are to be subordinated to this principle."[30] Thomas concludes from this the common destiny (*destinatio communis*) as well as the common use (*usus communis*) of the goods of this earth as principles of law and immutable natural law.[31] This position is reflected in Catholic social doctrine:

> God intended the earth with everything contained in it for the use of all human beings and peoples . . . attention must always be paid to this universal destination of earthly goods. In using them, therefore, man should regard the external things that he legitimately possesses not only as his own but also as common in the sense that they should be able to benefit not only him but also others.[32]

This "right to the common use of goods is the 'first principle of the whole ethical and social order.'"[33]

Two questions arise from this:

1. If Thomas himself emphasizes God's sole power over goods,[34] it is not evident why humans may possess goods at all when it is God who owns them. A quick consultation of the Bible delivers the answer to this question: God has the power to give people dominion over earthly goods. This power is transferred to humans with the purpose of subjugating the world.[35] At the same time, God sets out the limits of the freedom of disposal when he states: "The land shall not be sold in perpetuity, for the land is mine; with me you are but aliens and tenants."[36] God, then, enters into a lease with human beings that not only entitles them but also requires them to use it. Human beings do not acquire property because this is reserved for God. This becomes clear, for example, in the institutions of the jubilee year, in which every fifty years the existing property relations must be rearranged, and the sabbatical year, in which every seven years the crop harvest is due

to all.[37] God enters into the lease with human beings so that they can use the earth's goods responsibly.
2. The second question is more complex. How did Thomas come to add the right to private property? For even if God leases the goods of the earth to humankind, surely a common property system seems appropriate rather than the introduction of private property. How, then, according to Thomas, can there be private property despite the general destination of goods for all? After all, Thomas claims: "Man may use his property as he pleases."[38] The Aquinate explains it this way: According to natural law, the common property granted to humankind in God's lease is immutable natural law. No one may be excluded from the public use derived therefrom. The private property introduced by Thomas in STh II-II, 66, 2 refers to the cultivation and administration of goods. It is a natural law added out of rational consideration (*per adinventionem*).[39] In Thomas' sense, then, private property is subordinate to the original common property as a relative, secondary natural right.

Based on this gradation, the reasons why Thomas prefers private property to collective remain unclear. And also, why does Thomas speak of ownership at all when, in terms of the lease, God remains the sole owner, regardless of whether I subsequently determine the rights of disposal over the lease more collectively or privately? This is clarified in the following section.

Basic Rights and Obligations

Thomas' reasons are embedded in the idea of creation. They revolve around the materialized salvation of the individual in the here and now and not around an idealistic idea of humankind. "Radically taking the profane world seriously as God's creation implies that a path leads to the Creator via this world. . . . The concrete world remains the place allotted to man."[40] The order of goods is intended to enable humans to live according to their God-given destiny. Therefore, an understanding of the Thomasian train of thought on the justification of private property must start in the theological understanding of a successful life and thus in the relationship of humanity to God. Human nature (its general nature) is described in the story of creation. The human being is a moral existence because God gives humans the mission of salvation in the world,[41] including developing this against human nature (*natura corrupta*), which was damaged by the Fall, thus, for example, by the threefold responsibility (before God, oneself, and one's neighbor) and the sustainable use of creation.[42] A property system is just if it enables people to live in accordance with their salvation under the *conditio humana*. Social ethics is tasked with evaluating the order according to this standard. Relevant to individual ethics is the inalienable mandate of all humans not only to shape the social rules accordingly but also to give the salvific answers in the context of these rules and thus to pursue their destinies to the best of their abilities. For this purpose, the goods leased to humans by God are assigned rights and duties. Goods that people need according to their abilities as a minimum for a self-determined, dignified life must not be reduced or burdened by the rights of third parties (such as taxes). These are unconditional natural rights derived directly from dignity. For example, a public minimum level of care can be justified in the welfare state, as can care services for people with dementia or disabilities.

In the sense of Catholic social teaching, there is a conditional right of disposal over the goods that exceed the necessities of life, especially with regard to one's own family.[43] Any surplus beyond this can be justified as productive capital for job creation. It is then in the service of the mission of salvation if it creates free space for the joy of life.[44] If it is not productive capital in service to the livelihoods of otherwise needy people, the abundance is encumbered by third-party rights because it is owed to the poor: "What you have in abundance, give to the poor."[45] Thomas takes up this thought consistently when he emphasizes that, in an emergency, everything is common property.[46] RN 19 states: "But, when what necessity demands has been supplied, and one's standing fairly taken thought for, it becomes a duty to give to the indigent out of what remains over. 'Of that which remaineth, give alms.'"

If then the case arises in a society where some lack essential goods while others have abundance, the first duty of the rich is to help the needy. Soldiers give their lives for others in crises. All the more reason for a duty to give necessary goods to the poor! Where natural rights are not guaranteed, even a property-ethical right of self-defense can be derived from the *destinatio communis*. The famous "Fringsen" (i.e., the permission to steal coal out of dire need granted by Cardinal Josef Frings of Cologne following World War II) is an example of this. Therefore, when in great need, the poor have the right to take from the rich: "If one is in extreme necessity, he has the right to procure for himself what he needs out of the riches of others."[47] Thus, because of *destinatio communis*, status-based entitlements and abundance are encumbered by the unconditional natural rights of the needy. Despite this clarification, the problem of allocation remains unresolved. Because each person deems different goods to be absolute, conditional, or superfluous. There must, therefore, be a legally established property regime that fundamentally regulates the corresponding distribution. A collective property system and a private property system are conceivable for this purpose.

Between Ideal and Pragmatism

This leads me to a systematic overview of the theological foundations for a Christian understanding of property. God is the absolute owner of the earth. Humans, as natural moral beings, have the duty to develop their freedom and social determination. In goods, they have only usufructuary rights to achieve this goal. Human "property" is therefore never an end in itself because it does not correspond to the natural law. Ultimately, all goods are common to all. However, humans are allowed to use the goods of the earth entrusted to them based on the lease. The order must make this personal development in freedom before God feasible for every human being as far as possible through law and through the promotion of social virtues. This is the socio-ethical consequence. Morally, each person is responsible for living up to the contract and realizing the corresponding individual virtues. For social implementation, a form and order of ownership must now be found that optimally realizes the *usus communis* of the earth's goods with regard to the ethical destination in order to thus "put into effect the divine dedication of the earth's goods to all."[48]

In the following, the question is which property regime best enables this goal to be achieved. For Arthur F. Utz, the personhood of the human as an individual and social being grounds the right, formulated in STh II-II 66.1, "to use external things for his benefit."[49] The solution found in Thomas is the private property system. What the common good is to the social order, common use is to the property system. To ensure it, it makes sense to design the order of goods collectivistically.[50] Thomas initially follows this ideal:

> Anything that is against natural law is impermissible. According to natural law, however, all things are common property; but this commonality is contradicted by self-ownership. So man is not allowed to appropriate an external thing. . . . But the other thing that man is entitled to in relation to external things is their use. And in relation to this, man should not regard external goods as his own, but as common, to be easily shared with others in time of need.[51]

Utz concludes: "The Christian view of natural law doctrine even knows to report that the ideal communism of free personalities would have been in itself (!) the more advantageous solution to the tension between person and community."[52] This "ideal" is conceived as a negative communism in which there is no private property and everyone freely gives their best to the community.[53] The following applies to such ideal orders:

- The *usus communis* is realized in common property.
- The prerequisite is a self-responsible striving of every human being for perfection.

- There is a virtue of social love that unites people.
- All members of society voluntarily perform their best without coercion.
- No one takes more than they need from the common good.
- Knowledge, once acquired, is shared for the benefit of all.
- A theocracy prevails that demands and promotes private freedom and moral life.

Even if from the natural law private property is not allowed according to Thomas, Thomas does not transfer the ideal to a legally constituted communism. That is because he knows very well that this is an unrealistic utopia.

According to Utz, the ideal communism of free personalities would be in itself the more advantageous solution, "if the sin of the first men had not weakened the social instinct of the human nature of all."[54] From Thomas' point of view, the realistic view of the *conditio humana* means the end of negative communism. The decadence of humankind, the "tendency toward one's ego to the detriment of the community," are to blame because, according to Utz, "There's a little 'egoist' in all of us."[55] Theological and practical reasons speak against a collective property system.

Theological reasons:

- There is a danger of introducing a person's usefulness to the collective as a measure of dignity and material allocation. This contradicts the unconditional dignity of every person.
- There is a danger of a collective ideology when the collective comes before God's law as a legitimizing authority. The collective would then disempower God as the sole owner.

Practical reasons:

- Legally established common property prevents people from fulfilling their ethical mission. After all, people are more careful with private property:

"With regard to externalities, man is entitled to two things. One is the justification of acquisition and management. And to that extent, people are allowed to own property. This is also necessary for human life. . . . First, because people take more care to procure something that belongs to them alone than something that belongs to all or to many. Second, because chaos would ensue if everyone was responsible for everything with no differentiation whatsoever. Third, because in this way the peaceful condition of the people is better preserved, when each is satisfied with his own cause."[56]

- Care, order, and peace were already addressed by Aristotle, and performance incentives, clear responsibilities, and legal certainty are, according to Thomas, the advantages of a private property system.[57] Joseph Höffner and texts on Catholic social teaching reinforce this view.[58]
  - Incentives for creativity and work performance are lacking in a collective ownership system.[59]
  - Who applies what measure of goods allocation? The state? Who takes care of what? Without clear responsibilities, fighting and moral hazard can occur.
  - To let others work for you, although you could leverage your own talents to do so, is contrary to the mission of salvation.
  - Who guarantees the morally better distribution of goods for all by the state? Statism is also viewed critically for this reason: "It is only too evident what an upset and disturbance there would be in all classes, and to how intolerable and hateful a slavery citizens would be subjected."[60] Political interests have an inherent logic that also makes appropriate distribution difficult.
  - If everything is allocated by the state, then there is no need for a duty of love. This also contradicts the mission of salvation.

Theological and practical concerns, derived from the *conditio humana*, lead to the abandonment of what would "in itself" be the happier solution: "Thomas establishes property as a requirement of the social order, not as a subjective right of the human person."[61]

In Thomas and in the Catholic doctrine of property as a whole, the free human use of property is opposed by the unconditional obligation to help the poor, which is derived from the idea of *destinatio communis*.[62] The "twofold character of ownership, called usually individual or social according as it regards either separate persons or the common good"[63] reflects the tension already introduced at the beginning of the constitutional social obligation of private property.[64] "Legally, it defines exclusive disposition, but morally, it is to be considered common property to be used for the benefit of the whole."[65]

From a Christian perspective, this tension finds expression in different social bonds.

- The vertical duties under natural law are moral duties given by nature and legal duties to God based on the lease agreement—in the sense of divine law. Accordingly, the use of goods must be at the service of personal salvation, for which each person shares responsibility. Creation is to be made meaningful in this sense. Arguably, no material loss of rights to the goods

follows from a breach of these duties,[66] so that the fulfillment of these duties is of no legal relevance in the relationship between people.
- Horizontal natural law duties are nature-given moral (non-legal) duties toward other people. Among them are the moral duties of love to be fulfilled in freedom (giving alms, giving comfort, the seven works of mercy, etc.), by which people help others to develop their personhood.[67] "As for those who in the present age are rich . . . they are to do good, to be rich in good works, generous, and ready to share."[68]
- Furthermore, there are, as horizontal ones, the legally enforceable, natural law duties of justice. They arise from the human rights of third parties to the development of their dignity. For example, the right to a dignified life obligates the (private or collective) property of fellow human beings. The right of disposal is lost where the human rights of others to life and dignity are violated. For example, enforceable taxes can be justified to finance social transfers. Expropriation is also possible in the service of the public, or when private property may become a danger to the common good.[69]

"Yes" to Private Property

St. Thomas and the texts within Catholic social doctrine basically affirm the private property system, which is justified by the theological and practical criticisms of the alternative collective property system mentioned earlier in this chapter.[70] Incentives to creativity and diligence as well as personal freedom of action are better than a comfortable alimentation. Therefore, a "corporate economy" is also fundamentally in the spirit of Christian social ethics.[71] Higher performance creates efficiency, reduces waste of scarce resources, and thus serves the wise use of creation. In addition, this improves prosperity—all other things being equal—which, from a Christian point of view, is not an end in itself but a means to the end of human salvation with obligations. The decadence founded in the *natura corrupta* can thus be redirected to personal salvation as well as to the strengthening of the common good.[72] Since not all allocation of goods is left to the state, incentives remain for the formation of social responsibility out of the spirit of social love. At the same time, the personal human conscience is not released from the lifelong mandate to practice clemency and mercy.[73]

Nevertheless, with all these advantages, the private property system is also susceptible to theological and practical shortcomings that must be avoided. Theologically, God as the sole owner may not be detached any more than the original *destinatio communis*. As a protection against such a threat, the named social obligation of private property now applies instead of common property. Also, unconditional dignity must not be subordinated to individual or economic interests (such as social transfers as tolerance premiums). Christ had more than compassion and forbearance for the poorest: He himself was poor and gave dignity to the poor.[74] The way to achieve this within the framework of a socially organized private property system is the constitutional guarantee of unconditional rights, especially for the weakest. In practical terms, this means the need for a welfare state order in which, in a balance of solidarity and subsidiarity, unconditional rights and duties of people are established as legally enforceable. For example, social transfers (from fleeced property rights) to the needy can be legitimized as their human rights without diminishing their obligation to provide their own services (where possible). Obtaining emergency assistance is, therefore, not a flaw but a right.

The development of such virtues, which correspond to the purpose of salvation, must also not lead to a fight between one and all through avarice, greed, and profit-seeking or to physical as well as psychological overexertion on the one hand or to excessive abundance on the other. The masterminds of the social market economy counter this private-sector danger with the idea of social trust when they see social peace guaranteed by the spirit of cohesion in the Christian sense.[75] Within this property system, the key is to overcome envy toward the rich on the one hand and parasitic prejudice toward the poor on the other; it is undoubtedly an enduring challenge. Inner freedom from a seductive addiction to material goods motivated by Christianity can contribute to this. "For the sun rises with its scorching heat and withers the field; its flower falls, and its beauty perishes. It is the same way with the rich; in the midst of a busy life, they will wither away."[76] For Christians, earthly goods and their yields are only means to a higher end: "Store up for yourselves treasures in heaven" (Matthew 6:19). Salvation and *joie de vivre* are the goal, to which higher yields may be sacrificed under certain circumstances. Christians see their life as a gift and can therefore also acknowledge that not everything is humanly possible. In the competitive economy, this humility can protect against hubris and excessive demands on oneself.

These requirements of law and virtue must, in the Christian view, frame the private property system. At the same time, the concrete design of the legal order (as *ius gentium*) is morally bound only to natural law and natural rights and is quite variable in this context. For the concrete shaping of the *ius gentium*, it remains the task of the present and the future to implement the *usus communis* as optimally as possible in view of the *conditio humana*. The social market economy is currently the model of order chosen for this purpose.

Consequence and Compass

The fundamental Christian "yes" to the private property system against the background of the still valid divine order and the moral as well as legal rights and duties associated with it raises some questions, for each of which a compass is proposed here in conclusion.

- Is there a Christian alternative to the private property system?

"The distribution of created goods . . . is laboring today under the gravest evils due to the huge disparity between the few exceedingly rich and the unnumbered propertyless," Pius XI admonished in QA 58. However, a collective property system was far from a solution in the mind of Pope Pius. Nevertheless, the idea of Christian-based collectivism also as a model for a legally constituted property system is not dead. From a Christian point of view, we should take the systematic interpretations of Thomas from the postwar period seriously. Konrad Farner, for example, finds his arguments primarily in the Church Fathers and some confirmation in secular discussions of justice.[77] The fathers' criticism of wealth and greed must be interpreted "in a principled communist, topical social-reformist way."[78] In addition, quotes can be cited, for example, from Hieronymus: "All wealth comes from injustice"[79]; by Asterius of Amasea: "Greed is the mother of inequality, merciless, misanthropic"[80]; and by John Chrysostom: "The community of goods is to a greater degree the proper form of life than private property, and it is natural."[81] Cyprian also speaks only of the common use of the goods. Such references, in my opinion, confirm the concerns Thomas had about an unrestrained private property system, but they cannot eliminate the Aquinate's arguments of reason. It is true that alternatives to the Thomasian proposal for a solution are conceivable in principle, including for Christians. Even Utz finds charm in the ideal notion of negative communism. But this ideal remains, in view of the real conditions of humans in the world, a utopia, which, in the previous attempts of implementation, nevertheless often ended in positive communism and totalitarian horror. Given the nature of humankind and the mission of salvation in the world, therefore, Thomas' solution is plausible, even if it remains fraught with tension.

- Must the profit from abundance become common property?

What could speak for such an assumption is a view proposed by Wilhelm E. von Ketteler: "God created nature to feed all people, and this purpose must be achieved. Therefore, each shall restore the fruits of his property to the commonwealth, to contribute, as much as lies in him, to the attainment of this end."[82] So, can nonnatural law duties with respect to this abundance justify legally enforceable exploitation? What should be done when goods are abused in an irresponsible manner? Must abundance then become a common property?[83] Presumably, this can be justified from an idealistic point of view, but these demands fail when the *conditio humana* is taken into account. For who will judge the moral goodness of such dealings? This would also result in legal uncertainty. Abundance and the profits generated from it thus remain morally owed to others but legally only in the sense of natural law.

- What are the practical consequences of the right of self-defense, for example, also vis-à-vis the state?

Such practical consequences are difficult to verify. Does it follow from the right of self-defense that, for example, refugees seeking new material livelihoods in Europe have a legally enforceable claim to corresponding social transfers? State action must also be evaluated in the light of the *usus communis*: If the public sector accumulates debts, does this not, strictly speaking, give rise to natural rights and even self-defense rights of future generations vis-à-vis the state? Their redemption is probably a long way off. For this reason, too, Christian social ethics must recall good reasons along with their consequences before another way of thinking creeps in, which may be idealistically appealing, but leads us astray in the real world with corresponding demands and resulting conflicts.

- God leases the goods and remains the owner. Then, according to divine law, people are always just possessors. Would it not be better to speak of a private property system?

Under natural law, people have usufructuary rights to goods under the lease with God—that is, actual physical power. This is a right of possession according to natural law. Primary legal authority remains with God. He is and remains the owner. People are the possessors He has appointed. Ergo, strictly speaking, humans cannot "own" anything. For concrete coexistence, this leased property would then, in the positive legal sense of the German Civil Code (BGB), need to be divided into primary property (e.g., the landlord as owner according to human law) and secondary property (e.g., the tenant as possessor according to human law). Such a convention of speech could strengthen one's consciousness as a primary owner (and not merely an unattached owner), responsibility before creation as well as modesty, and the respect of fellow humans so as not to fall prey to hubris. Initially, this would not change anything about the legal system, but speaking differently in this way could actually foster a deeper sense of responsibility.

SOCIAL MARKET ECONOMY

Certain models of economic order, such as a planned economy or a free market economy, are fundamentally incompatible with the compass on property management. In the Catholic tradition, there has also been controversy in the past about a possible "Third Way." The Catholic Church long ago dispensed with the so-called corporativist professional order, which was still the basis of the encyclical QA, for example. In the meantime, a commitment to the social market economy has become a unanimous consensus in Christian social ethics, including in the ecumenical sense. But the content associated with this is again controversial, as the discussions concerning an understanding of social justice have already shown.[84] In socio-ethical discussions, the negative connotation of capitalism tends to cast a negative light on a market order with its economic instruments.[85] Moreover, references to statements by Pope Francis, such as "This economy kills,"[86] reinforce skepticism about the market economy. The social market economy does not fall under such suspicion. In order to clarify its semantic content, however, one must ask whether its popularity is not perhaps due to the fact that it—like social justice, for example—is sometimes used as a semantically empty weasel word for a wide variety of issues in the sense of Hayek so that everyone from liberals to leftists can identify with it. The once-successful model must also face the megatrends of our time: Globalization, digitalization, migration, nationalisms, inscrutable new models of order (such as truly capitalist communism in China), and so on are new challenges. So, is the idea of a social market economy the right concept for shaping the economic order of the present and the future in a way that is as economically successful as it is humane? Myriad attempts to conceptualize a "new social market economy" have failed. If Christian social ethics today continues to profess its support for the social market economy, good reasons must be presented for this. To present these reasons, we must recall the normative pillars of this idea of order. This allows for a systematic comparison with possible alternatives in order to transparently weigh the merits from the perspective of Christian social ethics and then address some key challenges that need to be considered in order for the model to remain viable in the future.

Basic Normative Concepts

Despite all the complexity of the social principles and values of the social market economy, over which the various founding fathers (including Alfred Müller-Armack, Walter Eucken, Alexander Rüstow, Wilhelm Röpke, or, politically, Ludwig Erhard and others) also engaged in controversial discussion, three basic pillars are to be identified here that simply describe the essence of the social market economy. Reducing the complexity to the topics of economic order, the view of humanity and coexistence helps prevent digressions into secondary factors in the ensuing discussion and instead promotes a comparison of the primary content of models of order. Here, then, is an overview of the three basic pillars:

- Economic order: According to its name, the social market economy is a market economy, as opposed to a collectivist planned economy. This is linked to a liberal "yes" to entrepreneurship, private property, consumer sovereignty, and to a methodological individualism that thinks of order in terms of the individual and of the market's allocation mechanisms, which are also normatively desirable.[87] The waste of scarce resources is avoided if the efficiency criterion is met. The price mechanism of supply and demand ensures welfare gains through consumer and producer pensions with incentives for increased quality, price reduction, and innovation. The state may make reallocative interventions in the market wherever the market itself could take its positive effects ad absurdum (e.g., anti-trust bans, correction of external effects, etc.). The value of so-called negative freedom protects people from arbitrary interventions of the general public in the private sphere. In principle, the individual must not be sacrificed to a collective interest. This is also roughly in line with the principle of personality.
- View of humanity: The market is framed by a normative idea of humanity, which demands the unconditional and inviolable dignity of every human being, primarily on the basis of the Christian view of humanity but also with echoes of categorical imperatives in Immanuel Kant. The framework is necessary 1.) because the market mechanism by itself cannot answer numerous questions relevant to economic ethics, such as the question of an appropriate rate of income tax, and 2.) because a merely negative freedom might leave the helpless to themselves, despite the fact that they cannot assume personal responsibility at all in the sense of subsidiarity. Therefore, in addition to negative freedom, there is also a need for an idea of positive freedom, which, in principle, enables everyone (including the disabled, sick, etc.) to make their own contribution to the community according to their own abilities.[88] Using the Christian view of humanity (Christian humanum) as a framework, a (market) economy is (socially) just if it enables people to fulfill their responsibility toward God, themselves, and their neighbors according to their possibilities and following Jesus' threefold commandment of love. Through order, people find support on their path to salvation before God in this context, both in their responsibility toward themselves and toward society, using the talents given to them and the

creation entrusted to them. This may also require distributive interventions in the market to establish such an empowerment of positive freedom: for example, adequate basic security for the otherwise destitute. Consequently, the relativization of human dignity, as carried out by social philosophers such as Peter Singer or Martha Nussbaum with references to disabilities that would thus destroy the essence of being human, is unthinkable.[89] After all, according to the Christian view, every human being is made in God's image, and it is not up to humans to relativize dignity, to assign or deny it and then to distribute resources (for example, in the financing of social and health care systems) in a discriminatory manner.

- Coexistence: Müller-Armack's irenic formula is a reminder that the social market economy, as a cultural style idea, strives to be far more than a mere economic order. Its goal for positive coexistence is the preservation of social peace through an affective feeling of social connectedness, for example, between rich and poor and between other divergent social poles.[90] Combat ideologies contradict this ideal, as does a purely anonymous coexistence of people ("Moral Order") or mere obedience to duty.

From its origins, the social market economy answers the question of the economic order with a "yes" to the market, the question of the underlying view of humanity with a Christian-based inviolability of dignity and the question of good coexistence with an irenic-affective idea.

Realistic Normative Humanism and Alternatives

There is no doubt that the social market economy, with its vision of the cooperation between the market and humanity, sets an ambitious goal for a desirable economic and social culture and thus, at the same time, a direction for real politics and real cohabitation.

In this context, the social market economy wants to understand its ideal as the goal of reality, without itself being an unrealistic utopia. This cooperation between ideal and reality was addressed earlier on in this volume in the economic thought of Thomas Aquinas and Adam Smith. Thomas did recognize that the goods of this world are ultimately the property of God and, therefore, intended for all people. However, from a realistic insight into the nature of humankind, he derives the legitimacy of private property, which is central to the market economy, not as a primary but as a secondary natural right.[91] A noble person in the sense of Smith is the person who is guided by altruism in day-to-day decision-making.[92] Like Thomas, Smith does not succumb to the temptation to make this ideal the standard for shaping a real economic order. For this entails reeducating humankind and overcoming egoism, which he—like Thomas—considers not only just harmful but also impossible. Attempts in history to base social orders on an idealized view of humanity have resulted in dictatorship. This experience likewise suggests combining the ideal with pragmatic realism. Smith thus reckons with humankind's egoism without normatively demanding it, as some contemporary business ethicists do (Gary Becker, Karl Homann, and others). And under the condition of the existing human egoism, he then conceives a liberal economic order that, without prescribed re-education, should nevertheless produce a good result. Similar echoes of such a tension between ideal and reality can also be found on the island of Utopia in Thomas More, where a collectivist order of goods entails the neglect of the old and the sick,[93] or in Kant, who, while wishing for the autonomy of humankind liberated from egoism and thus recognizing the moral law and the categorical imperatives as an ideal, at the same time imagines a real society in which, if necessary, even a nation of devils could be governed by mere obligation.[94] And Martin Luther, for instance, in his two-regiment doctrine, sees the real world as an intermediate state between the kingdom of heaven, where God's law of love reigns, and the kingdom of evil. As long as heaven and hell are at war, there is no paradise on this earth, and so there must be sanctions and rules here that are not necessary in the kingdom of heaven.[95] In the traditional line of such and other fields of conflict between ideal and reality, the social market economy claims to base the Christian-based humanum on the idea of a just economic and social order in a holistic and normative manner, taking into account not only the mission of God but also the imperfect nature of humanity. In this way, it aims to be oriented toward the ideal and yet practically realizable.

A collectivist planned economy and a radically liberal free-market economy are considered the main alternatives. Both models can and should be critically compared to the idea of a social market economy with the help of the three criteria identified here (i.e., economic order, view of humanity, coexistence).

First, let us examine the planned economy, which remains popular today even in places other than North Korea or Venezuela. The widespread failure of this economic order, especially in Eastern Europe, is well known. This is rooted not only in totalitarian party apparatuses and the rejection of entrepreneurship, the market and private ownership of productive goods but also in the system's inherent hostility toward innovation, which led to ruin in the medium term. This essential systemic flaw of socialist state economy was documented and elaborated on by Jürgen Schneider in his detailed trilogy on the economic history of the GDR.[96] According to normative collectivism, the value and dignity of human beings are measured according to attitude and arbitrary party power so that here, too, a fundamental contradiction to the concept of the social market economy emerges.[97] The same applies to the idea of coexistence: While collectivist models (red, brown, or even religious fundamentalist) emphasize a strong idea of affective social identity as well, this is grounded in an exclusive class, race, or religious affiliation. Combat ideologies of this kind contradict the irenic idea.

Even a radically liberal or libertarian form of a free market economy—now under the opposite sign—is distanced from the basic ideas of a social market economy. In the radically free market, there is room for negative freedom alone. Income tax, for example, can be rejected as forced labor following such thinking.[98] The radically liberal conception of humankind ultimately knows no responsibility to God or any other objective normative instance.[99] The normative prerequisites of a democratic society, which cannot produce them from itself, are lost from view. This makes the legalization of trade with one's own organs conceivable because the body is regarded as private property and thus as an individual and monetizable mass of disposal.[100] In accordance with the idea of normative individualism, social transfers to the needy can be justified only as premiums for acquiescence. Intellectually disabled people, the peace-loving poor, people on their deathbeds, or unborn children could be left to their own fate without a claim for solidary help, as long as no threat potential for other egoists emanates from them. This also contradicts the idea of unconditional human dignity because, if strictly and consistently thought through, these people would fall through the cracks without solidary legal claim to help. Finally, the idea of coexistence is content with selfish utility maximizers living side by side anonymously (moral order) since any kind of aspired affectivity is seen as paternalism and thus an attack on negative freedom.

Compass and Challenges

The simple comparison made here with collectivist and radically free-market models of order makes it possible to summarize solid reasoning behind a social market economy as a compass, and this reasoning bears significance for other perspectives beyond the Christian one:

- As the Third Way, the reality-based synthesis of market and humanity harnesses the benefits of the market for the common good,
- makes a well-founded unconditional human dignity the measure of justice, and
- rejects ideologies of struggle as well as an anonymous depersonalization of the human being.

The three pillars outlined in this section, with the consequences also covered, are subject to justification and are permanently challenged by alternative orders that compete with the social market economy. Various megatrends of our day are also calling into question the future viability of the social market economy. These include increasing secularization in many countries, an emotionalization of the media world, globalization, digitalization, and so on. Some of these challenges are addressed here—again, in the context of the three pillars of economic order, view of humanity, and coexistence.

1. Economic order:
    - The implementation of a worldwide social market economy with a global welfare state (with unconditional obligations and social entitlement rights) is far from being realized. Even in Europe, there is still a long way to go toward a common economic and social order oriented equally toward solidarity and subsidiarity, as is evident, for example, in monetary and fiscal policy.[101]
    - The often economically lucrative arms trade with authoritarian systems and corresponding deliveries to war zones remain a point of contention. The same applies to ecologically harmful production and problematic working conditions in non-member countries. Entrepreneurial freedom and the idea of humanity repeatedly come into conflict here. Balancing the two remains a challenge for a credible social market economy. Neither statism nor forgetfulness of humanity can be the solution.
    - Increasing digitalization potentiates human manipulability through monopoly-like platforms and thus endangers the freedom of the subject. This could mean an attack on the idea of methodological individualism, which is essential to the market economy, and opening the doors to the power of ideological elites beyond freedom (such as in China or the like). Here, reallocative regulation might become necessary to save the free individual, but it would have to be profiled as a competitive advantage in the global market.
2. View of humanity:
    - The Christian view of humanity is the normative basis of the idea of justice in the social market economy. German society is becoming increasingly secular, and there is no sign of the kind of rechristianization that Müller-Armack or Johannes Messner, for example, assumed was a prerequisite for stabilizing the social market economy.[102] Theological social ethics, which advocates a methodological atheism, does not have such proselytizing in mind.[103] We must seriously question how the humane foundation of the social market economy can be effectively justified in the future so that it can compete with alternatives. Does the social

market economy need a foundation of values other than Christian human values?[104] Which foundation should this be? Christian social ethics, in the sense represented here, is committed to recalling Christian humanity with its good reasons and justifications, even in a pluralistic context.
- Digitalization also challenges the view of humanity, for example, through artificial intelligence or humanoid robots, which are already ascribed human dignity. This is unacceptable—not just for Christians. Opposition to emerging technical developments is not enough to convince people. Therefore, such concerns must be articulated in a well-reasoned manner.[105] And there needs to be a serious debate about how to enforce those limits as well.

3. Coexistence:
   - Social anonymization fosters discontent and loneliness; exclusionary collective identities additionally promote a spirit of antagonism. This endangers well-founded Christian irenic thought.[106]
   - The diminishing relevance of the traditional family poses new challenges to intergenerational cohesion as well as to the transmission of values and virtues that are essential to the fathers of the social market economy.[107] More government as a panacea must be viewed critically in the spirit of subsidiarity.
   - It also needs a strong democratic culture of debate. Issues worthy of discussion must be debated with factual arguments.[108] This is especially true for even emotionally contentious issues such as the protection of life, family, social justice, entrepreneurship, and others, as addressed here in part III. Making controversy taboo damages democracy, to which the social market economy is closely linked.

It is by no means conclusive to say that the social market economy, with its idea of a well-founded and practically implementable synthesis of market and humanity, is also the model for the future from the point of view of Christian social ethics. But some of its foundations are in danger. What is at stake today, therefore, is nothing less than the future viability of this synthesis. It will depend essentially on Christians to continue or restore this humanity of the market for as many as possible.

CURRENCY

Following the fundamental contributions on the market, property, and the social market economy, a practical field of economic ethics can now be discussed on the basis of Christian social ethics. The currency crisis that has been going on in Europe for years is a good example of this. At the end of 2010, exorbitant mountains of debt in the eurozone came to light, which have since endangered the future of Economic and Monetary Union of the European Union and much more. This crisis is also fundamentally about the future of human coexistence in Europe. This is a classic challenge of Christian social ethics. Here, too, its mission is to help shape society with its values and principles in accordance with God's mission of salvation and to provide plausible ethical guidelines. I will attempt to expound on this here.

Both Sides of Neo-Socialist Social Ethics

So far, there has been no interrogable social discussion of Christian socio-ethical positions on this topic. There are probably several reasons for theology's reticence. Basically, it is not the task of Christian social ethics to take the role of politicians or economists. The social principles of solidarity and subsidiarity prove too unwieldy for fast-paced discussions of this crisis. After all, the Bishop of Aachen, Heinrich Mussinghoff, took a stand on this in his sermons on the awarding of the Charlemagne Prize to Jean-Claude Trichet in 2011 and to Wolfgang Schäuble in 2012. With explicit reference to the euro crisis, he ethically justified the goal of price stability and warned against a false solidarity that would forget subsidiarity.[109] Friedhelm Hengsbach was the first German voice of Catholic social ethics when, in 2011—unlike Mussinghoff—he called for not only a change in monetary policy but also a fundamental change in the regulatory system for the eurozone in the name of solidarity.[110] This position found an audience in Christian social ethics primarily because the stability-oriented idea of the European Monetary Union lacks its own socio-ethical foundation. According to Hengsbach, the European Central Bank's (ECB) restrictive monetary policy aimed at monetary stability is largely to blame for the plight of Greece and other (former) problem children in the eurozone, such as Ireland, Italy, Portugal, and Spain. The ethically required solidarity as a "form of social control" with the declared egalitarian goal of "justice as a presumption of equality" had to be interpreted in such a way that "supports the vulnerable according to their needs." In addition to generous debt relief, this would consistently include a monetary policy controlled by elected representatives. The monetary policy autonomy granted to the ECB on the model of the former Deutsche Bundesbank to guarantee price stability[111] was a "design flaw of the monetary union" that had to be eliminated. For the Union was mistakenly "built on the sands of secondary monetary control variables, the stability of the price of goods and the balancing of public budgets."[112] Instead, monetary policy, which has hitherto escaped democratic control, should in the future be geared in equal measure to the so-called magic square of price stability, high employment, external equilibrium, and steady economic growth, together with an overarching coordinated economic and social policy.[113] Public control of monetary policy with a relativization of the primacy of price stability (above all in favor of a high level of employment) are imperatives of solidarity. The Unification Treaty would, therefore, need to be substantially readjusted.

Since solidarity as a socio-ethical legal principle does not appeal to goodwill but certifies enforceable legal claims for help, solidarity understood in this way would not merely entitle highly indebted nations to help from more powerful economies so that they could help themselves. There would also be a nationalization of the advantages (of the debtors) that are as free of sanctions as possible, with simultaneous socialization of the debts, which is also systematically promoted as a "form of social control." Social justice, in this sense, calls for a monetary policy freed from the presumed paternalism of price stability, which largely leaves open to the weaker countries in particular expansionary options (above-average increases in the money supply and debt) for boosting their international competitiveness and for the publicly stimulated elimination of unemployment. Behind this is the widespread view that more money in circulation increases domestic demand and thus lowers unemployment. In the context of a European-coordinated economic and social policy, nationally generated debt could be incorporated into a large common European debt budget. Social transfers to the needy, which are to be guaranteed in order to safeguard human dignity, should also be financed through the common European social budget, which now relies on solidarity-based aid. The normative basis of this socio-ethical concept is the idea of needs-based justice, according to which a culture of balance is to be created under the primacy of solidarity. The demands made in the name of this idea of justice are thus:

- The ECB's monetary policy autonomy must be abolished and replaced by a democratically legitimized mandate of public control (of politics).
- The goal of price stability must lose its intrinsic value, become part of the catalog of economic policy objectives, and, in case of doubt, be subordinated as a service value to higher objectives, such as a high level of employment.
- The goal of public budgets that are as balanced as possible must be replaced by community liability.

The mere reference to solidarity does not make such a neo-socialist positioning plausible. For in the Christian socio-ethical sense, solidarity always exists only together with subsidiarity. To design such a compass that addresses both principles on equal footing, we can employ the familiar three-step see-judge-act method of analysis:

- See: In order to understand the alleged design flaws of monetary union, it is first necessary to present the basic ideas of European monetary policy, namely the convergence criteria, the requirement of price stability and the autonomy of the ECB, against which Hengsbach's criticism is directed. After a brief look at its history, the role and scope of action of the ECB are presented, which are important for understanding the basic ideas of the monetary union.
- Judge: Against the background of this assessment of the current situation, an evaluation of the monetary union and the crisis from an economic and socio-ethical perspective follows. In doing so, a reassessment of social justice for monetary policy is undertaken with the help of equal social principles of solidarity and subsidiarity.[114]
- Act: Finally, this section again includes consequences and a compass, this time in duplicate because the complex target question requires its own evaluation.

Basic Concepts of the European Monetary Union

The foundation for a common European market with a coordinated economic and monetary policy was laid in 1957 in the Treaties of Rome, establishing the European Economic Community.[115] The 1989 Delors Report, commissioned by the heads of state and government, drew up a concrete three-stage plan for realizing this project following a number of intermediate steps. The close coordination of economic, monetary, and financial policy (stage 1 from July 1, 1990), which followed the liberalization of domestic markets and was oriented toward monetary stability, was initially to be followed by a further intensification with the establishment of the European Monetary Institute (EMI) as the forerunner of the ECB (stage 2 from January 1, 1994), which was modeled on the German Bundesbank (prior to the monetary union). Finally, in order to complete the European Economic and Monetary Union,[116] the transfer of sole monetary responsibility to the ECB was slated to take place after the establishment of a single currency (stage 3 on January 1, 1999), which was then expressed in the introduction of the euro banknotes on January 1, 2002. Monetary policy, which focuses on the relationship of the euro to third currencies, is the responsibility of the Economic and Financial Affairs Council, while monetary policy is the sole responsibility of the ECB. Convergence, price stability, and autonomy are the basic ideas of the

European Monetary Union, which should inspire confidence if implemented credibly. Only under these conditions did Germany agree to the Treaty.

Convergence: The Maastricht Treaty, which was ratified in 1992 and merged into the Lisbon Treaty in 2009, laid down the following conditions to be met in the final year of examination for a country to join the European Monetary Union in order to ensure lasting convergence:[117]

- The country must have participated in the European Monetary Union exchange rate system for at least two years without currency devaluations with normal fluctuation margins.
- The inflation rate may not exceed 1.5 percent of the inflation rate of the three member states that have the greatest success in price stability.
- The interest rate on long-term public bonds may not exceed 2 percent of the corresponding interest rate in the three member states that have the greatest success in price stability.
- Public-sector debt may not exceed 60 percent of gross domestic product.
- The fiscal balance may not exceed 3 percent of gross domestic product.[118]

These regulations are designed to rule out unsound fiscal policy as far as possible. However, they were softened from the very beginning. Greece did not initially meet any of the conditions but was admitted as a full member in 2001 on the basis of overly optimistic calculations. Italy's public debt of 120 percent of GDP was accepted in consideration of a debt relief policy supposedly emerging there. In the event of violations of the last two criteria, the Council of Ministers must decide whether an excessive budget deficit exists and whether sanctions should be initiated. Article 126.1 dictates[119]: "Member States shall avoid excessive government deficits." In line with the subsidiarity principle, this requirement is underlined in Article 125 by the "no-bail-out clause": In order to safeguard long-term monetary and financial stability, community liability of the Member States is expressly excluded, even though Article 122 provides for the granting of financial assistance only on an exceptional basis in the event of exceptional difficulties. To resolve this conflict of objectives, the 1997 Stability and Growth Pact standardized a procedure that ties solidarity-based assistance to effective measures to be provided on a subsidiary basis to the goal of a nearly balanced public budget.

Priority of price stability: With the completion of monetary union, the ECB assumed sole responsibility for European monetary policy. Within the European System of Central Banks (ESCB), the national central banks (such as the Deutsche Bundesbank) primarily guarantee the implementation of ECB decisions, ensure the smooth operation of national payment systems and the provision of cash, and are represented via their governors on the ECB's Governing Council, which is responsible for the orientation of monetary policy. The ECB is given strong powers to achieve a clear objective:

> The primary objective of the ESCB is to maintain price stability. Without prejudice to the objective of price stability, the ESCB shall support the general economic policies in the Union with a view to contributing to the achievement of the objectives of the Union as laid down in Article 3 of the Treaty on European Union. (Art. 127.1)

Price stability must not be relativized by other objectives or even interests. It thus has a special priority in the European Union's catalog of goals, which makes it suspect for critics. It is an unconditional objective that must not be relativized even by the supreme objectives of the EU codified in Article 3. This includes, after all, the

> harmonious, balanced and sustainable development of economic activities, a high level of employment and of social protection . . . sustainable and non-inflationary growth, a high degree of competitiveness and convergence of economic performance . . . and economic and social cohesion and solidarity among Member States.[120]

The ECB uses instruments such as open market policy to fulfill its primary objective of price stability. The ECB sets the so-called key interest rate for the refinancing of banks, which is primarily carried out as a fixed rate tender in the form of repurchase agreements.[121] This is intended to control the money supply.[122] The setting of the minimum reserve ratio for deposits also alters the scope for money creation by banks.[123] A restrictive ECB policy to combat emerging inflation, with a high key interest rate and a high minimum reserve ratio, aims to reduce the money supply by lowering bank liquidity and reducing money creation, dampening the price level, and making credit more expensive, which tends to lead to a decrease in investment and an increase in savings.[124] However, the penetrating power of the instruments is fundamentally diminished by psychological delays in recognizing corresponding dangers and in the subsequent effect of the measures.[125]

Autonomy of the central bank:

> When exercising the powers and carrying out the tasks and duties conferred upon them . . . neither the European Central Bank, nor a national central bank, nor any member of their decision-making bodies shall seek or take instructions from . . . any government of a Member State or from any other body. The . . . governments of the Member States undertake to respect this principle and not to seek to influence the members of the decision-making bodies of the European

Central Bank or of the national central banks in the performance of their tasks. (Art. 130).

The steering of monetary policy is considered so important that, unlike in the French and even more so in the Italian central bank tradition, it must not be influenced by political interests (for instance, before elections or as demanded by climate activists), in line with the German model of independence. Thus, according to the Treaty, the European Central Bank is not bound by the instructions of any democratically elected government.

Perspectives on Economic Ethics Assessment

For an economic-ethical evaluation of the monetary union, a distinction is made between an economic perspective, a trust perspective, and further aspects of a socio-ethical perspective that considers solidarity and subsidiarity together on equal footing.

First, the economic issues:

- Price stability ensures the functionality of money as a medium of exchange, unit of measurement, and store of value. Relative prices of scarce resources can be determined, which enables efficient allocation of scarce resources. This allows the economic benefits of a stable euro to unfold. For intra-European trade, the transaction costs of currency exchange and, in the case of scheduled payments, the exchange rate risks are eliminated. This makes it possible to dispense with expensive exchange rate hedging transactions (currency swaps), for instance. It also enables a significant reduction in high-expenditure foreign exchange management.[126] When there is international confidence in the stability of the euro, the euro becomes a reserve currency for international trade, which, in turn, spurs investment and trade. These advantages stimulate international trade, from which exporting nations such as Germany benefit in particular.
- The centralization of European monetary policy has deprived member states of the opportunity to adjust exchange rates to economic strength by revaluing or devaluing their currencies. For example, before the monetary union, Italy, which was threatened by recession, was able to increase its international competitiveness by devaluing the lira because this made Italian goods more attractive for export. Such adjustments, which could have helped Greece and other countries during the most recent crisis period, are not possible in the single currency zone.
- "One-size-fits-all"—This principle states that the ECB's respective monetary policy affects all euro countries equally, whether they are currently experiencing a recession or a boom. The centralization of monetary policy

can no longer take account of national divergences and cultural characteristics as it did before. At the same time, an expansionary monetary policy can be an important aid to a country threatened by recession, while exposing another booming country to an inflationary spiral. Inflation differentials between countries highlight this issue. For example, the inflation rate in Germany averaged around 1.6 percent between 2002 and 2006, whereas, in Ireland and Spain, it was well over 3 percent.[127]

Now the discussion turns to the trust perspective:

- Trust has just as much ethical relevance as it has economical relevance. Without trust, both human interaction and all types of currency lose their value. Even more so since the final abandonment of the dollar's gold peg in 1971, the strength of a currency and its service functions stands and falls above all with the trust that people place in it. If confidence is lost, a run on bank deposits will probably set in, and the financial system will collapse. Inflation—if history is any indicator—is to a large extent also the result of a loss of confidence.[128] Respect for ECB autonomy on the part of policymakers and transparency of political interests in fiscal and monetary policy decisions, on the other hand, are good framework conditions for price stability. If they are adhered to, this strengthens a culture of contractual reliability in the eurozone characterized by mutual trust and honesty. In fact, a contrary development has progressed. It is true that the primacy of price stability and the autonomy of the central bank have been questioned time and again before.[129] In the meantime, however, the contractually defined competencies between monetary and fiscal policy have also been fundamentally blurred. For example, the purchase of bad government bonds by the ECB was significantly pursued on French initiative, thus shifting the responsibility for rescuing crisis-stricken states to the ECB.

"Averting a member country's insolvency or shoring up its financial system, however, is certainly not the task of the common monetary policy—but of fiscal policy."[130] Such averting was done in the awareness that the raising of the bailout umbrellas constituted an open breach of the Lisbon Treaty.[131] In 2011, former ECB President Jean-Claude Trichet even categorically ruled out Greece's exit from the monetary union with the following argument: "When a country enters monetary union, it shares a common fate with the other countries."[132] This may correspond to the idea of solidarity and political will emphasized in Articles 3 and 122. However, a contractually required consistent implementation of Article 125 and thus of subsidiarity cannot give way to a supply concept without damage to trust. The idea of a no-bail-out clause was gradually replaced by the idea of joint liability and legitimized as normative and factual.[133] The watering down of the convergence criteria is exacerbating the loss of confidence. Germany was one of the driving forces behind the lenient application of sanctions in the event of violations, especially of the criteria calling for budget discipline. The permanent zero interest rate policy has disempowered the ECB. The idea of the Treaty of Lisbon being highly binding strains credulity.

The breach of the Treaty caused by political intervention is a matter of concern for both economic and ethical reasons. It has shaken confidence in the euro and is fostering a culture of mistrust. This impedes the development of European social responsibility.

Other Christian socio-ethical arguments include the following:

- Christian social ethics articulates the content of its social principles as insights about human beings that—like human dignity—claim timeless validity. If the liberal idea of helping people to help themselves is replaced by giving them a handout, the principle of subsidiarity is ignored. Such an interpretation at the same time abandons the principle of mutual trust, which stabilizes not only the currency but also social peace. The neo-socialist solutions proposed are incompatible with this.
- Price stability has an economically justified socio-ethical quality because it prevents the waste of scarce resources on the market and counteracts poverty in old age by safeguarding savings and pension entitlements. A relativization of the primacy of price stability in favor of a policy trade-off in the magic square is conceivable only if the ECB's monetary policy autonomy is surrendered. The unpopular price stability in no way competes with the socio-ethical goal of high employment. This is because, as a result of expansionary monetary policy, demand on the market for goods and services may increase, driving up prices for them. However, this also increases labor and unit wage costs, which, in turn, cancels out the positive effects on the labor market.
- The ECB's autonomy receives its democratic legitimacy from the agreement in the Treaty of Lisbon. The presidents of the central banks are selected by the governments. The board of directors, as the highest decision-making body, is also appointed by political means so that the presumption of a lack of democratic legitimacy of its leadership can be rejected. Continued and/or expanded political and government influence on specific monetary policy will further exacerbate the crisis of confidence. If, on the other hand, a new treaty is concluded without safeguarding the ECB's autonomy, the ECB's dependence on political interests would become openly

apparent. But whether such transparency strengthens a culture of honesty and trust is doubtful in view of the inherent laws of political rationality.
- The requirement of budget discipline with mutual exclusion of liability seems only at first glance to be an unsolidary protective mechanism of the strong against the weak. Bundesbank President Jens Weidmann declared a two-stage condition to be a central principle for the exceptional granting of financial aid to highly indebted countries. The respective government, which is responsible for fiscal policy, must then present a convincing consolidation program ex ante, which must be implemented consistently ex post: "If a country fails to do so, further support should no longer be taken for granted and the country should be prepared to bear the severe consequences."[134]

On closer inspection, this supposed harshness follows the ideas of material freedom espoused by Wolfgang Kersting and enabling justice in the sense of Sen's capability approach, where solidarity and subsidiarity are closely intertwined, taking into account the causative principle.[135] Any government that knowingly accepts that its country's freedom of action is endangered, for example, by an unsound fiscal policy, should accept responsibility for this in the event of an emergency. Such a deliberate violation of one's freedom of action fulfills the condition of a sanction criterion. Anyone who acts in an obviously irresponsible manner cannot expect unconditional assumption of liability by the community of solidarity in the event of a crisis caused by this reckless behavior. According to this idea of justice, help is, therefore, linked to the condition that the party responsible for knowingly surrendering its own freedom must remedy the situation by any means necessary. Solidarity seen in this way, which is understood in a liberal sense, enables this act of liberation to be carried out and, at the same time, presents an obligation to assume responsibility. Help is limited to helping people help themselves. Those who do not help themselves in this way must bear the consequences mentioned by Weidmann in this understanding of equality.
- The implementation of this interplay of solidarity and subsidiarity, like the answers to the questions on the issue of trust, has consequences for the culture of coexistence. Here's an example: During the last major economic and financial crisis, low interest rates and the simultaneous search for new lucrative forms of investment on the financial market led many to believe that the Greenspan Doctrine was being practiced so

> that monetary policy would intervene and limit risks in the event of a crisis.... The very acceptance of such a promise of monetary policy left unchallenged promotes collective moral hazard and leads to the rise of

credit volume, asset prices and debt . . . within the financial system—and ultimately to the buildup of systemic risk.[136]

Europe finds itself in a similar trap.[137] An ECB that, as an extended arm of politics, reliably socializes the risks of private or state financial transactions or even fiscal decisions, creates incentives for the high risks in financial markets and fiscal policy. If the ECB must repeatedly provide deficit guarantees for the failures of irresponsible financial jugglers or politicians, it will not only violate its own autonomy but also undermine its task of ensuring price stability. Policies like these also incentivize a culture of ongoing irresponsibility:

> "By shifting extensive additional risks to the countries providing assistance and their taxpayers, however, the eurozone has taken a major step toward communitizing risks in the event of unsound public finances and macroeconomic slippages. This weakens the foundations of the monetary union built on fiscal ownership."[138]

This stability-oriented argument emphasizes the principle of subsidiarity, which must be taken into account from a socio-ethical perspective. The task of European fiscal and monetary policy should not be to foster a mentality of financial restraint and self-indulgence among governments, banks, and investors. After all, accommodating carelessness quickly unleashes wastefulness in light of short-term election tactics. It can obscure the view of agents in the financial world for the mere service character of money. It also kills the sense of creative personal responsibility and the spirit of social responsibility, including toward future generations.

- Subsidiarity, on the other hand, also calls for a culture of personal responsibility that promotes mutual trust between the strong and the weak. The goal here is for national self-interest to take a back seat. A coexistence of subsidiarity and solidarity strengthens both self-esteem and the European sense of unity. The prerequisite for this is the willingness to also assume responsibility. The consistent implementation of the normative idea of empowerment thus corresponds to a culture of accountability. It creates a climate of trust and responsibility.
- The scenario of socialized debt repeats the mistakes of collectivist economics, which underestimated humans' personal responsibility and thus their natural claim to the material development of their freedom. In the name of solidarity, regulation that provides for political needs theoretically creates more financial security. But it contradicts the idea of empowerment, incapacitates states and economic actors, stifles a culture of trust in the medium term, and nullifies the welfare effects of the market and price sta-

bility. A solidarity of responsibility, on the other hand, is the criterion for assessing the ongoing currency crisis. Options for action from a Christian socio-ethical perspective result from this for a new monetary policy, a more permissive determination of the status of the monetary union and for concrete social commitment.

Consequence and Compass 1

- Monetary policy could contribute to a culture of confidence if it proves that it has learned from past mistakes. Its powers would have to be enforced in accordance with the contract. In the United States, the 100 percent increase in the money supply initiated by the Federal Reserve's expansionary monetary policy from 2000 to 2008 (against real economic growth of 20 percent) combined with wage restraint led to a continuous increase in asset prices (real estate).[139] From today's perspective, the so-called Greenspan Doctrine of a wait-and-see monetary policy strategy is a mistake because the emergence of the bubble should have been countered by swift, restrictive measures.[140] Instead, the opposite happened: The lending rate was favorable, further price increases were expected, and real estate agents were paid according to the volume of loans they turned over. And so, high risks were also accepted for the acquisition of real estate. The banks resold their liability on the market with the attractively priced mortgages. As interest rates were low internationally, there was great interest in these securities until bank refinancing became more expensive and, at the same time, appreciation stalled. In addition to the moral hazard of banks and brokers and other unfavorable factors, the Fed's expansionary monetary policy allowed this bubble to emerge in the first place.[141] The ECB should be guided by such experience: "The question of what to do once a bubble bursts remains. But it should come only second, in case the evolution of a major bubble in spite of all efforts could not have been prevented."[142]

Europe is facing the risk of a bubble forming in the valuation of government bonds, for example. Speculation on politically motivated purchases of government bonds, especially those of crisis-stricken countries, by these countries or the ECB is driving up their price. If interest rates go through the roof, prices will fall, and a potential bubble would burst—with unforeseen consequences not only for the investing banks but also for the pension funds that have invested a lot of money in government bonds. It is possible to halt developments like this. Continued purchase of bad government securities is dangerous. Such securities must not be used as sham collateral for bank refinancing. Government guarantees by strong countries only offer weak assistance because they keep the value of the securities artificially high. Forced maturity extension of government bonds postpones repayment and, at the same time, lowers confidence in the bonds of other countries because corresponding coercion would have to be expected there in the future as well. Such an extension will also trigger liquidity problems for banks holding such government securities, especially in the countries concerned. And the pressure will increase to borrow these securities from the central bank. But that is precisely what is to be prevented. A passive strategy of waiting or even a politically desired tightening is economically and socio-ethically harmful. Responsible monetary policy should shrink the bond market bubble. In this way, the ECB could contribute in many directions to a culture of trust and responsibility.

- What is the use of financial sanctions against countries that are already illiquid to solve the ongoing crisis? And Keynesian-based public demand programs on credit remain no more than a flash in the pan without a credible will to consolidate on the part of the beneficiaries. Stalling economies through overly restrictive policies is also not a solution. A federal structure of monetary union, modeled on the Federal Republic of Germany, sounds tempting as a way out. In Deutschmark times, there was a single and largely stable currency despite cyclical divergences between the regions. Monetary policy alone, however, cannot provide this unity. The prerequisite for such federalism is political unity, in which tax and social systems are aligned. Transferred to Europe, this would mean that fiscal policy would have to become a centralized European power so that no country could incur debt at the expense of others at will. This, in turn, requires disciplining toward shared fiscal responsibility. By contrast, the consistent use of the exit option for crisis countries could restore confidence in the eurozone and, at the same time, open up opportunities to assist them with currencies that are now their own. The regained instruments of appreciation and depreciation, as well as independence from a leveling monetary policy that does not distinguish between booming and recessionary economies, can strengthen the competitiveness of such countries. New coalitions would emerge in the eurozone, making a change of course toward solidity more likely again. In the variant represented here, Christian social ethics can provide orientation to never consider solidarity without solidity in all proposed solutions: and this not first and foremost for economic reasons but to strengthen a culture of intergenerational justice with social and personal responsibility.
- Christians can also be socially practical in helping to find a solution. Here, for example, charitable work is needed for people who, especially in crisis countries, receive little to no support from social safety nets. At the same time, corruption and waste in such countries must be denounced. In the face of a spirit of national self-interest, Christian social ethics has the

opportunity and mission to strengthen a culture of shared responsibility. International meetings of church groups, especially at the local level, made a significant contribution to reconciliation between Germany and its neighbors, for example, after World War II. Above all, these meetings, along with national conferences in a spirit of mutual appreciation and integrity, serve the great vision of European peace.

Consequence and Compass 2: TARGET

For some time now, Hans-Werner Sinn, Joachim Starbatty, and other renowned economists have made it their business to warn against a companion to the euro crisis: the TARGET problem. This will be briefly explained here, followed by an ethical compass.

(Christian) social ethics must take a stand wherever there are potential threats to law and democracy. This also applies to the TARGET problem. The abbreviation TARGET stands for "Trans-European Automated Real-time Gross Settlement Express Transfer System" and refers to a balance arising, for example, after the settlement of an international payment transaction on the account of a central bank concerned with the ECB, which acts as a clearing house for such transactions. The fact that this Bundesbank account with the ECB accounts for a claim of almost 1,025 billion euros around July 2021 appears to be a threat.[143] On the other hand, the ECB accounts of the central banks of struggling euro-states have huge liabilities. The main reason for this has an ethical dimension: If there is mistrust in the creditworthiness of Spanish commercial banks, for example, they will no longer be able to obtain money on the market via interbank transactions. The resulting liquidity constraints are jeopardizing national payment transactions in Spain. And since each national central bank has the mandate to ensure this, commercial banks can now obtain liquidity from their central bank. This will also ensure that loans continue to be granted to Spanish companies, which use them to buy goods abroad. This secures international trade as well as the standard of living at home. The national central bank lends this money to its commercial banks against collateral, the standard of which it largely determines itself. It cannot simply create the money flowing to the banks out of thin air. Rather, their account at the ECB is debited for this purpose. The latter, in turn, offsets this by assigning a claim in the same amount to the Bundesbank, for instance. This is because the Bundesbank has a liquidity surplus since German commercial banks no longer lend their money to Spanish or other commercial banks in interbank trading on the market, preferring instead to safely park it at the Bundesbank. Once this operation is complete, the Bundesbank's book claim against the ECB is equivalent to a liability of the Spanish central bank to the ECB. Thus, in accounting terms, German money has flowed to Spain, which is used to maintain payment transactions in Spain. The German side has received a book claim for this, but it is not directly against Spain or its central bank but instead against the ECB.

Some socio-ethical evaluations will also be proposed as a compass for this in the context of the currency issue:

- Interbank trading is a market business. Commercial banks that are not afforded trust there are stealing away from the market mechanism by relying on replacement financing. There are no incentives for their own consolidation that could restore confidence in the market. These are then planned mechanisms that bypass the market and are thus ethically questionable both from the point of view of regulatory ethics and from the point of view of the principle of trust. The subsidiarity principle does not apply either.
- Lending to commercial banks is done with reference to the legally secured mandate of the national central bank to maintain domestic payment transactions. This ostensibly plausible explanation actually violates the virtue of honesty because the real issue is another one entirely. Ailing banks were and are being kept alive by such covert public support. To this end, the standards of collateral to be provided for an inflow of liquidity to commercial banks have also been lowered significantly in countries hit by the crisis.
- The more this security risk increases, the less likely the ECB will be to honor the debt. The argument sometimes advanced that, despite high target balances, a euro remains a euro, regardless of which central bank puts it into circulation, is not inherently wrong. But if such transfers ultimately turn what was originally safe money in Germany into dubious book claims whose redemption is becoming increasingly unlikely, the result is that good money has been transformed into bad. This bad money is used to buy good products in the marketplace. And this is not only questionable from an economic point of view but also from an ethical one as well. Monetary trust is exchanged for distrust, and the ethically desirable allocative outcomes of the market are distorted.
- The main concern here is that the risk of insolvency is being transferred from the taxpayers of one country to the taxpayers of another country without a democratic mandate. A great deal of money, for example, for maintaining the Spanish payment system ultimately comes from German taxpayers. The conditions for securing a repayment are determined in Spain. This goes against a basic understanding of democracy and can even lead to a form of expropriation that is not legitimized by the rule of law as an encroachment on personal freedom.

- The risk of the redemption of claims is initially borne not by the Bundesbank but by the ECB. If a default actually occurs, for example, if a country leaves the eurozone and cannot continue to meet its liabilities despite aid measures, the national central banks must step in proportionate to their capital share at the ECB. In this case, Germany would be severely affected. If the other owners can no longer step in due to their own crises, the contribution to be borne by German taxpayers could then quickly approach the level of the TARGET balances. One might consider this fair in terms of solidarity. But if, taking into account the balance sums, this also drags the German economy into the abyss, we should ask whether solidarity must be realized in the common demise of all, without any regard for the causative principle. Jewish social ethics, for example, would clearly contradict this.[144]
- Concerns about social peace in Europe should also not be underestimated. The high TARGET balances show that German taxpayers are already helping to finance living standards and payment transactions in crisis countries. Gratitude has been only one of many sentiments expressed for this over the years. Since the redemption of considerable portions of the receivables is no longer to be expected in the future, Germany would probably have been better off transferring subsidies directly from taxpayers' money to such countries in the past. This would have created more transparency for the support provided and thus a different awareness thereof. Consequences can be drawn from these experiences for comparable crises in the future.

The high TARGET balances are not the root cause but the result of a deep crisis of confidence. Therefore, building a new culture of trust is the order of the day. The six ethical consequences mark different courses of action. Creating new confidence in the banking systems in countries afflicted by the crisis is a priority. We must be honest with ourselves about one thing: Some banks will not survive. But in the case of many ailing credit institutions, so-called bad banks could be spun off, whose liabilities would then have to be settled not via European monetary policy but via fiscal policy. This would not only be in line with the contractually defined division of tasks between the ECB and the euro states but also with the imperatives of transparency and political solidarity. In the spirit of subsidiarity, the remaining good banks would have to be enabled—in terms of both material and human resources—to achieve sustainable solidity. Then they would once again be permanently marketable for interbank trading. If this is ultimately seen as a sign of a once again prosperous economic power and functioning markets, the TARGET problem will be solved.

RETHINKING ECONOMIC ETHICS

Finally, in this chapter, this section on behavioral economics will discuss a scientific challenge of the fundamental economic paradigm, which may provide a fundamentally new foundation for economic ethics. A corresponding fundamental reflection opens the door to this future. Behavioral economics, which is by no means young, has long challenged us to take up and discuss in depth its findings in the systematics of economic ethics.[145] The focus is not on the specific application contexts, such as the use of nudges or the consequences for successful marketing.[146] Instead, it is about the challenged exploration of a fundamentally new relationship between ethical and economic thinking.

Behavioral versus Standard Economics

Controversial discussions about so-called standard economic assumptions (such as the HO, the efficiency target, and others) have long dominated research at the foundation level of economic ethics. Such struggles with theories and approaches profiled therein were and continue to be necessary and fruitful. At the basic level of discussion within the subject area, which explores the interdisciplinary communication program of economic ethics, it is time to deal intensively and systematically with behavioral economics. There are already in-depth discussions at the application level.[147] This section, however, focuses on the theory of justification and outlines some essential behavioral economics challenges. We can subsequently identify basic ethical issues that are affected by this. These issues may then be raised for discussion, thus opening up some areas for normative reflections where Christian economic ethics can and should position itself.

The discipline of behavioral economics (*Verhaltensökonomie*) addresses fundamental doubts about the HO model.[148] To this end, we draw primarily on findings from psychology but also from sociology and neuroscience, which should help to revise or extend the counterfactual HO construct of an egoistic-rational utility maximizer, for example, with the help of experiments on humans. The aim here is to be able to predict human behavior in the market better than was previously possible with the standard model. Obviously, HO-based forecasts are often flawed because they misunderstand human decision-making. This deficiency is to be remedied because improved forecasts in favor of consistent welfare gain are the ultimate aim of economic research. Ulrich van Suntum, Alois Stutzer et al. offer this criticism of the HO in a German Research Foundation (*Deutsche Forschungsgemeinschaft* [DFG]) application in 2010:

A paradigm shift is emerging not only in terms of methodology, but also in terms of content. . . . The results of experimental economic research also pose a challenge to mainstream economics. In doing so, they exhibit altruistic and justice-driven behaviors that do not seem readily compatible with the HO paradigm.[149]

Since there is not only one interpretation of behavioral economics but also a wide variety of currents, the sought-after answer to this dilemma cannot simply be prefaced here. Depending on how criticism of the standard model is weighted, this may indicate a destructive departure from the HO or a constructive addition to it.[150] Behavioral economics does not aim to simply replace the HO with a differently modeled *homo*, whether *sociologicus* or any other.[151] It basically proposes a new paradigm, mainly with the help of alternatives to the three pillars of the standard model. These pillars, which, depending on the interpretation, seek to replace or supplement the standard theory, are briefly outlined here.[152] They include:

- experimentally accessed decision heuristics incorporating social utility instead of (strict) HO logic,
- the prospect theory profiled in particular by Daniel Kahnemann and Amos Tversky in lieu of the expected utility theory along with
- the calculation of future benefits using hyperbolic instead of exponential discounting.

New Heuristics

First, I will outline the fundamental questioning of a simply conceived HO rationality. The latter—in contrast to Gary Becker's economic imperialist view—is not aimed at being understood as a view of humanity but instead as a heuristic that allows the economic sciences to predict human behavior. For this reason, the HO assumption used is not primarily a normative but rather a descriptive statement.[153] On the basis of countless experiments on human decision-making behavior, behavioral economics counters the assumption of strictly rational-egoistic behavior (in the market), which can be identified as counterfactual by simple intuition alone, with the thesis that people (there) do not make use of HO rationality (alone) but of different heuristics, the use of which could even ultimately produce efficient results.[154] Heuristics in this sense is understood to mean strategies that reduce complexity to enable fast decision-making despite uncertainty—arising, for example, due to a lack of information. The advantages in terms of real-life application of these seemingly irrational biases are counterbalanced by the disadvantage that such decision-making using heuristics not only makes human behavior less predictable but could even cause individual or economic harm.

One take on heuristics, for example, might be the conclusion that it is sensible to thoroughly test new ideas before abandoning concepts that are tried and true. This preference for what is tried and true can have disastrous consequences, for instance, if an entrepreneur fails to seize an opportunity by being skeptical of introducing new technology and instead adhering to well-established yet outdated methods. Two sides of the heuristics coin become immediately apparent here: It is undoubtedly sensible not to abandon established theories too hastily, even if initial, plausibly delivered arguments suggest otherwise. As a result, the initial irrational preference could prevent a potentially inefficient reallocation. But then again, it might also underestimate the opportunities afforded by innovation, overlooking an efficient reallocation in the process. The use of such heuristics (the preference for established theories) in decisions offers opportunities and risks from an economic perspective of the criterion of efficiency. The same applies to a number of other heuristics identified in experiments, the list of which is constantly being expanded. Examples include the representativeness heuristic, a mental shortcut used to simplify the classification of other individuals or types in decision-making, the availability heuristic, which is used to make quick judgments on the basis of information provided by the media or similar channels, overoptimism with regard to one's own opinion and abilities, which can lead to courage or foolhardiness, overpessimism as a possible counter-model, and a distorted retrospective view of past decision-making situations, with which people tend to minimize their own mistakes. We can use the hypothesis that humans use heuristics such as these, along with others, to explain the many biases involved in real decisions (in the market) that were previously seen as purely irrational. Behavior economics thus contributes to novel forms of human decision-making that are superior to that of HO and seek to offer a more profound understanding.

There are three competing positions regarding the question of the compatibility of such findings with HO rationality.

- On the one hand, it may be necessary to replace the HO model, which would lead to a paradigm shift of unprecedented proportions for the economic sciences.
- On the other hand, the use of heuristics can be understood as an extension of the HO model, provided that one shares the assumption that humans have acquired and developed such decision-making patterns in the course of evolution.[155] Based on this reading of behavioral economics, it would be a proven strategy for reducing complexity whose ultimate aim would be efficiency, just like HO. According to such an interpretation, which does not mean a revolution in economics, the use of heuristics can then

be assumed as an expected human behavior alongside the traditional HO rationality that would otherwise be used in decision-making. Decisions (on the market) thus become easier to predict. And this could undoubtedly be seen as an important advance in economic research without sacrificing the at least relatively successful HO instrument. The negative consequences of bias, on the other hand, according to this interpretation, arise from the fact that the originally efficiency-oriented heuristics are exposed to new, more complex decision-making contexts today, for which they are no match. This would be an indication of the need to replace them with new heuristics in the course of evolution or through intervention.

- A third interpretation casts fundamental doubt on the informative value of behavioral economics.[156] Such a frontal critique denies the validity of experiments in which people behave artificially and according to the given framework conditions completely in line with the expectations of researchers, whose motivation is not so much to achieve progress in knowledge than to ride the wave of this fashionable trend, for example, to secure attention through the discovery of a supposedly new heuristic or bias and possibly to publish a highly ranked scientific article. Behavioral economics also lacks a mature theory of its own. Moreover, interpretations of these heuristics are pure speculation. This would lead scientists in the context of presumed heuristics to incorrectly objectivize subjectively perceived probabilities in decisions made in the face of uncertainty. All of this would discredit the rigorous standards of such research. On the other hand, one could also argue that, paradoxically, in the sense of a heuristic confirmation bias fallacy, such adherence to the conventional theory in the absence of an already mature alternative could render researchers unable to accept new insights.

In addition to the assumption of heuristically guided decisions, entire fields of research have addressed further questions regarding the HO model.[157] What Adam Smith already knew in his *Theory of Moral Sentiments* is now widely discussed in behavioral economics: for example, the admixture of motives such as altruism, fairness, sympathy, and antipathy, of emotions and feelings, a tendency toward performance equity, the avoidance of excesses in inequality, retribution, or even a non-defecting commitment to the provision of public goods.[158] However, social preferences—if made public—would only be used strategically in decision-making for the sake of appearances, thus enabling people to present themselves in a positive light. This could be understood solely as instrumental action in terms of HO logic. According to another inquiry of HO rationality, people evaluate their (economic) status in relation to others, which can lead to objective personal betterment over time not being perceived as such in cases where the betterment of society as a whole has progressed faster than one's own. This brief overview alone highlights the great complexity that behavioral economics presupposes in the field of human decision-making. Happiness research is also embarking on its own large-scale program to replace the HO utility paradigm with a new one that can be used to compare conditions of utility, income, or wealth.[159] The HO heuristic must be replaced by a happiness measurement because people are fundamentally concerned not with optimizing their utility but with optimizing their happiness, whereby the two can be correlated without being congruent. In this sense, we can explain the investment of time or money for family and friends, which may seem irrational in the sense of HO.

Standard economics criticizes such questioning of the HO heuristic primarily for the associated increase in complexity, which makes predicting human behavior much more difficult rather than easier. The deliberate reduction of the complexity of human rationality to the HO has, after all, been moderately successful as a solid foundation for standard economics. It thus satisfies the criterion of what Milton Friedman calls the F-Twist.[160] This states the following: If the model of HO enables us to adequately predict behavior, then the quality of the assumptions concerning human rationality is of negligible importance for economics. And as long as there is no model that allows a better prognosis, it should be avoided. After all, if the HO were to be abandoned, large swaths of economic science teaching would have to be completely rewritten. In addition, the criticism is often made that the measurement of happiness is not completely clear, for example, in happiness research, despite some suggestions[161]: "Most measures of happiness and well-being are based on surveys—and self-reported levels of happiness can be like a snapshot taken at an unlikely moment."[162] On the other hand, following the logic of Becker, for example, one could easily bring this field of research back into the standard paradigm by interpreting supposed happiness criteria, social preferences, or values such as family and friendship as ultimately all being derivatives of an HO logic.[163] Happiness researchers reject this economic imperialistic point of view, as this would involve the loss of their essential basis for argumentation.

Prospect Theory

Decisions made under circumstances of uncertainty are an integral part of economic research. Expected utility theory, in its descriptive interpretation, offers the tools of standard economics that are as proven as they are recognized. According to this theory, decisions turn out rationally in the way that humans weigh and optimize expectancy values (the utility of an act multiplied by the probability of its eventuation). The utility value that is decisive for choosing among alternatives can be objectively measurable (e.g., in €) or subjectively awarded. Experiments on human decision-making behavior are also used here to refine the theory. The result is that the utility function is not seen as linear as we rate a possible loss—for example, in a bet, with an equal chance of winning or losing (50 percent)—higher than a possible profit, although the amount and the probability of occurrence are even. Humans are thus risk-averse by nature.[164] This phenomenon could also be easily explained in a different way with decreasing marginal benefits and higher overall benefits. Moreover, the decision depends on how a problem pending decision is presented.

Behavioral economics contrasts this with the so-called Prospect Theory as an alternative to understanding.[165] Human decision-making first goes through a complexity-reducing editing phase, in which a fixed reference point is individually defined for all further considerations. Certain alternatives are categorically rejected as options unworthy of consideration. This is followed by the evaluation phase, in which the trade-off between losses and gains is far more complex than postulated in expected utility theory. Starting from the individual reference point as the zero-point of a value function, it is not the sums of benefits that are weighed here but instead only the probable gains or losses in benefits resulting from the corresponding actions. In the domain of loss, the curve is steeper as loss is estimated higher than equally high or equally probable profits. This is not surprising.[166] In the trade-off between lower probabilities of occurrence (>0 and <1), people are more venturesome, and in the case of higher probabilities, they are more risk-averse. In contrast to expected utility theory, the probability of occurrence drives the propensity for risk-taking, which has a decisive influence on decisions. Further determining factors must be added for observed falsifications, some of which are already known based on the discussion of heuristics. Framing—that is, presenting the problem as such a biased reason—is not new compared to standard theory. According to it, human preferences are anything but stable. For example, anchoring (i.e., trusting in the meaningfulness of evolutionary clues) makes people manipulable by providing external guidelines for decisions (e.g., in estimating amounts), which people use for orientation, even if these guidelines are far from a rational solution.[167] The status quo bias, on the other hand, describes the consequences of people's tendency to stick to established ways rather than venture into the unknown. It is also assumed that people allocate gains and losses to mental accounts, such as "leisure expenses." Then—according to the assumption—human decisions offset possible gains or losses on such partial accounts instead of weighting them in the sense of HO rationality in the context of an overall balance.

Criticisms of this theory are directed, on the one hand, at the fact that the individual determination of the key point of reference in the editing phase of scientific research is completely inaccessible. Some of the reasons given for bias are either banal or they are not only speculative but are, at best, only involved in superficially made decisions. Reflected decision-making, in contrast, could rapidly avoid such biases in favor of rational decisions.

Hyperbolic Models

The third pillar of standard economic thinking is the assumption that the utility of future acts is discounted exponentially in decision situations toward present acts such as discounted savings bonds.[168] It is a basic assumption that future consumption has less weight than immediate consumption—despite these having the same value. The higher the set individual interest rate based on personal preferences, the stronger the present preference. Thus, if I rate the payment of €100 in one year the same as an immediate payment of €90, I set my individual interest rate at 10 percent. If I rate €100 in one year the same as an immediate payment of €50, the interest rate is 50 percent, which indicates a stronger preference for the present. Discounting the utility available for consumption in the future is then performed over several years "n" with the interest rate "i" always by the same factor: $(\frac{1}{1+i})^n$. The discount factor $\frac{1}{1+i}$ remains constant at the same interest rate for all time periods. Starting from the future consumption value back to the present, the cumulative discount factor decreases.

Representatives of behavioral economics counter this with the effect of human impatience and of the amount of accurate discounting in individual (consumption) decisions. For example, if I were to decide how much money I would have to be given in order to forego a payment of €100 to me either tomorrow or in a year's time, the rate will certainly not be the same in all cases. Humans use lower rates when internally discounting in the distant future versus the near future. Assuming the willingness to forego €100 for a year might be worth €10 to me, it again corresponds to 10 percent compared to the future consumption value. Experiments have now shown that, in contrast, people are naturally prepared to do without less in absolute terms during the shorter period of abstention from consumption (in this case, one day) than during a waiting period of one year but are prepared to do without more in percentage terms. Then exponential discounting would no longer be appropriate for understanding human decisions. The discount factor proposed for this is now no longer constant because it decreases by $\frac{1}{1+in}$ with increasing n (i.e., with longer waiting times from year to year).

A simple example illustrates the difference. Discounting an amount of €100 over n=2 years and an initial interest rate of i=10 percent then yields the following values:

CALCULATION 11.1

Exponential: $\dfrac{100}{(1+0.1)(1+0.1)} = €\,82.64$

Hyperbolic: $\dfrac{100}{1+0.2} = €\,83.33$

The purpose of so-called hyperbolic discounting is to account for the fact that consumption in the distant future is discounted less than consumption in the near future.

In addition, it is assumed in this context that people tend to discount higher amounts more out of risk aversion. This could potentially run counter to the motivation that people enjoy the anticipation of future consumption and will therefore gladly wait for it, whereas they would pay off a speeding ticket faster in order to be rid of the negative feeling associated with it. Anticipation might thus be indicative of less discounting. All of these behaviors are also considered irrational in terms of the standard model and should be additionally considered from a behavioral economics perspective beyond the simple hyperbolic model. In this way, human behavior becomes easier to predict because it comes closer to the reality of decision-making processes than previous theories.

In addition to the fundamental skepticism about the validity of the underlying experiments, this model is criticized above all for the assumed theoretical arbitrariness and the speculative positing of the hyperbolic discounting factor.

Basic Ethical Issues

The three pillars briefly presented here are selected as examples for the review of the economic ethics discussion of behavioral economic challenges for the standard economy. Therefore, the focus is not on the coherence issues already alluded to. There is sufficient room for discussion of this outside the framework of economic ethics. Rather, the question here is explicitly ethical as to

- whether a basic normative aspiration of behavioral economics can be identified,
- what a possible value basis underlying this kind of thinking might be (view of humanity and social conception, idea of humane responsibility, etc.),
- how to prioritize the ratio of economic and non-economic values, and
- the normative consequences of the implementation of a theory yet to be systematized.

Economic research is primarily concerned with making human behavior (in the marketplace) as predictable as possible. This facilitates—through suitable theory formation—suggestions for rules and incentives on and for the market, as well as long-term—through better market operability—higher welfare gains resulting from an improved consumer surplus. This includes efficiency and, therefore, the prevention of waste of resources. Both standard and behavioral economics are committed to this market ethic. Normatively set, the obligatory aim is, therefore, expressly to be able to predict as accurately as possible human behavior (in the marketplace). HO heuristics is the standard economy instrument used here that does not lose its legitimacy in the sense of an F-Twist, as the hypotheses postulated there about human decisions do not reflect reality. A comparatively good prognostic potential ennobles the model viewed in this manner. Behavioral economics adheres to the basic economic predictability objective. This theory is also primarily about the optimization of the predictive potential of humans' decision-making behavior. However, for this purpose, a new or extended heuristic is now proposed instead of a simple HO model. This approach claims to better understand and reconstruct human behavior as a basis for understanding what was previously incomprehensible with the standard model. The inclusion of heuristics, social motives, and so on demonstrates the intention of understanding humans better not as an end in itself but rather as a means of achieving better predictability. Ethics that concerns humans is also about understanding humans. The normative aim of this understanding is to find out more about the (normatively understood) good life. The answer to this question can correspond to economic ethics with the best possible predictability. However, other ethics, such as the Platonic, Aristotelian, deontological, or metaphysical attempts, understand good as something else, namely the orientation toward obligations, law, tasks, or gifts that are predetermined for humans and that originate, for example, in an idea of reason or in a transcendent instance. Seen in this light, the simple congruence of goals is the exception. Therefore, it can be stated that behavioral economics and ethics seek to understand people. This understanding initially fulfills a higher purpose in each case. On the one hand, it serves the purpose of achieving better predictability (without questioning the quality), and on the other hand, it paves the way to a better life for humans, which may include consequences for the market. This is because inefficiency in the sense of wasting resources cannot, all other things being equal, be an ethically legitimate goal. In behavioral economics, understanding people is always a service value, not an end in itself. In Aristotelian, deontological, or metaphysical ethics, for example, this understanding of humankind can also be more than a service value, namely in the sense that it can be used to better understand the source of the good itself. Those who better understand human reason can thus better comprehend Kantian moral law, for instance. And those who see humans as being made in God's image can use their enhanced understanding of human nature to discover divinity throughout all of humankind.

Behavioral economic questioning does not share the normativity of the F-Twist by asking explicitly about the validity of the assumptions of human decision-making processes. Thus, it at least comes close to ethical thinking (not economically endogenized in the sense of Homann et al.) that does not simply equate the question of the good life with the question of better predictability. While standard economics usually explicitly does not want the HO to be understood in the image of humankind, behavioral economics explicitly seeks to shape such a view.[169] It reveals human heuristics but does not content itself with heuristics as an idea of human beings themselves. In principle, one could assume that behavioral economics represents a negative view of humankind. First of all, it identifies irrationalities in human behavior and tries to explain them, for example, with the help of heuristics and other motives. Hanno Beck, for instance, counters such a thesis of *homo irrationalis* when he identifies in the heuristics rather evolutionary strategies of complexity reduction.[170] Then the use of the numerous heuristics would be rational precisely as such. This reflection gleans something positive from the view of humanity in behavioral economics. However, it may be only a slight modification from the perspective of HO.

In prospect theory, assumptions are made about an irrational propensity for risk-taking and irrational risk aversion along with mental accounting. The model of hyperbolic discounting places a high value on human impatience and the action-guiding anticipation of future reward on the one hand and the desire to dispense with negative things as quickly as possible on the other. Such features are hypothetically inferred as descriptive in order to achieve the goal of better predictability with this knowledge. The moral goodness of such motives is not yet the issue here, nor is the question of whether these motives should be encouraged or discouraged, as the circumstances dictate. It could be asked normatively, for example, how risk aversion that is obviously based on fear or even impatience could be reduced—provided we see these as obstacles to a good life. This moral assessment would need to be very well justified.

Methods of generating supposed heuristics through behavioral economics must be fundamentally questioned in normative terms. In experiments, subjectively perceived probabilities that guide individual decisions are objectivized by researchers as heuristics, like stereotypes, and are formulated into new regularities that take the form of "if-then." In theory, they are considered a good explanation until another form of heuristics replaces them as a new social law that can more precisely explain human decision-making. Such simplification does not do justice to the individuality of human beings and is, therefore, itself at best a complexity-reducing heuristic. Human decision-making in the real world (not in the laboratory setting) is too complex to be accurately represented through stereotypes. This has been proved above all by systems-theoretical analyses of human behavior.[171] From this point of view, behavioral economics, contrary to what is claimed, cannot present a view of humanity but, analogous to HO, merely a heuristic modified in relation to it.

In behavioral economics, it is not possible to clearly identify to whom humans are and/or should ultimately be responsible for in their decision-making. For it does not claim to be a form of ethics that provides answers in and of itself. However, it does not exclude the possibility of connecting with ethical approaches, which themselves have demanding responsibility profiles. This means, for example, a responsibility of humankind to autonomy before the moral law in Kantian thinking, before an idea of the absolute good in Platonic and Aristotelian thinking, before a transcendent counterpart in religious thinking, before universal rules of communication in discourse-ethical thinking, and so on. If such responsibilities then semantically substantively determine people's preferences, these will only need to be identified again in terms of behavioral economics, thus preserving or improving the predictability of human behavior. If this is done with the help of social laws, which, like stereotypes, aim to make the influence of certain responsibility profiles on human decisions predictable, then the individuality of the individual decision-maker is once again pushed into the background, especially if the "irrationalities" identified here are again used for an economically justified paternalistic re-education.[172] For example, one could assume that the commandment to love one's neighbor always requires Christians to become organ donors. Those who are not organ donors would need to be re-educated. But such totality lacks nuance and depth, as there can also be good ethical reasons for some Christians not to be organ donors.[173] Otherwise, behaviors could be identified as irrational in the sense of the respective ethics, as they are irresponsible. For example, anyone who completely rejects charity as a Christian is acting irresponsibly in the context of Christian ethics. But ethics does not need help from behavioral economics to come to such a banal realization.

Prospect theory fundamentally adheres to the utility paradigm: It is still concerned with maximizing benefits. Just how this calculation takes place is debatable when compared with expected utility theory. If the identified behavioral-economic heuristics are also ultimately understood only as a modified form of HO rationality, the HO paradigm would survive as a basic idea of humanity. Thus, as long as the use of heuristics is then understood as efficient because it reduces complexity, it is rational in this sense. Countervailing biases, which the use of heuristics can also entail, would ultimately have to be identified as such in order to dissuade people from this. Thus, the efficient use of heuristics would still be permissible, as it is rational. Human behavior would be even more predictable under these circumstances. The inefficient use of heuristics would need to be inhibited in the sense of liberal or libertarian paternalism. Such an interpretation clearly implies a normative primacy of economic rationality over different social or other values. Social preferences, happiness motives, and so on would also be subsumed under this. And the question remains as to what kind of rationality the reference point in the editing phase of human decision-making, which is normatively important for prospect theory, should correspond to in the first place.

If the utility paradigm is to be replaced by a happiness paradigm, as is being considered in parts of happiness research, this would ultimately mean the end of HO and its normative effect on economic theory formation. The new standard of human decision-making (the optimization of happiness) would leave room for semantically substantial non-economic values such as family, love, friendship, religious faith, and so on. The consequence would be to give preference to these non-economic values for economically relevant decisions over the remaining HO arguments. This would henceforth be a new economic-ethical communication model for the dialogue of rationalities. Alternatively, these values, which are non-economic in origin, could now be defined as a new economic rationality, which would render any dialogue between economic and non-economic values superfluous. In a reversal of economic imperialism, this could mean a normatively problematic theory of happiness imperialism.

Depending on the objective, behavioral economics could set out to replace standard economics if it ultimately did not want its findings to be understood solely as modifications of the HO model and the theories derived from it. This would be a very strong imperative that would likewise face justified criticism regarding its methodology and systematic maturity. If, on the other hand, the goal remains to predict human decision-making in terms of social laws that basically follow only an extended HO efficiency rationality, the paternalistic conclusions already hinted at suggest that people should be induced to behave in this way if possible. Philipp Hacker considers this consequence to be compelling because the reception of behavioral economy concerns the

> question, how and in which direction human behavior should be influenced. This approach naturally raises not only the question of paternalism, but also the

need for a sound normative theory: Only such a theory can provide an indication of the ideal image of decision-making that should be used for the orientation and modification of behavior.[174]

This could lead toward economic normativity enhanced by behavioral economics, which, in the sense of Homann, warns against any morality that contradicts this rationality. Non-economic values would then merely be application fields of a modified HO logic to be treated as rationally as possible. The inefficiencies that arise through the use of heuristics, for instance, would need to be eliminated as far as possible. This could be done, for example, by reducing irrationality and bias in decisions (debiasing),[175] the use of nudges, and through appropriate educational measures. Such paternalism also justifies the interference of heuristics in evolution with the implementation of rationally improved heuristics and the demand for their use.[176] Taken to the extreme, this could lead to correspondingly complex programming of rationally decisive computers that take into account the optimal rational efficiency of heuristics. Their decisions could then be elevated to the normative model for good human decision-making—good because it would now be perfectly predictable. That would be the way to a rational world that only needs humans to better identify their own evolutionarily acquired efficiency strategies (heuristics) and purify them of their biased defects and could thus always inform humans on what must be done from a rational perspective. Deficits in evolution should be corrected. If anchoring, for example, was of evolutionary importance long ago but has now lost this meaning, such an interpretation implicitly attributes this change in virtues to humans. Can we thus say that humans were more trustworthy in ancient times than they are today? Such an interpretation undoubtedly raises significant questions about today's development and the quality of human virtue.

Consequence and Compass

After exploring some normative questions implied by a discussion of behavioral economics, we can conclude by suggesting some guidelines for fundamental reflection on economic ethics in the future, in which a Christian position can prove itself on the basis of its economic ethics values.

- We must ask the following: Must economics be content with a heuristic of humankind, regardless of how it is defined, for which its closeness to reality remains a subordinate question? To what extent can and should the anthropological perspective of a view of humanity, which, as with Smith, regards the understanding of humanity as an end in itself, find its way into

economic thinking and thus enrich or modify the goal of predictability? A Christian position welcomes such anthropological enrichment.
- A good prediction of behavior does not question the moral goodness of human motives. An economical perspective must question this too and should not simply relegate it to the realm of prediction objectives. Then again, prediction objectives should also not fall victim to simple ethical axioms. This would not do justice to the great service of economics to people and society. The question of what is good and the understanding of humans (in line with a view of humanity) would need to be introduced carefully to ensure that it does not interfere with the simplistic and, therefore, helpful complexity reductions of economic science methodology. In terms of economic ethics, the goal of good predictability is likely not understood as an end in itself but always as a service value to a higher human goal that requires definition. From the point of view of Christian social ethics, a renaissance of economic-philosophical reflection would be desirable.
- Behavioral economics findings are uncovering an ever-increasing complexity of human decision-making processes. Can and should the epistemological paradigm of critical rationalism that is so prevalent in the standard economy be replaced by a systems-theoretical methodology that takes exactly this complexity into account? So, is systemic economic ethics needed as a normative response to behavioral economics? From a Christian point of view, the associated apersonal view of humanity in systems theory must be viewed with skepticism.[177]
- To what extent—and behavioral economics must also address this question—can even a non-economically endogenized, substantial concept of responsibility infiltrate economic ethics research? From the point of view of Christian economic ethics, individual responsibility or concepts such as justice, dignity, freedom, and so on would also have to be considered as desirable values not just as an empty formula or as a cleverly handled black box but also in terms of the quality of their semantic substance.[178]
- Behavioral economics carries the risk of a latent paternalism that could disparage individuality and bring with it a re-education that serves the objective of predictability. From a Christian perspective, this challenge must also be taken seriously in the sense of good *Bildung*.[179]
- Can behavioral economics insights be adopted by standard economics? From a research ethics point of view, standard economics should not simply immunize itself against the likewise radical challenges of behavioral economics in service to its own paradigm by referring to its own elaborated theory. Honest research must also deal fairly with such a risk of the collapse of its own foundations.

- We must also pose another critical question: Does behavioral economics, for instance, offer a new dialogical communication model for economic ethics through happiness research, or is it embarking on the path of normative, behavioral economical happiness imperialism?
- Recognizing human characteristics in decision processes and their deficits might lead to calls to eliminate these deficits and condemn those who do not or cannot make such refinements. Appreciation of the irrational should also be an ethical issue from a Christian perspective.
- If the efficiency rationality modified by rational heuristics is normatively charged, the quality of real human rationality ultimately falls behind such an artificially perfected computer-based rationality. In the extreme case, it would amount to learning good decision-making from the perfectly rational PC as soon as it normatively legitimizes an "ideal model of human decision-making behavior."[180] Such a conceivable subordination of human rationality to algorithms is highly problematic, not only from the point of view of Christian social ethics.[181] Moreover, humans may be preparing to intervene in evolution in a corrective way with a corresponding normative interpretation. This hubris could lead to mistakes and/or, in the worst possible scenario, even to despotism. From a Christian point of view, it also contradicts the human mission of salvation, which presupposes humane (and not artificially generated) responsibility and the freedom of humans to make their own decisions.

NOTES

1. P. A. Samuelson and W. D. Nordhaus (1998): 28.

2. Pareto efficiency is named after the Italian sociologist and economist Vilfredo Pareto (1848–1923).

3. Clearly, one state is inefficient relative to another if, after reallocation, at least one affected party is worse off without even one other being better off. One state is indifferent to another if reallocations lead to better and worse positions (e.g., if a tax increase in favor of social transfers makes the recipients of the transfers better off but the taxpayers worse off). Better and worse are measured in terms of utility, whereby, according to economic understanding, having more money always brings a utility advantage. Benefit comparisons in this context cannot usually be assessed by offsetting, for example, by determining the increase in benefits of the transfer recipient against the decrease in benefits of the taxpayers in absolute terms and then comparing them with each other. Rather, the logic of Pareto efficiency is limited to a comparison of relative better and worse.

4. The simple assumption of economic HO rationality is an express reduction in complexity that deviates from the reality of life and is now being challenged in the behavioral economics discussed at the end of this chapter.

5. Cf. the analogous characterization of economic ethics via the efficiency goal and humanity goal in E. Fischer and O. Fischer (2007): 22.
6. See E. Nass (2018) for such a detailed distinction: 45–71.
7. See the chapter "Theological Humanism" in Part II, where the dialogue is addressed along with other conceptions of religious humanisms as ethical sets of values.
8. Cf. P. Ulrich (2000).
9. A. F. Utz (1994): 16.
10. See Part II for dialogue with these and other worldview concepts.
11. See the section on justice in the chapter "Creation, Justice, and Peace" in Part III.
12. In this case, a commitment to a metaphysical starting point of ethics in the sense of a desired connectivity may not be necessary. Cf. the chapter "Substantive Positioning in Dialogue" in the introduction.
13. Cf. E.-W. Böckenförde (1992).
14. See the section on Adam Smith in the chapter "Normative Humanism beyond Theology" in Part II.
15. Cf. the passage concerning discourse ethics in the section on normative relativism in Part II.
16. See A. Rich (1981) for this and other criteria: 36 et seq.
17. Cf. ibid. (1981): 41.
18. Instead of the humanum, the common good is sometimes demanded as a goal. But what is this specifically? It is so general that it cannot be concretized even philosophically. Thus, it is of little help here for a systematic outline of economic ethics.
19. See the section on Amartya Sen in the chapter "Normative Humanism" in Part II.
20. Of course, this could also be simply postulated the other way around, which would contradict the threefold commandment of love of Jesus. Cf. in the Bible, for example, Mt 22:37 et seq.
21. Cf. K. Homann (1993a): 41: "The overriding task of ethics will then be to warn against morality."
22. Cf. P. Battyány (2007).
23. Cf. STh II–II, 66, 1 et seq.
24. GG Art. 14 following Art. 153 Weimar Constitution.
25. German Civil Code (BGB) § 854.
26. W. Kerber (1986): Sp. 166.
27. BGB § 903.
28. German Federal Constitutional Court decisions (BVerfGE) 30, 292 (334 et seq.) (Petroleum stockpiling).
29. Cf. A. Rauscher (2008): 514.
30. PP 22, cf. QA 21 and, from Scripture, Lev 25:23.
31. Cf. STh 66.1 and W. Kersting (2008): 502. The demand for basic income is based on a one-sided interpretation of this premise. Since everyone has the right to the earth (soil, etc.), everyone must also have a right to an equal pension. However, this right also entails responsibility.
32. GS 69.

33. Compendium 172, cf. LE 19.
34. Cf. STh II–II, 66, 1. "Deus habet principale dominium omnium rerum."
35. Cf. Gen 1:26.
36. Lev 25:23.
37. See, for example, Lev 25:8.
38. Q. Quodlib. 6:12, quoted by: A. F. Utz (1992).
39. STh II–II, 66.2: "*Quorum unum est potestas procurandi et dispensandi. Et quantum ad hoc licitum est quod homo propria possideat. . . . Unde proprietas possessionum non est contra ius naturale; sed iuri naturali superadditur per adinventionem rationis humanae.*"
40. R. Heinzmann (1994): 67 et seq.
41. See the chapter "Sanctification of the World" in Part I.
42. On the notion of *natura corrupta*, see also the chapter "Ecumenical Perspective" in Part II in the section on the view of humanity as a set of values.
43. Cf. RN 19.
44. Rights to dispose of goods in abundance do not expire in the event of an unequal distribution of goods. "Private property, including productive goods . . . finds its guarantee and incentive [in the] exercise of freedom" (MM 108 et seq.). Rather, abundance is initially only "owed" to the poor (STh II–II 66,7). Augustine's exposition of Psalm 147:2 is somewhat sharper: "The superfluity of the rich is necessary to the poor. If you hold onto superfluous items, then, you are keeping what belongs to someone else." As quoted in C. Mayer (2018): 26. In contrast, Thomas initially retains the right to dispose of the surplus, but it is burdened with a debt. Joseph Proudhon speaks of abundance as theft, Karl Marx of robbery.
45. Lk 11, 41.
46. "*In necessitate omnia sunt communia, id est communicanda. . . . Et ideo res quas aliqui superabundanter habent, ex naturali iure debentur pauperum sustentationi.*" (STh II–II 66,7) Cf. STh II-II, 32,5: "*Quod bona temporalia, quae homini divinitus conferuntur, eius quidem sunt quantum ad proprietatem, sed quantum ad usum non solum debent esse eius, sed etiam aliorum, qui ex eis sustentari possunt ex eo quod ei superfluit.*"
47. GS 69.1.
48. O. von Nell-Breuning (1985): 208 et seq.
49. Cf. A. F. Utz (1953): 490 et seq., 516.
50. This idea can also be found, for example, in T. More's *Utopia* (2006).
51. STh II–II, 62.2.
52. A. F. Utz (1949): 139.
53. This does refer to positive communism, according to which the commonwealth appropriates either only the means of production (moderate) or all goods (radical).
54. A. F. Utz (1949): 139.
55. Ibid.: 101, 99.
56. STh II–II, 66,2 et seq.
57. Cf. K. Hilgenreiner (1931): Sp. 594 and W. Kerber (1986): Sp. 169.
58. Cf. J. Höffner (2011): 212–17.

59. Cf. CA 42 or RN 12:1: "The sources of wealth themselves would run dry, for no one would have any interest in exerting his talents or his industry."
60. RN 12.1.
61. A. Rauscher (2008): 516. And in doing so, he does not oppose the teachings of Jesus. The latter asks Zacchaeus to give up some of his property, but not all. Cf. Lk 19:1 and MM 108 et seq.
62. Cf. A. Rauscher (2008): 517.
63. QA 45.
64. Cf. GG Art. 14.
65. W. Kersting (2008): 503.
66. Cf. QA 47.
67. Ibid.
68. 1 Tim 17.
69. Cf. QA 114.
70. See, for example, S. Viotti (2007).
71. Cf. CA 42.
72. This derivation, not as a natural law end in itself but as a pragmatic necessity, can also be found, for example, in Adam Smith's economic philosophy, according to which the development of social empathy is an end in itself. Smith defends the market as a framework for self-interested (especially egoistic) behavior with his realistic assessment of human nature, not because egoism is good, but because it is inherent in human nature. Cf. in Part II in the chapter "Normative Humanism" in the section on humanism in Smith.
73. Parallels to this in Islam and Judaism are evident. Cf. in part II the chapter "Theological Humanism."
74. Cf., for example, 2 Cor 8:9.
75. Cf. the following section in this chapter on the social market economy.
76. James 1:11. See also MM 121.
77. Cf. K. Farner (1947).
78. Ibid.: 48.
79. Migne 22, 983 et seq.
80. Ibid.: 40, 209.
81. Ibid.: 62, 563.
82. W. von Ketteler (1849): 10 et seq.
83. This is what A. Horvath (1929) calls for: In case of abuse, first suspension, then a loss of rights. Pius XI (QA) and O. von Nell-Breuning oppose such a regulation because of the legal uncertainty it would create.
84. See the section on justice in the chapter "Creation, Justice, and Peace" in Part III.
85. For the logic of the market, see the section on the compass for the market earlier in this chapter.
86. EG 53.
87. See on the logic of the market, the section on the compass for the market earlier in this chapter.

88. See also, for example, Amartya Sen's idea of empowerment and the section on humanism in Sen in the chapter "Normative Humanism beyond Theology" in Part II.

89. See the section on normative relativism in the chapter "Ethics beyond Normative Humanism" in Part II.

90. See the section on social justice in the chapter "Creation, Justice, and Peace" in Part II. In table 9.2, the model of personal social love corresponds to the conception of human dignity and coexistence in the social market economy.

91. Cf. the preceding section on the property regime.

92. See the section on Smith's humanism in the chapter "Normative Humanism" in Part II.

93. Cf. T. More (2016).

94. Cf. I. Kant AK VIII, 366, as well as in Part II in the chapter "Normative Humanism beyond Theology" in the section on humanism in Immanuel Kant.

95. On Luther's idea of two regiments, see the section on the nature of the mission above in Part I in the chapter "Ecumenical Perspective."

96. Cf. J. Schneider (2017).

97. Cf. U. Huar (1979) and the section on normative relativism in the chapter "Ethics beyond Normative Humanism" in Part II.

98. Cf. J. Wolff (1991) and the section on normative relativism in the chapter "Ethics beyond Normative Humanism" in Part II.

99. See the section on organ donation in the chapter "Life, Work, and Death" in Part III.

100. See, for example, P. Oberender and T. Rudolf (2003) and, in more detail, in Part III in the chapter "Life, Work, and Death" the section on organ donation.

101. Cf. the following section on currency and finance.

102. Cf. A. Müller-Armack (1949/1981): 496 and J. Messner (1954/2001): 626.

103. Cf. in Part I in the chapter "Mission in Crisis."

104. See, for example, developments in the Netherlands. In 2015, only 17 percent professed a belief in God there. Cf. the corresponding statistics in Omics (2015).

105. See the section on digitalization in the chapter "Future Issues" in Part III.

106. On such social developments in Germany, with numerous references to corresponding empirical studies, see the section on education in the chapter "Life, Work, and Death" in Part III.

107. Cf. the section on family in the chapter "Life, Work, and Death" in Part III.

108. For the dangers of such a debate culture, see in Part I the chapter "Mission in Crisis."

109. Cf. H. Mussinghoff (2011), ibid. (2012).

110. Cf. on this and the following quotations F. Hengsbach (2011).

111. Cf. articles 127, 130 of the TFEU.

112. F. Hengsbach (2011).

113. B. Edmunds (2011) also emphasizes the need for "new instruments for solidarity-based management of economic development in the euro zone."

114. For an understanding of social justice, see the section on social justice in the chapter "Creation, Justice, and Peace" in Part III.

115. Cf. for overview P. Leipold (2008): 5.

116. Founding members are Austria, Belgium, Finland, France, Germany, Ireland, Italy, Luxembourg, the Netherlands, Portugal, and Spain.

117. Cf. Deutsche Bundesbank (1992).

118. Cf. Statista (2022c).

119. Cited in accordance with TFEU (2012).

120. The inflation rate is measured in the so-called Harmonized Index of Consumer Prices (HICP), which comprises a representative basket of twelve components (including energy costs). To calculate an inflation rate for the eurozone as a whole, a weighting is applied depending on the current importance of the economy (with Germany at around 30 percent). The objective of price stability is considered to have been achieved if inflation is below 2 percent. For the HICP model and the actual development of HICP inflation from 2002–2006, see P. Leipold (2008): 17–19, XVI–XIX.

121. The interest rate for lending is published by the ECB in the case of fixed rate tenders: Banks can make bids on how much they want to lend at that interest rate. If the total bids for loan amounts are higher than the total amount provided for by the ECB, the amount of the realized quotas is allocated to the banks in proportion to the respective quantity bid. Another instrument is standing facilities, with which the ECB offers banks one-business-day lending and deposit facilities in order to cushion interest rate fluctuations on the money market.

122. Cf. P. Fang (2006): 166 et seq. There are different measures for calculating the money supply. The most common of these is the M3 money supply. In addition to cash, demand deposits, deposits with an agreed maturity of up to two years, and deposits redeemable at notice of up to three months, it also includes money market instruments and debt securities with a maturity of up to two years. Cf. P. Leipold (2008): 38.

123. The banks create money by lending deposits as loans. For a deposit of €1,000, for example, the bank must deposit a minimum reserve ratio of, say, 10 percent with the ECB as collateral. Experience shows that a cash deduction of the deposit must be taken into account (e.g., 20 percent, depending on the form of deposit). Then a prudently calculating bank can lend €700 of this sum. If these funds flow back again as deposits, the whole cycle repeats itself and so on.

124. Such a constellation is counterfactual to the ECB's persistently experienced low interest rate policy at present.

125. The complexity of an increasing number of new financial instruments also makes management more difficult. Psychological components will be addressed later in the evaluation of trust issues.

126. Foreign exchange swaps are forward transactions as insurance against exchange rate risks.

127. Cf. P. Leipold (2008): 74.

128. In order to avoid such a loss of confidence, the German government, for example, declared the security of all bank deposits to be guaranteed by the state in 2008. More convincing than such government promises appears to be confidence in the credibility of stability-oriented policies. Price stability depends, to a large extent, on psychological factors. This is illustrated by the following simplified relationship:

According to the so-called quantity equation, the product of the money supply "M" and the velocity of circulation "v" is equal to the product of the real GDP "Y" and the price level "P." Formally, it follows: M*v=Y*P and, therefore, P= M*v/Y. The velocity of circulation, which is constitutive of the price level, is determined by psychological components. The lower the confidence in price stability, the more v will rise because money will be spent before the expected loss in value. This effect, in turn, increases the inflationary impact.

129. As early as 1972, German Chancellor Helmut Schmidt implied competition between price stability and high employment when he opined: "Five per cent inflation is easier to bear than five per cent unemployment." Quoted here from P. Leipold (2008): 20.

130. J. Weidmann (2011): 20.

131. See J. Starbatty (2012).

132. J.-C. Trichet (2011).

133. Cf. J. Starbatty (2012).

134. J. Weidmann (2011a): 8.

135. Cf. W. Kersting (1999), A. Sen (1988), as well as on the idea of capabilities in Part II in the chapter "Normative Humanism beyond Theology" in the section on Amartya Sen.

136. J. Weidmann (2011): 14.

137. Cf. ibid. (2011c).

138. Ibid. (2011b).

139. Cf. J. Starbatty (2011).

140. Cf. J. Weidmann (2011).

141. On the complexity of causes, see J. Weidmann (2011a): 3.

142. O. Issing (2011).

143. Cf. Statista (2022b).

144. See the section on Jewish social ethics in the chapter "Theological Humanism" in Part II.

145. An important pioneer well before D. Kahnemann and A. Tversky was, for instance, H. A. Simon (1955). Sometimes such a path is traced back as far as Adam Smith. See, for example, N. Ashraf, C. Camerer, and G. Loewenstein (2004).

146. The established literature has become virtually intractable. See, for example, R. H. Thaler and C. Sunstein (2008) and Sunstein (2015) on the use of nudges.

147. The applied ethical issues of behavioral economics are also undoubtedly highly relevant. For discussions on the libertarian paternalistic use of nudges and their influence on well-being, freedom, autonomy, and integrity, see, for instance, P. Hacker (2017): 205–392.

148. For the focus chosen here, I rely primarily on the foci of H. Beck (2014) and M. Baddeley (2017), where one may find numerous additional references to literature.

149. U. Van Suntum and A. Stutzer et al. (2010).

150. See H. Beck (2014) and M. Baddeley (2017), who argue for fundamental adherence to the HO.

151. Cf. on the construct of *homo sociologicus*, for example, R. Dahrendorf (2010).

152. Cf. the model principles in economics and psychology in C. Camerer (1999): 10576.

153. The situation is different in economic approaches to business ethics. Karl Homann, for instance, makes a normative call for HO behavior in the marketplace that is unburdened by morality in the context of rules, which, by the way, are themselves also designed according to HO rationality. This is because overcoming irrationality makes behavior more predictable and more fully exploits the positive allocative effects of the market through higher welfare gains. The economic imperialism suggested by G. Becker (1981) goes one step further by calling for instrumental action in egoism beyond the market context throughout all areas of life (for example, also when selecting friends or partners). Cf. the section on the compass for the market earlier in this chapter.

154. Cf. in more detail on different heuristics and the opportunities and risks associated with their use H. Beck (2014): 28 et seq.

155. See, for example, H. Beck (2014): 8.

156. Cf. on such criticism ibid.: 78 et seq.

157. Cf. ibid.: 255–347 and M. Baddeley (2017): 19–33.

158. See also, for example, the assumption of a deontological, utility-reducing motivation in A. Sen (2003): 9, as well as the comments on this in Part II in the chapter "Normative Humanism beyond Theology" in the corresponding section on humanism in Sen.

159. For an introduction to happiness research, see B. Frey (2017).

160. Cf. L. A. Boland (1997). Thus referenced in H. Beck (2014): 4.

161. See, for example, D. Kahnemann and A. Krüger (2006).

162. M. Baddeley (2017): 113.

163. See, for example, G. Becker (1981).

164. Cf. the presentation of the concave utility function and its explanation in H. Beck (2014): 105 et seq. and additions to this theory ibid. on the following pages.

165. Cf. D. Kahnemann and A. Tversky (1979).

166. Cf. ibid.

167. See, for example, N. Epley and T. Gilovich (2006).

168. See, for example, G. M. Angeletos, D. Laibson, A. Repetto, J. Tobacman, and S. Weinberg (2001) and numerous references to hyperbolic consumption in H. Beck (2014): 251–53.

169. See, for example, H. Beck (2014): 1, 76 et seq.

170. Cf. ibid.: 87.

171. See, for example, F. B. Simon (2007).

172. Cf. P. Hacker (2017): 17 et seq.

173. Cf. the section on organ donation in the chapter "Life, Work, and Death" in Part III.

174. P. Hacker (2017): 10 with reference to B. Fischhoff (1982): 442.

175. Cf. B. Fischhoff (1982).

176. See, for example, P. Hacker (2017): 17 et seq. On the phenomenon of the only seemingly adversarial relationship between paternalism and liberality, see, for instance, C. Sunstein and R. H. Thaler (2003).

177. See the section on systemic ethics in the chapter "Ethics beyond Normative Humanism" in Part II.

178. P. Hacker (2017): 19, on the other hand, proposes a postmodern variant with the principle of communicability. Cf. the chapter "(Post-)modern Contexts" in the introduction.

179. See the section on education in the chapter "Life, Work, and Death" in Part III.

180. P. Hacker (2017): 391 uses the idea of such a model to justify the concealed normative claim of behavioral economics, which at first glance appears descriptive.

181. See the section on digitalization in the chapter "Future Issues" further in Part III.

Chapter Twelve

Leadership and Organizational Culture

Organizations and companies are important carriers of the value culture in our society.[1] This undoubtedly includes the churches, constituted charitable organizations such as *Caritas* and *Diakonie*, as well as nonprofit or for-profit organizations (in a Christian spirit). Their socio-ethical relevance has many sides, for example, their organizational and management culture internally, their effect on society externally, whether as an employer or through the fulfillment of their core business or their core tasks, be it through corporate social responsibility (CSR) or through their economic or political networking and responsible exercise of power. This chapter outlines a model of a position taken by Christian leadership ethics designed for internal influence. In an excursus, both its internal and external consequences are applied to the area of church organization. A discussion of the socio-political responsibility of charitable organizations such as *Caritas* and *Diakonie* and comparable Christian organizations follows to highlight the external impacts.

COMPASS OF GOOD LEADERSHIP

In close connection with the compass of economic ethics outlined in the previous chapter, I will now briefly sketch a proposal for a compass of leadership ethics before using it to present basic features of Christian leadership.[2]

Systematics of Leadership Ethics

Leadership ethics is not just a catalog of virtues for managers. It encompasses individual and institutional ethical aspects and is the systematic normative reflection of leadership in organizations. Leadership is the effective influencing of individuals, relationships, and rules based on values. Leadership ethics evaluates leadership practice normatively with a transparent system of values, whereby these values are then themselves the basis for evaluating leadership practice. A distinction must be made between such generally defined leadership ethics in the broad sense and leadership ethics in the narrow sense: Using a transparent set of values and its subject area, the latter must additionally determine the relationship between economic efficiency and human service for its normative evaluation of the management culture, without instrumentalizing or replacing any of the objectives.[3] In other words, leadership ethics in the narrow sense must normatively evaluate how economic efficiency and human orientation in the field of leadership are to be understood and how they must relate to each other as non-substitutable ends in themselves. Accordingly, it is assumed that neither objective may be sacrificed entirely to the other. This would obviate the need to determine the relationship between the relevant objectives. If one of the two perspectives is lost from view, the implementation in the management culture leads, at least in the long term, either to an economistic depersonalization or to a utopian de-economization of entrepreneurial activity. How the relationship between the goals is then interpreted in concrete terms—based on the respective set of values—and which goal is given greater weight can, in turn, be used—analogously to the economic ethics system—to distinguish between different paradigms and approaches to leadership ethics.[4]

- A normative individualistic school, corresponding to the economic ethics of business, is based on HO heuristics.[5] From this, in the sense of efficiency, an idea of the workforce as human resources can be derived, which nevertheless does not seek to relativize the goal of serving people (precisely in the sense of heuristics). For the economic calculation serves—so the claim—the development of the human, who is outside the context of economy but not reduced to HO. Efficiency orientation, as an end in itself, initially counters a heuristically simplified notion that remains open to a more complex human orientation as an end in itself.
- Alternatively, complex anthropologically grounded human nature can be postulated that attempts to focus on humans as persons even beyond counterfactual HO heuristics. In addition to economic efficiency, the management culture should serve this personal development of people because such ethical models are not absorbed in the economics that endogenizes them. The optimization of the development of the human being as a person in dependence on fixed and variable personality factors must, therefore, definitely be taken into consideration. Then, in the sense of human service, personal development in this complexity is the end in itself that opposes

the goal of economic efficiency. As in economic ethics in general, a distinction must be made between deontological approaches based on Kantian or discourse ethics and models based on metaphysics, such as Christianity.

Any leadership ethic in the narrower sense must provide an answer, at least in the market context, for determining the responsibility dualism of human service and economic efficiency—this also applies to the nonprofit sector—founded in a transparent normative value basis on the one hand and related to concrete areas of application of leadership on the other. After all, that is the basic system.

In the set of values, the underlying view of humanity first identifies the relationship between individuals and the team or organization as a whole. Which should be given the highest priority in terms of its development? Which spirit should characterize how humans live together: more of an anonymous coexistence or opposition in competition, or cooperation out of a sense of duty or even affection? Is human service achieved when the individual is subordinated to a collective in the team or organization? Or is the team or the organization understood as the sum of individuals each realizing their own potential? Are there any interactions in the process? These and other basic ideas—in order to be transparent and comprehensible in their right—must, in turn, be flanked by an ideological justification, which can be interpreted in normative individualist, socialistic, gender-perspective, Kantian, metaphysical, discourse-ethical, or other terms. The formulation of the idea of responsibility also shapes the profile of leadership ethics in the set of values. We must ask this with a view to effectively influencing rules, individuals, and relationships: How are personal and social responsibility justified, understood, weighted, and in which culture should they be implemented? The set of values thus also presents a responsibility program that must clarify before whom and to what extent employees and managers must assume which responsibilities. This does not put aspects of hierarchy, delegation, or control first. Rather, it is first and foremost a question of whether, how, and why the managers concerned may or should feel responsibility for themselves, for the organization, for each other, for economic efficiency, or even for a (Christian or other) idea of good in corresponding leadership contexts of effective influence.

Based on the respective determination of the dualism of responsibility, the areas of application of the set of values make up the lived leadership culture that is aimed at by the respective conception of leadership ethics. Guido Palazzo distinguishes between the respective incentive structures, the culture of control and trust, and the design of decision-making channels.[6] This system is now continued in a three-part division based on it. Leadership in organizations essentially takes place in the cultures of personnel planning, deployment, and development of communication (including hierarchy, power, and delegation) and motivation (including loyalty, identification, control, and incentives). These three key areas of application are highlighted here as examples. In each case, the aim is to avoid losses in achieving objectives. However, depending on the set of values, priorities are set and interpreted differently in the individual application areas. They mark the respective areas of tension of the interpretations.

- Human resources planning, deployment, and development have a significant impact on management culture, for example, through the selection of managers and other employees, how teams are put together, and promotion and training programs or measures. Fundamentally different characters, different characteristics of people, and different team cultures must be sought depending on the set of values. In a consistent leadership culture, this also has a direct impact on decisions regarding education, training, and promotion.
- Communication and the organizational structures associated with it, such as the culture of hierarchy, power, and delegation, are basically used in the management culture, either primarily for rapid decision-making or, above all, for critical participation of as many as possible.
- A leadership culture is essentially characterized by its understanding of performance motivation. How does the ethics underlying it compare with Vladimir I. Lenin's imperative of "Trust is good, control is better!"? How is which culture of trust established and implemented? What forms of control are used, how, and why? And how can the willingness to perform and identification with the organization be positively and effectively influenced: more through extrinsic incentives or through a culture of intrinsic motivation? The goal of optimizing performance can be pursued through various incentive and educational structures.

The three areas of application of leadership ethics selected here thus have a direct impact on answering very practical questions in everyday organizational life: Which characters should prevail as leaders?[7] Which employees should be recruited, and which training measures should be promoted? Should leaders focus more on collaborative or top-down decision-making, more on control or trust, more on competition or teamwork in their area of responsibility? Are extrinsic financial incentives or intrinsic motivation through insight and identification to be favored here? Leadership ethics does not leave the answers to chance but should offer good reasons for a program of a coherent leadership culture derived from the set of values with its proposals for this.

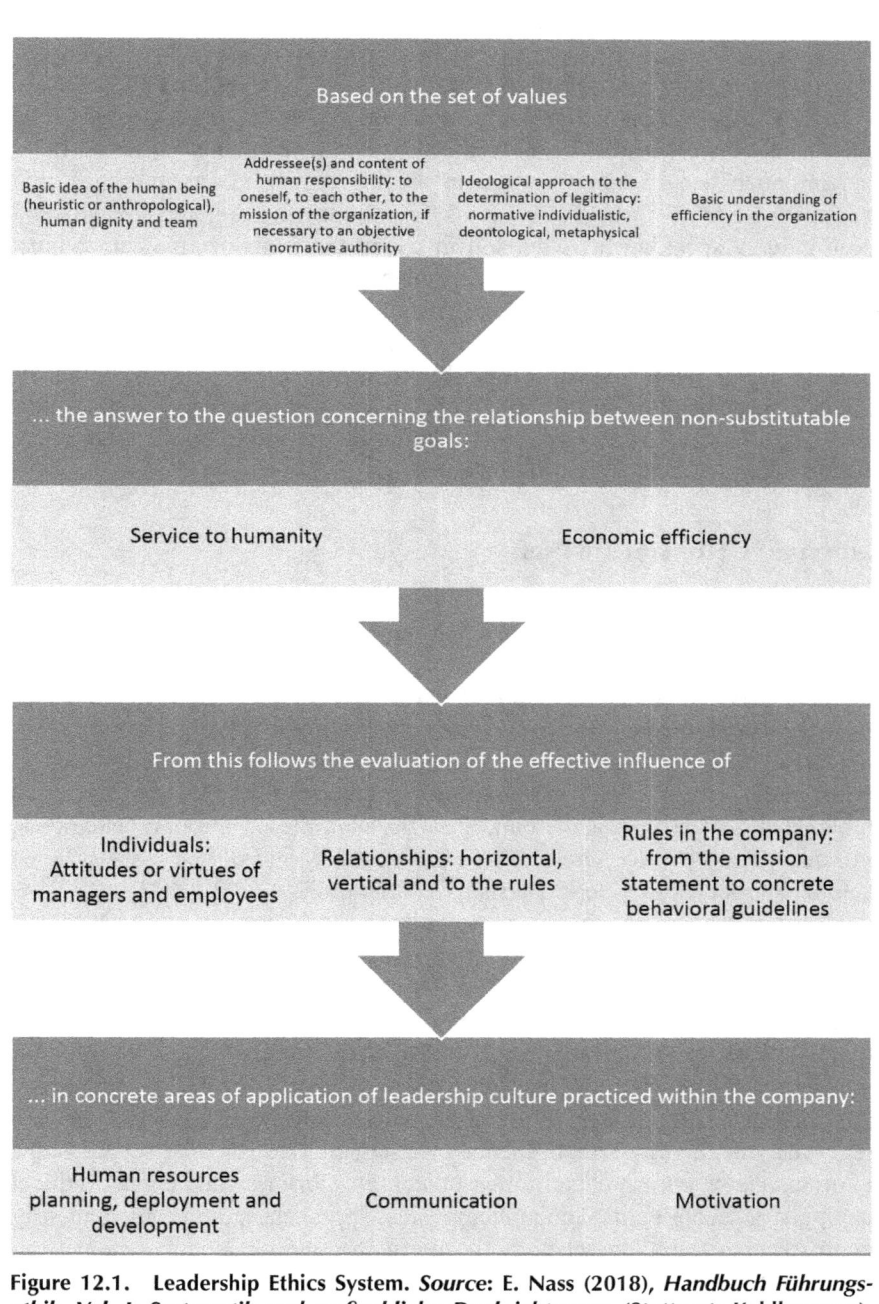

Figure 12.1. Leadership Ethics System. *Source*: E. Nass (2018), *Handbuch Führungsethik, Vol. I: Systematik und maßgebliche Denkrichtungen* (Stuttgart: Kohlhammer), 103.

Now we may turn our attention to systematics analogous to economic ethics, which expresses the need for credible leadership ethics to be coherent, and according to which the set of values and concrete applications follow a common, coherent normative logic. Because we must "strive for consistent internalization of ethical considerations in all management systems (e.g., performance incentive, performance appraisal, compensation, promotion, and control systems)."[8] The set of values is the soil that must be made transparent. Normatively speaking, it is the soil in which the fruits of application must also be measured. Leadership ethics, however, is not a closed system. It is quite possible that competing styles or organizational models may fit a set of values. Here, therefore, there is an openness and flexibility in the design, even within individual schools, possibly to adopt insights or perspectives of alternative leadership ethics models, provided they do not contradict one's own set of values. A syncretistically diluting set of values, on the other hand, would deprive the approach of this normative soil.

Normative Humanistic Profile

Christian leadership ethics bases its normative reflection on Christian values, in other words, the view of humanity founded in Jesus Christ, the ideal of responsibility inferred from this and the answers to the question of the relationship between economic efficiency and human service derived from this, with their consequences for the areas of application in the organization (e.g., personnel management, communication, and motivation culture). It thus systematically evaluates leadership cultures practiced on the basis of Christian ethics along with their value concepts (for example, in mission statements, missions, and visions). The set of values enables us to define these systems step by step in distinction to alternative paradigms.

Christian leadership ethics is close to the Kantian paradigm, which (in the moral law and the categorical imperatives) also presupposes an objective normative reference and argues in a normatively humanistic way. Like the leadership ethics models of the deontological school (integrative approach of Peter Ulrich, Kantian approach of Norman Bowie and others),[9] Christian leadership ethics must also presuppose in the set of values a complex anthropology with egoistic and non-egoistic rationality. Here and there, the legitimacy of the effective influence on rules, individuals, and relationships is oriented toward a predetermined objectivity. From a fundamental ethical perspective, deontological and metaphysical approaches, therefore, expressly compete with the approaches of the normative individualistic school from the perspective of the set of values. In contrast, they work together on a post-Taoist concept of rationality[10] to focus on a normative humanistic orientation with their own moral point of view on the ethics of leadership. The standard economic decision model derives human motivation first from the price effect (rewards, punishments, wages). However, from a normative humanistic point of view in contrast to behavioral economics, it neglects psychological findings according to which human behavior is also significantly controlled by intrinsic motivations.[11] Empirical studies by Bruno Frey and Alois Stutzer suggest that intrinsic motivatability, which is to be distinguished from egoistic utility maximization and whose development also has a cooperative and performance-enhancing effect, is an essential component of individual rationality.[12] Developing this motivation leads to greater satisfaction among people, which is accompanied by a greater willingness to perform.

Such evidence supports a personal-anthropological view for leadership ethics, as advocated today in deontological and metaphysical (e.g., Christian) approaches alike. Parallels such as these can be used to profile Christian leadership ethics: For this purpose, both schools present a complex anthropology with egoistic and non-egoistic rationality of humankind. In doing so, they can refer to Adam Smith, who, in his *Theory of Moral Sentiments*, explicitly places an altruistic rationality, including a moral conscience (inherent judge and impartial observer), alongside the egoistic one.[13] Under this condition, a human orientation of ethics cannot be limited to the development and promotion of egoistic self-benefit maximization (for whatever purpose) because this reduction depersonalizes the human being in the suppression of altruistic or even one's own deontological rationality.[14] If such an anthropology is accepted, then it is the task of normative humanistic leadership to take both rational dispositions equally seriously and to understand humans as dialogical beings in this way. Be it—coming from the tradition of the Enlightenment (especially Immanuel Kant)—a deontological ethics of reason or a metaphysically founded Aristotelian or, for instance, Christian theonomy, both schools categorically exclude the primacy of a self-referential economy.[15] Rather, it is assumed that selfish interests of individuals are not the sole measure of ethical legitimacy, even in the design of leadership. Therefore, such personal paradigms in good leadership are concerned with a comprehensive cultivation of non-egoistic human rationality. An ethically good, effective influencing of rules, individuals, and relationships (which equals good leadership) is oriented toward an objectivity that is obligatory in the moral or natural law, in the Bible or otherwise metaphysically, which humans can and should recognize by virtue of their reason or the like. Their content is derived either in terms of worldview from self-knowledge and the necessities of reason either transcendentally or from the knowledge of God or the Divine transcendent. Neither perspective is based on value-neutral assumptions but rather on ideologically founded, normative postulates that may or may not be shared.[16]

They presuppose an assumed objectivity by which morally good leaders and leadership cultures should be guided, along with an unconditional primacy of the human goal.[17] They are informed by the conviction that such a priority is neither unworldly nor need it contradict economic efficiency. Christian Müller, for example, counters the normative individualist credo of moral freedom by using game-theoretical considerations to show that individual morality in a dilemma can be just as rational and economically successful without everyone having to become a saint. "Expressed in the chic new style of 'German' spoken by management consultants: Ethics pays!"[18]

Both normative humanistic paradigms view not only the person with a moral mission in the business context but also represent a holistic personal view. For the dualism of responsibility, this means that the human service is realized in the assumption of the personal responsibility of leadership toward the appropriately identified addressees of this responsibility. In terms of virtue ethics, leadership ethics thus focuses first of all on the moral quality of managers or employees in the organizational context. In addition, there is the requirement, which must also be taken into account in terms of leadership ethics, that they (should) also effectively apply these morals in their other life contexts: "[The] successful business leader should have integrity in both his business and his personal life."[19]

From a Metaphysical to a Christian Profile

Christian leadership ethics is based on metaphysical arguments.[20] Deontological models do not necessarily exclude transcendence in terms of worldview (after all, Kant also thought of God as an idea that is necessary for thinking).[21] However, unlike the metaphysical models, they do not rely on the fact that managers can or even should derive norms of leadership from them. Herein lies the essential difference between the two otherwise related paradigms: Deontological approaches, like normative individualistic models, aim to remain free of metaphysics. In contrast, in a metaphysical set of values, normativity is explicitly derived from knowledge of transcendence, rather than transcendentally from necessities of reason. Transcendence can be understood as God (e.g., in the Christian sense) but also esoterically as the cosmos or platonically as an idea of what is good or similar. Good life in general and thus also good organizational leadership should be based on this transcendent good. This requires executives, in particular, to not only recognize and share but also to embody this standard of good habitually in order to use it effectively.[22] Metaphysical approaches assume a view and operationalize the content of a humanity that, for the determination of human service, can substantiate the human dignity sought in the leadership culture from a transcendentally given good that can be recognized as unconditional objectivity with the help of virtuous reason.

Above all, leaders, in their effective influence, are first responsible for the recognized divine power or idea of good and the universal ethical principles derived from it (such as the commandments of God, the cosmos, or the truth metaphorically recognized in Plato's Allegory of the Cave and the like). Good leaders, with their virtuous reason discerning the good, have a primary responsibility before the objective authority to follow its dictates. This is the result of responsibility before oneself and others so that here, too, the threefold responsibility toward which good leadership must first orient itself is effective. Metaphysical approaches—unsurprisingly—also have a missionary claim to liberate people to God or to the different transcendentally determined ideation of the good. But this is only a gradual difference to deontological approaches, which are no less missionary in their search for holistic autonomy. Even in the metaphysical approaches, it needs by no means to be a matter of a kind of religious conversion but possibly also of the empowerment of employees, made possible by effective influence, to a responsible freedom that leaves room for transcendence. Ferdinand Rohrhirsch, for example, understands Christian leadership with this outlook as "cooperation in preparing the way for what is to come."[23] In metaphysically based leadership ethics, human service consists of enabling ways to fulfill the given good but not forcing them. From a Christian point of view, for example, it is fulfilled in terms of virtue and institutional ethics in the threefold transcendentally founded responsibility. The market and the resulting economic viability are desirable with their service to the now metaphysical freedom of every human being. Economic efficiency, in turn, gains its legitimacy not only from itself but also from the morally preordained human service, which is now understood as a humane liberation to religiously promised salvation or otherwise transcendently prescribed good or salvation or sense. The cooperation between economic efficiency and human service follows neither an economic nor an ethical substitution of the other respective goal. Both have their own justification with their own logic.

From a Christian metaphysical point of view, human service is realized in the context of the mission of salvation in the threefold, biblically-based responsibility.[24] The goal of economic efficiency can be justified biblically on the one hand as the careful use of scarce resources (avoidance of waste) and on the other hand as the development of individual human talents. However, for dualism of responsibility, priority must be given to non-economically endogenous personal development, which economic calculus must serve. Human service and economy are related to the triune God of Jesus as the first goal.[25] The human development of social nature also unleashes social-creative potential for achievement as well as critical-creative decision-making in the workforce. A Christian synthesis of economic success and human service rewards performance as the development of individual nature and also promotes social development in teams: not chiefly for reasons of increasing profit but with the purpose of developing humans' natural personal destiny. Ultimately, it is the Christian perspective on the meaning of human existence, internalized both as an individual and as an organizational culture, which makes economic success a service value for personal development and thus systematically determines the interaction of efficiency and human service for organizational practice. Thus, economic efficiency in a leadership context is a necessary but not sufficient condition for the realization of Christian personal human service.

Consequence and Compass

Based on the essence of leadership ethics and the notion of a Christian set of values with its consequences, we may now conclude this section with a few results for the purposes of orientation.

- A good management culture must create room for development in the sense of Christian anthropology for the threefold responsibility (toward God, oneself, and one another). The premise is that Christian leaders are Christians so that they can justify and practice this threefold responsibility in this way. Not only do they have the threefold responsibility to allow their own potential to unfold, but they should also allow their employees the appropriate space to do the same.
- On the other hand, there is, of course, ample room for people of different worldviews and religions among staff members. Christian personhood is characterized precisely by the fact that even strangers and others are seen as individuals created in God's image with full dignity.[26]
- Following one's own destiny for salvation and empowering employees to follow their own destiny is the Christian vision of good leadership. The rules of the organization must also serve this purpose. Accordingly, what is good is a leadership culture with virtues, rules, and relationships that enable everyone to develop their God-given destiny for salvation even within the bounds of their working hours. Individuals are then responsible for the use of the corresponding space—according to their abilities. Thus, the freedom of Christians in their decisions must be taken seriously.
- In contrast to the anthroposophical-metaphysical organizational culture, personal appreciation in the organization also understands[27] the occasional imbalance or the lack of positive influence of employees not as a (refine-

ment) deficiency but as a human expression of the created, which, in biblical terms, may also have its time with Kohelet (preacher).
- In the areas of motivation and communication, the God-given individual and social nature of human beings must be considered with a high degree of individual responsibility and community. This requires a concept of helping people to help themselves, with an intense sense of social cohesion and individual commitment.
- The rules must first be designed in the service of mutual trust. Spaces where whistle-blowing might be desirable for breaking up conspiracies should not exist in such a leadership culture if possible. Because mistrust and fear fundamentally contradict the Christian ideal of unity.
- Accountable transparency of organizational goals and strategies is essential. However, the limits of a deliberative culture must also be kept in mind. Scrupulous moral brooding that blocks performance is just as worrisome as the inefficiency of overly long decision-making paths. Where possible, it is important to promote a sense of togetherness in the organization based on a sense of purpose, which is ideally fed by an affective sense of unity.[28]
- To this end, Christian confessors, as leaders, create spaces of freedom, including ideological diversity, based on their view of humanity. This culture thus makes heterogeneity and diversity possible from the source of Christian faith, which, however, must not poison the well from which this freedom originates in the first place.[29] This is the Christian idea of social love, which ultimately leads to the materialization of social peace in the spirit of togetherness. Undoubtedly, their realization remains a visionary idea, which at least sets an aspirational goal of a credible Christian leadership culture.
- In the case of a homogeneous staff (for example, under a commonly shared Christian vision), a tight hierarchy may also be conceivable. This, however, absolutely presupposes the self-determined voluntary nature of those affected, who in doubt can or even must eliminate the hierarchy. For even in homogeneity, the co-responsibility owed to the Christian understanding of personhood must not be relativized.
- In employee motivation, economic and ethical aspects should not be played off each other on the basis of the personal Christian view of humanity. For as soon as egoistic striving for self-interest must be suppressed by coercion, or if—vice-versa—it is assumed to be the sole maxim of action, the holistically understood responsibility of the free human being before God is not taken seriously. Even arguments that are not expressly Christian enrich the expressly Christian idea of personal motivation: Jonathan Wolff takes an anthropological view of the social side founded in a "human social nature," which, as a "sense of community" under consideration

of individual egoistic self-interest, nevertheless enables the formation of social responsibility.[30] Amartya Sen also recognizes this bipolarity.[31] These social motivations likewise have their own efficiency potentials, which can be activated by means of incentives if they are developed into an optimized allocation (i.e., into an efficient use of human resources). The Christian culture of a synergistic motivation seeks to challenge the advantages of competition and team motives equally with possible reference to such assumptions, now based on Christian personality. Efficient synergy effects follow from the fact that individuals motivated in this way are addressed comprehensively in their willingness to compete and in their ability to develop a team mindset with the full force of their own rationality. This allows for increased identification with the organization, reduces the copycat mentality, and realizes Christian personhood, the idea goes.

- Coercion to cultivate a dogmatically prescribed ideal of freedom contradicts the idea that the God of Jesus Christ expects a self-determined, free response from humans to His offer of love. Because *individualitas* and *socialitas* make human beings persons, focus must also be placed on competitive and group-rational team motivation. The shortening of economic endogenization, death, or re-education of competitive thinking result in a failed understanding of motivation, which violates the self-determined freedom of the Christian person and, at the same time, wastes efficiency potentials. This is where Christian ethical and business perspectives converge. For, according to the Christian view, the abridgments of the view of humanity lead to inefficient allocations in business management decisions because they are not oriented to the basic structure of human rationality (with competitive and team motivation) and, thus, neglect the holistic human perspective. This is because Christian personal motivation is to jointly tap the efficiency potentials of self-interest (competition) and collective integration (team spirit), from the point of view of human service and economic efficiency in equal measure. On the one hand, employees can be motivated more easily with such an approach. On the other hand, this human orientation of performance incentives is intended to optimally challenge the efficiency potential inherent in human rationality. The holistic nature of human rationality is the standard of leadership ethical legitimacy here.

EXCURSUS: COMPASS IN THE CHRISTIAN CONTEXT

The compass of Christian leadership ethics not only aims to but also has the potential to be applied in a wide variety of organizations and industries. Above all, it strives to be a benchmark for explicitly Christian organizations and their cultures. This affects not only organizations such as *Caritas* and *Diakonie*, for example, but also the church itself. For the church to win back followers today, it must radiate credibility. The answer to the question of how this can be achieved in concrete terms is less trivial. Some suggestions relate to being a church practicing within the professional sphere (i.e., the culture of togetherness in the context of church work). This message is sent out into the world and is either inviting or off-putting but does not comprehensively answer the question of credibility. The reason for this is that many other aspects, for example, in the areas of pastoral care, theology, or church constitution, are also of the utmost importance. By focusing on the culture of professional interaction in the church in the following brief excursus, a specific segment is singled out, the missionary impact of which should not be underestimated. Some facets of Christian leadership culture for the church are discussed as examples, in particular against the background of the mission in the world outlined in part I and the imperative of credibility. To facilitate this discussion, I will first sharpen the compass of leadership ethics just presented in this context before delving deeper into areas of application.

Church in the View of Leadership Ethics

In this section, the focus of the consideration of leadership ethics is on the lived relationships in the professionally constituted church. These include, for example, the culture of leadership and interaction with one another, whether in pastoral work and administration, in church associations, or in social educational institutions, or in the area of theological education and science. The three areas of application in which Christianity must prove itself in inner-church work relationships are, first and foremost—as was shown in the previous section—personnel work, communication, and motivation culture. Credible Christian leadership culture must answer the practice attached to it with its view of humanity and the values and principles derived from it.

The compass of values that should shape a winning Christian culture of professional interaction is well known. The basic orientation must be the image of every human being in the image of God, the threefold responsibility (before God, oneself, and one's neighbor), the human being as a social being of freedom and a moral person with talents given by God, weaknesses, hope in grace, and eternal life. Several principles for the culture of the church's existence in practice follow from this set of values. People who work in the church sector spend a more or less large part of their lives here. It must also be possible to fulfill the mission to find and walk a path to salvation before God as a moral person in the context of work. The employee is, therefore, never just an interchangeable human resource whose expertise and motivation must be optimized in order to achieve a higher output. This means, for example, that employees in the church—from financial administrators to the sexton of the parish—should also experience their work as part of their human fulfillment. Work is time spent throughout our lives and should be filled with meaning understood in this way. This is based on God's mission to open up paths to salvation for people in the workplace as well. Mere money-making jobs should not exist in the church. The point must be that togetherness must not be shaped as an anonymous coexistence or as an opposition in competition, nor as togetherness as merely the tiresome fulfillment of one's duty. Rather, people should develop a spirit of affection together in the workplace, derived from being the common children of God. We need to be able to experience for ourselves the simple fact that teams, in the context of church work, are more than the sum of individuals because they also feel connected to each other on a human level. However, individuals must not simply be subordinated to an abstract collective within the team or the institution. Because, as free individuals before God, they still bear responsibility themselves for the work they perform. Christian responsibility and rewarded performance are not contradictory if the respective possibilities of individuals are taken into account. In this context, egalitarianism contradicts the gift of individuality. Employees are to be given the responsibility that is reasonable for them because they are moral beings before God who should experience growth on the one hand but because they also have limitations on the other.

The desired salvation of humanity, the fulfillment of which includes life in the context of work, is not a Pelagian act of achievement. Rather, it is, ultimately, granted to humans by God. Thus, the weakness of the human being retains the same esteem as the freely developing successful spirit of creative design. From a Christian point of view, humans have a duty to God and to themselves to allow their individual and social personalities to unfold and to value every human life, especially the lives of the vulnerable.[32] This is true both of one's own weaknesses and the weaknesses of others. Performance and appreciation, even of the weaker members of a society, are thus inseparable parts of a Christian work culture, as is the recognition of performance in the service of the common mission. Unlike purely market-oriented companies, for example, the church and Christian organizations are well-advised to offer opportunities to people within their own ranks who would otherwise have no chance in the primary labor market, for example, in *Diakonie* and *Caritas* work, but also elsewhere. Of course, this must be justifiable financially, for cohesion within the team and in the service of the common mission, but where the possibilities exist financially, this is a credible sign of this option for the vulnerable.

Wasting time, money, and resources should also be avoided, as they could be better spent in other places under otherwise equal conditions in the sense of the salvation order and/or in the responsibility before creation. A working culture of Christian cooperation and decision-making is, therefore, based on the view of humanity founded in Jesus Christ and the resulting ideal of responsibility with its consequences for these areas of application. At the same time, there is always a missionary claim. This is not about aggressive conversion but instead about enabling employees to have a self-responsible freedom that leaves room in their working lives for encountering transcendence, whether in worship services or in fields of practical pastoral care with visible symbols or conversations that open this door. All of this constitutes a Christian set of values that must become concrete in the context of the areas of application if this lived culture is to be credible.

Now ways of implementing the ideal can be presented in the three application areas, assuming orientation to the compass for Christian leadership presented in the previous section.

Personnel Compass

Special character traits are generally expected in addition to confession for leadership positions and pioneers in theology in particular. When filling such positions, human quality should play an essential role in addition to professional suitability. This corresponds roughly to Aristotle's idea of justice. He had already proposed that public offices be awarded according to the moral fortitude of the applicants. This criterion should be applied comprehensively in the church and Christian organizations, supplemented by the profession of faith, which, however, coincides with goodness of character if it truly aims to be credible. In selection rounds for corresponding responsible positions, it is natural to also promote dissenters who share the spirit of the Gospel and are preferable in purely human terms to those who think alike ideologically. Personnel selection, especially in leadership areas, should, therefore, be carried out by taking into account the Aristotelian principle of goodness of character and shared belief.

For the personnel assignment, possible perhaps unconventional food for thought for the profession of the secular priest can be given from a Catholic perspective with parallels to the Protestant context intended. For a long time, there was an attempt to transform as many pastoral workers as possible into managers through the use of extensive training courses, even if these individuals neither wanted to nor were able to perform managerial duties. Many pastoral workers have been left behind and failed in the process. This experience may also have prevented some from taking such a path at all, even if they felt the call to do so within themselves later on. The social recognition of the priestly profession has also declined, which has further deterred some. It would be advantageous to be able to present priests with different profiles in the future. For example, young men with varying degrees of talent can and should be re-inspired to pursue this path. The following profiles could be advertised, for example:

- the classic full-time pastor who leads a large pastoral district and, despite some professional relief, must possess managerial talent;
- the missionary who goes through various communities where there is no longer a permanent priest. He holds catechesis, encourages the faithful on the ground, and celebrates the sacraments;
- the pioneer who moves to a secularized area and tries to rebuild the church and Christianity there; and
- the applied thinker who holds seminars for priests and full-time and volunteer workers and represents the winning side of faith on podiums, in the media, and in lectures.

Such images could be linked to clearly defined jobs that prospective students could align themselves with early on. It might also be possible to conclude attractive contracts with religious congregations. Secular priests, instead of living alone, could loosely join a monastic community, live there, share in the spirituality, and, in addition to being pastors to the bishop, contribute to the community. This is provided that both sides agree and that payment for it is also agreed upon. For elderly priests, there could be an option to move into the retirement home of a religious order and be cared for there in a spiritual atmosphere and community, for an appropriate fee. In their studies, in their seminar training, and, above all, in subsequent training courses, the candidates and priests could specialize in one focus area or another, in addition to the basic contents and attitudes assumed equally for all and prepared for a corresponding task in practice.

New forms of personnel development will likely be influenced by its impact. The conventional image that pastoral ministers must be able to do everything should be replaced. This does not mean, however, that everyone can simply do what they please in the sense of oft-aggrieved charisma orientation. This is a waste of resources and, therefore, inefficient. Self-serving privileges as mere self-fulfillment must be abolished. Instead, there are two sides to consider when speaking of the priority of personal development. After all, there are charisms on the one hand and necessary fields of action for a successful mission on the other. The two must come together. Proven experts could set out through communities and categorical areas in search of previously hidden talent. This could be a new route for finding outstanding preachers, for example. Or, in other places, there are parish priests who made excellent offers for days of reflection in their small local area. They could be appointed to the diocesan level for this purpose. This would offer an opportunity or possibly even a chance to experience a breakthrough to previously undiscovered talent. Apart from the fact that they are likely to flourish and be more effective than ever in their new roles, they might also report enthusiastically on their experiences to others.

Communication Compass

The culture of conflict is an essential part of the culture of communication. The church can also learn from the economy without importing its normatively charged view of humanity. In personnel interviews, there is more to praise than merely qualities and skills. In addition to this expression of positive appreciation, a communication of appreciative criticism must also be cultivated without being offensive. This helps individuals understand unexpected or disappointing decisions, work on themselves with purpose, and more clearly identify resulting successes in their own development.

Communication culture is also reflected in the coexistence of different opinions. Heterogeneity can be exhausting as long as there are no good rules of dialogue. In leadership teams, for example, or in theological faculties and academies, there are naturally people with different views of content, which are also fairly and constructively disputed beyond the common value basis of faith. The ideal would be the following: Representatives and supporters of different opinions, for example, on questions of liturgy, exegesis or social ethics, and so on, argue with each other in a cultivated manner on equal footing. And they recognize that it is possible to justify and defend a counter-position from an honest faith perspective. Thus, they also value each other personally. This is a tolerance by faith in freedom. Such a culture truly generates new ideas, thereby enriching cognition and decision-making.

With respect to the culture of decision-making in particular, leadership in ecclesiastical contexts, among others, expressly in Christian contexts, should create spaces of trust and transparency (at the right time). Important in the space of trust, besides professionalism and faith, is the aptitude of character already mentioned and a critical-creative loyalty. This is how personal responsibility and community spirit grow. Decisions do not always discuss Adam and Eve. For there is a consensus of content, like an ethical code, which is presupposed because it essentially founds the ecclesial community. This is the basis for discussion. This is desirable because it will continue the success of the mission. Managers and other decision-makers must treat their management teams with constructive criticism of their person or of their content in a professional and good manner, as well as separating the content and the personal as well as possible. Trust here means the following: In professional church teams, colleagues dare to express constructive criticism where it serves the cause.

At the same time, the space for this demanding, sanction-free culture of discussion at all hierarchical levels must be clearly defined. There is no room for a bureaucratic mentality. Lean decision-making processes and clear assignments of tasks are important.

Scrupulous moral brooding that blocks performance and decision-making should also be kept to a minimum. All this saves time, money, and nerves, frees up resources for other important tasks for the active implementation of the mission, and increases job satisfaction in administrative services as well because one's own actions are experienced as clearly more productive in service to the mission. These consequences radiate inward and outward. This does not mean that there should be no more discussion and that top-down rule should prevail.

Church leaders, in particular, are role models of culture down to the grassroots level, and again, this applies to church work in every context. As such role models, eyes are not only on the bishop, the vicar general, the director of the *Caritas* foundation, or the extended leadership team but ultimately all those who bear responsibility. As witnesses to the Christian faith, they create the spaces of freedom for diversity in the spirit of unity together, based on their view of humanity.

Motivation Compass

Motivation starts with the internalization of the Christian mission, for which employees in the church should stand together.[33] What connects all leaders and all employees in the church or Christian-theological areas of pastoral care, education, administration, social services, and science is, first, the common confession. Second, it is the common mission for which everyone shares responsibility. Third, the strength of character to do one's best and to stand up for one another (ideally) connects them. This identity is the reason for loyalty and also a willingness to sacrifice for the common mission. All creatively effective diversity, even if desired, is subordinated to this fundamental commonality. The free development of talents and individuality does not stand in the way of this but builds on it. The limits are: Whoever fundamentally loses faith in the triune God, whoever considers the mission to be fundamentally flawed, and whoever turns out to be conscienceless, egoistic, deceitful, and so on in terms of character is ultimately no longer acceptable. Corresponding loyalty rules should also be openly communicated. The goal is to be able to rely on one another when the going gets tough and to be able to celebrate all successes, even those of individuals, honestly and without envy. In case of doubt, everyone should and can assume co-responsibility according to their abilities. The strong protect the weak and defend them without intervening in their private lives in a paternalistic way, as is sometimes the case with sects. Such an overarching, collective idea does not contradict the notion of creative dialogue. On the contrary: It is the very foundation on which it is built. This understanding of heterogeneity on a transparent common personal basis attracts followers and offers orientation and space for boundless creative design. The most important prerequisite for such a good motivational culture is credible actors who appear and act on its behalf. Motivation arises from such a sense of community, of being in the same boat and jointly responsible for its visionary mission. In accordance with the motivational slogan "Be Know Do," the question of personal being is followed secondly by the question of knowledge and then by the question of concrete action.[34] However, motivational culture should not be thought of as exclusively corporate. Overemphasis on this brings with it the risk that the development of individuality and freedom might not be given the focus it is due. Ultimately, the goal is to provide everyone in the work context with a path to their salvation before God. No community, and certainly no normatively sanctioning collective, can take that away from them. In the end, each individual bears personal responsibility for this. Therefore, the liberal imperative "Take action and accept liability" also applies here with regard to personal salvation. Credible church motivational culture thus has an individual and a collective side. Synergetic motivation understood in this way leaves room for competitive and team motives alike.

Consistency to Compass

The goal of a credible culture of professional ecclesial participation can now be outlined as a compass that is worthy of attaining. It outlines an ideal:

- The spirit of the Gospel characterizes the togetherness of church work. Staff who are enthusiastic about this message appreciate the great freedom of thought, creativity, individual development, and critical dispute that the common confession offers. Paul would find the ideal of being a church from 1 Corinthians 12 well reflected in this culture. It is an appreciative tolerance from a faith in freedom with which the Christians inspired by it challenge the world around them. This has a credible effect both internally and externally. The influence of structural processes on this is manageable.

- The culture of togetherness in the work context of the church not only has an effect on the faith of those directly affected and their families but also on society. Issues regarding staff, communication, and motivation should be consistently implemented in the spirit of the Gospel and the mission.
- Above all, the common foundation of faith and honesty of character should be standards for filling positions in the spirit of Aristotle. They create a culture of freedom in faith that makes constructive discussions possible, especially between competing positions.
- Corporate and individual thought merge to help those involved in their daily work be of service to their salvation before God and to the Christian mission in the world.

Such aspects regarding staff, communication, and motivation can be inferred directly from the Christian confession and view of humanity. This makes it both compelling and challenging to those directly affected and to the outside world.

ADVOCACY IN OPINION FORMING

Christian organizations in the welfare sector such as *Caritas, Diakonie, Malteser, Johanniter,* and others must be measured against the compass of Christian leadership culture. On the other hand, they perform a service for the common good in following Jesus out of a credible Christian confession. They play a key role in shaping social values and opinions. In their respective areas of expertise, they have an important part to play in fulfilling the Christian mission to sanctify the world. This also includes their commitment to an appropriate awareness of values in society. This brief section provides this special responsibility with a compass guided by Christian social ethics.

Exemplary Faith

The following applies the principle in general and for the associations or organizations written with the same wording in particular with respect to the self-conception of Christian social work: *Caritas* or *Diakonie*[35] is an essential basic function of being a credible Christian and thus also a model for the common mission in the world. It arises from the encounter with Christ. This is why it starts from the altar, for example, in the sense of Wilhelm Löhe. It is thus connected to the liturgy. Christian welfare is always a witness to Christ in the world, which makes it a martyr. In this way, the Christian mandate of love is inseparable from the other two acts (liturgy and witness).

In the Christian welfare sector, *Caritas* and *Diakonie*, for example, also use their names to make an explicit commitment to this foundation of the Christian mission of salvation in the world.[36] The latter is concretely expressed in good arguments for inviolable human dignity in the social rules on the one hand and in the exemplary, appreciative cooperation, especially with the weakest members of society, on the other. In this way, Christian sponsors can be inviting markers of Christian credibility and, thus, at the same time, an audible voice in the field of moral opinion-forming, from hospital ethics committees to the German Ethics Council and beyond. Such genuine credibility succeeds when these bearers—like the church as a whole—understand themselves as sent into the world but without themselves being entirely of this world. The two must be thought of together. At times, however, the poles are pitted against each other as biases. Peter Beer, on the other hand, aptly outlines the challenging tension: "The Church should have a clear and prominent influence on this world, but it must always remember that is part of this world and that it does not simply stand opposite it."[37] Christian welfare agencies should also be leaven in the world—leaven that is understood. That is why, on the one hand, they need their roots in an increasingly secular environment. On the other hand, they must identify their profile, which goes beyond a mere appreciation of others. This includes a profile of making the world a better place in confession of Jesus Christ. Shaping the mission in this way as part of the practiced mandate for sanctification comes into view here, quite in the sense of the bipolar tension. The essential Christian contents of the Christian mission of salvation in the world were presented in part I. Christian welfare agencies can inspire our contemporaries with this mission to shape a better world.[38] Its impact can and should be felt as a Jesuan-based advocacy of empowerment, advocacy, and solidarity foundation precisely in the service of those in need of help. The linchpin of Christian social responsibility is the commitment to the origin of love.

Christian welfare agencies, as missionaries of a spirit of love, retain their practically effective relevance in the sense of their mission, if they neither lose touch with the world nor lose touch with God. The justification for the unconditional human dignity of the weak, the sick, the disabled, and the unborn and the commitment to its consistent implementation come into view precisely in the areas of expertise in Christian welfare work. It openly acknowledges inviolability as a matter of faith, justified in the Christian idea of likeness with the image of God and God's incarnation in Christ. Christian welfare thus has the task of taking an advocating and credible position in the world on the basis of its mission, as well as forming opinions and helping to shape society on this basis.

Credibility in Context

When Christian welfare organizations speak out publicly on their core social issues, they encounter secular or other positions in discussions about social justice, the right to life, family, health, education, care, and other issues. In order for their positions, which are based on normative humanism, to be heard, Christian sponsors must first radiate credibility and, to this end, also align their own organizational culture with the Christian ideal.[39] The following features are included:

- Adherence to cost-effectiveness serves to avoid wasting scarce resources, protect jobs, and preserve Christian sponsorship in the face of competition among providers.
- Educational initiatives for its own staff as well as open offerings should address the Christian social vision of dignity, social culture, and virtue.
- Active lobbying is needed for those who have no voice of their own in our society. Christian agencies must also network in order to fulfill their mission of empowerment, advocacy, and solidarity in the long term.
- Credibility also works through the people who represent the Christian sponsors internally and externally. These leaders should combine various virtues:
  - In addition to the good qualities required by leadership ethics, it takes courage to openly stand up for a Christian social vision of a just society.
  - Christian virtue lives from a habitus of joy in being endowed as God's image and in Christ as the human face of God.
  - In addition, there is a living spirit of love: given by God, lived in concrete terms, and passed on in a spirit of unity.
  - It is precisely into the brokenness of humans and the world that being a Christian should have an effect: as an attitude of well-founded gratitude to the divine.
  - Those who are not capable of this gratitude are left with the virtue of hope. Sources of a spirituality of hope are prayer, Holy Scripture, the church, and common confession therein. Christian confidence is not a consolation out of the world into the hereafter. On the contrary: It aims to help shape the here and now.[40]
  - Oswald von Nell-Breuning highlights prayer as a virtue in responsible decision-making: "The faithful Christian . . . will pray to the Holy Spirit for the right inspiration in such a situation." Christian welfare organizations will then successfully contribute to society if their decision-makers rely more on it than on power instinct or changing moods. For their credibility then lies in the radiating dignity that follows faith.

- The awareness that the origin and goal of human life are not earthly allows the Christian to live, think, celebrate, suffer, and even die with confidence where others might despair. Representatives in Christian welfare care, in particular, need this empathy. They must embody courage, gratitude, and hope, if they aspire to be credible.

EXAMPLE 12.1

Not long ago, I visited the *Kinderhaus* in Viersen, a home that cares for disabled children. Kristina, who was formerly active in the parish youth organization of my chaplaincy and is now the deputy director of the *Kinderhaus*, introduced me to her work with severely disabled children. These children live in the facility permanently and receive care there for the duration of their often relatively short lives. When I look into these children's eyes, I see no shortage of laughter, radiance, and hope. Kristina performs her work with the utmost dedication and passion for the children and her impressive service is a model for others. For her, the work is intentional, a conscious decision arising from her Christian faith, which has become a habitus for her. She sees the image of God in every child. I was deeply moved by this. When I am here, I experience witness for life in the most radical way possible, to the very end and, with unwavering hope, even beyond.

Consequence and Compass

Aware of the Christian social mission, which is not of the world but directed into it, denominational welfare agencies should act as advocates in the following way:

- For organizational culture, the orientations from the two preceding sections are applied in this chapter.
- Christian advocacy is reflected in different, also public, positions on socially and ethically relevant fields:
  - The orientations formulated earlier in each case in the compass, above all from the chapter "Life, Work, and Death," must be taken into account.[41] Any ideologies that would relativize human dignity in perspective are unacceptable. This is followed, for example, by a rejection of extremist war ideologies, whatever their stripes.
  - Utilitarian QALY criteria for rationing in health care should be rejected because they make the worthiness of human life dependent on a concept of utility. Socially just rationing in public health care requires, in

addition to human rights safeguards for minimum care with a ban on discrimination, the principle of responsibility to also be taken into account (for example, by considering individual health responsibility in the rationing debate).[42]
- Christian welfare organizations are committed to a social spirit of togetherness, in which help for the needy is not limited to legal claims that can be enforced. Raising awareness of basic values and social principles, as well as energetically contributing to a spirit of inclusive social cohesion, is a task of education that identifies the learning of ethical competence as an urgent goal.[43] A culture of (social) responsibility, which incidentally corresponds with the Jewish idea of helping the needy, requires mature people whose expertise always presupposes a capacity for socio-ethical judgment.[44]
- People in need of help have an unconditional right to be helped by the solidarity community. Of course, this includes people who legitimately seek protection and asylum in our country. An economic or collectivist relativization of this claim must be rejected. Subsidiarity must not be forgotten in solidarity. Thus, the requirement of helping people help themselves must not lead to luring people away from their homeland, where they are urgently needed for reconstruction.
- The disabled, the elderly, the sick, and the dying all belong at the center of our society. They enrich our culture with their charisma and experience, through their coping with neediness, frailty, or finiteness. Socially rich is the society that learns from these people, their questions, and their answers. Socially poor is a society that questions their dignity and right to live.
- Christian sponsors stand up for persecuted people and, in doing so, also make the persecution of Christians of our day an issue.

Such positions, which are sometimes also contentious, correspond to the Christian social mission in the sense of the acceptability represented here. The resulting task is to relate to them and to align social commitment with them.

NOTES

1. In the following, organizations are referred to comprehensively, which also includes companies that operate as businesses, whether in the profit or nonprofit sector.

2. Cf. in detail E. Nass (2018): 196–227.

3. On comparable ideas of such dualism of goals constitutive for leadership ethics, cf. T. Kuhn and J. Weibler (2012): 46 or P. Ulrich (1999): 230, 237. For human resource development, it is defined by M. Becker (2002): 492 in efficiency mode as

such: "HR development helps to achieve the goals of the business (economic efficiency) and the individual developmental goals of the employees (social efficiency)." Cf. also P. Ulrich (2010): 28, T. Kuhn and J. Weibler (2012a): 23, 94, 107, and L. Fischer and O. Fischer (2007): 22.

4. For a detailed account and distinction of authoritative schools of leadership ethics, see E. Nass (2018).

5. See the section on normative relativism in the chapter "Ethics beyond Normative Humanism" in part II and the section on the compass for the market in the chapter "Economy and Economic Order" in part III.

6. Cf. G. Palazzo (2007): 120.

7. T. Kuhn and J. Weibler (2012a), for example, criticize the fact that today's management positions are typically filled by Machiavellians, narcissists, or psychopaths.

8. P. Ulrich (1999): 244.

9. Cf. P. Ulrich (1999), N. Bowie (2005).

10. Cf. P. Ulrich (1999). 241.

11. See the section on rethinking economic ethics in the chapter "Economy and Economic Order" in part III.

12. Cf. B. Frey and A. Stutzer (2001).

13. See the section on Adam Smith's humanism in the chapter "Normative Humanism" in part II.

14. On deontological rationality, cf. A. Sen (2003): 9 and in part II, in the chapter "Normative Humanism beyond Theology" in the section on humanism in Amartya Sen.

15. See, for example, P. Ulrich (1999): 233, 235, 238 et seq.

16. See, for example, ibid.: 237. There, for example, such modern neutrality is asserted in distinction to supposedly pre-modern closed models.

17. In their Integrative Social Contracts Theory on Stakeholder Management, T. Donaldson and T. Dunfee (1994): 265 discuss so-called hypernorms, which can determine the legitimacy of contractualist norms because they are fundamental to human existence. This also presupposes a normative objectivity, which is beyond any constructivist or other kinds of relativization.

18. C. Müller (2017): 277.

19. N. Bowie (2005): 144.

20. Cf. E. Nass and E. Kreuer (2018).

21. Cf. in part II in the chapter "Normative Humanism beyond Theology" the section on humanism in Immanuel Kant.

22. A famous example of this is, for example, a non-egoistic attitude of "*Caritas in Veritate.*"

23. F. Rohrhirsch (2013): 95.

24. Cf. in part I in the chapter "Sanctification of the World" the section on the essential content of the good.

25. F. Rohrhirsch (2013): 29 points this out.

26. On the importance of diversity based on Christian values, see F. Rohrhirsch (2013): 84 with reference to H. Volk (2012).

27. Cf. in part II in the chapter "Theological Humanism beyond Christianity" in the section on belief in reincarnation.

28. On the sense-insight characteristic of Christian leadership, cf., for instance, F. Rohrhirsch (2013): 83–84.

29. Following this line of thought, which has already been mentioned several times, according to which, *mutatis mutandis*, a democratic society must also protect the normative sources that make the underlying freedom possible in the first place and that precede any democracy, see E.-W. Böckenförde (1992) and U. H. J. Körtner (2012): 83.

30. Cf. J. Wolff (1991). 29 et seq., 89.

31. Cf. A. Sen (2002).

32. See, for example, the sections on work and death in the chapter "Life, Work, and Death" in part III.

33. Cf. part I.

34. Cf. Leader to Leader Institute (2004).

35. Other Christian welfare organizations, such as *Johanniter, Malteser*, etc., are always included here when *Caritas* and *Diakonie* are mentioned as examples.

36. For a theological grounding, cf. DCE.

37. P. Beer (2018): 9.

38. Cf. ibid.: 11 et seq.

39. Cf. the excursus on the compass in the Christian context in the preceding section.

40. On this nature of the Christian mission in the world, see, for example, the section on "Responses to Crisis Phenomena" in part I in the chapter "Mission in Crisis."

41. Cf. the chapter "Life, Work, and Death" in part III.

42. Cf. in part II in the chapter "Normative Humanism beyond Theology" the section on humanism in Amartya Sen, as well as in part III in the chapter "Creation, Justice, and Peace" in the section on social justice.

43. See the section on education in the chapter "Life, Work, and Death" in part III.

44. See the section on Judaism in the chapter "Theological Humanism beyond Christianity" in part II.

Chapter Thirteen

Future Issues

DIGITALIZATION

The question of an ethical evaluation of new technology in the age of digitalization is a controversial one today and will probably remain so in the future. This applies, for example, to the use of robotics, technical assistance systems for the elderly (AAL: Ambient Assisted Living),[1] the further development of so-called artificial intelligence (AI), the concern about total surveillance (Big Data), the comprehensive networking of so-called smart systems, and the consequences of so-called Industry 4.0 with all its ramifications for people, the view of humanity, coexistence, the world of work (crowd work), and so on. Judicial legality, technical feasibility, mere acceptance on the market, and economic usability cannot be the only arguments in this highly complex field, at least from an ethical perspective. I will identify some areas of tension as examples here and provide various Christian orientations, first by making an understanding of ethical technology assessment transparent, then by pointing out some relevant dilemmas, and finally by questioning their acceptability from a Christian socio-ethical point of view.[2]

Fundamental Aspects of Ethical Technology Assessment Today

The term technology (τέχνη), originating from the Greek, refers to the mechanical, electronic, or digital auxiliary instruments artificially developed by the use of human mind (and hand).[3] Technology ethics in a narrower sense undertakes a normative evaluation of the use of such instruments or networks in which technology communicates and/or interacts with technology, people, nature, or the like. It is not the technology itself that is the subject of critical reflection but rather the immediate consequences of its application (e.g., the consequences of the use of a nursing robot on the well-being of the patient). The immediate ramifications are the basis for an appropriate ethical judgment. In addition, the indirect consequences must also be considered, such as the socially effective results of such use, a new understanding of the human-creation relationship, a changing view of humanity (for example, through the release of human cloning) or changing relationship behavior through new forms of communication (such as AI, robot use, or digitalization) or (for example, through prenatal selection processes) a change in the understanding of social responsibility, for instance, toward people with disabilities.[4] Thus, not only the immediate consequences of the specific use of technology on a micro level come into view but also questions about the changes in attitudes and relationships on the societal meso and macro levels that are triggered by it. These are the indirect consequences. Ethical technology assessment thus always has a social dimension. Individual ethical aspects (such as individual empowerment, privacy, etc.) must be taken into account as well as such relational and socio-ethical issues.[5] This is because the use of some technology changes horizons of human understanding and life. Sociality is newly realized and concretized, for example, by algorithms intervening in people's self-image and perception.[6] The more far-reaching normative questions associated with this are the subject of technology ethics in the broader sense or technology assessment. Here, it is precisely also concerned with "direct and indirect technical, economic, health, ecological, human, social, and other consequences of this technology and alternatives." In a general sense, however, it also questions "the state of the art and its development possibilities,"[7] with which the engineering sciences should be concerned. This latter field of assessment is beyond the scope of this section. In order to clearly define the intended field of ethical consideration, we will, therefore, speak of ethical technology assessment in the following, in order to avoid conceptual confusion with technology ethics in a narrow and broad sense.

The following contexts, for example, come into particular focus today, as they are understood as phenomena of the digitally self-controlling age (4.0): Self-driving cars will soon be a reality. Ethics committees discuss how algorithms are programmed when they are supposed to "decide" between colliding with a young or old person in a hopeless situation. Who is liable in the event of an accident caused by a self-driving car? These are new ethical questions. Virtual reality headsets are becoming increasingly realistic as they give users the feeling they are on the other side of the world. Not least, digital technology is influencing increasingly opaque financial flows and international trade in virtual securities and receivables. Algorithms, fake news, and artificial intelligence can manipulate the stock market over the long term. Fake news about people, armies, quotations, and so on spread by cyberattacks, by purposefully generated or possibly self-controlling algorithms can start wars and destroy people. Portals such as Amazon Mechanical Tank or Freelancer operate international labor markets, so-called "cloud labor markets" for "crowd-working." Beyond national labor law, protection of minors, minimum wages, and so on, sometimes very simple work orders are placed, for example, for web design or the like. On the one hand, this speaks in favor of flexible international contracting and enabling home work. It also opens up income opportunities for less highly skilled yet motivated people in disadvantaged regions of the world. In their imprudence, however, many of the activities contradict the personal meaning of human work demanded, for example, by John Paul II in his encyclical LE.[8] Wage dumping in the legal space, anonymization, loss of social relations, and portal dependence through exclusive, binding contracts are also conceivable. AI is constantly taking on new traits. It is also oriented toward human feelings. Humanoid robots can already caress, laugh, cry, and imply human closeness. Rational algorithms behind them influence human behavior, blur reality and suggestion, control vehicles, and make medical diagnoses. This also applies to skills of appropriate problem analysis and diagnosis, strategic decision-making in business and politics, and many other fields of science and coexistence.[9]

An ethical position on technology assessment must present a comprehensible concept of acceptability in order to thereby identify the use of a particular technology with its direct and indirect consequences as morally acceptable or unacceptable.[10] Numerous values and principles[11] can be brought into play here when it comes to making well-founded decisions about the opportunities and limits of such acceptability, for example: security, freedom, dignity, personhood, humanity, autonomy, self-determination, privacy, liberty, personal responsibility, environmental protection, sustainability, justice, transparency, economic efficiency, health, non-harm or welfare, and many more. This diversity alone is of little help for an assessment of acceptability. The ethical evaluation would only be simple if all conceivable normative criteria are equally fulfilled or if the improvement in one area of value can be clearly determined *ceteris paribus* through the use of technology (i.e., no losses in another area compete with it). However, the use of new technology has such different effects in terms of individual, relationship, and social ethics that such simplicity is usually not given. Therefore, normative guiding criteria must be well justified, semantically rich, and brought into a hierarchy that is also well justified so that they may be weighed. This is exactly what a concept of acceptability must do with the help of its disclosed set of values. Otherwise, the discussion gets stuck in semantic arbitrariness or normative indifference.

Ethical technology assessment must face these and many other challenges today and in the future. From this highly complex field, some dilemmas from the field of health care are now identified and subjected to such an evaluation. They aim to be a role model for making corresponding assessments in neighboring application areas as well.

Exemplary Dilemmas

Here are some examples of concrete dilemmas that challenge an ethical evaluation of the respective use of technology:

- The use of technology can give elderly people with dementia more security. For example, tracking devices help to quickly find confused people who lose their bearings. Silent commerce helps ensure that necessary purchases are made without active intervention. Digital networks (in so-called "smart homes") remind people to exercise, take medication, have meals and fluids, get necessary sleep, and so on. On the other hand, this can also be associated with deactivation because people blindly rely on technology and no longer make any effort to act (again) in a self-determined manner.
- What must be asked: If, for example, I assume an increase in safety through the use of a certain AAL technology (such as cameras for monitoring falls), define this as welfare and an increase in quality of life and set it against the autonomy or privacy endangered by this as a criterion of humanity, how should these diverging objectives be weighed?[12]
- Does the use of (humanoid) robots in care and artificial cuddly seals (PARO, the therapeutic robotic seal) in work with dementia patients not demonstrate a gain in perceived quality of life? After all, robots cushion constraints in nursing care caused by a shortage of skilled workers and thus also free up new time resources in nursing care for personal discussions. Cuddly seals give the impression of physical closeness. Humanoid robots of the future may be able to do this to an even greater extent. Such technology feigns closeness and feelings. Human-to-human or human-to-living-being contact becomes indistinguishable from simulating human-to-technology contact. This, in turn, has an impact on the understanding of the human person and of how lived relationships should be understood and what value truthfulness (e.g., of communication, closeness, etc.) has here.
- Many new opportunities for improved diagnostics are opening up through the personalized use of Big Data. It may also be possible to avoid the outbreak of diseases. Telemedicine makes diagnoses possible without the need for personal encounters. This saves time, money, and the patient the potentially arduous journey to the consultation. On the other hand, such

technology increases anonymity. Evidence-based interpretations of data sets by algorithms could make judgments based on data alone: The view of the human being is replaced by such calculations. There is no longer a holistic view of the human being obtained during personal encounters. Such depersonalization of medicine changes the image of human beings, social interaction and may not necessarily optimize diagnostics. What should now be the deciding factor when assessing such technology?
- Should health insurers be the hub where all digital patient information (e.g., on various therapies and medications) is collected in a comprehensive database to provide physicians with a more holistic overview? Possibly more knowledge on the part of the physician on the one hand contrasts with the idea of the transparent patient on the other. And the question of a possibly economically induced misuse of this information on the part of the health insurers should not be underestimated either.

These dilemma situations from the health care sector, which are only described as examples, cannot be left undecided in the context of an ethical technology assessment. They require resolution by a criterion of acceptability. Existing ethical evaluation systems can be reviewed and compared with a Christian system for this purpose.

Alternative Acceptabilities

A helpful tool for ethical technology assessment (especially in the field of AAL) has been presented in the form of the widely used MEESTAR procedure tool, which, however, does not itself offer any orientation in the sense of first-order acceptability.[13] In contrast, Tom Beauchamp's and John Childress's principles ethics, which is rooted in medical ethics, presents a concept of first-order acceptability, but the principles remain mere postulates, and concrete application to evaluate such complex dilemmas remains difficult.[14] It is precisely the indirect consequences of the use of technology that are given too little attention. Beyond this so-called principlism, understandings of first-order acceptability that prioritize individual values and principles are found for ethical technology assessment. Thus, it might also be natural to elevate the improvement of health to a supreme principle, provided there is an accepted definition of health. Then salutogenetic aspects could take precedence over all other criteria, and the use of technology in health care would always have to be measured last by its positive effect on the health promotion of individuals.[15] If health is regarded as the universalizable highest normative good to which everything else must be subordinated for an ethical evaluation of technology, this can, in the worst case, lead to a health dictatorship. In paternalistic terms, everything would then have to be done to ensure that health-promoting behavior of individuals is achieved with the help of incentives, sanctions, and also coercion. This could contradict an idea of freedom, unless one takes an objectified concept of freedom as a basis, which understands, for example, self-chosen health impairment as objective lack of freedom (such as smoking, lack of exercise, etc.). But that is likely to be highly controversial. And who determines exactly which health status should be achieved even with incentives or pressure? To avoid this dilemma and to exclude coercion as an evil as far as possible, voluntariness as an expression of self-determination could be elevated to the ultimate criterion. Then acceptance and acceptability could quickly become indistinguishable because the freely expressed will, even if it were freed from egoism in Kant's sense and thus had nothing to do with arbitrariness, might not have taken into account all the necessary information for a genuine assessment. Then such freedom would only be a sham.[16] If this concept of freedom is extended to include the requirement of being sufficiently informed, then, from a rational point of view, the acceptable use of technology should, for example, increase people's scope for options and decisions, their ability to comprehend, and their intelligence. Even such a final principle, however, would only *prima facie* be an unchallenged solution. For such autonomy as the ultimate criterion of acceptability could also include appropriate genetic manipulations, prenatal or other selection, personality-altering neuro-enhancement or other corresponding manipulations as legitimate, although this would significantly change the view of humanity and the understanding of the person. So even demanding autonomy as the ultimate criterion is not then the simple solution to the dilemma.

The normative starting point of Christian acceptability is the Christian view of humanity. The ultimate criterion is the ability of all persons to fulfill their God-given purpose of salvation according to the abilities given to them. Anything (including the use of technology) that serves this goal is to be encouraged. Anything that contradicts it must be rejected.[17] The use of technology is in principle a service value at the development of the given humanum. That is: Personhood understood in Christian terms should necessarily frame the self-logic of self-referential technology. The unconditionality of this transcendental rationale for a human(ly) just use of technology and thus the priority of this idea of human service is presupposed. Ethical evaluations of technology must always take into account the perspectives of those directly affected or patients, those responsible for them, the environment, as well as the consequences for the evolving view of humanity and society and, from a Christian perspective, also for the relationship of the affected individuals to God.

Consequence and Compass

Based on the Christian set of values, well-reasoned prioritizations for ethical technology assessment can now be made and acceptabilities can be formulated as orientations:

- Personhood is understood as God's gift and mission for salvation and is thus the highest principle. The use of technology that depersonalizes people must be rejected. Depersonalization occurs when human beings are cut down in their essential qualities that enable them to respond to the gift of God in their threefold responsibility. This includes the use of technology that seeks to wrest human life from God's discretionary power: for example, actively pursuing selective killing at the beginning or end of life or in the event of serious illness.[18]
- Manipulation of human beings that substantially changes the integrity and responsibility of the person is not permitted: Imagine, for example, a technique that could implant a new brain in humans. The assumption of responsibility presupposes freedom, but self-determination is not the ultimate criterion of acceptability. Personality-altering, artificial manipulations, while they might extend options and intelligence, are unacceptable if they undermine the continuity of human personhood and thus ultimately of responsibility (for example, to the Creator).[19] The self-determined desire to use violence against oneself or others (including suicide) is also unacceptable from a Christian point of view because it violates humankind's responsibility toward the life given by God.
- The use of technology should serve the good life (in the sense of the responsibly lived determination of salvation) and the state of health that would be of assistance to such a life. It is true that humans should develop a health consciousness in order to better understand and appreciate their creatureliness. However, coerced health must be rejected because the assumption of responsibility relevant to salvation must not be forced but instead must take place of one's own free will.
- Diagnoses and treatments should not be carried out solely by self-controlling algorithms because these no longer have human beings as a person (and God's image) in mind and reduce them to numbers and columns of data. Technology can and should have a relieving effect here, but ultimately, decisions must be made by human-to-human contact. Technology must not become independent because technology has no soul and does not recognize a soul in a patient. Nor can it take responsibility. It is impossible for autonomous technology to account for the working power of God because it cannot translate metaphysics, love and God's salvation

into its language. For this to happen, people must remain the ultimately decisive actors who use technology but are not soullessly determined by it.
- AAL technology in smart homes for old age or dementia should be rejected if it disables any remaining human abilities. This applies, for example, to the use of "silent commerce" with people who are basically still able to plan and implement purchasing decisions themselves. If activation of existing abilities is dispensed with, such a deployment curtails the individual's scope of responsibility to make the best possible use of their talents.
- We must reject technologies that replace personal contact (for example, between caregivers or relatives) with care robots or the like, without at the same time opening up new spaces for human encounters. Such techniques violate the basic human functions of social integrity and self-determined responsibility. They also diminish people's health consciousness by repressing the self-determined confrontation with one's own transience and the dying process and by relativizing the worthiness of fragile life. The use of technology should not feign health and therefore narrow the time and life spaces that are necessary to consciously prepare for death and the Christian hoped-for life afterwards.
- Security through the use of digital technology serves to protect the fragile life and is therefore a high good. Technology such as tracking systems may only restrict freedom if it creates greater freedom in terms of health and option spaces. Above all, such considerations must account for the consequences for the development of personhood of all those affected. Such weighing makes concrete evaluation difficult.
- Communication is only relevant to salvation if it can be assigned to one of the three levels of responsibility (toward God, oneself, and one's neighbor). Therefore, communication with a humanoid robot or a cuddly seal or the like is not a service to the salvation of the human being concerned. In addition: Such communication, with its possibly deceptive imagination, blurs the view of humanity. Fake feelings are perceived as real. The use of cuddle robots or the like is acceptable for people with dementia if it creates new spaces for honest human encounters. The emotional life of human beings must also not be deactivated by deception. The use of care robots (e.g., to perform basic care tasks) is generally unobjectionable as an aid. However, humanoid forms should be avoided because they only imitate human contact. They manipulate emotional life and relationships. And they contribute to relativizing the elevated dignity of humans in distinction to such machines.
- The possibilities for improving therapy and diagnosis through meaningful data storage are to be welcomed because they serve life. Health insurance companies may consider themselves to be the appropriate interfaces for

such data bundling. However, this entails risks of abuse, which arise from a realistic view of human beings and their egoistic dispositions.[20] It would be desirable to have an independent body that brings together such data from health insurance companies and so on to serve people and prevent misuse.
- The use of digital technology is problematic if it leads to people being overwhelmed by it, for example, in the evaluation of infinite amounts of data or in practical handling. As a result, the reasonable assumption of responsibility is in jeopardy in many ways. Because people have a responsibility to themselves even in view of the talents they have been given, they should reject such use of technology because they are negligently violating the commandment of self-love in view of the experience of failure it causes.
- For the problem of digital labor markets, lower limits on international labor wages, the formation of communities of "crowd workers," or transparent ID identifiers against the spreading anonymity of workers could be solutions.[21] Above all, to solve these problems in the spirit of Pope Francis as well as his two predecessors, Benedict and John Paul II, the idea of global regulation seems worth considering. After all, the popes are also calling for an internationally legitimized body with sanctioning power to enforce fundamental human rights.[22] Regulating digital labor markets should be part of their scope of work.

FURTHER QUESTIONS FOR THE FUTURE

The areas of application discussed here in part III are a selection of central socio-ethical questions of the present with prospects for the future. Many other challenges could be discussed in detail, such as the following questions:

- Autonomous weapons systems
- Peaceful international order
- Colonialism, neo-imperialism
- Migration and refugees
- Society's fight against sexualized violence
- Pandemic ethics
- Critical race theory, DEI (diversity, equity, and inclusion), and movements such as Black Lives Matter
- LGBTQIA+
- Corruption
- Hunger
- Democratic culture of dispute

- Media ethics and opinion forming
- Political radicalization and social cohesion
- Globalization and new protectionism
- Ethics of the financial markets
- Demographic development and the future of social systems
- Energy politics of the future

Such highly topical questions and many other globally and regionally important issues are, of course, also the subject of Christian social ethics. The orientation and guide for these issues can be developed and proposed with the systematics presented in part I. The relevant discussions were not included in this volume because they are highly topical, which, of course, should not completely exclude them from a volume with a fundamental socio-ethical focus such as this but should exclude them as far as possible. Another key reason for this is the European perspective I have taken on many of the issues outlined here, which is simply not sufficient for an in-depth discussion of specific regional challenges. However, I do hope that this universal guide will offer regional subject experts orientation and enable them to engage in productive discussions in their locales.

NOTES

1. AAL Germany (2016): "Ambient Assisted Living (AAL) stands for concepts, products and services that introduce new technologies into everyday life, thereby enhancing the quality of life for people in all phases of life, especially in old age. AAL seeks to offer age-appropriate assistance systems for healthy and independent living." What is meant by AAL, for example, is an application of fall monitor and sensor mats, surveillance cameras or refrigerators that make purchases independently when food runs low (silent commerce) in the home, among other things.

2. On the ethical evaluation criterion of acceptability (in principle as well as from a Christian point of view), cf. in part I in the chapter "Sanctification of the World" the section on socio-ethical efficacy.

3. To this end, H. Jonas (1987): 17–21 helps make a distinction between pre-modern forms, which can be understood more as a stable possession of something, and modern forms, which are regarded as a dynamic enterprise or restless phenomenon, extending beyond themselves for further development and networking.

4. Cf. for the inclusion of such perspectives B. Städtler-Mach (2016):17–19. For consideration of indirect consequences as well, cf. the discussion of values in part III in the chapter "Life, Work, and Death," the section on organ donation.

5. Cf. B. Städtler-Mach (2016): 20.

6. Cf. M. Braun and P. Dabrock (2016): 315, 319.

7. G. Ropohl (2001): 15.

8. Cf. the section on work in the chapter "Life, Work, and Death" in part III.

9. A. Armbruster (2018), however, with reference to the high-tech pioneer Chris Boss, still sees such creations in the distant future.

10. Cf. in part I in the chapter "Sanctification of the World" in the section on socio-ethical efficacy.

11. Values and principles are summarized below as normative criteria for the sake of focusing the argument.

12. Cf. T. Henking (2016): 22.

13. Cf. the section on postmodern discourse ethics in the chapter "Ethics beyond Normative Humanism" in part II.

14. Cf. the sub-section on principle ethical acceptability in the section on Immanuel Kant in the chapter "Normative Humanism beyond Theology" in part II.

15. Cf. the salutogenetic model of A. Antonovsky (1979).

16. Cf. T. Henking (2016): 22.

17. See the chapter "Sanctification of the World" in part I.

18. Cf. the section on death in the chapter "Life, Work, and Death" in part III.

19. Under these conditions, for example, forms of so-called transhumanism must also be assessed ethically. Cf. on this topic, for example, J. Hughes (2013) and M. Rose (2013).

20. Such a realistic anthropology led Thomas Aquinas, for example, to establish private property as a secondary natural right, although it was not intended to be so in the order of creation. See the section on the property system in the chapter "Economy and Economic Order" in part III.

21. On these proposals, see, for example, M. Sendker (2016) and, in part III, the chapter "Life, Work, and Death" in the section on work.

22. Cf. in part II the chapter "World Authority for Unconditional Human Dignity."

Conclusion

Relevance of the Christian Perspective

With this volume, a Christian social ethics is positioned in the environment shaped by (post-)modernity, which sees itself self-confidently—and from a Catholic perspective with ecumenical accents—as a possible normative compass from its mission to sanctify the world founded in Jesus Christ. In the critical dialogue with (post-)modernity, it simultaneously takes a step out of its thinking, challenges it itself, seeks constructive dialogue with other religious and non-religious positions, and offers concrete answers that seek to convince with solid reasoning. It sees itself as an argumentative-dialogical invitation to the people of our era to discover Christian social ethics as an acceptable orientation compass for numerous social dilemmas of our time, either once again or completely anew. With its commitment to its origin, mission, and goal all oriented toward human salvation, it is thus a curious pioneer on the path to a new dawn of socio-ethical reflection.

With its proposal of the set of values made transparent in the Christian understanding of human dignity and responsibility (part I), it builds bridges to some socio-ethical positions of other origins (part II). Proximity and distance, and thus the connectivity of non-Christian religious and secular positions to Christian social ethics, are also explored here. The central question is to what extent sustainable bridges can be built from such ethics to the Christian idea of humanity and society. Christian social ethics thus sets out in search of socio-ethical positions that can and should fight together with it for the assertion of universal human rights and the unconditional dignity associated with them. At the same time, with its transparent value profile, it aims to be found by alternative socio-ethical positions that are also committed to the implementation of an essentially comparable idea of humanity (with different value justifications in each case). Religious and other normative humanistic positions can form such a coalition with Christian social ethics. In contrast, well-founded and controversial positions should reach a binding result in a communicative procedure (second-order acceptability), and even after such an agreement, they should not give up their own figure of justification but instead keep it present for the time being for their own plausibility as well as for a further dialogue on questions of justification. Otherwise, the ethics would remain mere postulates. In this sense, the coalition is united by an inspiring vision of content.[1] That is: Third-order acceptability (a common humanistic synthesis, for example, within the framework of a normative world authority) presupposes first-order acceptabilities (such as an expressly Christian social ethic).

Once the synthesis is found, the constructive dialogue on the competing rationales for this humanistic content continues. These would include, for example, Christian, Islamic, Jewish, or secular images of humanity and society. When religions and worldviews communicate with each other in this way, they value both each other and that which is foreign by engaging in such an open exchange of good reasoning on equal footing. This idea of acceptability is an alternative to secularism and saves the idea of human dignity from possibly being ignored, relativized, or perverted as a postulate. In this context, Christian ethics cannot be satisfied with the secular role assigned to it, for example by Charles Taylor (to be tolerated). For in its service to people, it is not essentially at the service of a secularity to be stabilized but at the service of the message of Jesus. That is why it will strengthen its value foundations.

From the perspective of Christian social ethics, transparency in the justification of values and an invitation to a normative humanistic dialogue on values are two sides of the same coin. At the same time, the contours of first-order acceptability enable the formulation of orientations for complex socio-ethical dilemmas (part III). On the one hand, this is intended to show a logically stringent path from a good value rationale via the formulation of corresponding values and their compatibility with alternative positions to concrete proposals for solutions that at the same time remain open to dispute. The compass formulated in each case in the fields of application is thus non-arbitrary, non-relative, and, therefore, also disputable. These characteristics are due to Jesus' equally non-arbitrary, non-relative, and disputable mandate to Christians, to which Christian social ethics, as its meta-compass, must ultimately always be oriented.

NOTE

1. Cf. P. Beer (2018): 11.

Bibliography

LITERATURE

Legal Sources

Basic Law for the Federal Republic of Germany in the revised version published in the Federal Law Gazette Part III, classification number 100-1, as last amended by Article 1 of the Act of September 29, 2020 (Federal Law Gazette I p. 2048), www.gesetze-im-internet.de/englisch_gg/englisch_gg.html#p0083 (February 10, 2022). (GG)

European Union. (2012). Consolidated versions of the Treaty on European Union and the Treaty on the Functioning of the European Union—Consolidated version of the Treaty on the Functioning of the European Union—Protocols—Annexes—Declarations annexed to the Final Act of the Intergovernmental Conference which adopted the Treaty of Lisbon, signed on December 13, 2007, Official Journal C 326, 26/10/2012 P. 0001—0390, http://data.europa.eu/eli/treaty/tfeu_2012/oj (February 10, 2022). (TFEU)

Herdegen, Matthias. (2003). Kommentar zu Artikel 1, Absatz 1. In: Thomas Maunz and Günter Dürig (Ed.), Grundgesetz. Kommentar (Loseblattsammlung), München.

United Nations. (1948). Universal Declaration of Human Rights (December 10, 1948). www.un.org/en/about-us/universal-declaration-of-human-rights (February 10, 2022).

Magisterial Ecclesiastical Texts[1]

Pius XI. (1931). Encyclical letter *Quadragesimo Anno* (May 15, 1931), Vatican City. (QA)

John XXIII. (1961). Encyclical letter *Mater et Magistra* (May 15, 1961), Vatican City. (MM)

Paul VI. (1965). Declaration on the Relation of the Church to Non-Christian Religions *Nostra Aetate* (October 28, 1965), Vatican City. (NA)
Paul VI. (1965). Pastoral Constitution on the Church in the Modern World *Gaudium et Spes* (December 7, 1965), Vatican City. (GS)
Paul VI. (1967). Encyclical letter *Populorum Progressio* (March 26, 1967), Vatican City. (PP)
John Paul II. (1981). Encyclical letter *Laborem Exercens* (Sepember 14, 1981), Vatican City. (LE)
John Paul II. (1981). Encyclical letter *Familiaris Consortio* (November 22, 1981), Vatican City. (FC)
John Paul II. (1987). Encyclical letter *Sollicitudo Rei Socialis* (December 30, 1987), Vatican City. (SRS)
John Paul II. (1991). Encyclical letter *Centesimus Annus* (May 1, 1991), Vatican City. (CA)
Leo XIII. (1991). Encyclical letter *Rerum Novarum* (May 15, 1891), Vatican City. (RN)
John Paul II. (1995). Encyclical letter *Evangelium Vitae* (March 25, 1995), Vatican City. (EV)
Benedict XVI. (2005). Encyclical Letter *Deus Caritas est* (December 25, 2005), Vatican City. (DCE)
Benedict XVI. (2009). Encyclical letter *Caritas in Veritate* (June 29, 2009), Vatican City. (CiV)
Francis. (2013). Apostolic Exhortation *Evangelii gaudium* (November, 24, 2013), Vatican City. (EG)
Francis. (2015). Encyclical letter *Laudato Si* (May 24, 2015), Vatican City. (LS)
Francis. (2016). Post-Synodal Apostolic Exhortation *Amoris Laetitia* (April 8, 2016), Vatican City. (AL)
Francis. (2020). Encyclical letter *Fratelli Tutti* (October 3, 2020), Vatican City. (FT)

Other Religious Sources

Aurelius Augustinus. (ed. 2008). De Civitate Dei. Chapter XXII, 17, www.hs-augsburg.de/~harsch/Chronologia/Lspost05/Augustinus/aug_cd22.html#17 (February 10, 2022).
Benedict XVI. (2008). Address to Participants at an international Congress organized by the Pontifical Academy for Life (November 7, 2008), www.vatican.va/content/benedict-xvi/en/speeches/2008/november/documents/hf_ben-xvi_spe_20081107_acdlife.html (February 10, 2022).
Benedict XVI. (2011). The Listening Heart. Reflections on the Foundations of Law. Visit to the Bundestag (September 22, 2011), www.vatican.va/content/benedict-xvi/en/speeches/2011/september/documents/hf_ben-xvi_spe_20110922_reichstag-berlin.html (February 10, 2022).
Benedict XVI. (2012). Die Ökologie des Menschen: Die großen Reden des Papstes, München.

Congregation for Catholic Education. (2019). "Male and female He created them." Towards a path of dialogue on the question of Gender Theory in education, Vatican City.

Congregation for the Doctrine of the Faith and the Dicastery for Promoting Integral Human Development (2018). "Oeconomicae et pecuniariae quaestiones." Considerations for an ethical discernment regarding some aspects of the present economic-financial system http://press.vatican.va/content/salastampa/en/bollettino/pubblico/2018/05/17/180517a.html (February 10, 2022).

Council of the EKD. (2013). Zwischen Autonomie und Angewiesenheit: Familie als verlässliche Gemeinschaft stärken. Eine Orientierungshilfe des Rates der Evangelischen Kirche in Deutschland, Gütersloh.

Council of the EKD and DBK. (1997). Für eine Zukunft in Solidarität und Gerechtigkeit. Wort zur wirtschaftlichen und sozialen Lage in Deutschland (Gemeinsame Texte 10), Hannover/Bonn.

Council of the EKD and DBK. (1997a). "Und der Fremdling, der in deinen Toren ist." Gemeinsames Wort der Kirchen zu den Herausforderungen von Migration und Flucht (Gemeinsame Texte 12), Hannover/Bonn.

Council of the EKD and DBK. (2000). Verantwortung und Weitsicht. Gemeinsame Erklärung zur Reform der Alterssicherung in Deutschland (Gemeinsame Texte 16), Hannover/Bonn.

DBK. (2013/2000). Gerechter Friede. DBK Publications No. 66, Bonn.

Francis. (2015). General Audience (April 15, 2015). www.vatican.va/content/francesco/en/audiences/2015/documents/papa-francesco_20150415_udienza-generale.html (February 10, 2022).

Francis. (2016). Conferral of the Charlemagne Prize (May 6, 2016), www.vatican.va/content/francesco/en/speeches/2016/may/documents/papa-francesco_20160506_premio-carlo-magno.html (February 9, 2022).

John Paul II (Ed.). (1983). Codex Iuris Canaonici. Code of Canon Law, www.vatican.va/archive/ENG1104/_INDEX.HTM (February 10, 2022). (CIC)

John Paul II (Ed.). (1997). Catechism of the Catholic Church, www.vatican.va/archive/ENG0015/_INDEX.HTM (January 4, 2021). (CCC)

Migne Patrologie Latina. (*sine anno*). www.documentacatholicaomnia.eu/1815-1875,_Migne,_Patrologia_Latina_01._Rerum_Conspectus_Pro_Tomis_Ordinatus,_MLT.html (February 10, 2022). (Migne).

Pontifical Council for Justice and Peace (Ed.). (2006). Compendium of the Social Doctrine of the Church, www.vatican.va/roman_curia/pontifical_councils/justpeace/documents/rc_pc_justpeace_doc_20060526_compendio-dott-soc_en.html (February 10, 2022). (Compendium).

Ratzinger, Joseph Cardinal. (2005). Mass "Pro Eligendo Romano Pontifice" (April 18, 2005), www.vatican.va/gpII/documents/homily-pro-eligendo-pontifice_20050418_en.html (January 14, 2021).

The Koran. (1955). Interpreted, translated by Arthur J. Arberry, 2 vols, London/New York.

Zentralkomitee der deutschen Katholiken. (2015). Zwischen Lehre und Lebenswelt Brücken bauen—Familie und Kirche in der Welt von heute. Vollversammlung in Würzburg am 9. Mai 2015. www.zdk.de/veroeffentlichungen/erklaerungen/detail/Zwischen-Lehre-und-Lebenswelt-Bruecken-bauen-Familie-und-Kirche-in-der-Welt-von-heute-225w/ (February 10, 2022).

Other Source Texts

Aristoteles. (ed. 1888). Opera. 2 Bände. Edited by August I. Bekker, Berlin.
Engels, Friedrich. (ed. 1962). Die Entwicklung des Sozialismus von der Utopie zur Wissenschaft. In: Karl Marx and Friedrich Engels - Werke. Vol. 19, Fourth Edition 1973, Ost-Berlin, www.mlwerke.de/me/me19/me19_210.htm (February 10, 2022).
Fichte, Johann G. (ed. 1970). Gesamtausgabe der Bayerischen Akademie der Wissenschaften. Edited by Reinhard Lauth a.o., Series I, Vol. 4, Stuttgart.
Kant, Immanuel. (ed. 1900 et seqq.). Kant's gesammelte Schriften. Edited by the Preußische Akademie der Wissenschaften, Berlin, https://korpora.zim.uni-duisburg-essen.de/kant/ (February 10, 2022).[2]
Kant, Immanuel. (ed. 1781/1922). *Critique of Pure Reason*, New York/London.
Kant, Immanuel. (ed. 1785/1998). Groundwork of the Metaphysics of Morals. Edited by Mary Gregor, Cambridge/New York/Port Melbourne/Madrid/Cape Town.
Kant, Immanuel. (ed. 1788/2002). Critique of Practical Reason, Cambridge.
Kant, Immanuel. (ed. 1795/1996). Toward Perpetual Peace. In: Mary Gregor (Ed.), Practical Philosophy (The Cambridge Edition of the Works of Immanuel Kant), Cambridge.
More, Thomas. (ed. 2006). Utopia. Latin Text and English Translation, Cambridge.
Smith, Adam. (ed. 1790/2006). The Theory of Moral Sentiments. Edited by Sálvio M. Soares São Paulo.
Smith, Adam. (ed. 1789/2007). An Inquiry into the Nature and Causes of the Wealth of Nations. Edited by Sálvio M. Soares, São Paulo/Amsterdam/New York.
Thomas Aquinas. (ed. 1933–1962). Deutsche Thomas-Ausgabe. Edited by Albertus-Magnus-Akademie Walberberg, Heidelberg, Graz, www.corpusthomisticum.org/ (February 10, 2022).

STATISTICS

Eurotransplant. (2022). Statistics Report Library, http://statistics.eurotransplant.org/ (March 10, 2022).
Omics. (2015). Religions in the Netherlands, http://research.omicsgroup.org/index.php/Religion_in_the_Netherlands (January 12, 2021).
Statista. (2017). Sollte Sterbehilfe Ihrer Meinung nach in Deutschland erlaubt werden? https://de.statista.com/statistik/daten/studie/442893/umfrage/umfrage-zum-thema-legalisierung-von-sterbehilfe-nach-altersgruppen/ (February 10, 2022).
Statista. (2022). Anzahl der Auszubildenden in Deutschland von 1950 bis 2020, https://de.statista.com/statistik/daten/studie/156916/umfrage/anzahl-der-auszubildenden-in-deutschland-seit-1950/ (February 10, 2022).

Statista. (2022a). Anzahl der Hauptschulen in Deutschland von 2005 bis 2020, https://de.statista.com/statistik/daten/studie/235849/umfrage/hauptschulen-in-deutschland/ (February 10, 2022).
Statista. (2022b). Anzahl von Geburt an schwerbehinderter Menschen in Deutschland nach Geschlecht in den Jahren 2001 bis 2017 (in 1.000), https://de.statista.com/statistik/daten/studie/449656/umfrage/von-geburt-an-schwerbehinderte-menschen-in-deutschland-nach-geschlecht/ (February 10, 2022).
Statista. (2022c). Finanzierungssaldo des deutschen Staates (Defizit-bzw. Überschussquote) in Prozent des Bruttoinlandsprodukts (BIP) von 1992 bis 2020, https://de.statista.com/statistik/daten/studie/2213/umfrage/finanzierungssaldo-des-staates-in-deutschland-in-prozent-des-bip-seit-1991/ (February 10, 2022).
Statista. (2022d). Target2-Salden der Länder des Eurosystems im Juli 2021 (in Milliarden Euro), https://de.statista.com/statistik/daten/studie/233148/umfrage/target2-salden-der-euro-laender/ (February 10, 2022).

FURTHER LITERATURE

Abu Zaid, Nasr Hamid. (2008). Gottes Menschenwort. Für ein humanistisches Verständnis des Koran, Freiburg i.Br.
Aghajari, Hashem. (2002). Uns fehlt ein islamischer Humanismus, www.zeit.de/2002/52/Aghadscheri (January 14, 2021).
Albert, Mathias, Klaus Hurrelmann, Gudrun Quenzel, and TNS Infratest Social Research. (2015). 17th Shell Youth Study: Youth 2015, Hamburg (Flyer).
Alsheimer, Martin and Beate Augustyn. (2006). Sterbehilfe: Modell Holland? Regelungen, Entwicklungen und Motive unter der Lupe, www.dgpalliativmedizin.de/images/stories/pdf/fachkompetenz/Sektion%20Pflege%2060914%20PCLLL%20Sterbehilfe%201%20FachKomp.pdf (January 17, 2022).
Ambient Assisted Living Deutschland (Ed.). (2016). Technik die unser Leben vereinfacht, www.aal-deutschland.de/ (January 9, 2022).
Amnesty International (Ed.). (2018). Amnesty International Report 2017/18, www.amnesty.org/en/documents/pol10/6700/2018/en/ (January 2, 2022).
Angeletos, Georg M., David Laibson, Andrea Repetto, Jeremy Tobacman, and Stephen Weinberg. (2001). The hyperbolic consumption model: Calibration, simulation, and empirical evaluation. In: Journal of Economic Perspectives 15 (3): 47–68.
Antonovsky, Aaron. (1979). Health, Stress and Coping, San Francisco.
Apel, Karl-Otto. (1986). Grenzen der Diskursethik? Versuch einer Zwischenbilanz. In: Zeitschrift für philosophische Forschung 40: 3–31.
Apel, Karl-Otto. (1996). Die Vernunftfunktion der kommunikativen Rationalität. Zum Verhältnis von konsensual-kommunikativer Rationalität, strategischer Rationalität und Systemrationalität. In: Karl-Otto-Apel and Matthias Kettner (Ed.), Die eine Vernunft und die vielen Rationalitäten, Frankfurt a.M.: 17–41.
Apel, Karl-Otto. (1997). Diskurs und Verantwortung. Das Problem des Übergangs zur postkonventionellen Moral, Third edition, Frankfurt a.M.

Armbruster, Alexander. (2018). Künstliche Intelligenz. Große Gefahr, übertriebene Angst—was denn nun? Frankfurter Allgemeine Zeitung (May 18, 2018).

Arrow, Kenneth. (1972). Gifts and Exchanges. In: Philosophy & Public Affairs 1 (4): 343–62.

Asendorf, Ulrich. (1988). Die Theologie Martin Luthers nach seinen Predigten, Göttingen.

Ashraf, Nava, Collin Camerer, and George Loewenstein. (2004). Adam Smith—Behavioral Economist, Cambridge.

Baddeley, Michelle. (2017). Behavioural Economics. A Very Short Introduction, Oxford University Press, Oxford.

Baeck, Leo. (1913). Gottesebenbildlichkeit und Menschenliebe. In: Michael Brocke and Jobst Paul (Ed.). (2015). Nächstenliebe und Barmherzigkeit. Schriften zur jüdischen Sozialethik, Köln a.o.: 46–49.

Baeck, Leo. (1914). Die Schöpfung des Mitmenschen. In: Verband der deutschen Juden (Ed.), Soziale Ethik im Judentum, Second Edition, Frankfurt a.M.: 9–15.

Bauer, Axel W. (2012). Der lebende Mensch ist keine Sache. In: Frankfurter Allgemeine Sonntagszeitung (October 28, 2012): 15.

Bauer, Joachim. (2009). Neue Einsichten in das Wesen Mensch, Köln.

Beauchamp, Tom L., and James F. Childress. (2001). Principles of Biomedical Ethics, Fifth edition, New York.

Beck, Hanno. (2014). Behavioral Economics. Eine Einführung, Springer Gabler, Wiesbaden.

Beck, Roman. (2013). Syrien und die Frage nach dem Bellum Iustum, https://iwm.sankt-georgen.de/syrien-und-die-frage-nach-dem-bellum-iustum/ (January 10, 2022).

Becker, Gary S. (1981). A Treatise on the Family, Cambridge.

Becker, Gary S., and Julio Jorges Elias. (2006). Introducing Incentives in the Market for Live and Cadaveric Organ Donations. In: Journal of Economic Perspectives 21 (3): 3–24.

Becker, Manfred. (2002). Personalentwicklung: Bildung, Förderung und Organisationsentwicklung in Theorie und Praxis, Third edition, Stuttgart.

Beckmann, Jan. (2012). Ethische Aspekte der Organtransplantation. In: Jan Beckmann, Günter Kirste, and Hans-Ludwig Schreiber: Organtransplantation. Medizinische, rechtliche und ethische Aspekte, Second edition, Freiburg i.Br.: 93–159.

Beer, Peter. (2018). Welche Mitarbeiter brauchen Caritas und Diakonie? Christliche Organisationskultur zwischen Identität und Diversität. Grundlegende arbeitsrechtliche Perspektive in Theorie und Praxis, Neuendettelsau.

Beestermöller, Gerhard. (1991). Möglichkeiten und Grenzen einer ökumenischen Sozialethik. Eine Tagungsnachlese. In: Catholica 45: 296–308.

Beestermöller, Gerhard. (2003). Krieg gegen den Irak—Rückkehr in die Anarchie der Staatenwelt? Ein kritischer Kommentar aus der Perspektive einer Kriegsächtungsethik, Second edition, Stuttgart.

Belardinelli, Sergio. (2007). Traditionelle Familie. In: Päpstlicher Rat für die Familie (Ed.), Lexikon Familie. Mehrdeutige und umstrittene Begriffe zu Familie, Leben und ethischen Fragen, Paderborn a.o.: 737–41.

Berndt, Christinane. (2013). Ärzte bringen Kind von toter Frau zur Welt. In: Süddeutsche Zeitung (November 14, 2013), www.sueddeutsche.de/gesundheit/ums trittene-medizin-aerzte-bringen-kind-von-toter-frau-zur-welt-1.1818932 (February 6, 2022).
Beutin, Melanie. (2013). Der internationale Transplantationsmarkt. Eine ökonomische Analyse, Bayreuth.
Bischof-Köhler, Doris. (2006). Von Natur aus anders. Die Psychologie der Geschlechtsunterschiede, Third edition, Stuttgart.
Böckenförde, Ernst-Wolfgang. (1992). Die Entstehung des Staates als Vorgang der Säkularisation. In: Ernst-Wolfgang Böckenförde: Recht, Staat, Freiheit. Studien zur Rechtsphilosophie, Staatstheorie und Verfassungsgeschichte, Second edition, Frankfurt a.M: 92–114.
Böckenförde, Ernst-Wolfgang. (2003). Die Würde des Menschen war unantastbar. In: Frankfurter Allgemeine Zeitung (September 3, 2003): 33, 35.
Böckle, Franz. (1989). Ethische Probleme der Organtransplantation. In: Arzt und Christ 35: 150–57.
Boisard, Marcel A. (1982). Der Humanismus des Islam, Kaltbrunn (CH).
Boland, Lawrence A. (1997). Critical economic methodology: a personal odyssey.
Bowie, Norman. (1998). A Kantian Theory of Meaningful Work. In: Journal of Business Ethics 17: 1083–92.
Bowie, Norman. (1999). Business Ethics. A Kantian Perspective, Oxford.
Bowie, Norman. (2005). Expanding the horizons of leadership. In: Joanne B. Ciulla, Terry L. Pierce, and Susan E. Murphy (Ed.), The Quest for Moral Leaders. Essays on Leadership Ethics, Cheltenham/Northampton: 144–60.
Bowie, Norman, and Patricia Werhane. (2005). Management Ethics, Oxford.
Braun, Matthias, and Peter Dabrock. (2016). Ethische Herausforderungen einer sogenannten Big-Data basierten Medizin. In: Zeitschrift für medizinische Ethik 4/62: 313–29.
Breger, Claudia. (2013). Identität. In: Christina von Braun and Stephan Inge (Ed.), Gender@Wissen. Ein Handbuch der Gendertheorien, Third edition, Köln: 55–66.
Breyer, Friedrich, and Hartmut Kliemt. (1995). Solidargemeinschaften der Organspender: Private oder öffentliche Organisation? In: Peter Oberender (Ed.), Transplantationsmedizin. Ökonomische, ethische, rechtliche und medizinische Aspekte, Baden-Baden: 135–60.
Brocke, Michael. (1976). "Nachahmung Gottes" im Judentum. In: Abdoldjavad Falaturi, Jakob J. Petuchowski, Walter Stolz (Ed.), Drei Wege zu dem einen Gott, Freiburg i.Br. a.o.: 75–102.
Broumand, Behrooz. (1997). Living donors: the Iran experience. In: Nephrology—Dialysis—Transplantation, No. 12: 1830–31.
Buber, Martin, and Karl Ludwig Schmidt. (1933). Kirche, Staat, Volk, Judentum. Zwiegespräch im jüdischen Lehrhaus in Stuttgart (January 14, 1933). In: Theologische Blätter 12 (1933), edited by Karl Ludwig Schmidt: 257–74.
Buber, Martin. (1964). Nachahmung Gottes. In: Werke, Vol. II, München: 1055–64.
Buchanan, James. (2001). Moral Science and Moral Order, Carmel (USA).

Butler, Judith. (1990). Gender Trouble, Feminism and the Subversion of Identity, New York 1990.
Byrne, Paul A., Cicero G. Coimbra, Robert Spaemann, and Mercedes Arzú Wilson. (2005). Brain Death is Not Death. Essay - At a meeting of the Pontifical Academy of Sciences in early February 2005, www.chninternational.com/brain_death_is_not_death_byrne_paul_md.html (January 7, 2021).
Camerer, Collin. (1999). Behavioral Economics: Reunifying psychology and economics. Proceedings of the National Academy of Science Vol. 96: 10575–577.
Chiodi, Maurizio. (2006). Etica della vita. La fide della practica e le questioni teoriche, Milan.
Christlich Demokratische Arbeitnehmerschaft (CDA). (Ed.). (2015). Grundsatzprogramm. Nachhaltig christlich-sozial. Der Mensch ist wichtiger als die Sache, Berlin.
Coleman, James S. (1986). Social theory, social research, and a theory of action. In: American Journal of Sociology 91: 1309–35.
Cowell, Alan. (1994). Pope Seeks a Disarming of Aggressor in Bosnia. In: New York Times (January 13, 1994), www.nytimes.com/1994/01/13/world/pope-seeks-a-disarming-of-aggressor-in-bosnia.html (March 12, 2022).
Dahrendorf, Ralf. (2010). Homo sociologicus: Ein Versuch zur Geschichte, Bedeutung und Kritik der Kategorie der sozialen Rolle, VS Verlag für Sozialwissenschaften, Wiesbaden.
Darwin, Charles. (1871). The Descent of Man, and Selection in Relation to Sex. In two volumes, London/New Jersey.
Demmer, Klaus. (1995). Naturrecht und Offenbarung. In: Marianne Heimbach-Steins (Ed.), Brennpunkt Sozialethik, Freiburg i.Br./Basel/Wien: 29–44.
Deutsche Bundesbank. (1992). Die Beschlüsse von Maastricht zur Europäischen Wirtschafts- und Währungsunion. In: Monatsberichte der Deutschen Bundesbank, 44. Vol., Issue 2: 23–28.
Dietz, Karl-Martin. (2008). Jeder Mensch ein Unternehmer. Grundzüge einer dialogischen Kultur, Karlsruhe.
Donaldson, Thomas, and Thomas Dunfee. (1994). Toward a Unified Conception of Business Ethics: Interative Social Contracts Theory. In: Academy of Management Review 19 (2): 252–84.
Dorji, Sonan. (2015). Fraternity, a prerequisite for overcoming social evils: a Buddhist perspective. In: Pontificium Consilium pro Dialogo inter Religiones: Pro Dialogo 2015 (1–2): 200–207.
Ebeling, Gerhard. (1992). Dogmatik des christlichen Glaubens, Vol. I, Third edition, Tübingen.
Eckert, Willehad P. (1967). Erasmus von Rotterdam. Werk und Wirkung, Köln.
Eckstein, Walter. (1994). Einleitung. In: Adam Smith (1926/1994). Theorie der ethischen Gefühle, Hamburg: XI–LXXXIV.
Englert, Rudolf. (2003). Was bringt uns Bildung? In: Uta Pohl-Patalong (Ed.), Religiöse Bildung im Plural. Konzeptionen und Perspektiven, Schenefeld: 19–29.

Epley, Nicholas, and Thomas Gilovich. (2006). The Anchoring and Adjustment Heuristic—Why the adjustments are insufficient. In: Psychological Science 17–4: 311–18.
Fang, Paul. (2006). Die Europäische Zentralbank, Zürich: Metropolis.
Farner, Konrad. (1949). Christentum und Eigentum. Bis Thomas von Aquin, Bern.
Fernando, Emmanuel. (2018). Redeeming the Past: Going Beyond the Wounds. Healing historical, physical, psychological and spiritual wounds. In: Pontificium Consilium pro Dialogo inter Religiones: Pro Dialogo 2018 (1): 76–81.
Fischer, Lorenz, and Oliver Fischer. (2007). Sind zufriedene Mitarbeiter gesünder und arbeiten härter? In: Personalführung 40 (3): 20–32.
Fischhoff, Baruch. (1982). Debiasing. In: Daniel Kahnemann, Paul Slovic, and Amos Tversky (Ed.), Judgement under Uncertainty: Heuristic and Biases, New York: 422–44.
Foerster, Heinz von. (1988/1998). Abbau und Aufbau. In: Fritz B. Simon: Lebende Systeme, Frankfurt a.M.: 19–30.
Franco, Giuseppe. (2016). Economia senza etica? Il contributo di Wilhelm Ropke all'etica dell'economia e al pensiero sociale Cristiano, Soveria Manelli.
Frey, Bruno S. (2017). Wirtschaftswissenschaftliche Glücksforschung: Kompakt—verständlich—anwendungsorientiert, Springer, Berlin.
Frey, Bruno, and Reto Jegen. (2001). Motivation Crowding Theory. In: Journal of Economic Surveys (15) 5: 589–611.
Frey, Bruno S., and Alois Stutzer. (2001). Happiness and Economics. How the Economy and Institutions affect Well-being, Princeton/Oxford.
Frey, Christofer. (1998). Die Ethik des Protestantismus von der Reformation bis zur Gegenwart, Gütersloh.
Frick, Marie-Luisa. (2017). Menschenrechte und Menschenwerte. Zur Konzeptionellen Belastbarkeit der Menschenrechtsidee in ihrer globalen Akkommodation, Weilerswist.
Habermas, Jürgen. (1984). Moralität und Sittlichkeit—Was macht eine Lebensform 'rational'? In: Herbert Schnädelbach (Ed.), Rationalität, Frankfurt a.M.: 218–35.
Habermas, Jürgen. (1996). Über den inneren Zusammenhang von Rechtsstaat und Demokratie. In: Jürgen Habermas: Die Einbeziehung des Anderen, Frankfurt a.M.: 293–305.
Habermas, Jürgen. (2001). Glauben und Wissen, Frankfurt a.M.
Habermas, Jürgen, and Joseph Kardinal Ratzinger. (2005). Dialektik der Säkularisierung. Über Vernunft und Religion, Bonn.
Hacker, Philipp. (2017). Verhaltensökonomik und Normativität. Die Grenzen des Informationsmodells im Privatrecht und seine Alternativen, Tübingen.
Hallaq, Wael B. (2013). The Impossible State: Islam, Politics and Modernity's Moral Predicament, New York.
Heidegger, Martin. (ed. 2000). Über den Humanismus, Frankfurt a.M.
Heimbach-Steins, Marianne. (1994). Unterscheidung der Geister: Strukturmoment christlicher Sozialethik: Dargestellt am Werk Madeleine Delbrels, Münster.
Heimbach-Steins Marianne. (2015). Die Gender-Debatte—Herausforderungen für Theologie und Kirche. Köln.

Heimbrock, Hans-Günter. (2007). Empirie, Methode und Theologie. In: Astrid Dinter, Hans-Günter Heimbrock, Kerstin Söderblom (Ed.), Einführung in die Empirische Theologie - Gelebte Religion erforschen, Göttingen: 42–59.

Heinle, Johannes. (2017). Immanuel Kants Selbstzweckformel, www.sapereaude pls.de/2017/07/23/immanuel-kants-selbstzweckformel/ (January 10, 2021).

Heinzmann, Richard. (1994). Thomas von Aquin. Eine Einführung in sein Denken, Stuttgart, Berlin, Köln.

Hengsbach, Friedhelm. (2011). Europäische Solidarität—nicht zum Nulltarif, edited by Oswald-von-Nell-Breuning Institut, Frankfurt a.M.

Hengsbach, Friedhelm, Bernhard Emunds, and Mattias Möhring-Hesse. (1993). Ethische Reflexion politischer Glaubenspraxis. Ein Diskussionsbeitrag. In: Friedhelm Hengsbach, Bernhard Emunds, and Mattias Möhring-Hesse: Jenseits Katholischer Soziallehre. Neue Entwürfe christlicher Gesellschaftsethik, Düsseldorf: 215–91.

Hengsbach, Friedhelm, Bernhard Emunds, and Mattias Möhring-Hesse. (1993a). Jenseits Katholischer Soziallehre. Neue Entwürfe christlicher Gesellschaftsethik, Düsseldorf.

Henking, Tanja. (2016). Technik im Alltag und im Alter—Gewinn für die Autonomie oder Gefahr der Entmenschlichung? In: Zeitschrift für medizinische Ethik 1/62: 21–31.

Her, Rey-Sheng. (2018). The path of Nonviolence of the Buddha in: Pontificium Consilium pro Dialogo inter Religiones: Pro Dialogo 2018 (1): 49–50.

Herre, Petra. (2003). Die Genderperspektive in der Bildung. In: Uta Pohl-Patalong (Ed.), Religiöse Bildung im Plural. Konzeptionen und Perspektiven, Schenefeld: 183–201.

Hilgenreiner, Karl. (1931). Art. Eigentum. In: Michael Buchberger (Ed.), LThK Vol. 3, Freiburg i.Br., 593–98.

Höffe, Ottfried. (1981). Sittlich-politische Diskurse. Philosophische Grundlagen—Politische Ethik—Biomedizinische Ethik, Frankfurt a.M.

Höffner, Joseph. (1960). Soziale Sicherheit und Eigenverantwortung. Der personale Faktor in der Sozialpolitik, Second edition, Paderborn.

Höffner, Joseph. (1962/1997). Christliche Gesellschaftslehre. Edited by Lothar Roos, Kevelaer.

Höffner, Joseph Kardinal. (2011). Christliche Gesellschaftslehre, Third edition, Erkelenz.

Höver, Hendrik. (2016). Kommentar aus Sicht des St. Galler Management-Modells: Klärung des normativen Sinnhorizonts als Fundament für wirksames Management. In: Alexis Fritz, Michael Fischer, Wolfgang Heinemann, and Georg Beule (Ed.), Entscheidungen im Management christlicher Organisationen, Freiburg: 203–17.

Höhn, Hans-Joachim. (2014). Postsäkulare Gesellschaft? Zur Dialektik von Säkularisierung und De-Säkularisierung. In: Thomas M. Schmidt and Annette Pitschmann (Ed.), Religion und Säkularisierung. Ein interdisziplinäres Handbuch, Stuttgart/Weimar: 151–63.

Hollerbach, Michael. (2011). Wann beginnt menschliches Leben? Die Haltungen der Weltreligionen im Vergleich. In: Deutschlandfunk Kultur (April 2, 2011),

www.deutschlandfunkkultur.de/wann-beginnt-menschliches-leben.1278.de.html ?dram:article_id=192726 (February 10, 2022).
Holyoake, Georg Jakob. (1896). English Secularism. A Confession of Belief, Chicago.
Homann, Karl. (1988). Rationalität und Demokratie, Tübingen.
Homann, Karl. (1993). Art.: Wirtschaftsethik. In: Georges Enderle, Karl Homann, and Martin Honecker (Ed.), Lexikon der Wirtschaftsethik, Freiburg i.Br.: 1286–96.
Homann, Karl. (1993a). Wirtschaftsethik. Die Funktion der Moral in der modernen Wirtschaft. In: Josef Wieland (Ed.), Wirtschaftsethik und Theorie der Gesellschaft, Frankfurt a.M.: 32–53.
Homann, Karl, and Franz Blome-Drees. (1992). Wirtschafts-und Unternehmensethik, Göttingen.
Homann, Karl, and Ingo Pies. (1996). Sozialpolitik für den Markt: Theoretische Perspektiven konstitutioneller Ökonomik, in: Ingo Pies and Martin Leschke (Ed.), James Buchanans konstitutionelle Ökonomik, Tübingen: 203–39.
Honecker, Martin. (2005). Gerechter Friede oder gerechter Krieg, Theologische Rundschau Neue Folge 70 (2): 228–36.
Horvath, Alexander. (1929). Eigentumsrecht nach dem hl. Thomas von Aquin, Graz.
Huar, Ulrich. (1978). Mensch und Politik in Geschichte und Gegenwart. Zum Verhältnis von Individuum, Klasse und Politik, Ost-Berlin.
Huber, Wolfgang. (2001). Unantastbare Menschenwürde—Gilt sie von Anfang an? www.ekd.de/gesellschaft/Huber_011207.html (January 7, 2022).
Hümmeler, Hans. (*sine anno* ca. 1935). Helden und Heilige, Bonn.
Hughes, James. (2013). Transhumanism and personal Identity. In: Max More and Natasha Vita-More (Ed.), The Transhumanist Reader, Oxford/Malden: 227–32.
Huifeng, Shi. (2015). We belong to One Human Family: a Buddhist Perspective. In: Pontificium Consilium pro Dialogo inter Religiones: Pro Dialogo 2015 (1–2): 168–76.
IGFM. (2012). Hinrichtungen von Lagerhäftlingen für Organhandel? Medieninformation der Internationalen Gesellschaft für Menschenrechte (IGFM). (November 7, 2012), www.igfm.de/news-presse/aktuelle-meldungen/detailansicht/?tx_tt news%5Btt_news%5D=1794&cHash=e70147a37aaaee796dd9f3904df50d6f (January 3, 2021).
Issing, Otmar. (2011). Lessons for Monetary Policy: What Should the Consensus Be? IMF Working Papers 11/97, April 2011.
Izetbegović, Alija. (2014). Islam zwischen Ost und West, Wien.
Jesse, Horst. (2005). Leben und Werk des Philipp Melanchthon. Dr. Martin Luthers theologischer Weggefährte, München.
Jonas, Hans. (1987). Technik, Medizin und Ethik. Praxis des Prinzips Verantwortung, Frankfurt a.M.
Jozuka, Emiko. (2018). Beyond Dimensions: The man who married a hologram. In: CNN Health (December 29, 2018), https://edition.cnn.com/2018/12/28/health/rise-of-digisexuals-intl/index.html (March 13, 2022).
Jüngel, Eberhard. (1997). Meine Zeit in Gottes Händen. Zur Würde des befristeten Menschenlebens, Heidelberg.

Kahnemann, Daniel, and Alan B. Krueger. (2006). Developments in the Measurement of Subjective Well-Being. In: Journal of Economic Perspectives 20 (1): 3–24.
Kahnemann, Daniel, and Amos Tversky. (1979). Prospect theory—an analysis of decision under risk. In: Econometrica 47 (2): 263–92.
Kaufmann, Franz-Xaver. (2008). Ehe und Familie zwischen kultureller Normierung und gesellschaftlicher Bedingtheit. In: Anton Rauscher (Ed.), Handbuch der Katholischen Soziallehre, Berlin: 257–72.
Kerber, Walter. (1986). Art. Eigentum III. Sozialphilosophie des Eigentums. In: Görres-Gesellschaft (Ed.), Staatslexikon Vol. II, 7. Ed., Freiburg/Basel/Wien: 166–71.
Kersting, Wolfgang. (1999). Verteilungsgerechtigkeit oder politische Solidarität? Über die Schwierigkeiten einer philosophischen Sozialstaatsbegründung. In: Petra Kolmer and Harald Korten (Ed.), Recht-Staat-Gesellschaft. Facetten der politischen Philosophie, Freiburg i.Br.: 112–39.
Kersting, Wolfgang. (2002). Kritik der Gleichheit. Über die Grenzen der Gleichheit und der Moral, Weilerswist.
Kersting, Wolfgang. (2008). Das Eigentum und seine Formen—Philosophische Begründungen. In: Anton Rauscher (Ed.), Handbuch der Katholischen Soziallehre, Berlin: 501–10.
Ketteler, Wilhelm E. Freiherr von. (1849). Die großen sozialen Fragen der Gegenwart. 6 Predigten gehalten am Hohen Dom zu Mainz, Mainz.
Khorchide, Mouhanad. (2012). Gott ist kein Diktator. Interview von Arnfrid Schenk und Martin Spiewak. In: DIE ZEIT (October 4, 2012), www.zeit.de/2012/41/Mouhanad-Khorchide-Islam-Gewalt (January 2, 2022).
Klafki, Wolfgang. (2007). Neue Studien zur Bildungstheorie und Didaktik. Zeitgemäße Allgemeinbildung und kritisch-konstruktive Didaktik, Sixth edition, Weinheim.
Klein, Rebekka A. (2018). Hat die theologische Ethik eine interdisziplinäre Verfassung? In: Zeitschrift für Evangelische Ethik 62 (4): 308–12.
Kluxen, Wolfgang. (1999). Das Allgemeine und das Gemeinsame. Moralische Normen im konkreten Ethos. In: Peter Koslowski (Ed.), Das Gemeinwohl zwischen Universalismus und Partikularismus, Stuttgart-Bad Cannstadt: 17–29.
Knoepffler, Nikolaus. (2018). Ethische Fragen zu Transplantationsmedizin, www.uniklinikum-jena.de/studiendekanat_media/Downloads_%C3%B6ffentlich/ME_4_2_Organ_1803-p-15102.pdf (January 13, 2021).
Körner, Felix. (2008). Modernistische Koranexegese in der Türkei. Eine Diskussion mit Mustafa Öztürk. In: Peter Hünseler (Ed.), Im Dienst der Versöhnung. Für einen authentischen Dialog zwischen Christen und Muslimen, Regensburg: 13–22.
Körtner, Ulrich H. J. (2012). Evangelische Sozialethik. Grundlagen und Themenfelder, Third edition, Göttingen.
Korff, Wilhelm. (1977). Die ethische und theologische Relevanz der Humanwissenschaften. In: Martin Hengel and Rudolf Reinhardt (Ed.), Heute von Gott reden, München/Mainz: 25–49.
Kornwachs, Klaus. (2013). Philosophie der Technik. Eine Einführung, München.
Korsgaard, Christine. (1996). Creating the Kingdom of Ends, New York.

Kropač, Ulrich. (2019). Religion—Religiosität—Religionskultur. Ein Grundriss religiöser Bildung in der Schule, Stuttgart.
Kühnlein, Michael. (2018). Ausblick: Nach der Entzauberung der Entzauberungstheorie—Wo stehen Politik, Ethik und Religion heute? In: Michael Kühnlein (Ed.), Charles Taylor: Ein säkulares Zeitalter, Berlin/Boston: 213–23.
Kühnlein, Michael. (2018a). Einführung: Taylors Gegenwart. In: Michael Kühnlein (Ed.), Charles Taylor: Ein säkulares Zeitalter, Berlin/Boston: 1–15.
Kuhn, Thomas, and Jürgen Weibler. (2012). Ethikbewusstes Personalmanagement. Erfolgsstrategische Selbstverständlichkeit oder moralische Herausforderung? In: Stephan Kaiser and Arjan Kozika (Ed.), Ethik im Personalmanagement. Zentrale Konzepte, Ansätze und Fragestellungen, München/Mering: 45–62.
Kuhn, Thomas, and Jürgen Weibler. (2012a). Führungsethik in Organisationen, Stuttgart.
Lapide, Pinchas. (1984). Wie liebt man seine Feinde? Mainz.
Lauer, Simon. (1995). Verteilungsgerechtigkeit—aus jüdischer Sicht. In: Kurt Abel and Martin Hüneburg (Ed.), Friede und soziale Wirtschaftsordnung. Juden, Christen und Muslime in gemeinsamer Verantwortung, Hamburg: 68.
Leader to Leader Institute. (2004). Be Know Do. Leadership The Army Way, San Francisco.
Lehmann, Karl. (2000). Das christliche Menschenbild in Gesellschaft und Kirche. In: Reinhold Biskup and Rolf Hasse (Ed.), Das Menschenbild in Wirtschaft und Gesellschaft, Bern/Stuttgart/Wien: 51–78.
Lehmann, Karl Kardinal. (2005). Geleitwort "Seelsorge lernen in Studium und Beruf", zu: Georg Köhl (Ed.), Seelsorge lernen in Studium und Beruf, Trier: 13–15.
Leipold, Peter. (2008). Fünf Jahre gemeinsame Geld- und Währungspolitik. Eine Erfolgsgeschichte? Hamburg.
Lenzen, Verena. (2013). Der jüdisch-christliche Dialog heute. In: Zeitschrift für Missionswissenschaft und Religionswissenschaft 97 (3–4): 203–10.
Leonhardt, Rochus. (2006). Luthers Rearistotelisierung der christlichen Ethik. Plädoyer für eine evangelische Theologie des Glücks. In: Neue Zeitschrift für Systematische Theologie und Religionsphilosophie 48/2: 131–67.
Linke, Anna. (2013). Autonomie bei technischen Assistenzsystemen. Ein Trade-off zwischen Privatheit, Unabhängigkeit und Sicherheit. TU Cottbus: non-published Master Thesis.
Lintner, Martin. (2007). Organ-Spende oder Organ-Handel? "Gaben-theologische" Anmerkungen. In: Zeitschrift für medizinische Ethik 53: 66–78.
Luhmann, Niklas. (1971). Sinn als Grundbegriff der Soziologie. In: Jürgen Habermas and Niklas Luhmann (Ed.), Theorie der Gesellschaft oder Sozialtechnologie—Was leistet die Systemforschung? Reihe: Theorie-Diskussion, Frankfurt a.M.: 25–100.
Luhmann, Niklas. (1985). Sinn als Grundbegriff der Soziologie. In: Jürgen Habermas and Niklas Luhmann (Ed.), Theorie der Gesellschaft oder Sozialtechnologie—Was leistet die Systemforschung? Frankfurt a.M.: 25–100.
Luhmann, Niklas. (1988). Ökologische Kommunikation, Second edition, Opladen.

Luhmann, Niklas. (1994). Die Tücke des Subjekts und die Frage nach dem Menschen. In: Peter Fuchs and Andreas Göbel (Ed.), Der Mensch—das Medium der Gesellschaft. Frankfurt a.M.: 40–56.
Luhmann, Niklas. (1997). Die Gesellschaft der Gesellschaft. 2 Volumes. Frankfurt a.M.
Luhmann, Niklas. (1998). Selbstreferentielle Systeme. In: Fritz B. Simon (Ed.), Lebende Systeme, Second edition, Frankfurt a.M.
Luhmann, Niklas. (1999). Die Wirtschaft der Gesellschaft, Third edition, Frankfurt a.M.
Lyotard Jean-François. (1988). Beantwortung der Frage: Was ist postmodern? In: Wolfgang Welsch (Ed.), Wege aus der Moderne. Schlüsseltexte der Postmoderne-Diskussion, Weinheim: 193–203.
Maaser, Wolfgang. (2003). Gerechtigkeitshermeneutik bei Luther. In: Peter Dabrock, Traugott Jähnichen, and Lars Klinnert (Ed.), Kriterien der Gerechtigkeit, Festschrift für Christopher Frey, Gütersloh: 68–85.
Mack, Elke. (2015). Tötet diese Wirtschaft wirklich? Katholische Wirtschaftsethik zwischen dem II. Vatikanum und *Laudato Sí*. In: Theologie der Gegenwart 58 (4/2015): 303–16.
Malthus, Thomas M. (1789). Essay on the Principle of Population, London.
Manzeschke, Arne. (2011). Tragen technische Assistenzen und Robotik zur Dehumanisierung der gesundheitlichen Versorgung bei? Ethische Skizzen für eine anstehende Forschung. In: Kirsten Brukamp, Katsiaryna Laryionava, Christoph Schweikardt, and Dominik Groß (Ed.), Technisierte Medizin—Dehumanisierte Medizin? Ethische, rechtliche und soziale Aspekte neuer Medizintechnologien, Kassel: 105–11.
Manzeschke, Arne, Karsten Weber, Elisabeth Rother, and Heiner Fangerau. (2013). Ergebnisse der Studie. "Ethische Fragen im Bereich altersgerechter Assistenzsysteme," München.
Marschütz, Gerhard. (2014). Trojanisches Pferd Gender? In: Kerstin Schlögel-Fierl and Gunter M. Prüller-Jagenteufel (Ed.), Aus Liebe zu Gott—im Dienst am Menschen, Münster.
Marquart, Manfred. (1995). Ehe—Raum des Lebens. In: Wilfried Häre and Reiner Preul (Ed.), Marburger Jahrbuch Theologie VII: Sexualität, Lebensformen, Liebe, Marburg.
Maturana, Humberto. (1999). The organization of the living: A theory of the living organization. In: International Journal of Human-Computer Studies 51: 149–68.
Mayer, Cornelius. (2018). Augustinus-Zitatenschatz. Kernthemen seines Denkens, Basel.
Meinefeld, Werner. (1995). Realität und Konstruktion. Erkenntnistheoretische Grundlagen einer Methodologie der empirischen Sozialforschung, Opladen.
Merleau-Ponty, Maurice. (1966). Phänomenologie der Wahrnehmung, Berlin.
Messner, Johannes. (1954/2001). Kulturethik. Mit Grundlegung durch Prinzipienethik und Persönlichkeitsethik. Reprint, Vienna/Munich.
Meuthrath, Annette. (2014). Wenn ChristInnen meditieren. Eine empirische Untersuchung *über* ihre Glaubensvorstellungen und Glaubenspraxis, Münster.

Michel, Thomas. (2008). The mystery of human responsibilty according to Daid Nursi. In: Peter Hünseler (Ed.), Im Dienst der Versöhnung. Für einen authentischen Dialog zwischen Christen und Muslimen, Regensburg: 77–86.
Mitchell, Donald W. (2018). Beyond Secularism and Fundamentalism: Re-Inventing Global Citizenship. In: Pontificium Consilium pro Dialogo inter Religiones: Pro Dialogo 2018 (1): 68–75.
Modehn, Christian. (2010). Humanistischer Islam. Menschenrechte sind wichtiger als religiöse Gesetze, http://religionsphilosophischer-salon.corbida.de/749_humanistischer-islam-menschenrechte-sind-wichtiger-als-die-religiosen-gesetze_interkultureller-dialog (January 21, 2021).
Möhring-Hesse, Matthias. (1993). Tradition verpflichtet. Typen christlicher Gesellschaftsethik in der Folge Katholischer Soziallehre. In: Friedhelm Hengsbach, Bernhard Emunds, and Mattias Möhring-Hesse (1993). Jenseits Katholischer Soziallehre. Neue Entwürfe christlicher Gesellschaftsethik, Düsseldorf: 57–87.
Müller, Christian. (2017). Wieviel Moral kann sich ein Unternehmen leisten? Einige spieltheoretische Überlegungen. In: Elmar Nass, Wolfgang H. Spindler, and Johannes H. Zabel (Ed.), Kultur des Gemeinwohls, Trier: 262–80.
Müller, Gerhard Ludwig. (2010). Katholische Dogmatik. Für Studium und Praxis der Theologie, Eighth edition, Freiburg i.Br. a.o.
Müller, Maria Caroline. (2019). Überall weht Gottes Geist. Die Ordensspiritualität der Steyler Missionsschwestern als Konkretion einer Theologie der Säkularität. Unpublished academic term paper as part of the first state exam for the teaching profession at International Baccalaureate Schools in the subject Catholic Theology, Hessische Lehrkräfteakademie Frankfurt.
Müller-Armack, Alfred. (1949/1981). Diagnose unserer Gegenwart. Zur Bestimmung eines geistesgeschichtlichen Standorts, Second edition, Bern/Stuttgart.
Mussinghoff, Heinrich. (2011). Sermon for the Feast of the Ascension on June 2, 2011. Charlemagne Prize Award to the President of the European Central Bank, Mr. Jean-Claude Trichet. In: Generalvikar des Bistums Aachen (Ed.), Karlspreispredigten von Bischof Heinrich Mussinghoff, Aachen: 106–10.
Mussinghoff, Heinrich. (2012). Sermon for the Feast of the Ascension on May 17, 2012. Charlemagne Prize Awarded to the Minister of Finance of the Federal Republic of Germany, Mr. Wolfgang Schäuble. In: Generalvikar des Bistums Aachen (Ed.), Karlspreispredigten von Bischof Heinrich Mussinghoff, Aachen: 112–16.
Nass, Elmar. (2006). Der humangerechte Sozialstaat. Ein sozialethischer Entwurf zur Symbiose aus ökonomischer Effizienz und sozialer Gerechtigkeit, Tübingen.
Nass, Elmar. (2012). Vision Mensch—Mission Hoffnung. Glauben, der wieder gewinnt, Paderborn a.o.
Nass, Elmar. (2015). A Christian Theory of Leadership Ethics. In: Catholic Social Science Review 20: 3–19.
Nass, Elmar. (2018). Akzeptabilität als Kriterium ethischer Technik-Bewertung. Methodologie und eine christliche Anwendung. In: Zeitschrift für medizinische Ethik 64 (4) 2018: 383–95.
Nass, Elmar. (2018a). Handbuch Führungsethik. Vol. I: Systematik und maßgebliche Denkrichtungen, Stuttgart.

Nass, Elmar, and Ellen Kreuer. (2018). Methodology and Applications of Christian Leadership Ethics. In: Journal of Values-Based Leadership II-XI (2018): 71–88.
Nawroth, Egon E. (1961). Die Sozial-und Wirtschaftsphilosophie des Neoliberalismus, Heidelberg/Löwen.
Nell-Breuning, Oswald von. (1985). Gerechtigkeit und Freiheit. Grundzüge katholischer Soziallehre, Second edition, Vienna.
Nell-Breuning, Oswald von. (1987). Unsere Verantwortung—Für eine solidarische Gesellschaft, Freiburg i.Br.
Nida-Rümelin, Julian. (2001). Bio-Ethik. Wo die Menschenwürde beginnt. In: Der Tagesspiegel, January 1, 2001.
Nigg, Walter. (1982). Gespräch mit den Heiligen. In: Walter Nigg: Heilige und Richter, Olten/Freiburg i.Ue.: 11–27.
Nussbaum, Martha. (1988). Nature, Function, and Capability. Aristotle on Political Distribution. In: Oxford Studies in Ancient Philosophy Special Issue: 145–84.
Nussbaum, Martha. (1990). Aristotalian Social Democracy. In: R. Bruce Douglas, Gerald M. Mara, Henry S. Richardson (Eds.). Liberalism and the Good, New York: 203–52.
Nussbaum, Martha. (1993/1999). Menschliche Fähigkeiten, weibliche Fähigkeiten. In: *ibid.* (Ed.), Gerechtigkeit oder Das gute Leben, Frankfurt a.M.: 176–226 (not published in English).
Oberender, Peter, and Thomas Rudolf. (2003). Das belohnte Geschenk—Monetäre Anreize auf dem Markt für Organtransplantate. Discussion Paper 12-03 University of Bayreuth: Faculty of Law and Economics, Bayreuth.
Ockenfels, Wolfgang. (1990). Vermittlungsprobleme der Katholischen Soziallehre. In: Anton Rauscher (Ed.), Katholische Soziallehre im politischen und gesellschaftlichen Prozeß, Köln: 66–85.
Orthey, Frank Michael. (2013). Systemisch führen. Grundlagen, Methoden, Werkzeuge, Stuttgart.
Oslington, Paul, and Kim Hawtrey. (1996). Some Questions and a Bibliography on the Relationship between Christianity and Economics. In: History of Economics Review 24: 84–94.
Pagode Path Hue. (Ed.). (2018). Der Edle Achtfache Pfad, www.phathue.de/buddhismus/die-grundlehren-des-buddha/der-edle-achtfache-pfad/ (January, 16, 2022).
Palazzo, Guido. (2007). Organizational Integrity—Understanding the Dimensions of Ethical and Unethical Behavior in Corporations. In: Walter C. Zimmerli, Klaus Richter, and Markus Holzinger (Ed.), Corporate Ethics and Corporate Governance, Berlin/Heidelberg: 113–28.
Pannenberg, Wolfgang. (1996). Grundlagen der Ethik. Philosophisch-theologische Perspektiven, Göttingen.
Papaderos, Alexandros K. (2005). Aspekte orthodoxer Sozialethik. In: Ingeborg Gabriel, Alexandros K. Papaderos, and Ulrich H. J. Körtner: Perspektiven ökumenischer Sozialethik. Der Auftrag der Kirchen im größeren Europa, Mainz: 23–126.
Pfordten, Dietmar von der. (2005). Normativer Individualismus und das Recht. In: Juristen Zeitung 22 (60): 1069–1120.

Polaino-Lorente, Aquilino. (2007). "Ehe" Homosexueller. In: Päpstlicher Rat für die Familie (Ed.), Lexikon Familie. Mehrdeutige und umstrittene Begriffe zu Familie, Leben und ethischen Fragen, Paderborn a.o.: 377–86.
Preusche, Bernhard. (2017). Sozialstaat im Überlegungsgleichgewicht. Die Kohärenz von Sozialrecht, Gerechtigkeitsvorstellungen und katholischer Soziallehre zur Erarbeitung sozialstaatlicher Qualitätskriterien, Baden-Baden.
Rahner, Karl. (1980). Zum Verhältnis von Naturwissenschaft und Theologie. In: Schriften zur Theologie XIV, Zürich: 63–72.
Rauscher, Anton. (2008). Die christliche Lehre über das Eigentum. In: ibid. (Ed.), Handbuch der Katholischen Soziallehre, Berlin: 511–22.
Rauscher, Anton (Ed.). (2008a). Handbuch der Katholischen Soziallehre, Berlin.
Ratzinger, Joseph. (1964). Naturrecht, Evangelium und Ideologie in der katholischen Soziallehre. In: Klaus von Bismarck and Walter Dirks (Ed.), Christlicher Glaube und Ideologie, Mainz: 24–30.
Rawls, John. (1971/1999). A Theory of Justice. Revised edition, Cambridge.
Rawls, John. (1993/2005). Political Liberalism. Expended edition, New York.
Reingold, Rebecca, and Leticia Mora. (2020). Child Euthanasia in Belgium. Edited by O'Neill Institute for national & global Health, Georgetown (February 10, 2020), https://oneill.law.georgetown.edu/child-euthanasia-in-belgium/ (March 12, 2022).
Rendtorff, Trutz. (1990). Ethik. Grundelemente, Methodologie und Konkretionen einer ethischen Theologie, Vol. 1, Second edition, Stuttgart/Berlin/Cologne.
Rich, Arthur. (1970). Das ‚Humanum' als Leitbegriff der Sozialethik. In: Trutz Rendtorff and Arthur Rich (Ed.), Humane Gesellschaft. Beiträge zu ihrer sozialen Gestaltung, Berlin: 13–45.
Rich, Arthur. (1981). Grundlagen der Sozialethik. In: Armin Wildermuth and Alfred Jäger (Ed.), Gerechtigkeit, Tübingen: 30–54.
Röpke, Wilhelm. (1965). Gefährdungen der freien Welt. In: Aktionsgemeinschaft Soziale Marktwirtschaft (Ed.), Was müssen wir für die freie Welt tun? Ludwigsburg: 9–19.
Rohrhirsch, Ferdinand. (2013). Christliche Führung—Anspruch und Wirklichkeit. Führen mit Persönlichkeit und Ethik, Berlin.
Ropohl, Günter. (2001). Das neue Technikverständnis. In: ibid. (Ed.), Erträge der interdisziplinären Technikforschung. Eine Bilanz nach 20 Jahren, Berlin: 11–30.
Rose, Michael R. (2013). Immortalist Fictions and Strategies. In: Max More and Natasha Vita-More (Eds.). The Transhumanist Reader, Oxford/Malden: 196–204.
Rosenzweig, Franz. (1935). Briefe, unter Mitwirkung von Ernst Simon. Selected and published by Edith Rosenzweig, Berlin: 662–75.
Sacks, Jonathan. (1992). Wohlstand und Armut. Eine jüdische Analyse. In: ZEDEKA: 14–29.
Samuelson, Paul A., and William D. Nordhaus. (ed. 2009). Economics, New York.
Sandel, Michael J. (2012). How Markets Crowd out Morals. In: Boston Review May 2012, www.bostonreview.net/forum-sandel-markets-morals (January 22, 2022).
Satel, Sally. (2006). Organs for Sale. In: The American Magazine (October 14, 2006), www.american.com/archive/2006/november/organs-for-sale (January 9, 2021).

Schlögel, Herbert. (1998). Unterschiedliche Zugangsweisen zum Personbegriff. Ein Beitrag zur ökumenischen Ethik. In: Andreas Fritzsche and Manfred Kwiran (Ed.), Der Mensch, München: 12–25.

Schmergal, Cornelia. (2011). Ökonom fordert Börse für Organhandel. Interview mit Peter Oberender. Wirtschaftswoche (October 15, 2011), www.wiwo.de/politik/deutschland/organspende-oekonom-fordert-boerse-fuer-organhandel-/5758800.html (February 9, 2022).

Schneider, Jürgen. (2017). Die Ursachen für den Zusammenbruch der Sowjetunion und der DDR (1945–90). Eine ordnungstheoretische Analyse, Stuttgart.

Schockenhoff, Eberhard. (2007). Theologie der Freiheit, Freiburg i.Br.

Schockenhoff, Eberhard. (2008). Das kirchliche Leitbild von Ehe und Familie und der Wandel familialer Lebenslagen. In: Anton Rauscher (Ed.), Handbuch der Katholischen Soziallehre, Berlin: 291–310.

Schockenhoff, Eberhard. (2013). Ethik des Lebens. Grundlagen und neue Herausforderungen, Second edition, Freiburg i.Br.

Schüssler Fiorenza, Elisabeth. (2011). Gender, Sprache und Herr-schaft. Feministische Theologie als Kyriarchatsforschung. In: Renate Jost and Klaus Raschzok (Ed.), Gender Religion Kultur. Biblische, interreligiöse und ethische Aspekte, Stuttgart: 17–35.

Sen, Amartya. (1993). Capability and Well-Being. In: Martha Nussbaum and Amartya Sen (Ed.). (2002). The Quality of Life, Eighth edition, Oxford: 30–53.

Sen, Amartya. (1988). The Standard of Living, Cambridge.

Sen, Amartya. (2002). On Ethics and Economics, Oxford.

Sen, Amartya. (2003). Commodities and Capabilities, Seventh edition, New Delhi.

Sendker, Michael. (2016). Economic Decision Making and Ethical Attitudes. Five Studies in the Fields of Institutional Economics, Behavioral Economics and Economic Education. Dissertation at the Faculty of Economic Sciences of the Westfälische Wilhelms-University Münster, Münster: 50–78.

Sharstri, Lobsang Norbu. (2015). From a "Culture of Diversity" to a "Culture of Solidarity": A Buddhist Perspective. In: Pontificium Consilium pro Dialogo inter Religiones: Pro Dialogo 2015 (1–2): 186–89.

Shell Deutschland (Ed.). (2002). 14. Shell Jugendstudie. Jugend 2002. Zwischen pragmatischem Idealismus und robustem Materialismus, Frankfurt a.M.

Shell Deutschland (Ed.). (2006). 15. Shell Jugendstudie. Jugend 2006. Eine pragmatische Generation unter Druck, Frankfurt a.M.

Shell Deutschland (Ed.). (2010). 16. Shell Jugendstudie. Jugend 2010. Eine pragmatische Generation behauptet sich, Frankfurt a.M.

Shell Deutschland (Ed.). (2019). 18. Shell Jugendstudie. Jugend 2019: Eine Generation meldet sich zu Wort, Weinheim.

Shewmon, D. Alan. (2009). Brain Death—Can It Be Resuscitated? In: Hastings-Center Report 39 2009: 18–24.

Simon, Fritz B. (2007). Einführung in Systemtheorie und Konstruktivismus, Second edition, Heidelberg.

Simon, Herbert A. (1955). A behavioural model of rationality choice. In: Quarterly Journal of Economics 69: 99–118.

Singer, Peter. (2011). Practical Ethics, Third edition, Cambridge.
Sinus Institute. (2005). Milieuhandbuch. Religiöse und kirchliche Orientierungen in den Sinus-Milieus 2005, Munich.
Sinus Institute. (2018). Information on Sinus Milieus 2018. Status 10/2018, Heidelberg/Berlin, www.sinus-institut.de/fileadmin/user_data/sinus-institut/Bilder/Sinus-Milieus_092018/2018-10-31_Information_on_Sinus-Milieus_English_version.pdf (February 26, 2022).
Southern, Richard W. (1997). Scholastic Humanism and the Unification of Europe, Oxford/Cambridge.
Städtler-Mach, Barbara. (2016). Medizin für den Menschen: Moderne Techniken für Patientenunterstützung. In: Zeitschrift für medizinische Ethik 1/62: 13–20.
Starbatty, Joachim. (2011). Geld verdirbt den Charakter. Wie es zu den Exzessen in der Welt des Geldes gekommen ist. Vortrag zum Studium generale vom 12.1.2011 an der Universität Tübingen, www.tele-akademie.de/begleit/video_ta110313.php (January 9, 2021).
Starbatty, Joachim. (2012). Vom Währungswettbewerb zur Haftungsgemeinschaft. In: Harald Enke and Adolf Wagner (Ed.), Zur Zukunft des Wettbewerbs, Marburg.
Stegmann, Franz-Josef, and Peter Langhorst. (2005). Geschichte der sozialen Ideen im deutschen Katholizismus. In: Walter Euchner a.o.: Geschichte der sozialen Ideen in Deutschland, Wiesbaden: 597–862.
Steiner, Rudolf. (1995). Die Philosophie der Freiheit. Gesamtausgabe 4, Dornach.
Sunstein, Case. (2015). Choosing Not in Choose: Understanding the Value of Choice, University Press, Oxford.
Sunstein, Case, and Richard H. Thaler. (2003). Libertarian Paternalism is not an Oxymoron. In: The University of Chicago Law Review 70: 1159–1202.
Taylor, Charles. (2007). A Secular Age, Cambridge.
Thaler, Richard H., and Case Sunstein. (2008). Nudge—Improving Decisions about Health, Wealth, and Happiness, Yale University Press, New Haven, CT.
Tietzel, Manfred. (2001). In Praise of the Commons: Another Case Study. In: European Journal of Law and Economics 12: 159–71.
Titmuss, Richard. (1970). The Gift of Relationship. From Human Blood to Social Policy. In: New Press, New York.
Trichet, Jean-Claude. (2011). Interview in: DER SPIEGEL 20/2011: 79.
Tück, Jan Heiner. (2016). Anschwellendes Unbehagen. In: Neue Züricher Zeitung (November 25, 2016), www.nzz.ch/feuilleton/zeitgeschehen/deutsche-bischoefe-ohne-kreuz-auf-dem-jerusalemer-tempelberg-anschwellendes-unbehagen-ld.130529 (February 2, 2022).
Ulrich, Peter. (1995). Demokratie und Markt. Zur Kritik der Ökonomisierung in der Politik. In: Jahrbuch für christliche Sozialwissenschaften, Vol. 36: 75–95.
Ulrich, Peter. (1998). Integrative Wirtschaftsethik. Grundlagen einer lebensdienlichen Ökonomie, Second edition, Bern/Stuttgart/Vienna.
Ulrich. Peter. (1999). Führungsethik. In: Wilhelm Korff a.o. (Ed.), Handbuch der Wirtschaftsethik, Bd. 4: Ausgewählte Handlungsfelder, Gütersloh: 230–48.

Ulrich, Peter. (2000). Wirtschaften heißt "Werte schaffen": Die Wirtschaft in einer wohlgeordneten Gesellschaft freier Bürger. In: Schweizer Personalvorsorge 13 (1): 43–44.
Ulrich, Peter. (2010). Zivilisierte Marktwirtschaft. Eine wirtschaftsethische Orientierung, Bern a.o.
Utz, Arthur F. (1953). Kommentar zu Thomas von Aquin: Recht und Gerechtigkeit. Deutsche Thomas-Ausgabe Bd. 18, Heidelberg.
Utz, Arthur F. (1985). Johannes Messners Konzeption der Sozialphilosophie. Die Definition der Sozialnatur und der Gesellschaft. In: Alfred Klose, Herbert Schambeck, and Rudolf Weiler (Ed.), Das Neue Naturrecht, Berlin: 21–62.
Utz, Arthur F. (1992). Francisco de Vitoria und das Naturrecht. In: Die Neue Ordnung 46: 382–88.
Utz, Arthur F. (1994). Wirtschaftsethik, Bonn.
Vaaßen, Susanne. (2010). Das Ende von Mann und Frau? Geschlechtsidentität in dekonstruktivistischen Gender-Theorien, https://logoi.de/wp-content/uploads/2010/07/Susanne-Vaaßen_Geschlechtsidentität-in-dekonstruktivistischen-Gender-Theorien.pdf (January 17, 2021).
Vanberg, Viktor. (1986). Individual Choice and Institutional Constraints. The Normative Element in Classical and Contractarian Liberalism. In: Analyse und Kritik 8: 113–49.
Van Parijs, Philippe. (1997). Real Freedom for All, Oxford.
Van Parijs, Philippe. (2001). Real Freedom, the Market and the Family. A Reply to Seven Critics. In: Analyse und Kritik 23: 106–31.
Van Suntum, Ulrich, and Alois Stutzer a.o. (2010). Normative und positive Grundlagen der Glücksforschung. Unveröffentlichter Antrag zu einem bei der DFG eingereichten Forschungsprojekt, Münster/Basel/Bochum.
Viscusi, W. Kip, and Joseph E. Aldy. (2003). The Value of Statistical Life: A Critical Review of Market Estimates throughout the World, AEI-Brookings Joint Center for Regulatory Studies.
Viotti, Sabastiano. (2007). Una lettura del liberalismo da parte della dottrina sociale della chiesa. In: Studia Moralia 54/2: 257–94.
Volk, Hartmut. (2012). Die offene Auseinandersetzung mit der anderen Meinung ist die Voraussetzung für die Zukunftsfähigkeit des Unternehmens. In: DMW—Die Milchwirtschaft 4/2012: 134–35.
Wagner, Ralf. (2008). Die Soziale Marktwirtschaft—eine schlechte Idee? www.wagner-berlin.de/artikelwiesel.htm (January 23, 2021).
Weidmann, Jens. (2011). Aktuelle Herausforderungen für Zentralbanken—Betrachtungen im Licht der Finanz- und Wirtschaftskrise. Rede beim Center for Financial Studies in Frankfurt a.M. (June 20, 2011), edited by Press Office of the Deutsche Bundesbank, Frankfurt a.M.
Weidmann, Jens. (2011a). Concluding remarks at the Banque de France/Deutsche Bundesbank Spring Conference on "Fiscal and Monetary Policy Challenges in the Short and Long Run" (May 20, 2011) in Hamburg, edited by Press Office of the Deutsche Bundesbank, Frankfurt a.M.

Weidmann, Jens. (2011b). Erklärung zu den Ergebnissen des Europäischen Rates, Press Notice of the Deutsche Bundesbank (July 22, 2011).
Wielandt, Rotraut. (1993). Menschenwürde und Freiheit in der Reflexion zeitgenössischer muslimischer Denker. In: Johannes Schwartländer (Ed.), Freiheit der Religion. Christentum und Islam unter dem Anspruch der Menschenrechte, Mainz: 179–204.
Witschen, Dieter. (2005). Die Organspende eines Lebenden als supererogatorische Handlung betrachtet. In: Zeitschrift für medizinische Ethik 51: 277–89.
Wolff, Jonathan. (1991). Robert Nozick. Property, Justice and the Minimal State, Stanford.
Zahavi, Dan. (2007). Phänomenologie für Einsteiger, Paderborn.

SOURCES SINE NOMINE

Sine nomine. (2004). Did Eskimos put their elderly on ice floes to die? In: The Straight Dope (May 4, 2004), www.straightdope.com/21343302/did-eskimos-put-their-elderly-on-ice-floes-to-die (March 13, 2022).
Sine nomine. (2008). Berechnung nationaler Armut, www.armut.de/armut-in-deutschland_berechnung-der-armut.php (January 21, 2021).
Sine nomine. (2012). Illegaler Organhandel boomt: Bis zu 160.000 Euro für eine Niere. In: Der Standard (May 30, 2012), http://derstandard.at/1336698138449/Schwarzmarkt-Illegaler-Organhandel-boomt-Bis-zu-160000-Euro-fuer-eine-Niere (January 22, 2022).
Sine nomine. (2016). Papst besucht katholische Kirche in Tiflis—Absage an Gendertheorie. In: Radio Vatikan (October 1, 2016), www.archivioradiovaticana.va/storico/2016/10/01/papst_besucht_katholische_kirche_in_tiflis_-_absage_an_gende/de-1262114 (January 13, 2022).

NOTES

1. Magisterial ecclesiastical texts are cited in the order in which they appear, indicating their abbreviation with chapter number.
2. Works by Immanuel Kant are cited based on the numbering system using the Academy Edition (AK).

Index

acceptance and acceptability, 26, 27, 312
affective: and social cohesion, 22, 137; and social cooperation, 137, 219, 238
affectivity, 240
agents, 7, 14, 18, 26, 82, 88, 252
allocation, 128, 183, 187, 191, 209n122, 216, 217, 218, 228, 230, 231, 232, 237, 248, 292
altruism, 187, 192, 193, 194, 222, 238, 285
anonymity, 25, 70, 202, 311, 339
anthropology, 35, 37, 43, 44, 45, 79, 88, 141, 143, 160, 221, 286, 287, 290, 317n20
anthroposophy, 61, 73, 75–77
Apel, Karl-Otto, 101–2, 104, 115nn21–23
apersonal, 109–12, 271
Aquinas, Thomas, 3, 5, 7–9, 31, 35, 38, 65, 67, 70, 132, 145, 171, 174, 211n175, 225, 238, 317n20
arbitrariness, 45, 47n24, 93n30, 158, 199, 265, 309, 312
Aristotle, 9n8, 31n22, 38, 91, 114, 135, 231, 295, 300
Arrow, Kenneth, 192
artificial intelligence, 242, 307–8
atheism, 43, 52, 57n2, 77n45, 114, 241
atmosphere, 107, 109, 296
Augustinus, Aurelius, 205n36
autopoiesis, 115n29

Batthyány, Philipp, 273n22
Beauchamp, Tom L., 83, 91, 93n17, 311
Becker, Gary S., 127, 190–91, 194, 239, 262, 279
behavioral economics, xviii, 215, 258–72, 278n147, 280n180, 287
bellum iustum theory, 144, 149–50
Benedict XVI (pope), 17–18, 20, 25, 30n18, 35–36, 95, 117, 126, 130, 148, 151nn2,4,17, 179, 209n127, 315
Bible, 1, 18, 22, 45, 55, 126, 133, 159, 200, 206n46, 223, 226, 273n20, 287
Bildung, 173–75, 178–80, 271
black market, 182, 184, 189, 194, 209n127
Böckenförde, Ernst-Wolfgang, 97, 100, 198, 211nn166–68, 221, 273n13, 306n29
Bonhoeffer, Dietrich, 16
Bowie, Norman, 286
Brother Roger, 16
Buber, Martin, 68,
Buchanan, James, 128, 137
Buddha, 72
Buddhism, 71–72, 75, 77n46, 121

343

business ethics, 279n153
Butler, Judith, 205n35

capability approach, 84, 86, 93nn20–21,26, 113, 115n16, 152n27, 251
capitalism, 236
categorical imperative, 80–82, 91, 199–200
Catholic doctrine, 53, 146–47, 151n17, 231
Catholicism, 14, 33, 35
Catholic Social Teaching, 7, 24, 25, 30n18, 171, 228, 231
charity, 6, 19–20, 22, 25, 69–70, 124, 151n17, 159, 168, 170, 185, 189, 197–98, 268
Childress, James F., 83, 93n17
China, xiii, 72, 182, 209n127, 236, 241
Christian faith, 48n40, 55, 68, 70, 150, 179, 195, 291, 298, 303
cohabitation, 137–40, 156, 159, 164, 203n6, 238
Coleman, James S., 204n18
collectivism, 34, 98–100, 134, 138, 140, 152n20, 187, 199, 224, 234, 239
compassion, 6, 22, 36, 87, 160, 233
competition, 28, 139, 157, 217, 278n129, 283–84, 292, 294, 302
complexity reduction, 267
conscience: as a standardized norm, 5, 9n2
consensual discourse, 103
constructivism, 105–9, 112, 114, 162
consumerism, 128, 130, 172
convictions, 39, 59, 118
crisis phenomena, 26, 51, 54, 57n2, 127, 213n180, 306n40
critical rationalism, 108, 271
culturelessness, 25
currency, xxi, xxii, 242, 245–46, 248–50, 253–54, 256

Dabrock, Peter, 316n6
Darwin, Charles, 99, 157

Darwinism: market, 222; social, 99–100, 157–58
deconstruction, xix, 25, 147, 205n35,38
deism, 86
dementia, 24, 98, 100, 139, 228, 310, 314. *See also* people with dementia
deontological, 64, 83–84, 93n23, 222, 266–67, 279n158, 283, 286–89, 305n14
desubjectivization, 111
dialectics, 112
digitalization, 123, 236, 241–42, 307–8
disabilities, 86, 98–100, 114, 115n14, 139, 175, 180–81, 188, 198, 201, 228, 238, 308. *See also* people with disabilities
disabled people, 72, 100, 139, 240
discourse: socio-ethical, 39, 162
discursive, 87, 102, 104, 157, 162, 221
discrimination, 59, 66, 72–73, 188, 304
distributive interventions, 238
divine law, 64–68, 225, 231, 235
Donaldson, Thomas, 305n17
dualism of goals, 304n3
Duldungsprämien, (tolerance premiums), 97, 100, 115n34, 122, 140, 142, 233
Dunfee, Thomas, 305n17

ECB. *See* European Central Bank
economic efficiency: as a goal of business ethics, 168, 218–19, 224, 282–83, 288–90, 292, 305n3
economic imperialism, 127, 133, 158, 177, 189–94, 222, 269, 279n153
economic philosophy, 221, 224, 275n72
ecumenism, 56
ego tactics, 176
Enlightenment, xviii, 66, 135, 287
Erasmus of Rotterdam, 40, 178
Erhard, Ludwig, 236
ethical salary, 293

ethics: business 279n153; of conviction (*Gesinnungsethik*), 7, 46, 149; of duty, 79, 82; of leadership, 4, 77n44, 281–90, 292–93, 302, 304n3, 305n4; of responsibility (*Verantwortungsethik*), 7, 147; secular, xii, xxi, 60, 117, 157, 220. *See also* leadership ethics
Eucken, Walter, 236
Euro (currency), 243, 245, 248, 250, 255–57, 276n113
European Central Bank (ECB), 243–57, 277
European Union, 243, 247
Eurotransplant, 181–83
euthanasia, 5, 99, 182, 195–98, 201–2, 209n127, 211n165,170, 213n178
evangelical, 203n6
evolution, 99, 101, 157, 159, 223, 260–61, 270, 272
externalities, 230

family: marriage and, 75, 156, 160, 164, 203n6, 204nn13,21; traditional, 204n15, 242
feelings, 55, 74, 108, 176, 192, 197, 222, 261, 309, 310, 314
finality, 36
Foerster, Heinz von, 116nn38,46
foundations, xvii, xx, 29n9, 59, 229, 242, 252, 271, 320
France, 156, 277n116
Francis (pope), xx, xxiiin15–16, 25, 61, 76n2, 117, 125–26, 128–34, 141, 151n11, 160, 163, 204n16, 206n45, 236, 315
freedom: of contract, 224; from metaphysics, 113–14; from random valuation, 221
Frey, Bruno, 210n153, 279n159, 287
Frey, Christopher, 43
Frick, Marie-Luisa, 60n4
fundamentalism, 99, 149

gametes, 212
Gandhi, Mahatma, 148
gender, 4, 53, 161–63, 165, 205n35, 206nn45,47, 207n56, 283
goodwill, 153n43, 244
Gospel, xxii, 1, 14–15, 42–43, 46, 179, 295, 299–300
greed, 6, 19, 127, 233–34

Habermas, Juergen, xviii, xix, 41, 101, 105, 162
habitus, 15, 19, 24, 37, 46, 112, 302–3
hamartiological, 30n15, 31n27, 47nn20,30, 151n9
Harari, Yuval, xix
Hayek, Friedrich A. von, 97, 113, 135–36, 236
healthcare system, 102, 176
hedonism, 176
Heidegger, Martin, 88, 90, 116n47
Hengsbach, Friedhelm, 243, 276n110, 151n15
heterogeneity, 220, 291, 297, 299
hierarchy, 132, 219, 283–84, 291, 309
Hitler, Adolf, 105, 150
Hoeffner, Joseph, xxiin1, 195, 207nn71,72, 231
homo economicus, 45, 127, 217, 260–63, 266–70, 272n4, 278n150, 279n153, 282
homogeneity, 75, 291
Huber, Wolfgang, 60n1
human ecology: holistic, 25, 126–30, 132
humane ethos, 21
humanism: normative, 59–60, 64–65, 68, 71–73, 76, 79–82, 84, 88, 90–91, 95, 105, 113–14 117, 119–21, 126, 136–38, 141, 152n20, 156, 178, 199, 202, 221, 302
human race, 24, 38, 99, 157
human self-definition, 87, 93

humanum, Christian, 40–41, 46, 221, 223–24, 237
Husserl, Edmund, 88
hyperbolic models, 264–65

idea of good, 9, 11, 33, 90, 283, 289
Imago Dei doctrine, 34
imitatio Christi, 14, 39
imperialism, economic, 127, 133, 158, 177, 189–94, 222, 269, 279n153
incentive: logics, 128; structures, 172, 176, 283
individual ethics, 3, 16, 228
individualism: methodological, 114n2, 237, 241; normative 31n21, 96–100 114, 138–40, 152n20, 157–58, 189, 191, 217, 240
information policy, 186–87, 210n138
intrinsic value, 38, 128, 138, 169, 172, 177, 244
Ireland, 243, 249, 277n116
Islam, 61–66, 68, 71, 75, 120, 144, 146
Islamism, 59, 62

Jaspers, Karl, 88
Jewish, 61, 68–71, 75, 120, 257, 304, 320
John Paul II (pope), 40, 95, 145, 159, 166, 209, 212n176, 309, 315
John XXIII (pope), 30n18, 117
Jonas, Hans, 316n3
Judaism, 68–69, 71, 75, 224, 275n73
Juengel, Eberhard, 201

Kahnemann, Daniel, 259, 278n145
Kant, Immanuel, 5, 9nn2,8, 44–45, 79–83, 87–88, 91–92, 92nn1–7, 9–10, 93nn16,32, 96, 113, 135, 151n16, 199–200, 208n89, 211nn173–74, 223, 237, 239, 287–88, 341n2
Kersting, Wolfgang, 251, 273
Ketteler, Wilhelm von, 6, 234

killing, 5, 147–48, 181, 183, 200, 212, 224, 313
King, Martin Luther, 16
Knoepffler, Nikolaus, 195
Körtner, Ulrich H. J., 48n40, 306n29
Koran, 62, 64–68, 76nn4,8

labor: forced, 140, 167, 240
law of reason, 112, 199–200
leadership ethics, 4, 77n44, 281–90, 292–93, 302, 304n3, 305n4. *See also* ethics of leadership
leaven, xx, 1–2, 12, 14, 26, 33, 51, 56, 179, 301
legitimacy of rules, 95–96, 114n2
legitimation, 37–38, 102–3, 114, 117, 201, 202
Lehmann, Karl, 2n1, 47n23
Lenin, Vladimir I., 284
lex aeterna, 8, 18–19, 31n24, 35–36
LGBTQAI+, xiv
liberalism, 34, 86
loneliness, 55, 242
love: of God, xx, 12, 24, 29n9, 69, 148, 150; of oneself, 29n9, 69, 132, 141, 150, 169; of one's neighbor, 22, 29n9, 141, 150, 185, 227, 268, 293, 314
Luhmann, Niklas, 54, 55, 106, 110, 115n29, 116n45
Luther, Martin, 14–15, 35–36, 39, 41, 43–45, 48n40, 147, 203n6, 239

Machiavellian, 45, 175, 305n7
Malthus, Thomas, 157, 203n8
market economy perspective, 216
marketing, 177, 258
Marx, Karl, 169, 274n44
Maturana, Humberto, 106
meaningful experience, 111
medical ethics, 83, 91, 195, 311
Melanchthon, Philipp, 14–15, 30n15, 36, 40–41, 43–44, 47nn13,30, 178

Messner, Johannes, 241
meta-ethics, 223
metaphysics, 9n8, 36–38, 44, 79, 90, 92nn1–4,7, 93n16, 101, 112–14, 157, 211, 221, 283, 288, 313
micro-macro model, 204n18
migration, xiv, 128, 236, 315
missionary, 1, 11, 26, 33, 37, 41, 51–52, 54, 64, 74–75, 82, 146, 150, 205n27, 289, 293, 295–96
moral: community, 137–38; freedom 223, 288; law, 5, 6, 80, 82–83, 87, 93n32, 114n2, 199, 200, 239, 267–68, 286; order, 128, 137–38, 158, 219, 238, 240; point of view, 224, 287
More, Thomas, 16, 199, 239
Mother Theresa (Saint), 16
motivation: intrinsic, 284, 287
Muhammad, 62, 67, 76n16
Müller, Christian, 114n9, 288
Müller, Gerhard Ludwig, 29n9, 30n15, 32nn35,37, 47nn29–30, 49n49, 203n6
Müller-Armack, Alfred, 236, 238, 241

narcissism, 175
national central banks, 246–48, 255–57
nationalism, 236
natural law, 299
nature of humankind, 35, 64, 80, 95, 234, 238
Nell-Breuning, Oswald von, 30n21, 38, 275n83, 302
Nicolaus of Myra, 16
normativity, 8, 31n21, 60, 75, 88, 97, 103, 105–6, 114n2, 129, 157, 159, 167, 267, 270, 288
Nozick, Robert, 140
nursing, 308, 310
Nussbaum, Martha, 93n20, 100, 113–14, 115n16, 116nn51,53, 238

opportunism, 16, 176
organ donation, xxi, xxii, 31n33, 181, 184–85, 187, 189, 194–96, 209n127, 212n175, 316n4
organizational culture, 123, 208nn98,109, 281, 290–91, 302–3
orthodox, 5, 33, 46n1, 63–64

pacifism, 147, 150
Pareto priciple, 216, 272nn2–3
participation, 15, 19, 22, 35–37, 71, 75, 103, 144, 191, 221, 284, 299
paternalism 74, 103, 134, 161, 219, 240, 244, 269, 270–71
paternalistic, 75, 163, 268–69, 278n147, 299, 312
Paul (Apostle), 15, 29n10, 162–63, 168, 207, 299
Pax Islamica, 63
peace: just, 143–44, 150, 212n177
people with dementia, 24, 98, 100, 139, 228, 310, 314. *See also* dementia
people with disabilities, 86, 98–100, 114, 115n14, 139, 175, 180–81, 188, 198, 201, 228, 238, 308. *See also* disabilities
personality, 73, 82, 170–77, 208n98, 237, 282, 292, 312–13
perturbations, 110
phenomenological transcendental revelation, 89
phenomenology, 88–89, 91–92
Pius XI (pope), 234, 275n83
Pius XII (pope), 185
Plato, 9n8, 35, 38, 87, 135, 174, 266, 268, 288–89
positivism, 38, 72
principlism, 83, 311
property: private system, 129, 132, 228–29, 231–35; rights, 233
prospect theory, 259, 262–63, 267–69
psychology, 258, 279n152

Rahner, Karl, 37
Ratio Christi, 15–17, 42, 46
Ratzinger, Joseph, 43, 151n2
Rauscher, Anton, 119, 275nn61–62
Rawls, John, xviii, 32n55, 102, 113, 116nn51–52, 135, 139
refinement, 74, 157
reincarnation, 61, 71, 74–75
relativism: normative, 20, 31, 49n53, 71, 95–96, 99–100, 113, 129, 137, 156, 198–99, 208n100
responsibility: threefold (transcendentally founded), 22, 26, 29n9, 39, 69, 86, 132, 141, 173, 227, 289–90, 293, 313
revelation, 6–7, 15, 29n9, 43, 45, 88–89, 91, 112, 164
Rich, Arthur, 37, 221
robots, 165, 242, 307–10, 314
Roepke, Wilhelm, 236
Ruestow, Alexander, 236

saints, 13–16, 29n10, 30n11, 178
salvation, 7, 21, 23, 30n18, 40, 43, 46, 63, 159, 163, 165, 174, 180, 294–95, 204n19, 207n73, 227, 228, 231–34, 237, 243, 272, 289–90, 293, 299–301, 312–14, 319
Sandel, Michael, 184–85, 193, 209n132
Schockenhoff, Eberhard, 2n2, 22, 31n33, 164, 185–86, 195, 202n5, 203nn6–7, 204n26, 207n57, 212nn175,77–78
scholasticism, 9n8, 36–37
school system, 85, 180
secularism, xix, xxiin7, xxiiin11, 52, 54, 71, 90, 96, 120, 180, 320
self-love, 69, 72, 132, 150, 170, 172, 224, 315
Sen, Amartya, 47n28, 48n33, 79, 84–85, 91–92, 93nn20–25, 113–14, 115n16, 135, 152n27, 204n14, 222, 251, 276n88, 278n135, 279n158, 292, 305n14

sense of duty, 85, 222, 283
sense of purpose, 291
servant, 17, 65
service to humanity, 218–19, 221–23
Shell Germany, 47n18, 155–56, 175–76, 178, 180
Simon, Herbert A., 278n145
Sinus Millieus, 47n18, 155
Smith, Adam, 5, 9n2, 86–88, 91, 92, 93n30,32, 221–24, 238–39, 261, 270, 275n72, 278n145, 287
social cohesion, 22, 136–37, 160–61, 247, 291, 304, 316
socialist, 53, 98, 141, 220, 239, 244, 250
social justice, xxi, xxii, 4, 5, 24, 34, 38, 133–36, 138–43, 151n15, 173, 219, 225, 236, 242, 245, 276n90, 302
social laws, 108, 268–69
social market economy, 40, 130, 133, 135, 173, 233, 236–42, 276n90
social philosophy, 113, 135
solidarity (principle), 185
Solus Christus 33, 43
Spaemann, Robert, 211n162
spirituality, 73, 131, 296, 302
Stalin, Josef, 105
Starbatty, Joachim, 255
Steiner, Rudolf, 73
Subsidiarity, xxiiin16, 4, 23, 24, 69, 91, 139–41, 166, 168, 224, 233, 237, 241–46, 248–52, 256–57, 304
subsidiarity (principle), 246, 256
Sunstein, Case, 278n146, 279n176
sustainability, 156, 309
systems theory, 54, 95, 105–7, 109–10, 112, 163, 271

TARGET (Trans-European Automated Real-time Gross Settlement Express Transfer System), 255, 257–58
Taylor, Charles, xix, xxiiin10, 55, 90, 92, 94n42, 320

terrorism, 143, 147
Thaler, Richard H., 278n146, 279n176
theonomy, 62, 163, 221, 287
transcendence, xix, xxiiin10, 5, 9n8, 15, 17–19, 25, 30n18, 45, 53–55, 61, 65, 67, 71, 76, 77n46, 89–92, 96, 101, 107, 112–13, 151n17, 157, 174, 179–80, 219, 288, 289, 295
Trichet, Jean-Claude, 243, 249
Tversky, Amos, 259, 278n145

Ukraine, 145
unborn, 24, 75, 81, 98, 139, 198, 201, 240, 301
United States, 186, 190, 253

utilitarianism, 133
Utz, Arthur F., 219, 229–30, 234

value basis, 8, 27, 69, 116n45, 117, 132, 218, 266, 283, 297
Van Parijs, Philippe, 139, 171
visio Dei, 14–15

war: just, 143, 145, 147–48, 150, 212n177
weasel word, 135, 173, 236
Weber, Karsten, 102
Weidmann, Jens, 278n141, 251
welfare state, 24, 70, 72, 86, 139, 217, 228, 233, 241
Weltanschauung (worldview), xx, 4, 5, 8, 119

About the Author

Elmar Nass holds the chair of Christian Social Sciences in Cologne. He was ordained a Catholic priest in Rome in 1994, holds a doctorate in theology and social economics, and completed his Habilitation (postdoctoral thesis and postdoctoral lecturing qualification) in social philosophy. He is an external scientific expert on welfare issues for the Christian Democratic Union of Germany (CDU) and scientific advisor to the CDU workers' wing. He is a board member and advisor to numerous socio-ethical societies and publishes on value issues of the social order.

www.ingramcontent.com/pod-product-compliance
Lightning Source LLC
Chambersburg PA
CBHW061422300426
44114CB00014B/1502